STUDENT WRITERS AT WORK

STUDENT WRITERS AT WORK

The Bedford Prizes

SECOND SERIES

Edited by

Nancy Sommers & Donald McQuade

Rutgers University   University of California, Berkeley

A Bedford Book

ST. MARTIN'S PRESS · NEW YORK

Library of Congress Catalog Card Number: 85-61300
Manufactured in the United States of America

9 8 7 6
f e d c b a

For information, write St. Martin's Press, Inc.,
175 Fifth Avenue, New York, NY 10010
Editorial Offices: Bedford Books of St. Martin's Press,
29 Commonwealth Avenue, Boston, MA 02116

ISBN: 0-312-76940-7

Acknowledgment

Sylvia Plath. Lines from "Daddy" from *The Collected Poems of Sylvia Plath* edited by Ted Hughes.
Copyright © 1963 by Ted Hughes. Published by Harper & Row, Publishers, and Faber and Faber,
London. Reprinted by permission of Harper & Row, Publishers, Inc. and Olwyn Hughes, repre-
senting the estate of Sylvia Plath.

PUBLISHER'S NOTE

The Bedford Prizes in Student Writing is now an annual nationwide contest for essays written for a freshman composition class. It is sponsored by Bedford Books, an imprint of St. Martin's Press. Contest rules can be found at the back of this book.

The first Bedford Prize contest was open to essays written in 1982. It drew over twelve hundred entries from over five hundred colleges and universities in forty-eight states. A list of the thirty-one winners, who came from twenty-nine schools in twenty states, is printed on the inside back cover.

The second contest, which produced the winning essays reprinted in this book, was open to essays written in 1984. It drew almost two thousand entries from over six hundred colleges and universities in all fifty states. All the entries were read at least twice by a panel of experienced composition instructors, and this preliminary screening produced the essays sent to the seven contest judges for a final reading. In neither the preliminary nor the final judging were the readers aware of the students' names or schools.

The thirty-five winning essayists come from thirty-two two- and four-year schools in twenty-two states across the country. They and their instructors received cash awards as well as formal certificates. (Students who performed additional writing tasks in connection with the preparation of this book received additional compensation.) We congratulate our winners, their instructors, and their writing programs. We also thank everyone who entered or otherwise supported the contest for helping to make it such a success.

We at Bedford Books are grateful to the distinguished panel of writers and educators who served as our judges—Frederick Crews, Janet Emig, Donald McQuade, Donald M. Murray, Nancy Sommers, Lynn Quitman Troyka, and William Zinsser. We thank them for their enthusiastic support and participation in the contest. To Donald McQuade and Nancy Sommers, who have been at the heart of this project from its onset—not only as contest judges but also as contest coordinators and co-editors of this anthology and its bestselling predecessor—we offer special thanks for their good will and good spirits, their high standards and hard work, for their belief in the worth of such a contest and their vision of the potential in a book containing its winners.

PREFACE

The second series of *Student Writers at Work* continues our commitment to making student writing the *primary* text in a composition course. The new edition reflects what we have learned from the Bedford Prize winners, from their instructors, from our own students, and from instructors who have enthusiastically used the first edition. *Student Writers at Work* has been more successful than we dared anticipate: we are told it is the most widely used collection of student writing ever published. We take this as confirmation that a steadily increasing number of freshman composition programs have begun to see students as *writers* and to place student writing at the center of their composition courses.

In its second series, *Student Writers at Work* again celebrates the writing of students and particularly the accomplishments of the thirty-five winners of the Bedford Prizes in Student Writing. But the book is more than merely celebratory. It accords student writing the attention and regard it deserves, not only by publishing it, but also by subjecting it to critical attention like that brought to bear on professional essays in the typical composition anthology. And it explores the composing processes of the prize-winning writers, letting them speak in their own voices about their purposes and strategies, their struggles and satisfactions.

The book is designed to serve either or both of two functions in the classroom. First, it provides a collection of accessible essays comparable to those students will be asked to write, essays that can be used in place of or along with a collection of professional essays. Second, it provides a comprehensive instructional resource for courses in which the primary focus is on student writing.

The collection of Bedford Prize winners in *Student Writers at Work* is in some ways similar to the traditional composition reader and in other ways very different. On the one hand, these essays are as diverse as any group of professional essays. The writers vary widely in age, background, and experience; each of their voices is distinctive. Their subjects include political and social issues, twentieth-century phenomena, and literature as well as personal experience. Their aims and purposes range from expressive to explanatory to argumentative. On the other hand, unlike the writing in professional collections, these essays were written by students for the freshman composition course and thus represent readily accessible and attainable models. Because of the contest's scope, these models reflect a broader demographic range than could be found in any single school or classroom.

Moreover, the material surrounding the student essays is unprecedented in a reader. Because the Bedford Prize contest rules stipulated that all entries be accompanied by preliminary notes and drafts, and because all the winning essayists and their instructors completed detailed questionnaires, the headnotes and discussion questions explore the writers' composing processes as well as their finished products. The headnotes provide not only biographical information about the writers but also quotations from them about their intentions and their writing habits.

The questions after the essays fall into two groups. Those questions on reading address the standard rhetorical concerns of content and form. The questions on revising focus on revision in one of two ways: either by highlighting the writer's strategies and choices or by posing "What if" questions that invite students to consider the effects of further changes in the essay. Together, the two groups of questions are intended to encourage students to read critically and to evaluate carefully the relative success of various writing strategies in particular circumstances. The suggestions for writing that follow each essay include at least one topic related to the essay's rhetorical form, one related to its theme, and one that extends its thematic implications in a different rhetorical form. More particularly, each personal experience essay is followed by an expository or argumentative topic, in keeping with our conviction that the real challenge of the freshman composition course is to show our students how to move from personal experience essays to exposition and argumentation.

We have created a completely new—and unprecedented—part for this second edition entitled "Moving from Personal Experience to Exposition and Argument." The part guides students step by step from writing firsthand accounts of their own experience to broader and more objective approaches to the same material. We asked two Bedford Prize winners, Beverly Dipo and Julie Reardon, to develop new essays from the ones they had originally submitted. The part records their progress: Dipo's from narration to argument,

Reardon's from description to exposition. Each writer kept detailed notes on her writing process, from brainstorming to outlining and then to drafting and revising. Reinforcing these examples are specific advice on how to make the transition from personal to expository or argumentative writing and exercises to help students get started.

We have retained and refined four special sections from the first edition of *Student Writers at Work* designed to help students strengthen their own writing:

Students on Writing. This introduction provides an overview of the writing process through the voices of the winning essayists. They discuss their satisfactions and frustrations as writers and their specific strategies for getting started, drafting, and revising. In the second edition we have included more student comments on invention, along with an example of brainstorming.

Three Student Writers at Work. This part focuses on the composing processes of three prize-winning essayists. Guided by editorial comments, students first examine the complete notes and the rough draft of one of the prize-winning essays, along with the writer's own explanations of her intentions. Then, guided by questions, students analyze the choices of two other prize-winning writers as their essays developed from rough drafts to final versions.

Peer Editors at Work. This part prepares students to be effective peer editors and to respond as writers to the editing of their fellow students. We begin with an explanation of the principles and procedures of peer editing. Next, students see the comments of four composition students on one of the winning essays. Through questions, they are then guided to analyze the peer editors' comments and to evaluate the essay on their own. The writer of the essay responds to the peer editors' comments and revises his essay, and students are again invited by questions to examine the results. Further exercises in peer editing with a second example of peer editing are also included.

The Professional Editor at Work. The final part demonstrates what happens to writing when it is prepared for publication. We found that many users of the book appreciated this demonstration of close critical editing as an example of the kinds of comments professional editors make to encourage writers to revise. The professional editor's work also illustrates—and emphasizes—how even first-rate essays can be revised. After an introduction explaining the goals and procedures of editing, the professional editor offers specific recommendations for two of the winning essays, focusing on how to improve communication between the writer and the reader. Both writers then revise their essays, commenting on the revision and on the experience of being edited. Through a series of questions, we help students examine the editing of each essay and the writer's response to it.

An additional feature in this edition of *Student Writers at Work* is a glossary of rhetorical terms. We have included a particularly full discussion of each rhetorical pattern to help students recognize these forms in the essays they read and to work with them in those they write.

Each of the distinctive features of *Student Writers at Work* as well as *in the company of other writers* receives special attention in the complimentary *Instructor's Manual* prepared with the expertise of Miriam Baker of Dowling College. The manual discusses each feature as well as each essay thoroughly and offers teaching suggestions, discussion questions, and writing topics. It also provides a syllabus with ideas for using *Student Writers at Work* as well as *in the company of other writers* throughout a semester and a detailed arrangement of the essays by elements of composition.

We continue to be influenced by the more than two hundred members of the Council of Writing Program Administrators who responded to our survey on the uses of student writing in the classroom. Among many other ideas, the respondents shared their almost unanimous belief that student writing should be the primary text in the composition class; as one administrator put it, no book can replace "the living, breathing student in the class who is there to speak up, to argue, to defend, to explain, to accept, and to reject." *Student Writers at Work* and *Student Writers at Work and in the company of other writers* do not attempt such replacement. Instead, each offers a collection of essays that are both worthy of emulation and possible to emulate. And each supplements the work of students in the class with the work of their peers across the nation, giving them an opportunity to sharpen their critical skills, to study how successful writers make the composing process work for them, and to see themselves as members of a community of writers that extends well beyond the classroom walls.

Acknowledgments

Sherwood Anderson once said that "the whole glory of writing lies in the fact that it forces us out of ourselves and into the lives of others." Behind this second edition of *Student Writers at Work* stands a large—and steadily increasing—number of colleagues and friends who graciously allowed us into their already crowded lives to seek advice and encouragement.

Before we could prepare this new edition of *Student Writers at Work*, we conducted a second national contest to determine the winners of the Bedford Prizes in Student Writing. And before there could be a contest, there were rules to be checked and written. For their counsel during this phase of the project, we would like to thank David Kaye, Paul Slevin, and Hans Smit, Esq. Most importantly, we would like to acknowledge both the instructors across the country who supported the contest by submitting their students's work as well as the nearly two thousand students who wrote essays worthy of submission.

We are indebted to the kind people who kept track of the essays as they were submitted and who prepared them to be read anonymously by our judges: Chitrita Banerji, Janet Campbell, Judson Evans, Alison Luterman, and especially Carla Johnson. The generosity of Joe McDermott, the Vice President of Local 237 of the Teamsters Union in New York, and Ed Quinn, the former Director of the Center for Worker Education in the City University of New York, provided us with a warm shelter from February snow to read—and re-read—essay after essay.

We are also grateful to the writers, editors, and teachers of writing who served as judges in the first reading: Carla Asher, Deborah Asher, Carol Bamdad, Donald Billiar, Gerald Coleman, Catherine Costa, Jaqueline Costello, Anthony DeLuca, Robert DiYanni, Linda Farhood-Karasavva, Pam Farrell, Beverly Fenig, Bruce Forer, Halima Gutman, Patricia Haag, Barbara Hardy, George Held, Virginia Hlavsa, Siri Hustvedt, Dexter Jeffries, William P. Kelly, Kathleen Kier, Lori Lefkovitz, Mitchell Levenberg, Norman Lewis, Blaise Marino, Phyllis McCord, Catherine McKenna, Stephen Olsen, Barney Pace, John Pufahl, Judi Sandler, Stephen Schmidt, Jonna Semeiks, Susan Stock, Joyce Warren, Robert Webb, Peter Weiss, Gordon Whatley, and Scott Zaluda. Once again special thanks are due Deborah Asher, who helped recruit many of our first-round judges, and especially to Sue Shanker, who also helped recruit judges, then trained them, and choreographed with great skill and delightful humor the multiple readings of each essay. Working with the distinguished panel of judges who chose the winners of the Bedford Prizes in Student Writing remains one of the special pleasures of this project. For their careful readings and thoughtful comments, we would like to thank Frederick Crews, Janet Emig, Donald M. Murray, Lynn Quitman Troyka, and William Zinsser.

We would also like to thank the many instructors who so generously shared with us their experience of working with *Student Writers at Work* in their classes over the past two years: William Arfin, University of North Carolina, Chapel Hill; Eugene Baer, Wisconsin Lutheran College; Dennis Baeyen, Iowa State

University; Carol Bamdad, Union County College; Sheila Bender, Seattle Central Community College; Daryl Coats, University of Mississippi; Terri Cook, Westmont College; Donald Daiker, Miami University, Ohio; Patricia Daire, Pima Community College; Dorothy Fillmore, Virginia Commonwealth University; Paulette Flowers, Vanderbilt University; Beth Franklin, University of Minnesota; J. L. Funston, James Madison University; Margie Garner, Freeman Junior College; Lt. Jill Garzone, United States Naval Academy; E. R. Gelber-Beechler, University of North Carolina, Charlotte; George Greenlee, Missouri Southern State College; Quay Grigg, Hamline University; Susan S. Hankins, University of Mississippi; Susanne E. Hill, Maria Regina College; John K. Hoernig, Niagara County Community College; Diane Horan, Montgomery County Community College; David Jolliffe, University of Illinois; Jim Kolsky, Western Nevada Community College; Mary Beth Lake, Normandale Community College; Sherry Mon Lidaka, Northern Illinois University; Pamela Liebing, Harper College; Darlene Lister, California State University, Dominguez Hills; Nancy G. Little, Motlow State Community College Theresa L. McLain, University of Texas, San Antonio; Barbara C. McMillan, University of Mississippi; Adelio F. Maccentelli, Essex Community College; Harry Marks, Temple University; Vernon G. Miles, University of Arkansas, Fayetteville; Mary Frances Minton, Virginia Commonwealth University; Kathy Morris Murray, University of Mississippi; Edward M. O'Keefe, Niagara County Community College; J. Daniel Patterson, Kent State University; Paul Perry, University of Texas, San Antonio; Douglas Roycraft, Erie Community College; Joseph Sanders, Lakeland Community College; Judi Sandler, Union County College; Paul Sladky, University of Texas, Austin; Mary Ann Smith, Boston College; Cheryl A. Staunton, Mary Washington College; Mary Kathryn Stein, University of Arkansas, Little Rock; Mary Stein, Evergreen Valley College; Judith Straffin, Rock Valley College; Edward F. Sundberg, Cabrillo College; Marilynn Talal, University of Texas, San Antonio; Gilbert Tierney, W. R. Harper College; Erskine S. White, University of North Carolina, Charlotte; Gerald C. Wood, Carson-Newman College.

We are also extremely grateful to the following colleagues for their detailed readings of *Student Writers at Work* and for their many helpful suggestions: Carolyn Beck, Kent State University; Thomas Blues, University of Kentucky; Margaret Butler, Motlow State Community College; Robert Connors, University of New Hampshire; Michele Czosnek, University of Wisconsin, Milwaukee; Anne Hall, University of North Carolina, Chapel Hill; Miriam Baker, Dowling College; Marge McMinn, University of Arkansas, Little Rock; Steven Rayburn, University of Mississippi; Bonnie Rudner, Boston College; John

Ruszkiewicz, University of Texas, Austin; and Judith Stanford. For their advice
and encouragement, we'd like to thank Deborah Asher, Robert DiYanni, Edward Dornan, Betsy B. Kaufman, William P. Kelly, Elaine Maimon, Robert
Roth, and Mimi Schwartz. Laura Novo, Columbia University, helped us locate
an elusive text, and David Richter, Queens College, C.U.N.Y., generously
made his vast knowledge of fiction available to us. We admire his intelligence
and appreciate his help. Gary Goshgarian graciously consented to let us print
drafts of one of his many first-rate essays on culture in the chapter on the
professional editor. We'd also like to acknowledge Edward P. J. Corbett. His
collegiality, accomplishments in print, and intellectual integrity stand as models
for our profession.

We continue to be indebted to Jane Aaron, who was once again an eloquent
and encouraging voice in "The Professional Editor at Work." Miriam Baker,
Dowling College, has lived through two editions of this book with us, and she
has been a constant friend and a limitless source of first-rate ideas and teaching
strategies. Hers is the strongest of our three voices in the *Instructor's Manual*,
and reports of its success in the first edition are a tribute primarily to her
accomplishments as an outstanding teacher and writer as well as to her vision
of the book's potential.

We would like to acknowledge our colleagues in England and the United
States whose work helped shape the section on peer editing: M. L. J. Aber-
crombie, Lil Brannon, John Clifford, Richard Gebhardt, Thom Hawkins, Ed-
win Mason, Stephen Tschudi, and especially Ken Bruffee, Rosemary Deen,
and Marie Ponsot. For their invaluable help on this section, we would also
like to thank the student writers and peer editors at Queens College, C.U.N.Y.:
Nicholas Balamaci, Jason Eskenazi, Nelson Farias, and Frances Osborne. Their
intelligent, sensitive readings of another, and rather distant, student's writing
broadened and enriched the limits of a productive community of writers.

For helping us to recognize the need for the new part on moving from
personal experience to exposition and argument, asking us difficult questions,
and offering generous advice, we would like to add a special note of thanks to
Ron Strahl, Barbara Cambridge, and their colleagues at Indiana University/
Purdue University at Indianapolis. Anne Middleton pursued a similarly helpful
and rigorous series of questions in conversation at the University of California,
Berkeley for which we are grateful. The work of James Moffett as well proved
helpful in developing this new part. We would also like to acknowledge the
generous cooperation of Nancy Jones of the University of Iowa and Joyce
Kinkead of Utah State University.

For the elegant look of their work, we would like to thank Anna Post, who once again designed the book and contest poster, and Richard S. Emery, who deftly repeated his success in designing the book's cover. Linda Howe skillfully copyedited the manuscript, and Anne Richmond was an outstanding proofreader. John Repp, University of Pittsburgh, and Rebecca Saunders, Tufts University, contributed first-rate research to the professional writing supplement. Virginia Creeden Bogucki skillfully managed assembling the permissions for the professional writing included in the supplement, and Sue Dunham graciously did the necessary typing.

One of the most important contributors to this new edition is Carol Verburg. She most generously allowed us to enter her life on the shortest of notice, and she has worked tirelessly on our behalf ever since. This new edition could not have gone to press without her help, we are grateful for her innumerable contributions to *Student Writers at Work and in the company of other writers.*

Our continuing thanks go to the kind people of Bedford Books. Chris Rutigliano coordinated the complex administrative work of the contest and helped see the book through production with a remarkable blend of intelligence, efficiency, and good cheer. Karen Henry coordinated the book's review program and assisted in setting up the contest's first round of judging with great skill and intelligence. Stephen Scipione deserves an MVP as a utility infielder; he played an important role in virtually every phase of this project. The uncommon energy, skill, and irrepressible good humor of Nancy Lyman, Advertising and Promotion Manager, helped keep both the contest and the book on course since their inception. Elizabeth Schaaf, Managing Editor, guided the manuscript through a maze of production problems with an extraordinary amount of intelligence and energy and with an unflappable professionalism. Joan Feinberg, Associate Publisher, not only gave us generous, rigorous comments on every aspect of the manuscript but also repeatedly encouraged us to take the kinds of intellectual risks that made working on this book at once exhausting and yet enormously satisfying. She is the kind of editor every writer hopes to work with and the kind of reader every writer hopes to write for. And Chuck Christensen, Publisher, who enticed us with the idea of the Bedford Prizes, has continued to offer us wise and genial support and the kind of confidence in his authors that makes each sentence easier to write. Both *Student Writers at Work* and *in the company of other writers* have been truly collaborative enterprises.

Finally, we would like to thank the friends who gave us either time to work or ideas to work with or, in several cases, both: Robert Atwan; Hans Dieter, Sarah, and Amelia Batschelet; Fred, Jill, and Alexander Buell; William Harris; Janine Karoly; William P. Kelly; Helene Kessler; Robert and Bridget Lyons;

Judy and Amanda Myers; Kurt Spellmeyer. Gerry McCauley once again helped at both ends of this project. Most importantly, we can only hope that in this sentence Patrick, Rachel, and the recently born Alexandra Hays as well as Susanne, Christine, and Marc McQuade will know how much they have helped us and how much their help has meant to us.

Nancy Sommers
Donald McQuade

CONTENTS

> To "know thyself" is not always to like what you see. Benson's encounter with George Kelly's *Theory of Personality* revolutionizes her concept of herself and everyone around her. CAUSE AND EFFECT

> In this chilling vignette, pressure to succeed turns a military recruit's daytime buddies into his nighttime enemies. NARRATION

CONTENTS **xxi**

STUDENT
WRITERS AT
WORK

STUDENTS
ON WRITING

Part I

ONE OF THE MOST reassuring discoveries any student of writing can make is that there is no single way to write, no fail-proof formula to produce successful essays. Anyone seriously interested in learning to write can benefit from listening to what other writers have to say about the challenges and pleasures of the composing process. The pages that follow will give you a special opportunity to examine the writing process from the point of view of student writers. The thirty-five winners of Bedford Prizes in Student Writing explain their successes and frustrations as writers as well as their particular methods of composition. From their detailed responses to a questionnaire on their specific habits and goals, their strategies and concerns as writers, we have drawn practical information on many aspects of writing—from how these student writers search for an idea and then develop it in a first draft to how they revise and then prepare that idea for presentation in a finished essay.

What do these student writers talk about when they are invited to discuss writing? Like all writers, they invariably speak of the problems and the pleasures of struggling to convey a clear sense of their ideas. They also talk about the purpose and structure of their essays, their use of language, and their relation to an audience. They frequently touch on their respect for and anxiety about mastering the skills required to write good prose. And they describe in detail the distinctive ways in which they compose: how they go about generating ideas for a paper, how they brainstorm and freewrite about that idea, how they organize and develop their first drafts, how they contend with the procrastination and the dead ends that threaten their progress, how they revise, and how they determine when their essays are finished and ready to be read by their peers and submitted to their instructors. Given the academic context within which they work, they also touch on their concern about grades and discuss their perceptions of the place of writing in their career goals.

The perspectives these student writers present on the composing process are as varied as their backgrounds and interests. But the procedures they follow when writing can be grouped into three general phases: getting started, drafting, and revising. Writers usually start by searching for and then deciding on a subject to write about, developing their ideas about the subject, clarifying their purpose in writing, organizing their thoughts, and considering the audience they want to address. In the drafting phase, they usually carry out their detailed plan in a first draft; in the revising phase, they study what they have written and determine how they can improve it. These designations are not a lockstep series of discrete stages that writers work through in exactly the same manner each time. They are simply patterns of activities that describe what happens when writers write. As every writer knows, at least intuitively, writing is not a linear but a recursive process. Writing rarely proceeds neatly from one phase to the next. Rather, the phases frequently overlap, making the process often appear messy. Many writers, for example, revise what they have written as soon as the word or the sentence appears on the page. Each writer participates in the writing process in a different way, at a different pace, and with a different result. In tracing the exact movements of a writer's mind at work on an idea, it is possible to discover and describe patterns, but the specific circumstances and the particular moves are never exactly the same every time.

Yet reading what other students have to say about writing should assure you that all writers — whether they are professionals, prize-winning student essayists, or classmates — grapple with many of the same basic problems. You may be surprised — and pleased — to learn that in many instances the observations and solutions of the prize-winning student writers are similar to those you may have developed in your own writing. In addition, these prize-winning student writers may offer new suggestions that can help you improve your writing. Recognizing both the unique and the shared elements of the writing experience will enable you to place yourself in the company of other writers while distinguishing your own voice from theirs. What follows is not a comprehensive survey of every facet of the writing process but a detailed report on what happens when successful student writers work productively.

GETTING STARTED

In the first of the three phases of the writing process, a writer usually chooses a subject to write about if one has not been assigned, discovers a purpose for writing about the subject, generates a thesis or a controlling idea about the subject, considers the audience to be addressed, and then develops that idea in freewriting and brainstorming exercises, in an outline, or in some other form that will be the basis of a first draft of an essay. This is the most difficult phase of writing for most people. Because they usually face so many problems and obstacles here, most writers seem to have more to say about it than any other phase.

Procrastination

Perhaps the single most common obstacle the prize-winning student writers face when they write is their tendency to procrastinate — a trait they share with most other writers, students and professionals alike. For many writers, the easiest part of writing is putting it off. Matthew Holicek identifies the problem quite succinctly: "About the easiest thing for me to do when I write a paper is getting out a sheet of paper and a pen. After that, nothing is really *easy.*" Holicek may well also speak for many when he recognizes his own tendency to delay writing. "I'm a chronic procrastinator," he observes, "I'll say things like 'Oh, the paper isn't due until next week,' but that soon turns into 'It's due on Monday, so I'll start on the weekend.' " He usually starts writing an essay "one or two nights before it is due. I try to put the thought of writing out of my head until the last possible moment. . . . Then, when I've put it off long enough, I just sit down and force myself to do it, constantly reminding myself about when it is due, and that if I don't do it I'll fail. That usually works." As Holicek suggests, some writers apparently can produce only under great pressure, usually the looming presence of a deadline. Johnna Lynn Benson observes: "I like to procrastinate, but I don't know any cute tricks for that bad habit. It usually takes a panicked glance at the calendar to make me decide to start." Frances Taylor elaborates on much the same point: "I try to avoid writing by answering the phone, calling people I suddenly decide I'm worried about, turning on the TV, or playing my guitar. I don't overcome it on my own primarily because most of the things I want to write about are too painful and the rest is boring. So I need classroom deadlines. I need orders."

The stratagems these student writers use to put off writing are often almost as ingenious as the methods they finally discover to write successfully. Ravenel Boykin Curry's account of his preparation for writing includes a catalogue of procrastination techniques, several of which may be familiar to other students: "I do anything to avoid writing. . . . I stand up and pace. I read, reread, and reread. . . . I eat. I daydream. I chew my pencil. I chew the paper. I tell myself that I have to let my ideas 'settle' for a while. . . ." Sandra Casillas would add "drawing pictures" to that list, while Brenda Jacobs explains her reasons for her procrastination this way:

> I avoid writing seriously at all times for two principal rea-
> sons: (1) the process is so very difficult, requiring more
> effort and time that I am normally willing to give; (2) I
> am never fully satisfied with anything that I write, feeling
> that in the end I am pursuing an impossible dream. I avoid

writing in many ways: reading "how to write" books, reading magazines, rereading old assignments. Anything at all
is a good excuse. I have found only two ways to overcome
this — either an obligation to someone or a deadline that
absolutely must be met. Then, and only then, am I able
to sit down and actually complete a particular essay.

The road Ann Field routinely travels on her way to a first draft includes a few
visual and gastronomic detours: "First, I make sure there is nothing on TV
that I have to watch, because once I get started I can't stop. Then I make
sure that my other homework is completed or can wait without putting me
too far behind in my studies. Then I make sure I'm running on a full stomach
and then I begin. I always eat shortly before I begin writing." As Ann Field's
comment suggests, the kitchen is an especially appealing place for student
writers both to prepare for writing and to procrastinate, and eating is the most
common source of pleasurable distraction for writers intent on postponing the
work they need to do.

Eating is hardly the only sure-fire way to avoid writing. Erik Field recounts
a simpler, fail-safe, method: "I avoid writing essays by enrolling in a minimal
number of composition courses. I write well when I have to. I prefer not to
have to."

The student writers whose essays are gathered in this book could identify
any number of equally successful tactics to combat procrastination. Barbara
Carter explains: "My body gets nervous when I don't want to write. With a
will of its own, it needs a walk, or a drink, or a change of pace. When this
happens, I usually take a walk and think about what I'm writing. Often I
return with a different perspective on my work that helps me to get going."
Ravenel Boykin Curry also tries to refresh his mind "and cast away nervous
energy and restlessness with exercise. Fifteen minutes of jumping rope intensely
can make sitting down to a desk far easier." David Christman relies on an
equally determined but less strenuous method for battling his tendency "to put
off writing in lieu of other things. I have partially overcome this by leaving
my typewriter on the table where I can't avoid it," quickly adding, "I don't
live alone, so I can't leave it there all the time." Earnestine Johnson imposes
deadlines on herself and scrupulously, if somewhat "begrudgingly," observes
them.

The Writing Environment

Most writers are as finicky about the circumstances of where and when they
write as they are about whether they will start writing at all. Kelly Mays

describes a rather elaborate ritual for postponing—and then completing—the first draft of an essay:

> I will usually do anything to avoid actually sitting down to do this first writing. . . . I look down at the empty paper, knowing that I have to write this paper tonight. I get up, pour myself a glass of orange juice and sit back down. I tap the pen on the desk several times, then get up and call my mother or a friend. I complain about the paper and then talk about anything else that I can think of. I soon feel guilty or the other person makes me get off the phone. Then I pace around the room, sometimes cleaning it up. Finally, I gather up what little determination I possess along with my materials and drive to the library.
>
> At the library, I always go up into the book stacks and sit in the same carrel. I like it because it is on the floor with the art and literature books and because it is in the very back corner so that there is no human traffic to create distractions. I always eat before I go to the library and smuggle a drink in with me. These two precautions give me no excuse for leaving, except for going to the bathroom (which I usually allow myself). I prescribe for myself an amount of the paper to complete, taking the available time into consideration. Usually I have four hours because I tend to write from 8:00 to 12:00 at night. I always use the same notebook, a plastic folder with a clipboard full of notebook paper and a pocket to hold notes, index cards or assignment instructions. I never bring anything else with me (except the text and a pen) because I will use it to distract myself.

The student writers in this book seem to be divided on the issue of whether writers need a quiet work space to concentrate on practicing the skills required to write successful essays. Judy Jennings represents one extreme when she reports that she needs "total quiet" to write. William Malley's ideal enviroment for writing is "perfectly quiet and absolutely free from distractions." For Brenda Jacobs, writing best takes place near midnight, when the only break in her concentration might come when "the night sounds of crickets ricochet against the open-screened window." The relative stillness of the night envelops her as she works: "Paper covers the round oak table — page after page, coffee-stained and dog-eared, some crumpled into vindictive wads, each white sheet desecrated front and back with inky scribble and crisscrossed with long, bold lines. A still life composed of precariously balanced dictionaries and reference books, coffee cups, overflowing ashtrays, and a pencil sharpener completes the writer's work table. Trancelike, the writer sits in her ladder-back chair, staring at the paper before her, the word puzzle the focus of her attention."

At the other extreme, many students need some form of sound in the background to offset the silence and solitude of writing. Some students prefer to work in front of a television set, and a few even report that they write only during the commercials. Terry Burns's sound is the stereo: "I know most people like it quiet when they write, but I just can't think when it's quiet. Crank up the stereo, and I'm in business." Amber Kennish amplifies this point when she explains: "I usually listen to music when I write because silence only makes distracting thoughts louder." Karen Kramer describes herself in her "ideal" environment for writing: "in my room, alone, with a stereo on, playing some kind of music that I won't feel inclined to sing along with, dance to, or stare out the window and reminisce with. I like it dark, too, with just one desk light on. Makes it cosier somehow." John Mason prefers to "surround myself with pictures of people that have influenced me and that I care about."

Discarded food and packaging, half-filled coffee cups, jugs of Kool-Aid, three-liter bottles of soda, crumpled papers, mangled pencils, disgruntled expressions, furrowed brows, and lingering curtains of cigarette smoke are fairly common features of the productive writing environment many students describe. Linda Lavelle describes a representative sampling of such circumstances for composition: "If someone walked into my room and observed me trying to get started, the first thing they would notice is the mess. Books and papers are scattered on the table; cigarettes, crackers, and a coffee mug fill in the spaces. In the middle of this confusion I sit, tapping my pen on the dictionary, staring into space for long stretches of time. This is followed by bouts of frantic writing. This person would also observe me gulping coffee, chain smoking, crumpling papers, and (so I am told) making faces, twirling my hair, and talking to myself."

Yet student writers do get started on their papers, however perilously close to the deadline they may be, and even if it means, as some report, using "favorite" pens or pencils, wearing "lucky" clothes, or consuming special foods while writing. Julie Reardon, for example, usually wears "a fuzzy blue robe and fuzzy pink slippers" while writing during what she calls "Minnesota's eleven months of winter." She always writes, as she explains, with "treats close at hand. . . . Chocolate is necessary to the writing process, as is diet caffeine-free Coke. A black hard-tip magic marker and lined pad complete my required list of items to write with." Karen Kramer reports that when she writes "sometimes I do like to wear a silly hat and sunglasses." Whatever the quirk, the superstition, the ritual, or the curious concern, many writers feel that certain circumstances must be present before they can even begin to write.

William Malley reports that he relies almost exclusively on determination to complete his writing assignments: "Writing is hard work that requires concentration and effort. For this reason, I never eat, listen to music, or carry on a conversation while writing. I do attempt to write at a time when my head is clear and I am well-rested. I never drink coffee or take any stimulant to keep me awake; that just fools the body and muddles the mind."

Some writers find the time and circumstances of composition unimportant. Nelsy Massoud, a recent émigré from war-ravaged Lebanon, reports, almost casually, that "I write my essays anywhere — a bomb shelter, a car, a bar — and at any time — four in the morning or three in the afternoon — whenever the feeling is there." And she is always prepared: "I always carry on me a very small notebook and pen." Ann Field offers a more tranquil version of the same conviction: "I can write anywhere. If I don't have a place to sit and a surface to rest the paper on, then I just write in my head. I've written brilliant essays while washing dishes, pulling weeds, and scrubbing the bathtub."

Finding a Topic

For many writers, ideas often come when they least expect them — while taking a shower, riding a bicycle, or reading a newspaper. Sandra Casillas reports, for example, that she has little difficulty writing "when I'm ready. But getting ready is something that can go on for days or weeks. It is not a process anyone can observe. It goes on only in my head. It takes time. The 'voice in my head' talks when I'm driving, washing dishes, and doing things completely unconnected with writing." In contrast, Karen Kramer explains that "if getting started means picking a topic, then the best thing for me to do is to sit and wait. It'll come to me. If I try to think actively about it, I usually panic because I feel under the gun as the assignment deadline nears. However, after several of these intense little panic sessions, interspersed by my doing something completely unrelated to the task at hand, I usually end up with a good topic. I know it's a good topic if I get excited about it, or if I just smile in anticipation of writing about it."

Writing invariably involves a great deal of both patience and self-discipline. Barbara Seidel explains the difficulties of each: "If the subject is not of my choosing, I have to wait until an idea hits me like a ton of bricks, and I am not good at waiting. If the subject is of my choosing, I have to restrain myself to get one word at a time out, rather than one paragraph at a time, and I am not good at self-control."

The number of different tactics the student writers use to find their topics and to get started on exploring their ideas about them is virtually endless —

from deliberate reading and research to peer group discussions and random mental association. Ravenel Boykin Curry has found that "the best way to get ideas (and a more interesting way to live your life) is to look for some kind of significance in little things you observe each day":

> A mother slaps her whining kid on the beach. You can pursue the aesthetic — the sun is shining on thousands of people laughing and playing in the water, but all that fills this kid's being right now is the pain and anger. . . . You can be psychological — is the child a brat because the mother responds with violence? Or could negative incentive help the kid to understand that the world doesn't tolerate a whiner? Take a political angle — should the state be able to intervene in minor family violence? What if the husband slapped the wife? What constitutes child abuse, and who should decide? You can expand anything; ideas are endless.

Monika Jerabek has found that the best way to generate ideas to write about is to read in areas of personal interest. Other students prefer to review the material they are studying in either their writing class or in the other courses they are taking. The assigned reading in these courses may well provide a subject to focus on. Magazines and television news and documentary programs also offer ready sources for topics to write about, subjects that will engage your interest — and your reader's. Have confidence in your ability to decide on an interesting subject to write about. As John Mason observes: "The easiest thing for me to come up with is an idea to write about. The world is filled with subjects to write about." But Mason also reminds us that writing involves a good deal of hard work: "Sitting down and explaining that idea in writing is another matter."

A *journal* is one excellent way to keep track of your ideas about a subject. A journal is a daily record in writing of your experiences and thoughts on particular subjects. Journal entries are usually more focused and related than those in a diary, which poses no restrictions on subject or focus. Beverly Dipo uses her journal to discover — and rediscover — her hopes and aspirations, her fears and anxieties: "I keep my journal hidden as if it were top secret. I feel this writing stuff bares my innermost self to the world and that is uncomfortable for me. How does one go about overcoming that? . . . Writing in a journal is a free psychiatric session that would cost upwards of $50.00 an hour. It recalls feelings you thought were buried long ago, returns your mistakes to haunt you, and for me, it gives me an insight into a self that I am surprised to find." Earnestine Johnson connects her journal entries more directly to her essay assignments. Keeping a journal provides her with useful starting points for writing: "What works best for me is sitting down and writing whatever comes to mind on the subject. I may write ten pages, and once I have reviewed them all, I may find that only two or three pages are useful, but they give me a starting point."

Many writers find that they can discover ideas about a subject by writing down everything they know about it. Barbara Seidel relies on a technique known as *freewriting,* also called *nonstop writing.* She begins writing by "pouring out words, thoughts, feelings down on paper, without concern for grammar or punctuation or neatness. I write in a mad rush and want to be undisturbed at this point in the writing process." Seidel's work as a writer comes later, "in organizing those poured-out feelings and thoughts, in getting them to make sense to someone other than me. Words trip over each other, each demanding to be first." As Seidel implies, the key to using freewriting successfully is to put your pen to paper and continue writing without pausing between words or sentences to consider such elements of composition as grammar, sentence structure, word choice, and spelling. Should you find yourself stuck along the way, repeat an important word and expand on it. For Amber Kennish, freewriting "allows my ideas to work and build upon themselves. To write a paper from these ramblings is usually only a matter of lifting a section of the freewriting from my journal and organizing and focusing it into a coherent essay." She finds it especially useful to freewrite "at different times of the day, while I'm in different moods. From these notes it should be easy to form some kind of thesis."

Many writers follow up on their initial thoughts with another round of freewriting, often called *focused freewriting.* In focused freewriting, the writer reviews the first round of freewriting, selects what seems to be a promising lead in it, and then freewrites about that more limited topic. Judy Jennings offers an instructive sample. Having spent some time freewriting about her marriage and children, Jennings decided to loop back over the subject of her stepchildren to focus more deliberately on, as she says, "the injustices of stepparenting" and "to make a few clarifications about a very misunderstood role."

I don't really know what to say or where to start when I try to talk (or write) a logical something about my relationship with my stepchildren! I think all the time "How did I get myself into this?" When Les and I got married, I was an extremely naive 24 and never realized that I was marrying not only a man, but a man with three kids — a package *deal so to speak. The first thing I think of when I remember back to our early marriage is the second weekend after we were married. It was Les' weekend to have his children. The older son rode with him to pick up the other two. On the way back they came across an old man on the side of the road selling (or rather giving away) puppies — Mongrel dogs if ever there were such. Some awful mixture that looked like a cross between a bloodhound and a chihuahua. They stopped and took not one but two of the horrible bloodshot-eyed pups.*

These notations, still in rough form, served as the basis for Jennings's first draft of her essay "Second-Class Mom." Freewriting and focused freewriting are effective means to deal with what Ravenel Boykin Curry calls the "horrible experience" of having a "piece of paper [that] sits there empty, that white sheet just staring back at you." Frances Taylor aptly summarizes the value of freewriting: "freewriting helps because it liberates ideas at their source while they're still connected up with a great deal of raw power. A lot of writing is generated from which to cull all sorts of marvelous notions."

Other writers prefer to develop ideas through *brainstorming.* Unlike freewriting, which produces ideas by linking or associating one thought with another, brainstorming records thoughts as they come, with no regard for their relation to one another. When writers brainstorm, they often leap from one thought to another without stopping to explore the connections between what may well be two completely unrelated ideas. When Brenda Jacobs set out to write an essay on regional expressions, she decided to brainstorm to come up with a list of words and phrases. Here is what part of it looked like:

Regionalistic expressions
flip flap — fly swatter   pitch a fit — mad
britches — pants
poor — skinny   fixin to go
                             hand down grace — say

chaps ⎫
chill'un ⎬ Kids
younguns ⎭
yonder - far, there
sister / brother
ailing - sick
liter - kindling
sang - community
    singing affair
pot liquor - from greens
⎧ took up with
⎨ took a cold
⎩ <u>took</u> sick

Black dog bit - depressed
2 much sugar for a dime
   tuckered out - tired
I swanee - I declare
  chopping ax
squarehills (squirrels)
   risen - boil
  hollerin - crying
skirttail - hem
     coattails
  ya'll
colorful
rural Southern mystique

Brainstorming, like freewriting, is a writing exercise that can be done virtually anywhere, at any time, and at any pace. When Petrea Galloway is at work developing ideas for an essay, she is concerned that she will get, as she notes, "too much ahead" of herself: "so I hurry and write it anywhere. I've written on the bottom of Kleenex boxes, in book matches, on theater tickets, my shoe. . . ." Her advice about this stage of thinking in writing is simple: "just get it down."

Exercises such as freewriting and brainstorming are excellent confidence builders, especially for relatively inexperienced writers. Such writers can produce a great deal of writing in a very short time. These exercises also enable writers to see rather quickly just what they have to say about a subject while resisting the urge to edit their work prematurely. Whether you write in a leather-bound journal or on the inside of a matchbook, doing your thinking in writing is perhaps the best way to discover a subject. A practiced writer is usually an effective writer.

Purpose

Once they have settled on a subject, most student writers decide on a purpose for writing about that subject; they make decisions about what to say and how to say it. The first of these concerns establishes the general content and the overall goal of the essay. The second focuses on the structure and tone of the essay. Whether an essay is designed to narrate, describe, explain, convince, or persuade, a clearly stated purpose helps ensure its effectiveness and marks most of the essays printed in this book. In most cases, the students' motives for writing include, but are rarely restricted to, the understandable desire to earn an outstanding grade. For some student writers, the pure pleasure of working with words is an added attraction of writing. For others, writing offers the prospect of helping change attitudes and behavior: to defeat a prejudice or upset a stereotype, to underscore the dignity of the oppressed or the terminally ill, to change long-standing opinion on public issues. Steve West wanted to demonstrate "the inadequacy of the Reagan administration's justifications for the Grenada invasion"; Greg Weekes "to show others the horrors of the modern whale hunt and to impress upon my readers that the 'romance' of the nineteenth century whale hunt is gone"; Linda Lavelle "to show that blue-collar workers are not necessarily illiterate or lacking in ambition. I wanted the reader to remember to view people as individuals, not write them off as a group."

A clear purpose need not be as public or as issue-oriented. For many writers, the principal purpose for writing is as simple as wanting to narrate or describe an experience, record a personal anecdote, remember a family story, or recover the pleasure of reading a book, hearing a concert, or seeing a film or play. Just as there is no single, sure-fire way to succeed at writing, there is no single definition of an appropriate subject or purpose in writing. Whatever your purpose, try to make it as clear as possible. As Kelly Mays reminds us, "It is important to gain the reader's interest with a clear and interesting statement of purpose, which then should be heightened and fulfilled by careful and organized evidence within the body of the paper." Deciding on a clear purpose for writing can be, as she notes, "a very creative process."

Audience

Imagining an audience looms large in the mind of every writer. The writer's view of the reader invariably helps determine the extent of an essay's success. The writer usually asks, "Who is my reader? What do I have to do to lead that person to understand what I want to say about the subject?" The first question addresses the knowledge, background, and predispositions of the reader toward the subject. The second points to the kinds of information or appeals that the reader is most likely to respond to. Yet, not all writers begin to concern themselves with the issue of audience from the beginning of their work on an essay.

The primary concern of most writers, however experienced they may be, is to establish authority over their own experience, to express as clearly and as deliberately as possible a sense of control over their own ideas. Johnna Benson puts it this way: "When I start, I'm trying to find my ideas and make them meaningful to myself. I try to get a hold of what I want to say, but my ideas don't always make sense to other people in that form. Then I start trying to present the ideas, but the ideas are set." For William Malley, the initial stage of the composing process is "a very private thing." Like many other student writers, he doesn't consider the issue of audience until he feels that he understands fully what he is trying to say in an essay. Karen Kramer underscores this point when she notes: "The fact that someone is going to read my writing doesn't really influence me as far as I'm aware. . . . I don't think about my audience when I'm getting started. When I begin writing, I set out to produce something that I enjoy writing and reading, and I hope everyone else will enjoy it too." As Terry Burns explains, writing with an audience in mind initially "made me very nervous. But as I gained confidence, the nervousness lessened. Now I encourage people to read my writing. The influence an outsider can have on your work can be invaluable. I usually don't think much about my reader until my last couple of drafts; the first drafts are for me."

Since all student writers prepare papers to satisfy course requirements, they are also mindful of their instructor's presence in their audience. Some student writers deal with what they regard as their instructor's intimidating presence by imagining themselves writing for teachers with whom they can relax. Others, practiced in and encouraged by the principles of collaborative learning, write specifically for their peers. But whether they are writing for a teacher, their peers, or an audience beyond the classroom, the fact that someone is going to read their writing imposes a good deal of discipline on most student writers. Thinking about their readers will help student writers make decisions about appropriate subjects, the kinds of examples to include, the type and level of language to use, and the overall organization of the essay. Every writer wants to be clear and convincing; most consciously try to minimize the risks of being misunderstood.

Outlining

To reduce the possibility that they will be misunderstood and to maximize the likelihood that they will appreciate the implications of their own ideas, all writers find it particularly useful to plan the scope and sequence of their ideas carefully before or during the course of writing a first full draft. For many students, outlining figures prominently in that effort. Yet *when* they turn to outlining varies greatly. Some student writers routinely outline their essays in their minds before they ever set pen to paper. David Christman, for example, notes his habit of composing "the main idea and some supporting ideas in my head." Amber Kennish creates "a basic outline in my head of where the paper will start, progress, and end. The actual writing is a matter of fitting my ideas logically into this outline." Linda Lavelle lets "the idea for an essay rattle around in my head for a few days until a few key phrases or sentences develop. With these few key phrases in mind, I can sit down to plan and write an essay and then come up with something that resembles a first draft."

Beverly Dipo reports "My writing process may be unique. I can write, and have written, an entire outline and the first paragraphs of an essay at night, in bed, in my head." As she explains, "I pretty well have my outline in my head before I actually start writing. I sit down at the typewriter and start typing my thoughts on paper. I'm a pretty organized person, so my first thoughts seem to organize themselves; sentences fall into paragraphs naturally for me. I some-times use an outline to get an idea going, but I seem to outline in my head better. This was easy with the short essays we were required to do. I imagine it would be difficult for longer works." Carol Oberhaus describes a method of composing that is equally unique: "I make an outline to help me limit the topic. When that is done, I study it for a few moments, then put it aside. My next step is always to do a lot of freewriting and note-taking. I simply empty my mind onto the paper. Later on, I fit the ideas I've made notes on into the framework. I *have* to have a very tight outline because my ideas come from all over the place when I am freewriting and brainstorming. Having the outline gives me the freedom to think because the disciplined part of the essay is done for me."

Other student writers reserve outlining until their writing is well under way. John Siegrist suggests that "brainstorming and freewriting help to select a topic and to determine if it can be adequately covered in a paper. Outlining works well after this because it divides the material into paragraphs." Similarly, Brenda Jacobs's method of composing usually starts with "a list of ideas or words associated with the topic. Depending on the length of the paper, the list is often expanded into an outline — a fairly brief one for short essays, a detailed one for term papers." For Pamela Garrettson, outlining is a handy device to use when a writer gets "stuck": "When I am stuck on a first draft, a rough outline helps me organize my ideas into a coherent order. Also to write down anything, no matter how badly worded or thought out, is preferable to staring at a blank piece of paper. I can always go back and change it later."

Kelly Mays describes an even more intricate system for organizing her essays:

> "Despite the fact that I have always been told of the necessity of an outline, I have never been able to write one. Instead, I tend to brainstorm, thinking about the paper for a long time, even unconsciously, before I actually sit down to write. By the time I do begin, this thinking process has usually helped me to fully formulate my ideas into some cohesive order in my mind and to assemble the evidence which I think supports those ideas. Sometimes for the latter process I also use index cards with quotations and evidence on them which I think are important and pertinent. Physical sorting of these cards can help to organize the evidence when it begins to become too complex to be arranged mentally. When I have gotten to this stage of my thought process, I simply have to make myself sit down and begin to write. The actual process of writing helps further to organize my thoughts and evidence.

In contrast, Johnna Benson finds outlining inhibiting: "Outlining encourages me to discard ideas. I use it later in revising sometimes, but never in the beginning." Matthew Holicek reports that he starts a paper by "just throwing ideas around in my head until I feel I've come up with a satisfactory opening. The rest of the paper works basically the same. I'm one of those people who just hates to waste paper, and I would rather get it right the first time. I hate outlining and brainstorming. However, sometimes I have to if they are required, but in the end I rarely go back to my outline. I don't think I need an outline: I've already got a basic master plan inside my head once I begin writing."

The student writers whose work appears in this book would not be likely to agree on whether it is most helpful to outline an essay before, during, or after writing a first draft. Yet no doubt they would agree that all writers should develop a clear sense of the particular strategies for getting started that work best for them. Practicing these strategies frequently should result in increasing skill and confidence.

DRAFTING

It would not be practical to enumerate all the different ways writers work during the second phase of the writing process—completing a full draft of an essay. Instead, both the introduction to each essay printed in Part II and the Questions for Reading and Revising, along with the Suggestions for Writing that appear after each essay, include detailed information about the specific circumstances in which each essay was written. Here we present just a few general statements from the student writers on their characteristic styles of drafting.

Some writers write to discover what they want to say. In one sense, such writers must see their ideas on paper in order to explore, develop, and revise them. They must write in order to discover and shape their own meaning. William Malley's description of his writing process exemplifies the main features of this style of composing:

> I write the paper in longhand—I never compose at a typewriter, and I do not own a computer. . . . I sometimes sketch a brief outline, but more often I simply begin to write. The first few paragraphs are almost always fairly rough, but within a few minutes I usually fall into a groove. The writing then comes in spurts. I'll write a paragraph or even a page, then go back and look things over. Usually, I write pages and pages in this manner, several of which say the same thing in different ways. The process is time-consuming but worthwhile, because it is in these brief spurts that I churn out the good sentences, the nuts and bolts that can be rearranged and reworked into a good paper.

Writers like Malley usually need to examine their ideas as they are unfolding to clarify, develop, or revise them. Johnna Benson describes herself as "definitely a person who needs to see her ideas on paper before she can evaluate them." To this end, Terry Burns reports that he writes as much as he can in his first draft, without paying "any attention at all to things like punctuation, spelling, and grammar. I just write whatever comes into my head and worry about the mechanics later. I guess this works for me because it frees my mind for writing what I feel, and I don't get bogged down in technicalities." Nelsy Massoud extends Burns's point: "The easiest thing to do is to fill up pages and pages. It's like drawing, the lines must be on the paper." Such writing works incrementally: the writer quickly produces a very rough first draft to sketch out, explore, and develop the controlling idea of the essay and then focuses in subsequent drafts on organizing and polishing that idea. Here is how Beverly Dipo puts it: "Writing for me now is like painting a picture. I have a painting of horses that I did hanging in my living room. It turned out fairly well, but only after much effort. Writing is also something I can accomplish fairly well, with some effort. I am not a 'natural' at anything, including writing."

Some writers proceed at a slower pace. They think carefully about what they are going to say before they commit themselves to writing it out. These writers generally are more comfortable composing in their heads than on paper. They usually regard thinking and writing as separate, and in fact sequential, intellectual activities. David Christman summarizes this method of drafting when he notes: "For the most part I develop the idea in my mind and then sit down at the typewriter and just start in. . . . Most of the time my organization is mental, and I don't put anything down until I start typing." Kelly Mays describes her composing style in slightly different terms:

> I tend to compose in my head a good deal. I often compose whole sentences of the introduction mentally before I sit down to write. By having a very good idea of this portion of the paper prior to actual composition, I order my ideas into the form which they will take in the body of the paper. I think that this process becomes an almost mental outline by which I organize the paper before writing. It is true, however, that the actual writing of the paper greatly aids me in exploring and clarifying my ideas. As they take shape on paper, they often seem to change and take a clearer form in my own mind.

For Terry Burns, careful planning can sometimes produce surprising results: "Most of what I write has been carefully thought out. I can spend weeks turning an idea over and over in my head, until I know exactly what I want to write. Then I sit down and write something totally different."

Many student writers feel most comfortable creating their own distinctive blends of both the write/rewrite and think/write styles of drafting. Matthew Holicek is most comfortable writing when he has worked out beforehand the basic ideas and direction of his essay: "If I know basically what I am going to say and the direction I'm headed, I can usually come up with some lively and somewhat complex sentences right out of my head." Yet, as he explains, he also follows those sentences to wherever they may lead him: "Many times I just get on a roll and everything spills out into place almost perfectly. That's why when I start writing I don't like to stop until I finish the paper or at least that paragraph — for fear of losing my train of thought and the ideas that are floating around in my head." Ann Field makes a similar point when she describes her method of composition:

> I do most, if not all, of my prewriting in my head so it looks as if I'm starting in the middle when I sit down and write. I also try to write my first draft in one sitting. Once I get to the sit-down-and-write stage I know what I want

> to say and how I want to try to say it. And once I get
> started I just can't stop. It's as if the ideas are running away,
> and if I don't get them down on paper in some crude form
> they will be lost forever. In the past I have forced myself
> to stop in the middle of a first draft, and when I've come
> back I have been unable to pick up where I left off.

Karen Kramer prepares her essay carefully enough to be able to rely confidently on writing two drafts: "Generally speaking, the body of the essay was already in my head before I sat down and started typing. Once I think up an introduction, the rest just flowed naturally from there. . . . I typed the paper out, and then I went back and reread it, out loud, and added what I thought was appropriate, changed a few words here and there, etc. I only write two drafts, a rough draft and a final draft. . . . I know I'm finished with the essay when I read it and I wouldn't change, add, or delete anything." And as is the case with most accomplished writers, Kramer knows better than to violate the methods that work best for her.

Most of these writers continue to be aware of their audience as they write, and that awareness helps shape the ways in which they write. But for some, the anxiety about having their work read continues to haunt their efforts to compose. Barbara Carter, for example, pictures her readers as "a passionate group of red-pencil-slashing freshman English students." And Steve West's consciousness of an audience for his writing exacerbates, as he says, "my tendency to want to work out in a first draft every little imperfection as it comes up. I have a hard time leaving something that doesn't sound right, even though I'm aware that I can come back and fix it up later." For many writers, such issues help expedite the process of writing an essay. For an equally large number of others, such questions prompt them to revise.

REVISING

Many writers appreciate the power and permanence that revision can add to the act of writing. When writers revise, they reexamine what they have written with an eye on strengthening their control over their ideas. As they revise, they expand or delete, substitute or reorder. In some cases, they revise to clarify or emphasize. In others, they revise to tone down or reinforce particular points. And, more generally, they revise either to simplify what they have written or to make it more complex. Revising gives writers an opportunity to rethink their essays, to make them accomplish their intentions more clearly and fully. Revising includes larger concerns such as determining whether the essay is logically consistent, whether its main idea is supported adequately, whether it is organized clearly enough, and whether it addresses its intended audience in engaging and accessible terms to satisfy their specific needs or demands. Revising involves looking at the whole essay as well as at each part, at paragraph as well as sentence structure, at ideas as well as specific word choice. Revising enables writers to make sure that their essays are as clear, precise, and effective as possible.

Although revising is often the most painstaking phase of the writing process, it is crucial to successful writing. The student writers included here value the opportunity revising provides to clarify their ideas, sharpen their purpose in writing, tighten and strengthen the structure of their paragraphs and sentences, and refine their selection of examples and word choices. In describing her own procedures for revising, Brenda Jacobs offers an informative overview of this phase of the composing process. For her, revising involves:

> eliminating superfluous words, and sentences that sound terrific, but either don't fit or are redundant. It also means rearranging sentence patterns for smooth, even flow, improving paragraph transition, finding more precise wording, and rearranging paragraphs in a more logical sequence. . . . Normally, while revising, I find myself adding details that I hope add character to the work—description, examples, etc.—things I tend to leave out in the beginning. . . . Each progressive draft deals with smaller details, until finally (ideally) the little bells that go off in my head when something strikes a wrong note quit sounding.

Pamela Garrettson turns to a different metaphor to explain how she knows she is finished revising her essays: "when I read and start grinning like a fool. I get a big kick reading anything I have written well." As Garrettson reports, there are fundamental differences between drafting and revising an essay: "When I begin writing, I have to think divergently, opening my mind to various possibilities and writing techniques. When I revise, however, I must progress toward a particular goal or point and express my arguments and examples in clear, concrete terms." Barbara Seidel underscores this point by observing that revising provides writers with the occasion to distance themselves from their work: "Revising means taking my emotional likes and dislikes out of the writing process, and looking at my work objectively. This is truly difficult to do, because, like most creative people, I am insecure and therefore uncertain of what should stay and what should go."

Writers like Ravenel Boykin Curry revise as they work on their first drafts: "I usually revise as I write, with about three or four sentences to a page (unless I'm using a word processor). My main structure doesn't usually change too much—if something just doesn't work I'd rather start with something fresh. When a page becomes so messy with arrows and cross-outs that I can't read anything on it any more, I'll recopy it on a new sheet, but otherwise I really only have two drafts — my original and my final one, which is written a few days later." Erik Field also rereads each sentence and paragraph several times before moving on to the next one, adding, "the degree to which I revise is directly proportional to the degree of difficulty of the essay."

Other writers revise after they have written a very quick and usually very rough draft. Once they have something on paper, they revise for as long as they have time and energy. Patrick Kinder Lewis accentuates this point when he describes how he revises: "Length and overall development of structure seem the first factors which I weigh. Then I move slowly through the text actually listening to how it sounds to me. Sometimes I just have to take a breather, or I lapse into verbose stiltedness." Beverly Dipo's method of revision produces numerous drafts, each less messy than the preceding: "I take my typewritten rough draft with its double or triple spacing and wide margins and a red pencil. Then I proceed to thoroughly mess up the rough draft with slashes, marks, underlines, parentheses, arrows, exclamation points, secret codes, doodles, and assorted expletives. I will then retype what is left and repeat the procedure until I produce a whole essay without one single red mark!"

Still other student writers require more distance from their first draft in order to revise effectively. Earnestine Johnson reports that "I try to give myself several days between my first draft and my revision. The several days allow me to return to my writing, after what I call putting my work in 'cold storage.' I can review it later with a more critical eye." Petrea Galloway uses a similar method: "I try to get away from my piece for a few days. If that is not possible, a complete change of scenery for a few hours will help. When I return and read it, I may say, 'Really great!' or I might laugh at it and start over." As Ann Field notes, distance from a first draft enables her to "see the essay as if I were not the one who wrote it. Passages that are unclear or unnecessary are easier to see. And sometimes I have thought of new things to write or new ways to write the old things."

Many of the student writers mention the value of reading their work aloud as an aid to revision. Karen Kramer enumerates the benefits of reading essays aloud:

> I read the paper *out loud*. This is very important. I could read a paper a hundred times to myself and never catch something, but if I read it out loud, I'll catch it. Sometimes you have to actually *hear* what you wrote before you realize that it sounds like something a fourth-grader wrote. So, I read it aloud and change what doesn't sound right. Clumsily constructed sentences, weak words, questionable modifiers, etc. all come to light when I read it aloud to myself.

Other students remind themselves of an audience for their writing by asking family or friends to read their essays aloud to them. Johnna Benson, for example, reports that "I recruit people who live on my floor, members of study-groups, and anyone I can get to read my drafts. I have my victims read for the sense of it, not for grammar, though many can not help but comment on grammar. I also ask them to read aloud. That way I can tell if they get the jokes, understand the phrases, etc., without asking them if they noticed it. This technique really helps me . . . because I knew my readers were mainly unwilling, and that forced me to rework anything boring, technical, or that sounded like dead space."

Barbara Carter thinks about her potential readers in very different terms. "Honing down an essay is always difficult for me. I try to picture a classroom filled with students yelling 'Who cares?' when I revise my work." Jonathan Schilk no doubt speaks for many other students writers on the issue of audience in revision when he observes:

> When I first start a paper, the reader is not really that important. I feel at that stage, subject matter is most important. When the first draft has been completed, then it's time to consider readability. . . . Knowing that it is possible that I may have an audience for my work does influence me and my writing. The audience is just as important as the subject material and must be treated with all due regard given to the subject matter. I feel the reader must be treated as an intelligent person with common sense and at the same time I feel obliged to help him or her along on little-known subjects.

Thinking about an audience for their writing also helps many writers revise and edit their essays. When writers and publishers *edit* a piece of writing, they read it with an eye to preparing it for publication, whether that occurs literally in a newspaper, magazine, or a book, or figuratively in the exchange of essays within the community of a classroom, department, college, or university. When writers *proofread*, they reread their final drafts to detect any errors — misspellings, omitted lines, inaccurate information, and the like. Several student writers recommend what they call a "fail-safe" method for proofreading their essays — "read the essay backwards." Doing so enables writers to see the words more clearly outside the context of the sentence.

In general, more experienced writers concentrate on the larger concerns of writing — their purpose, ideas, evidence, structure — before they give attention to such matters as strengthening syntax and searching for the "right word." The student writers here tend to be interested in both when they revise. And they revise well because they are both practiced writers and readers.

An increasing number of students use word processors when preparing their essays. Yet, for Ravenel Boykin Curry, writing with a word processor comes only after he has written his first page: "I still need a pen and paper to write out the opening paragraph with scratches and cross-outs and arrows and scribbles. I have to face the machine with something *real*." For many other students, using a word processor makes revising simpler and less time-consuming. As Ann Field notes, word processors eliminate the drudgery of retyping and offer an added attraction: "The hardest part of revising is cutting out unnecessary parts. It feels like I'm throwing away something important. Now that I have a word processor, I can save all the unnecessary parts and use them someday somewhere else."

When asked to offer some final, general advice to first-year college students to help them improve their writing, the thirty-five Bedford Prize winners gave responses as varied as their descriptions of the distinctive ways in which they compose. Common responses were such good-natured imperatives as "Trust your own experience," "Write about what you know or about what you are interested in learning," "Don't be too critical of yourself," "Don't fear failure," "Listen to your teachers," and "Keep it simple!" Steve West amplifies this last recommendation when he notes that "the biggest problem I think young writers have is a tendency to try to sound too polished and artificially intellectual." "It's not hard," he adds, "for readers to tell when authors are trying to adopt a voice they are not comfortable with, and I would advise students to stick to a simple style that seems natural for them." Perhaps not surprisingly, "Write and write and write" and "rewrite, again and again" are the most frequent refrains in the advice these Bedford prize winners offer their peers. Barbara Carter puts the point most simply: "Write! I've heard it said that no one could write 365 bad essays a year; if you write every day, you are bound to come up with something that is good."

These student writers also urge their peers to read as widely, voraciously, and rigorously as possible. "Be curious about everything," Sandra Casillas urges, "and read everything, even cereal boxes." Earnestine Johnson underscores this advice when she says, "Read as much and as often as possible. I would also encourage other student writers to take as many writing courses, labs, and workshops as possible. I believe growth is through knowledge, be it in life experience or in writing experience."

These prize-winning writers take this advice and enjoy reading—for knowledge *and* pleasure. Asking Petrea Galloway what she likes most about reading is, as she explains, "like asking what I like most about food. First, it keeps the body alive. Then there are the different flavors of the various foods. In reading, I like the learning, the discovery, the thoughts provoked, the pleasure of a good tale, the laughing at great humor, and even the sadness of a tragedy." For Linda Lavelle, "Every well-written story is a teacher, and I love to learn."

Yet these student writers often distinguish between reading for pleasure and reading for an assignment. "Reading for pleasure is direct enjoyment," John Siegrist observes, "while reading for an assignment is indirect enjoyment (getting a good grade)." Terry Burns draws the distinction in slightly more wry terms: "The main difference is that reading for pleasure can keep me up late; reading for an assignment can put me to sleep early." Barbara Carter pushes the distinction even further: "When reading for an assignment, you need to keep a grip on reality and study the structure and composition of the work. This does pay off in your writing process."

Nearly all of the student writers recognize the benefits of reading. Patrick Kinder Lewis, for example, describes himself as *not* being a "reader in the traditional sense in which writers seem to be. That is not to say I don't read: I read voraciously—I can almost never be caught anywhere without a book in my possession. But the habit is more a thirst for wisdom than from any learned-pleasure of reading for its own sake. I didn't grow up reading, but thinking and doing instead." Yet, as he explains, he recognizes in reading the opportunity to "look out of a different window onto the same wonderfully complex world. Like learning a new language, reading is truly liberating." Reading also provides, as Brenda Jacobs notes, the possibility to be "transported to other places and times, allowing me to experience vicariously those things apart from my own reality." "Reading," Barbara Seidel explains, "relaxes me, teaches me, reaches my heart, makes me think about people and lifestyles different from me and mine. It expands my limits of tolerance and makes me realize how fortunate I am in life. I could not think of a life without words." The motivations for writing vary widely among these student writers—from the reasonable desire to earn a good grade to the understandable need to discover more about oneself and one's relation to the larger world. Karen Kramer is fully aware that writing can sometimes be a "chore," but she also regards it as "an incredibly enjoyable experience. I know no greater pleasure than when I have written something I really like. Writing is also one of the easiest ways I know of obtaining a sense of accomplishment." "Besides," she quickly adds, "someone has to keep the liquid paper people in business." For Barbara Seidel, writing is "an emotional release, a very selfish pleasure. It is the only time in my life I am totally selfish. I write for my own sanity."

Most important, these writers are all students who write because they have something to say. "I find," Kim Sport says, "that many, many students fear writing courses and do not see the advantage of taking such a course. Learning to write is the most important element in their education. If they can write, they can pass all other courses that require writing with ease. . . . The ability to write is also a measure of a person's qualifications. It is not to be feared or taken lightly. Everyone should always be proud of what and how they write." "Be a person when you write," Johnna Benson urges. "The more you write what you think, the better you think." Finally, as Frances Taylor explains, the act of writing is a truly distinctive way to assert your presence in the world: "Writing belongs to you. There is no voice on earth like your own, and that equals power, so learn to craft it, and read, read, read."

QUESTIONS FOR THINKING AND WRITING

This exercise gives you an opportunity to examine your own attitudes toward writing in general and, more specifically, toward each stage of the composing process outlined in this chapter. Respond in writing to each of the following questions in as much detail as possible.

1. What are your earliest recollections of writing?

2. Have any members of your family, teachers, or anyone else encouraged you to write? Explain the circumstances.

3. What is the easiest thing for you to do when you write an essay?

4. What is the most difficult aspect of writing for you?

5. What method of getting started is most successful for you? Why do you think that method works for you?

6. If someone walked into your room and observed you trying to get started writing, what would this person see? Write your answer in a paragraph or two.

7. Do you try to avoid writing? If so, what do you do to avoid it?

8. What special habits do you have when you write?

9. What is the ideal environment for you as a writer?

10. How does the fact that your writing has an *audience* influence the way you write? How do you take an audience into account when you are writing an essay?

11. Describe in detail the specific procedures you follow when writing the first draft of an essay.

12. What does revising mean to you? Describe your methods of revision. How

many drafts do you usually write? How do you decide when a paper is finished and there is nothing more that you can do with it?

13. How would you describe yourself as a writer? As a reader?

14. What do you like most about reading? What do you like least? What have you learned about writing as a result of your reading? Identify what you do when you read that helps you when you write.

15. What general advice would you offer other first-year students to help them improve their writing?

16. Add any comments on or clarifications of any aspect of your writing that was not addressed adequately in these questions.

THE ESSAYS

Part II

JOHNNA LYNN BENSON

Brigham Young University
Provo, Utah
Brian S. Best, instructor

Johnna Lynn Benson reports that she drafts most of her papers late at night in her dorm room, a place that "has privacy and yet is near people who will listen to drafts and make comments. . . . I wouldn't recommend my method for writing papers. I need more time to write a paper than most of my friends would. I have to start soon after an assignment is given, and I need time between drafts for my ideas to soak down. I like writing this way because I end up with papers no one else would write—papers that sound like me. And even though I agonize over my papers, I enjoy working at them more than throwing together forgettable papers I never thought about. Some people don't like my kind of paper, and some people includes some professors. It's a choice I made."

Benson's choice to express her own distinctive voice marks virtually every aspect of her life. The eldest of six children, she was born in Santa Monica, California. She explains that the "biggest influence on me was my name, Johnna. It's a combination of my Dad's little-used first name and an unrecognizable portion of my Mom's first name. I always felt like I could take the components of my life and put them together in my own new way." A 1984 graduate of El Camino Real High School in Woodland Hills, California, she has earned two academic scholarships—the Mattel Foundation Scholarship and the Presidential Scholarship at Brigham Young University. "I don't have a major, but it won't be English," she notes. "I don't have a career goal, except to have a career and be able to write in it."

Benson explains that the assignment for her paper was "basically to pick any topic we'd studied in the writing colloquium and talk about it. In a class that jumped from evolution to psychology to philosophy, . . . I should have felt like I was at a topic banquet. But I didn't feel like I had anything to say. In connection with the class, I had an advisor who had the title 'writing lab instructor,' whom I was supposed to meet by such-and-such a date, topic in hand, to plan my paper. I mixed up my appointments and showed up without a subject as my advisor, Chris, was leaving for work. She sat on her moped and made suggestions for topics—all ideas I had looked at and discarded in disgust. I tried to explain to her that I needed a topic I could 'soapbox' on, yell and scream about injustice and ignorance. (My previous paper had been on homosexuality.) She asked me why, and I tried to explain that I was different, that I couldn't present an idea someone else might have thought of. In groping for an example of how I am unique I remembered a book we had been reading, George Kelly's A Theory of Personality. Chris said, 'Look at you, you're yelling at me. I think you'd better do your paper on Kelly.' And she buzzed off to work."

"By now," Benson reports, "I had not only made my writing lab instructor late for work but I had also made myself late to math. I found an empty seat in the back of the class, but I have a weakness in not paying attention to a teacher when more than one hundred people separate us. I turned over my homework and started writing about Kelly,

31

or more accurately, about the things I wanted to say to Chris when she had escaped. I ended up with a page and a half of sarcasm and jokes, mainly about myself. Later I . . . ended up showing a friend what I wrote. . . . He said he also felt different than everyone else. . . . He showed me that he understood what was under the sarcasm. From then on, I wanted to write the paper using Kelly's Theory of Personality only for what light Kelly threw on the topic of myself. I wanted to make my sometimes abstract sense of uniqueness understandable."

For an exercise in peer editing, see Benson's essay in Part V.

Rotten at the Core

George A. Kelly's *Theory of Personality* has scrubbed me on a washboard   1
and put me through the wringer. Discovering what I actually am under the dirt and debris has been bewildering and has left me wondering if I would be better off blissfully ignorant. I had thought "to know thyself" an admirable pursuit, especially since I believed truth was beauty. Now I see I have been beautifully wrong about who I am and who everybody else is.

When the colloquium introduced me to *Theory of Personality*, I was sure we   2
would get along great. I have always loved dabbling in psychology. My friends and I would make Freudian jokes or play shrink-games, using those little tests in women's magazines designed to save on psychoanalysis costs. You could say I won those games; my free associations were always more bizarre than anyone else's. I wasn't even trying to be shocking or clever. That is just a bad habit. My only feud with psychology was that I aspired to be more than a product of my environment, a multiplication of Mormonism by a materialistic middle-class suburb. *Theory of Personality* eliminated that limitation for me.

I loved it instantly. Kelly's treatise holds that people create their own per-   3
sonalities. As a person tries to make sense of the circus around him, he picks up on recurring themes in his life and makes deductions about what is going on. The individual creates these explanations, called "constructs," for his convenience in anticipating what the world is going to hit him with next. As a person construes, he builds an inner road map of himself, of life, and of what he can expect from it. The psychology I had been exposed to before treated man like an organism poked and prodded into reactions. I found the concept of deciding for yourself who you are and what you can expect from life far more palatable. Claiming total responsibility for my outlook on life filled me with satisfaction.

Theory of Personality created a little garden paradise in the corner for me,   4
but it also unearthed something upsetting. As part of our colloquium study of

constructs, we were asked to write about our core roles, or how we viewed ourselves. I kept putting the assignment off because every time I started it, my query led me down the same path. If you do not want to go to Rome, finding that all roads go there is rather dismaying. Suddenly it was the day to hand in the assignment, and I discovered, as I frantically wrote the thing in the Harris Fine Arts Center an hour before class, that I had spent enough time trying not to think about it that I knew exactly what I didn't want to know.

With Fresh, Original, and Bizarre as my highest ideals, my core role seems 5 to be that I must be different. And I am different, which makes me exceptional, though not in a way the general population appreciates. This arrogant idea actuates my every thought and emotion, a realization that makes me shudder. Exploring the fact that I'm rotten at the core reduced me to tears.

Yet I can't seem to get around it. I look at how I hate get-acquainted parties. 6 To adhere "Hello, my name is . . ." on my lapel is to assume common ground exists between these strangers and me. But my core role says my lifeline runs geometrically askew to theirs. Kelly defines guilt as an awareness of contradicting one's core role structure, and guilty well describes the uncomfortable feeling I get pretending such parties aren't futile. I forget that I actually do share significant parallels and intersections with family and friends. I like the differences. By the time I was six I introduced myself by saying, to the consternation of my playmates, that I did not like chocolate cake or soda-pop. For years my favorite color was chartreuse, sienna, or puce. My favorite number is 3.02875×10^{14}. I took up origami because I thought no one had heard of it. In short, anything popular was not worth my time, while anything obscure or new was mine by right.

Moreover, I felt unique enough to assume that although rules were necessary 7 to keep the regulars in line, they did not apply to me. Because rules were necessary, I never quite broke them but found interpretations to suit me. For example, when an elementary class punishment to copy five pages from the dictionary was handed down, my paper always included a few words outside the assigned alphabetical range, like "despot," "toupee," or "maltreatment." Lights-out at camp meant it was dark enough to leave the cabin unnoticed and go for a moonlight walk. Going to parties where friends were too drunk to really notice my abstinence was showing my love and understanding for people with problems, not to mention making them aware of the Mormon Church. And of course, as long as my boyfriend and I didn't go all the way, whatever we wanted to do was fine. We were toying with the idea of marriage anyway. Other people needed rules. I did not.

I have been carried away with my own individuality enough to hypothesize 8 that when I was a zygote, some stray cosmic ray zapped my DNA, making me a daughter of chance and not of Terry and Dianna Benson. On a similar note, I latched onto the idea that I have always existed, that before I was a spirit I was an entity, an intelligence bobbing out somewhere like a chartreuse soap bubble. I did not want to be someone else's creation. I figured God recognized the special and distinctive thing I was and handpicked me to be his child.

Being Mormon has been convenient in other ways. It is a guaranteed way to stick out like a sore thumb. I always felt a swell of pride as I answered astonished cries of "You've never done such and such?" I could spend hours elaborating on LDS precepts with the sole intent of blowing an innocent Protestant mind. I have had so much fun being Mormon that I have to wonder how much of my testimony is based on faith and how much on the attention it garners. I created my outlook on life according to my convenience, says Kelly. My convenient testimony thus becomes as meaningful as my green argyle earrings; I would probably join any group that boasted of being a peculiar people.

Yet my testimony of the gospel encapsulates some of my strongest emotions and most important rational convictions. I founded my belief on study, contemplation, and prayer, not whim. If such a testimony is invalid, there is little I think or feel that is valid. But I must consider I may have forced my personality to grow in unnatural and indirect ways because I wanted to be different, cultivating a taste for mustard on my french fries and a taste for LDS doctrine. I have created my personality and maybe I could have done a better job. Yet the thought of supplanting myself with a new and improved model based on different criteria scares me. It would be personality suicide; although someone would be here named Johnna, I would cease to exist.

And what about all these other people? I always pictured my intelligence as a chartreuse bubble in contrast with their monochromatic assembly of lemon yellow bubbles. If Kelly gives me the right to be self-made, he also extends that right to all those dumb slobs. Besides, I doubt Kelly was lemon yellow. If he and I can be different, then probably everyone else is on a slightly different wavelength, can be a slightly different color. This means I probably don't stand out at all. I have always understood why people were worried that God might not know them specifically. There was no reason for him to bother when they were all the same. But if everyone is a unique individual, how does Heavenly Father remember which fingerprint I am? In my place in the sun, I did not notice all those stars out there, each one shining bright for someone. I do not feel important or special while gazing at billions of stars.

For the first time in my life I feel truly lost, an electron carrying practically no weight, fairly indistinguishable from any other electron, whose orbit is an unknown in a probability cloud. I am looking at life in a new and startling way, and this is the ultimate test of my taste for the new and startling. I find myself attempting to straddle the importance of my uniqueness and the existence of 4.5 billion other unique individuals. I do not like wondering who I am. I could always tell before by the stark contrast between me and anyone else. I had three dimensions and the other person only had two. Now I see that I just had no depth perception.

How everyone can be different intimidates and amazes me. Without its 13 former base, my sense of identity has become as fragile as the chartreuse soap bubble I imagine as its beginnings. I fear the existence of all the variegated personalities that might crowd and pop it. Yet in returning to that sense of fragile newness, I see the world freshly. I have bemoaned the fact that no one could appreciate my special outlook. Now I see there are countless other outlooks for me to explore, each a world as strange and wonderful as mine. For the first time there is an impetus for me to get to know people. This potential soothes my battered psyche and fills me with wonder in proportion to my fear.

QUESTIONS FOR READING AND REVISING

1. Johnna Benson's instructor, Brian Best, reports that her interdisciplinary writing colloquium had been reading George Kelly's *A Theory of Personality*, "which discusses the roles, or 'constructs,' people adopt and stresses that all of us have alternative possibilities if we are willing to re-examine our constructs and experiment with other ways of going about creating our self-identity. We had also read Lao Tse, the *Tao Te Ching*, and the *Book of the Hopi*, with the intent of getting some idea of how other cultures view their world. All of this apparently worked for Johnna, and she found herself in something of an identity crisis. Her journal and her rough drafts of this paper became her personal battleground with some long-held personal constructs which she began to question." Outline the major points that Johnna Benson makes in her essay. How is each of these points specifically connected to George Kelly's book, *A Theory of Personality*? How does Benson use Kelly's book to help organize her essay?

2. What assumptions does Benson seem to make about her audience's familiarity with *A Theory of Personality*? Where and how does Benson provide her readers with information about Kelly's theory? Consider, for example, paragraph 6. In writing it, Benson notes that she "spent a great deal of time trying to find concrete examples to back up the connection between Kelly's theories and my own." How successful is she in this paragraph at accomplishing that goal? What overriding point does she make about herself in this essay? What examples does

she offer to support it? How does she connect it to Kelly's theory? What exactly does she mean when she judges herself to be "rotten at the core"? How does she expect her *audience* to react to her use of this phrase?

3. Benson reports that one of the goals of her essay is "to make my sometimes abstract sense of uniqueness understandable." What specific examples does Benson use to make this abstract notion understandable to her audience? Do these examples suggest that her self-awareness increased gradually or occurred suddenly in a moment of revelation while reading Kelly? Point to specific words and phrases to verify your response.

4. One of the strengths of Benson's essay is the lively, honest voice she uses to address her readers. Figurative language helps make this voice memorable. See, for example, paragraph 1, where she notes that "Kelly's *Theory of Personality* has scrubbed me on a washboard and put me through the wringer." What is the nature of this metaphor? Why is it particularly appropriate to Benson's overall *purpose* in writing? Point to other examples of Benson's use of metaphors and assess what each contributes to the points she wants to emphasize.

5. In describing how she writes, Benson notes: "I also cram initial drafts with jokes and cynical parenthetical comments. They keep me entertained and sometimes evolve into relevant subtopics." For example, in paragraph 2, she speaks of how "My friends and I would make Freudian jokes or play shrink-games, using those little tests in women's magazines designed to save on psychoanalysis costs." What is the nature of the cynicism expressed here? Reread Benson's essay and identify other moments when her voice seems to be marked by lingering traces of "jokes and cynical parenthetical comments." What does each contribute to the overall effectiveness of her essay?

6. Benson explains that she drafted this essay "in sections rather than just plodding through the whole paper. I spent a lot of time on the third paragraph, trying to explain Kelly without getting overtechnical or breaking the tone." Reread that paragraph carefully and evaluate how successful she has been. What writing strategies does she use to avoid being "overtechnical"? How successful is she in maintaining the overall *tone* of her essay in this particular paragraph? Point to specific words and phrases to support your response.

7. In discussing the satisfactions and frustrations of writing this essay, Benson observes: "Finding a way to say what I really mean plagued me in the paragraphs on religious attitudes. I would draft and ask myself, 'Is that what I think?' " Reread paragraphs 7 through 10. What role have her religious beliefs and practices played in her increasing self-awareness? What exactly does she mean at the end of paragraph 10 when she talks about "personality suicide"?

8. Benson explains that she worked her way through "one package of notebook paper and half a package of typing paper" as she prepared the multiple drafts of this essay. "I write on every other line in drafts and then cross most every-

thing out. I'm hard on trees." Here is one of Benson's earliest drafts of what became paragraph 6:

> Yet I can't seem to get around it. Kelly defines guilt as "awareness of dislodgement of the self from one's core role structure," a realization that you've contradicted your core role. Guilt can act as a trailmaker pointing to the core role maligned. No wonder I feel guilty at parties where everyone runs around with "Hello, my name is." It's not right for me to act that way, anxious to meet and make friends because people are not my peer group. My lifeline runs geometrically skew, no parallels and no intersections. Of course a logical voice in the back of my head will intone that for me to be so alien to the human race is simply not true. Interactions with family and friends deny the possibility. Logic is thereby, however, ignored. Since I believed I was so set apart, I set myself apart; the conviction was a self-fulfilling prophecy.

Compare and contrast this very early version of paragraph 6 with the final draft of Benson's essay. Which points from this early draft does Benson preserve in the final version and how is each developed? What are the choices she made as a writer in moving from one draft to another? In what specific ways does Benson's revised version more successfully support the overriding point of her essay? How might her final draft of this paragraph be strengthened further?

9. The conclusion of her essay posed special problems for Benson. "Since I don't draft straight through, there is no exact number of drafts. Some parts were only worked about three times, but the ending had at least twenty attempts. . . . Ending the essay was difficult because I felt I had really reached no conclusions; I had a diagnosis but no prescription." Reread Benson's essay carefully, with special emphasis on the relationship between the final paragraph and the rest of the essay. Show how she is—or is not—accurate in her assessment that her essay provides a "diagnosis but no prescription" and point to specific words and phrases to support your response. If Benson had the opportunity to revise her essay, what specific recommendations would you offer her to help strengthen her final paragraph?

SUGGESTIONS FOR WRITING

1. In paragraph 7, Johnna Benson notes: "I felt unique enough to assume that although rules were necessary to keep the regulars in line, they did not apply to me. Because rules were necessary, I never quite broke them but found interpretations to suit me." She then offers as an example to support this point

an anecdote about "an elementary class punishment to copy five pages from the dictionary" and that she included several words "outside the alphabetical range." Consider an incident in your own experience in which you thought that, "although the rules were necessary to keep the regulars in line, they did not apply" to you and write an expository essay in which you recount an incident that illustrates this point. What "lesson" did you learn about yourself— and rules—as a result of this experience?

2. Each of us has had one or more experiences that have fundamentally changed our perceptions of ourselves and of our relationship to those around us. This changed perception might well have also led to substantial changes either in our way of doing something or in our relationships with others. Write an essay in which you re-create that experience. Show how it changed not only your perception of yourself but also your behavior.

3. One of the features that makes Benson's essay effective is her deft use of humor. Psychology and psychiatry have often been the subjects of both cynical and good-spirited humor. Gather as many "professional" jokes about one occupation as you can. What traits do these jokes have in common? Write an *expository* essay using these jokes as *examples* to illustrate what you take to be the general public's prevailing perception of this profession.

TERRY L. BURNS

Canisius College
Buffalo, New York
Robert Durante, instructor

"Being the youngest in a large family made it hard to be taken seriously. I always had things to say, but it was difficult to get anyone to listen. I find writing a better way to say what is on my mind. If I get words just right, I can make people listen." Terry Burns needs no special circumstances or environment to write. *"I can write just about anywhere,"* he notes, *"at work, on the bus, in a bar, anywhere but at my desk. . . . All I need is a pen, some paper, and a very large ashtray."* Given the size of his family, Burns has no difficulty writing in the midst of commotion: *"I know most people like it quiet when they write, but I just can't think when it's quiet. Crank up the stereo and I'm in business."* He writes his drafts in longhand, and then types only his final version: *"I don't type well, and I can lose a thought before I can put it on paper."*

Terry Burns was born in Buffalo, New York, the youngest of nine children. A self-described apathetic student in his *"younger"* years, Burns has become increasingly interested in writing. He plans to major in English and pursue a career as a free-lance writer. Reading a great deal of fiction occupies a good portion of his time away from classes, and he includes Edgar Allan Poe, Dick Francis, and Kurt Vonnegut among his favorite writers. *"The main difference between reading for pleasure and reading for an assignment,"* he observes, *"is that reading for pleasure can keep me up late and reading for an assignment can put me to sleep early."*

In the following essay, Burns re-creates the response of *"a scared eighteen-year-old, far from home,"* to a violent initiation into military life and ritual.

The Blanket Party

Crickets chirped in the grass surrounding the compound as four men, dressed 1 only in white government issue underwear, made their way through the dark barracks. Airman Goodrich woke as the rough, military blanket settled over his head and chest. He tried to move, but the four men held the blanket securely, pinning him to his bunk. His feet kicked as a fifth man rose from his neighboring bunk and began to pummel him to unconsciousness. Goodrich's screams shattered the night, yet no one moved a muscle to help. Though the snoring, which was incessant at night, had stopped abruptly and completely, everyone pretended to sleep. When the screaming and pleading had finally died away, Goodrich was motionless. The moonlight poured through the windows, casting unearthly shadows across his body.

After ten minutes of total silence, the taps on Sgt. Siat's shoes could be 2
heard echoing in the long, tile hallway. The fluorescent, overhead lights blinked
on, momentarily blinding the entire flight. Everyone was standing at "Attention," as Sgt. Siat, perfectly creased and polished, walked the length of the
barracks, the taps on his shoes adding an exclamation point to each step. He
stopped at Goodrich's bunk and pulled the blood-soaked blanket from his face.
As he turned and surveyed the entire flight, Sgt. Siat's lips bent to form a
smile that didn't quite reach his eyes. If any concern showed on his face it
was certainly not for Goodrich. Why should he waste his concern on Goodrich? He couldn't march, he couldn't make his bed, he couldn't even shine
his shoes right. The Sergeant threw the blanket on the foot of Goodrich's
bunk, turned on his heel, and headed toward his office to call the base ambulance.

The ambulance arrived, along with two Military Police officers. As the 3
ambulance attendants piled the broken, battered body of Goodrich onto a
stretcher, the MPs finished their cursory investigation and left, thinking nothing of the fact that a man could be mercilessly beaten as one hundred men
slept on in the same room.

The "Blanket Party" was a rarely mentioned, but highly encouraged method 4
of dealing with malingerers and incompetents. It was the favorite method of
some of the "best" instructors. Give extra duty to everyone when one man
consistently made mistakes, and eventually some of his peers would visit him
in the night. The training missed while in the hospital would cause him to be
recycled into a younger flight and then he was someone else's problem. The
"Blanket Party" seemed to work just fine when a man could do the work but
wouldn't. Airman Goodrich, a meek, nervous, unhealthy-looking young man,
just could not do the work. He was easily shaken and seemed on the verge of
tears anytime anyone raised his voice. But the men who are your comrades
and buddies can easily become your enemies when deprived of even a few of
the already meager privileges.

The young men who had joined this organization with the dream of becom- 5
ing "men" had been betrayed by the people they had trusted. They had in
reality become a mob, skulking in the darkness, preying on people as they
slept, always making sure to cover their victim's face, not so much to avoid
being seen as to avoid seeing. The act of felonious assault is much easier when
your victim is faceless. Back at the barracks, life went on as usual, but not for
Goodrich; two flights and two "Blanket Parties" later, Goodrich was discharged
for a defective attitude. The men who had assaulted him, as well as those who
had looked on, went on to graduate. But Goodrich, his face still swollen and
his hair just a shadow on his head, was sent home to face his family.

QUESTIONS FOR READING AND REVISING

1. Terry Burns's advice to other students in first-year writing courses is to "get a good first sentence. A reader can decide if he likes a story very quickly, and you have to hook them as soon as possible." Reread the opening sentence of Burns's essay carefully. In what specific ways does that sentence demonstrate the soundness of his own advice? What features of the sentence encourage—and even impel—his readers to continue reading?

2. Characterize Burns's *point of view* in this essay: Is he detached and objective? Involved and subjective? Some other combination? Where and how is his point of view established? Does it remain consistent throughout the essay? If not, when and how does it change, and with what effect? Support your response with an analysis of specific words and phrases from the essay.

3. What larger significance does Burns find in the ritual of beating Airman Goodrich? When and how does he signal this significance to his readers? What overall point is he trying to make in his essay?

4. Reread Burns's first two paragraphs. How does his choice of phrasing reinforce the ominous story he tells? What, for example, is the effect of his repeating *taps* in paragraph 2? In what other ways is this an effective word choice? Point to additional examples of phrasing in these two paragraphs that heighten the effect Burns tries to create.

5. Consider Burns's final paragraph. What is the effect of using "organization" in sentence 1? What attitude toward the military does this word choice express? Toward Airman Goodrich? Does Burns's attitude toward the military—and toward Goodrich—remain the same throughout this paragraph? What issue is embedded in the final sentence? Why would Goodrich's facing his family be an issue—either for him or for Burns? What does the last sentence tell his readers about Burns's attitude toward Goodrich?

6. Burns wrote several drafts of this essay. The following is his first draft of the opening paragraph:

> Screams shattered the sleep of one hundred men in the dark barracks as Airman Goodrich pleaded for help. Everyone knew what was happening. Three men were holding a blanket over Goodrich's upper torso and head as the fourth pummeled him into unconsciousness, yet no one moved a muscle to help. Everyone pretended to be asleep, though the snoring, which was incessant at night, had stopped abruptly and completely. When the screaming finally stopped the room was deadly silent. The only sounds to be heard were the chirping of the crickets in the grass surrounding the compound and the ominous buzz of the

locust in the trees. Goodrich lay still on his bunk, the moonlight pouring through the windows, casting eerie shadows across his body.

Compare the two drafts of the opening paragraph of this essay. What specific changes do you notice? Comment on the effectiveness of each change. Which version do you prefer? Why?

7. Burns notes that, "while revising is not the easiest part of writing, I find it to be the most satisfying part. Rearranging sentences and searching for just the right word or phrase until I have a clear and concise finished product is very gratifying to me." Here is Burns's last sentence as it stood *before* the final draft: "Airman Goodrich was sent home to face his family, discharged, according to his separation papers, for a 'Defective Attitude.' " Reread the final draft sentence of Burns's essay and consider the revisions he made as he prepared the final draft. Which version do you prefer? Why? How well do the terms *clear* and *concise* apply to his revisions?

SUGGESTIONS FOR WRITING

1. In an earlier draft of his essay, Terry Burns added a series of sentences to his final paragraph that read, in part: "Goodrich, as well as the rest of these young men had been betrayed by a group of people they had trusted to show the way to adulthood, to lead them away from the simple world of childhood to the complex world of men." Write an essay in which you *argue* that the "way to adulthood" should (or should not) include experience with violence. What role should violence play in the move from "the simple world of childhood to the complex world" of adulthood? Support your position with evidence from your own experience and from contemporary world events.

2. The world we live in is filled with various rituals: hazing for fraternities and sororities, joining a team, preparing to jog, studying for exams, and the like. Choose a ritual that is part of your own life and write an essay in which you explain your participation in—and reaction to—this ritual.

3. In the final paragraph of his essay, Burns notes that the soldiers who had beaten Airman Goodrich acted like a mob, "preying on people as they slept, always making sure to cover their victim's face, not so much to avoid being seen as to avoid seeing." Choose a contemporary example of such "faceless" violence and write an essay in which you re-create the nature of the incident and draw some conclusions about the effects of this incident on those involved and on American society in general.

BARBARA J. CARTER

Rogue Community College
Grants Pass, Oregon
Mary Slayter, instructor

"Early evening is the best writing time for me," reports Barbara Carter. "The thoughts of the day are still with me; the commitments of the day are behind. If someone walked in and observed me writing they would see a woman (me) with one hand on a coffee cup and the other gripping a pencil, staring alternatively from the window to the pages spread before her with a mildly mad look in her eye. In spurts of decision, she gulps her coffee and rapidly scribbles words on the paper until her shoulders relax and the madness seems to be replaced with a bemused smile."

Barbara Carter was born in Whittier, California, into a "solid middle-class family that encouraged artistic expression." She is interested in music and theater, and manages a dinner theater in Santa Barbara that encourages the production of plays by new playwrights. Her advice to fellow writers is to "Write! No one could write 365 bad essays a year; if you write every day, you are bound to come up with something good."

Asked to write a "snapshot" description of a person or place, Carter reports: "I wanted my memories to speak to the memories of others. The way that I remember the cupboard is not the same as others do—it may not even be the way it was—but I wanted to promote the idea that our recollections shape our future. My essay is written primarily from a childhood perspective and should be read with that in mind. We all have a cupboard of some kind in our mind."

Momma's Cupboard

In the back of the house, down the long hall between bedrooms and past the laundry chutes, the pantry squatted cramped and dark. It looked like a wart on the house, an architectural afterthought. It was ugly with its weak-tea-stained-plywood veneer and wonderful with its bounty and visions.

Momma called her crowded pantry the guest cupboard and under threats of a sound shaking, we knew better than to sneak a treat. How longingly we children dreamed of the delicacies stacked up in there; how patiently we awaited the guests that never came to relish and sup the goodies that lay within. With every Christmas the gift packs of smoked meats would arrive, make their way into the pantry, and never come out again. Valentine's Day meant one more can of Almond Roca to be set on the second shelf. Every birthday that went by meant one more bottle of vanilla flavoring bought in good faith for the cake to come—but it seemed there was never a child that was good long enough for it to be made.

Sometimes, late in the evening when Momma was at school, we would line   3
our little bodies up at the pantry door like stacking dolls and dream of the
dinner party that was sure to come some day. Stored on the bottom shelf were
my favorite supplies: canned sardines, oysters, salmon packs, and Dinty Moore
Beef Stew. My big sister liked the second shelf with its Almond Roca, candies,
mandarin orange segments, and maraschino cherries. Jim wanted the salty stuff:
pretzels, shoestring potatoes, peanuts, and pecans. Linda settled for whatever
was left over: popcorn kernels, canned clam chowder, apricot nectar, Beeman's
Gum. Robert, the oldest and tallest, lay general claim over it all as befitted
his position. We never ate anything from Momma's pantry, but I remember,
on one occasion, my eldest brother passing around a bottle of vanilla flavoring
that we ceremoniously drained dry.

There weren't a lot of shared plans and dreams in my childhood home, but   4
that pantry was a focal point for everyone. We have all developed opinions
and theories about its effect on our lives—the denials and broken dreams, the
promise that never came. No guest ever did arrive in time for dinner; to my
knowledge no one was ever invited. The day we drank the vanilla flavoring
was the day we stopped believing in birthday cakes or cupboard fantasies.
Although we kept up the illusion for a while, by the time I was in my teens
the pantry was only mentioned when new supplies arrived. We could all be
trusted by then to put the goodies away into that little back room, pausing
only long enough to wipe the shelf dust off our fingertips.

Last year when I moved my parents out of the old childhood home, I   5
followed Momma's explicit instructions, packed up the contents of the pantry
into little cardboard boxes, and donated them all to the church. Someone,
someplace, is having dreams for dinner. Someone is eating my sardines.

QUESTIONS FOR READING AND REVISING

1. Barbara Carter creates a picture of her childhood by focusing on her mother's
   pantry. What did the pantry represent to Carter as a young girl? What does
   the pantry represent to her now as an adult?

2. Carter's essay reflects on an important place in her childhood. It is easy to be
   sentimental and romantic about such places; how does Carter avoid sentimentality?

3. Carter never comes out and makes any direct statements about her mother.
   Rather, we learn everything indirectly through Carter's *description* of the pantry. For instance, in paragraph 4 Carter writes: "No guest ever did arrive in

time for dinner; to my knowledge no one was ever invited." What does this detail tell the reader about her mother? What other passages are similarly indirectly revealing? How is this an effective strategy?

4. One of the most powerful pictures in Carter's essay is that of Carter and her siblings: "Sometimes, late in the evening when Momma was at school, we would line our little bodies up at the pantry door like stacking dolls and dream of the dinner party that was sure to come some day." Why does Carter tell us what each sibling liked in the pantry? How does this information advance her purpose?

5. Carter uses details very effectively. Find specific details and explain what they tell us about the pantry, about Carter's family, and about Carter herself. To what senses do these details appeal?

6. Does Carter maintain a clear, definite *point of view* toward her subject? If so, how?

7. Compare Carter's description of the pantry in paragraph 1 with her reference to it at the end of paragraph 4 as "that little back room." Why is each *description* appropriate for her *purpose?*

8. Carter ends her essay with these simple, but powerful lines: "Last year when I moved my parents out of the old childhood home, I followed Momma's explicit instructions, packed up the contents of the pantry into little cardboard boxes, and donated them all to the church. Someone, someplace, is having dreams for dinner. Someone is eating my sardines." Why is this an effective *conclusion?*

9. In an earlier draft, the last sentence in paragraph 2 read: "Every birthday that went by meant one more bottle of vanilla flavoring bought in good faith for a cake never made." Compare this sentence with her revised version. What is the effect of the change?

10. Carter begins her description of the pantry in her introductory paragraph. Yet in an earlier draft, these two paragraphs introduced the essay:

> There were seven of us tugging, shoving, and scrambling up together in a medium-sized home in a very large sub-urban track. Our neighborhood—in its vast pretense of privacy—was one where you could walk for miles without getting anywhere and yet always feel a little lost. Inside our cluttered home, filled with elbows, secrets, and twenty years of *National Geographic,* that same feeling prevailed.
>
> I have few vivid memories of my childhood. Most of the years and the times that were my youth are a mist in my mind. I am the youngest child; many of my memories are stories that I heard so often I made up my own recol-lections for them. Some of my memories might not be true.

But then there are those few that are grounded in their
childlike perception—persistent in their visits—and real.
One of these is the memory of Momma's pantry.

Why do you think Carter dropped these two paragraphs? What effect does
the revised introduction have on the reader? What is the effect of beginning
in such a direct way?

SUGGESTIONS FOR WRITING

1. Select a place that represents the color and texture of your childhood. Write
an essay *describing* this place and showing how it represents some important
aspect of your childhood.

2. Consider an important person or place from your childhood. Interview your
siblings, if possible, to see what this person or place meant to them. Write an
essay *describing* this person or place that incorporates the various perceptions
of each sibling. *Compare and contrast* these various perceptions.

3. Choose an incident in your life that marked the turning point between childhood and adulthood. Write an essay in which you reflect on this turning point
and explain its significance to you.

4. *Compare and contrast* two kitchens or bedrooms or any two rooms in a house.
Explain how the personalities of the inhabitants are reflected in the possessions
and arrangement of the rooms.

SANDRA CASILLAS

University of Texas at El Paso
El Paso, Texas
Alicia Gaspar de Alba, instructor

"Writing was a magic I could hardly wait to learn," Sandra Casillas confesses. *"I used to get my older cousin to write words for me on my drawings, and then I would copy them and go over them when they faded."* Sandra Casillas traces her interest in writing to the encouragement of her mother but decided early on to concentrate on art. *"Writing took second place,"* she notes. Now an art major at the University of Texas at El Paso, Casillas combines her study of art with work in advertising and art instruction at a nearby Episcopal school.

Born in Phoenix, Arizona, Sandra Casillas grew up in an artistic family. Her father was a jeweler, her mother a poet, her brother a sculptor. Art remains a central fact in her life:

> To be an artist, it is necessary to be as serious and as free in
> your thinking as possible. I have always kept a journal since
> high school but I have never done any writing for other people
> until I was forced to take freshman English courses.

Asked by her instructor to write a research paper about a ceremony or ritual from a foreign culture, Sandra Casillas was determined to write about a subject related to her major interest.

She began her research by focusing on the beauty of Raku pottery, which, she later discovered, plays a prominent role in the Japanese tea ceremony. *"My idea developed as I read, and each book and bit of information led me to new ideas and questions, as well as a few answers. It was very exciting to immerse myself in this completely new and unknown subject."* The result is an essay that examines the fascinating process of an ancient Japanese ceremony, a ceremony used for centuries, as Casillas notes, *"to teach the people of Japan tranquility, respect, aesthetics, and restraint."*

Cha-No-Yu,
the Japanese Tea Ceremony

Imagine yourself in a loose flowing robe of pure silk, sitting on a cushion 1
in a small austere room so sparse of decoration that you might compare it with
a cell but for the warmth of the lovely woodwork and the delicate balance of
its simple lines. Imagine that you came to this quiet room in a series of modes
of travel so foreign to this setting that you might have come by sheer magic.

The manner in which we matter-of-factly accept the incredible heights and speeds of transoceanic flight and ride across Japan at over 100 mph in the futuristic "Bullet," electric miracle of public transportation, is an act of faith in modern technology, if not an acceptance of magic.

The transition from chaotic modern life to the tiny tranquil chamber in which you now find yourself has been provided by entering through a rustic gate into a miniature garden of almost other worldly charm. Each paving stone has been set in a carefully thought-out design. You feel that each pebble in the garden has been counted and has a special significance. The sand around the large rocks to one side of the path has been raked into a pattern of ridges that represent ocean waves. Each tree and shrub has been carefully pruned to perfection. Though foreign, you cannot help but admire the controlled beauty of the scene and forget the outside world. You are asked to sit on a small bench with a rustic shelter overhead in case of rain. The spot has been carefully chosen to give you a moment for quiet contemplation of this garden-of-an-other-world. When you continue on your way, you will find you are noticing more of nature than you thought possible in so small a garden. Even the sound of the pines is intriguing in this tight little area. Small is big, you think, as you look at the lovely details of landscape design reflected in a single pool. A rock tied up like a gift with a single rope is found sitting at forks in the path to show where you need not travel (Nishihara 99). Very near the tea house is a stone basin with water running through for the purification ritual of washing your hands and rinsing your mouth.

The entrance to the tea house is an opening three-feet tall. By sitting on the threshold and removing your shoes, you can easily swing your feet inside and enter. The patina of the wooden floor is soft and glowing, mellow and smooth, never touched by anything but stockinged feet. The room is small, a bare ten feet square. You remember what you read about a tea room where the very holy Manjushiri received 84,000 disciples of Buddha and it was fine since space is of no consequence to the truly enlightened (Repplier 140). The empty room, a place "to create your own universe of calm and peace away from the world (Nishihara 96) is reminiscent of the isolation tanks used by many to find tranquility ("Nirvana"). You admire an ancient scroll in the tokonoma (sanctuary) that has been especially chosen for this occasion. A slight noise of the host outside at the purification basin is your cue to be seated.

Now, as the ceremony proceeds, you observe each detail of the meticulous ritual, each precise movement of incredible economy and grace. Little tea cakes, subtle of taste, close and firm of texture, are served first. You are impressed with the gentle, quiet courtesy with which each guest is treated, the gracious appreciation of each response. You are impressed with the silence.

You realize that you have slowed down to a time so quiet and peaceful that time does not exist. The only sounds are the boiling of the water on the hearth. You are told later this is called the sound of the soughing of the pines and at times pieces of iron are placed in the iron kettle in order to enhance the sound (Okakura 35). The tea bowl is passed around. It is thin tea.

Imagine that now it is your turn to taste the tea. Your first sip reveals that which you had already observed by its strange green color, its frothy texture— Lipton's, this is not! As your tastebuds evaluate the unique, rather bitter flavor, you remind yourself to appreciate its delicate quality as well and assume that this tea is something for which you must acquire a taste.

Contemplating the flavor and aroma of the tea, you become aware of the small, simple tea bowl held on the palm of your left hand. Your right hand cradles the cup and enjoys the smooth, slightly pebbly surface of the cup. Its shape is so humble, almost prehistoric in essence. Its balance and weight seem just right; it is pleasant to the hand. You express your admiration of the tea bowl to your host and you are told, as you suspected, that it is a Raku tea bowl of a shape designed by Chojiro, a potter of the sixteenth century. There are seven of these traditional designs by Chojiro that are used by modern potters. They have whimsical, descriptive names such as: fast ship, priest's peach blossom, wet crow, and iris (Chikamatsu 149). The word *raku* means enjoyment, pleasure, ease, and Raku pottery is considered the perfect tea bowl for this ceremony. A continuous line of craftsmen in Kyoto have been producing these bowls since the technique was evolved by Chojiro.

Until now, the conversation has been formalized statements, which began with the main guest saying, *Osakini*, meaning, "Excuse me for preceding you" (Ross 55). You are forgiven, being a foreigner, for breaking the pattern, but your questions are really not that out of line. As each guest finishes his tea, he admires the tea bowl, comments on the tea and its very special preparation, and compliments the host. This is an appropriate time for the host to comment on the history of the article mentioned and even to include an account of how it came to belong to his family. Often the tea bowl may be a valuable treasure dating back for several generations. There are times during an informal tea ceremony that you exchange pleasantries with your neighbor between formalized comments, but never are you "to mention work, politics, or topics pertaining to human glory or vanity. You discard rank or station at the door. Each present is free" (Nishihara 99). This is one of the reasons special training in the tea ceremony is sought, even today, by many Japanese as a necessary social grace. Important family occasions, such as contracting a marriage, are negotiated in this way. It helps the families of the young couple begin their relationship in a positive way (Kawashima). Training, besides enhancing your enjoyment of the ritual, teaches you grace and economy of motion. It is no mean trick to sit around on your knees for two or three hours at a time. Even modern day Japanese have a problem with this. You need to be in top physical condition to enjoy the Way of the Tea.

If you were taking part in a more formal situation and the tea ceremony was to include a dinner, this would only be a beginning. The guests would retire to the garden after partaking of the thin whipped tea, *Usuda*, and would relax, smoke, or maybe converse a bit. The sound of the gong, struck gently but firmly, would signal the time to return. The purification ritual at the water basin would be repeated and shoes again removed before entering. Stopping at the *tokonoma*, you would admire and contemplate a special flower arrangement of remarkable simplicity in a quaint bamboo vase, replacing the scroll previously displayed (Fukukita 29). 8

Flower arranging is an art, like the making of the tea bowl, that has forms particular to the tea ceremony. Bamboo vases of this type, a simple hollowed out section of bamboo, have been favored since the time of Rikyu, the Zen teacher who first formalized the tea ceremony as it is practiced today. Rikyu favored the artless and natural such as leaving droplets of water on the flower to enhance the freshness of the bloom—as if just plucked from the garden (Okakura 57). In keeping with his teachings, showy or loud flowers are avoided as are flowers with obvious meanings that would be inappropriate—such as white plum blossoms on a snowy day. These would be considered an excess, too much of a good thing, in the same way as would displaying a scroll at the end of autumn with the inscription, "Leaves fall down like raindrops" (Chickamatsu 50). This aspect of the tea ceremony, like all its aspects, is studied in Japan as part of understanding culture. The Flower-Masters, the Tea-Masters, potters, and poets are proclaimed National Living Treasures and are supported and protected. Schools are formed under their leadership to insure their art forms for posterity. 9

After absorbing the significance of this flower, you again take your place at the hearth. Your host serves the dinner himself. The tea this time is *Koicha*, thick tea, about the consistency and appearance of creamed spinach soup. (Both types of tea are made from powdered green tea.) The procedure this time is also a bit different. With the thin tea, the cup was passed back to the host each time and a new cup was prepared for the next guest in line. With *Kiocha*, the same tea bowl is passed around from person to person in a tedious ritual of turning the cup slightly each time and wiping the rim. The folding of the cloth, the *Fukasa*, in a careful ceremonial fashion is so difficult to learn that it is called "taming the *Fukasa*" (Ross 54). 10

It is curious to note that the sharing of the tea bowl with attendant for- 11 malized ritual is more than reminiscent of the Catholic ceremony of Holy Communion. However, any modern Japanese person (and indeed all reference material) will assure you that *Cha-No-Yu* is a completely secular ritual with no religious overtones inherent or intended. The lessons to be learned from *Cha-No-Yu* are harmony, respect, purity, and tranquility. This communion service with a tea-bowl, while definitely not a Christian communion, is indeed a true communion of these goals for those present. The ideals of life and art as taught through the disciplines of Tao and Zen are found in the tea ceremony. Tao is the Way, the essence of all life and divine order. One who knows the Way goes with the flow, so to speak. Zen is a manner of being in contact with this Way, as through meditation. It is said that "Taoism furnished the basis for aesthetic ideals and Zennism made them practical" (Okakura 29). The original tea ceremony is believed to have begun in southern China by a group of Buddhist monks who incorporated many Tao doctrines with their Zen beliefs. For them the tea ceremony was a profound holy sacrament in which they drank tea from a single bowl (Okakura 15–16). It was this Zen ritual that was finally developed in Japan by Rikyu, the celebrated Tea-Master of the sixteenth century, as a way to instill in his people an ethic of humility and tranquility and respect for one another—so needed for survival for a group living so closely on such a tiny island.

It was a Zen Buddhist teacher who is said to have discovered tea after an 12 act of self-mutilation. Daruma, while wandering through China, attempted to meditate for nine years. After seven years, he fell asleep. Realizing what had happened, in anger he ripped off his eyelids, so as not to sleep anymore, and threw them on the ground. The next day he noticed they had been transformed into a plant. Chewing the leaves, he found they kept him alert and he slept no more while meditating. Zen Buddhists used tea often as an infusion to assist in their meditation, and gradually the use of tea spread around the world (Seeger 168–70).

Another island nation, Great Britain, also has its tea ceremony, consisting 13 of a litany of "One lump or two?" and "Do you care for cream?" accompanied by a chorus of banal small talk and scones, rolls, and bread and butter. Tea became so popular it was a taxable necessity, even in the New World in the eighteenth century, where Americans invented their own famous tea ceremony, the Boston Tea Party, that rebellious act that heralded the beginning of the American Revolution.

The refinement of the Japanese tea ceremony has given an ethic of dignity, 14 restraint, and refinement to peasant and wealthy alike. As the world grows smaller, the population more condensed, and the pollution runs rampant, we all might learn ceremonies of self-restraint, courtesy, and tranquility—to preserve our sanity and to relate more fully to our neighbors. These ceremonies might well be an escape from our environment. The Japanese will do well to continue to treasure their tea ceremony and their master artisans. They will need them more than ever with the future they are creating of computers and transportation like the Maglev (magnetic train) now being perfected to travel at 300 mph. Who can relate to that speed? (Sato 95).

Imagine yourself in the year 2084, in a small cubicle with subdued lighting. 15 Six other people are in sitting position levitated on magnetic mats seven inches above the floor around a microwave oven. Tiny, cordless Walkmen in their ears transmit the sound of boiling water. The scroll in the sanctuary is a Dow Jones printout from a Wang computer. The garden you just passed through, though very tiny, boasted of lovely hydroponic tea gardens under glass belljars. The host passes you a humble Raku tea bowl and you turn to the guest next to you and politely ask, "Osakini?"

Works Consulted

Blaser, Werner. Japanese Temples and Tea-Houses. New York: F. W. Dodge, 1956.
Bruce, William. Religions in Japan. Rutland, VT: Charles E. Tuttle, 1962.
Chikamatsu, Shigenori. Stories from a Tearoom Window. Trans. Kozaburo Mori. Rutland, VT: Charles E. Tuttle, 1982.
Fukukita, Yasunosuke. Tea Cult of Japan. Tokyo: Board of Tourist Industry, 1934.
"History of Tea," World Book Encyclopedia. 1976 ed.
Hutchison, Mike. "Isolation Tanks: The State of the Art." Esquire Aug. 1983: 124.
"Japan." Encyclopedia Americana. 1979 ed.
"Japanese Tea Ceremony." Encyclopedia Americana. 1979 ed.
Kawashima, Dr. Yasuhide. Personal interview. 15 June 1984.
King, Francis. "Japan." Man, Myth and Magic. Ed. Richard Cavendish. 24 vols. New York: Marshall Cavendish, 1970. 11:1486–94.
Lilly, John C. The Center of the Cyclone. New York: Julian Press, 1972.
Mano, D. Keith. "Sensory Deprivation." National Review 10 Dec. 1982: 1564.
McFarland, H. Neill. The Rush Hour of the Gods. New York: Macmillan, 1967.
"Nirvana in a Dank, Dark Tank" Time 24 Mar. 1980: 105.
Nishihara, Kiyoyuki. Japanese Houses, Patterns for Living. Trans. Richard L. Gage. Tokyo: Japan Publications, 1968.
Okakura, Kakuzo. The Book of Tea. New York: Dover, 1964.
Repplier, Agnes. To Think of Tea. Boston: Houghton Mifflin, 1932.
Rhodes, Daniel. Clay and Glazes for the Potter. Rev. ed. Radnor, PA: Chilton, 1975.
Riegger, Hal. Raku: Art and Technique. New York: Van Nostrand Reinhold, 1970.
Rosenthal, Ernst. Pottery and Ceramics. London: Penguin Books, 1949.
Ross, Nancy. "Chanoyu: The Art of Tea." Sphere Feb. 1974: 54–56.
Sadler, A.L. Cha-No-Yu: The Japanese Tea Ceremony. Rutland, VT: Charles E. Tuttle, 1963.
Sato, Akihiro. "Beyond the Bullet." Popular Mechanics Apr. 1980: 95.

Seeger, Elizabeth. *The Pageant of Chinese History.* New York: Longmans, Green, 1944.
Terry, Charles S. *Contemporary Japanese Houses.* Tokyo: Kodansha, 1968.
Thompson, Bob. *Shiga the Potter.* New York: Van Nostrand Reinhold, 1983.
Woodhouse, Charles Platten. *The World's Master Potters.* London: Pitman Publishing, 1974.

QUESTIONS FOR READING AND REVISING

1. The overall purpose of Sandra Casillas's essay is to *explain* the process of an ancient Japanese ritual. Outline each step in the tea ceremony. Which does Casillas handle most effectively? Why? Reread paragraph 9 on flower arranging as an art. Explain why this paragraph does/does not digress from her purpose. How does it reinforce the overall *purpose* of the essay?

2. Casillas's essay opens with a direct address to the reader. Point to other instances later in the essay where she maintains this form of address. What is its effect? When and how does she vary this direct address? With what effect? What would be the advantages/disadvantages if Casillas had written the essay consistently in either the first or third person? Before responding, rewrite one of Casillas's paragraphs using the first or third person *point of view.*

3. In discussing how she sharpened the focus of her essay, Casillas notes: "Sometimes getting too close to a subject can narrow your vision and cause tunnel vision. The opposite proved true in the case of Cha-No-Yu. I developed 'Grand Central vision.'" Given the context of her essay, what do you suppose Casillas is suggesting here? Point to specific words and phrases that illustrate your reading of her *metaphor.*

4. Casillas explains that one of the aims of her research paper is to describe "an atmosphere of escape into an inner world"—and that "contrast at times was used to help the reader visualize" this idea. Reread Casillas's essay carefully and identify the nature—and the effect—of the *contrasts* she uses. At which points in her essay are these contrasts especially effective? Why?

5. One of the strengths of this essay is the writer's effective use of *description.* Choose one paragraph in the essay that highlights Casillas's successful use of description and list each example of *concrete,* sensory *detail.* In the second paragraph Casillas notes, "you will find you are noticing more of nature than you thought possible in so small a garden." Where—and how—does she use description to help her readers fulfill the promise created in this sentence?

6. Imagine that you are the writer of this essay and that one of the peer editors in your class recommends that you eliminate the section on the history of the tea ceremony as distracting and irrelevant. On what grounds would you defend the inclusion of this particular section of the essay? What does it contribute to the overall *purpose* of the essay?

7. Look carefully again at the opening paragraph. What are its strengths? How, for example, does Casillas capture her reader's attention? What is the function of the second sentence in this paragraph? Of the third sentence? Explain what each contributes to the paragraph and to the essay as a whole.

8. Reread the opening sentence of paragraph 11. In the previous draft it read: "The sharing of the tea bowl and attendant ritual accomplished by formalized strict ceremony is more than reminiscent of the Catholic ceremony of Holy Communion." What specific changes do you notice in these two drafts? Which version do you prefer? Why? Characterize the verb forms in the same paragraph and identify their strengths and weaknesses. Rewrite the paragraph, making the verbs as effective as possible.

9. Review the final paragraph of Casillas's essay. In what specific ways does the paragraph return to—and recapitulate—the *themes* and syntax of earlier parts of the essay? How—in its *tone* and *diction*—does the paragraph head off in a new direction? Explain why the essay would/would not be stronger if the final paragraph were omitted.

SUGGESTIONS FOR WRITING

1. Near the end of her essay, Sandra Casillas observes that "as the world grows smaller, the population more condensed, and the pollution runs rampant, we all might learn ceremonies of self-restraint, courtesy, and tranquility—to preserve our sanity and to relate more fully to our neighbors." Examine carefully some ceremony that emphasizes one or more of these qualities—"self-restraint, courtesy, and tranquility." Write an essay in which you *explain* the process of the ceremony and the specific ways in which it emphasizes these qualities.

2. What ethnic rituals did you and your family participate in on a regular basis during your childhood? Write an expository essay in which you re-create with detail the specific steps in the *process* of that ceremony and the occasion on which it was performed. Explain why the ritual was important to you as a child and how you view it today. What did you learn—either positively or negatively—about your own ethnic heritage and about yourself from having participated in it?

3. Write an *expository* essay in which you explain in detail the precise nature of some social ritual you engage in each year—preparing Thanksgiving dinner, making New Year's Eve resolutions, sending Valentine's Day cards, and the like. How does this social ritual serve as an expression of a particular cultural sensibility? What does it reveal about the culture in which it functions?

DAVID A. CHRISTMAN

New York University
New York, New York
Tony Giffone, instructor

"Don't limit yourself to only the easiest, most obvious topics," David A. Christman urges other students of writing. *"Try to be original in your approach to assignments. Not only will it impress teachers, but, more importantly, it will make writing a much more vital and rewarding experience."* Christman's essay, *"Nietzsche and the Art of Tattooing,"* demonstrates the soundness of his advice. Having read Nietzsche's definitions of *"Dionysian"* and *"Apollonian"* in A World of Ideas, edited by Lee A. Jacobus, Christman was asked to *"choose some form of cultural manifestation"* and write an essay analyzing *"its Dionysian and Apollonian aspects."* Christman quickly settled on the art of tattooing. *"How exactly I arrived at tattooing for this, I'm not sure. My awareness of tattooing had been somewhat heightened by a trip to the Museum of Tattooing in San Francisco and also by a chance meeting at a party with Spider Webb, one of the better known American tattoo artists."* Christman's interest in tattooing converged with his reading of Nietzsche to produce an essay that compares and contrasts, as Christman notes, *"tattooing as both an ancient and modern art and as a personal and cultural phenomenon."*

In addition to tattooing, Christman cultivates several other, and equally *"visible,"* artistic interests. A movie buff, he is also an accomplished singer and songwriter. Born in New York City and educated at Northfield Mount Herman School in Massachusetts, Christman has played with a rock band, Debroy Rebop, and has cut a record:

> My musical abilities influenced me in a number of ways. For one, the success my band enjoyed gave me a sense of confidence in my own ability to succeed. Secondly, it was really songwriting that led me to writing: first to poetry, then to fiction, and on to nonfiction. My writing is an extension of my total self, including all my experiences and abilities.

Christman is majoring in English at New York University, principally because, as he explains, *"NYU does not offer a degree program in writing."* And while his career goals remain somewhat uncertain at this point, he quickly adds: *"I am sure they will include writing in some capacity."*

Nietzsche and the Art of Tattooing

It is a sorry development of modern civilization that the art of tattooing 1 has come to be associated with only the lowest members of the social strata. Despite a lengthy tradition as a symbol of nobility and achievement, it is regarded by many as a sign of either low self-esteem or of low moral character. Yet to deny this unique form of self-expression the term "art" would be to do it an injustice. One glance at the powerful imagery of the traditional Japanese full-body tattoo makes this clear. It is a discipline that requires not only unerring dexterity, but an eye for both the beautiful and the grotesque.

I have long been interested in tattooing, having been tattooed twice, once 2 in 1977 and then again in 1981. But it was only this past summer (1984) that I began to learn about some of tattooing's history. The catalyst for this, and the reason for my intensified interest in the field, was a visit to Lyle Tuttle's Museum of Tattooing in San Francisco. The museum is a fascinating compendium of tattooing history, both in folklore and in fact.

Where the art of tattooing differs from more traditional artistic efforts is 3 that it requires not one, but two willing participants. That is, both the artist and his "canvas" must agree on the work to be performed. Without question though, the "tattooee" is the more active participant in the primary decision of whether to be tattooed at all.

Although by no means an acid test for tattooing's worthiness as art, it is 4 interesting to note that many aspects of it can be related to Nietzsche's concepts of Apollonianism and Dionysianism, both in terms of tattooing's historical development and, more importantly, the individual's decision to be tattooed.

Although Nietzsche states that Dionysos represents the "non-visual art of 5 music," (212) Dionysianism can be extended, as we will see, to encompass the visual arts as well, especially one that requires an actively collaborative effort, as tattooing does.

Tattooing is an ancient art. The mummy of the Egyptian princess Hathor, 6 believed to have died around 2000 B.C., was found to be tattooed. In its present day form, tattooing is usually done with an electric tattooing needle which cuts through the skin, injecting pigments below the epidermis. However, different cultures have developed other methods for tattooing. The tribal Moko tattooing practiced by the Maori tribes of New Zealand used chisel-like pieces of ivory which were hammered into the skin, the cleaved flesh then rubbed with soot or dyes. In Japan, long bamboo sticks with anywhere from one to thirty needles protruding from them are slipped effortlessly in and out of the flesh by hand.

The reasons for tattooing vary widely. In most of its early manifestations, 7
tattooing was primarily for chiefs and warriors of tribal cultures, including the
Incan and Mayan Indians. In Borneo, only the upper-class women of the
Kenyah and Kayan tribes were allowed to be tattooed. This habit permeated
Western civilization as well, when, around the turn of the twentieth century,
much of Europe's nobility and aristocracy was tattooed, including King George
V and Kaiser Wilhelm II.

Nietzsche states that Apollo is the "apotheosis of the principium indivi- 8
duationis" (223) or as text commentator Lee Jacobus elucidates, "the god in
whom the concept of the individual is best expressed" (223). Is not the tattooing of nobility an embodiment of this Appolonian trait—that those people,
who either by birthright or bravery are chosen to rule, should wish to reinforce
their superior "self" by indelibly marking their bodies as a reminder of "the
beguiling image of their own existence" (220)? That these members of nobility
would hope for a long and prosperous reign would be no surprise. And a tattoo
against which to continually mark the successful passing of time would seem
to be representative of what Nietzsche calls "man's . . . desire to remain on
earth" (221), another Apollonian trait, as well perhaps as a veiled attempt to
defy mortality. Princess Hathor's tattoos outlived her by four thousand years.

Of course the majority of tattooed people are not royalty. So for what 9
reasons might an "average" person get tattooed? This too varies with different
cultures. In Japan, the tattooed person (usually a man) enters a type of particularly close-knit club, called a *nakama*, once tattooed. So, as Donald Richie
points out in *The Japanese Tattoo*, it is a rite of communal membership. In the
Maori culture it was a rite of passage required by all members of the tribe. A
man or woman without Moko was held in low esteen by the rest of the community. In the West, many people are tattooed simply because their friends
or associates are tattooed. This differs somewhat from Japan in that in the
United States, oftentimes the person who is tattooed is not trying to associate
himself with tattooed people in general but rather is tattooed to identify himself
as a member of some other group, for example: motorcyclist, musician, or
sailor. It is interesting to note that these people are often tattooed in a group
and that it is not uncommon for them to be drunk. Dionysos is the god of
wine and drunkenness.

In all these instances the underlying motive for being tattooed is conformity, 10
either to friends or tradition, or as an initiation to a fraternal setting. This
notion of conformity is one of the fundamental concepts of Nietzsche's Dionysianism. "Man now expresses himself . . . as a member of the community,"
says Nietzsche (216). In Japan, where a strong sense of unity exists between
tattooed people, this is especially true. In the annual Buddhist festivals, thou-

sands of fully tattooed men come together, usually wearing nothing more than their fundoshi (loincloths), dancing and swaying to traditional music. And so as Nietzsche states, "the abrogation of the principium individuationis become(s) an esthetic event" (218).

Tattooing is not an aesthetic event only in Japan, though the festivals have [11] an obvious association with the Dionysian celebrations that Nietzsche talks about, but the conformity, the Dionysianism of tattooing, can be seen in other ways too. For instance, it is often noted that most tattoos are based on a rather limited number of motifs. Flowers, animals, and religious imagery are among the most common. This is another tenet of Dionysianism. Nietzsche says that the Dionysiac dithyramb incites "the desire to express the very essence of nature symbolically" (219). What more obvious way to do this than to wear these symbols as adornments of the body? And it is interesting to note that these symbols are rarely the accurate Homeric representations of nature inherent in Apollonianism but rather are caricatures or approximations of nature.

The decision to be tattooed need not always be of a Dionysian nature, [12] though obviously many aspects of the art are. To observe or enjoy the art from afar is a much different thing than to wear it. To consider or conceptualize about being tattooed is an Apollonian exercise, one of fantasy and illusion. But to be tattooed steps over what Nietsche calls the "thin line which the dream image may not cross" (214) and becomes the Dionysian. That is, the conceptualizer, considering the motifs or their placement on his body, by choosing them and being marked with them, is "no longer the artist, he has himself become a work of art" (216).

Although Eastern and tribal tattooing is largely an exercise in conformity, [13] as is a lot of tattooing in the West, many people are tattooed for precisely the opposite reason. These are people who see tattooing as an individualistic and nonconformist exercise. Sometimes they feel they are outcast from society and their tattoos reflect this: "Hell Raiser," "Born To Lose," etc. are common manifestations of these feelings. Other times people see tattooing as an aesthetically pleasing thing to do. They like tattoos and they like they way they themselves look, or would look, with tattoos.

This relates closely to some of Nietzsche's Apollonian concepts. He men- [14] tions an "Apollonian need for beauty" (221), which is really what this aspect of tattooing is all about; the beautification of the body. And an "unabashed delight in colors" (217) is an inherent part of this, for these are people who are being tattooed not simply to carry a mask but to carry a symbol that embodies their ideas of fashion and beauty. They work closely with the tattooist in conceptualizing this custom piece of work, usually ignoring standard tattoo motifs and concentrating instead on brightly colored, highly detailed works of their own design.

Over the past ten years tattooing has been enjoying a renaissance of sorts, 15
especially in the United States. Custom tattooing has generated some beautiful
pieces of work which in turn have been accorded a lot of attention and respect
by the media. In part this is due to the fact that many of today's top tattooists
were trained in "traditional" art schools like Pratt and the Rhode Island School
of Design. It is also due to the rising sentiment that tattooing is not just for
bikers and sailors but is a respectable and legitimate art form for all types of
people.

Though it is unlikely that Nietzsche's work was even remotely connected 16
to tattooing, it is startling that so many passages from his work seem perfectly
suited to this discussion. For instance, in his discussion of the Dionysiac cel-
ebration, which correlates closely to the Buddhist festivals of Japan, Nietzsche
describes nonparticipating onlookers as "cadaverous and ghostly" (215) when
compared with "the intense throng of Dionysiac revelers" (215), perhaps in
much the same way that nontattooed spectators might seem to appear at a
Buddhist festival. And later Nietzsche describes what could be a scene from a
Westernized version of the Japanese iconographic tattoo, "the savage beasts of
mountain and desert approach . . . the chariot of Dionysos is bedecked with
flowers and garlands; panthers and tigers stride beneath his yoke" (215).

More importantly, would Nietzsche have even acknowledged the Apollon- 17
ian and Dionysian elements of tattooing? Or would he have been one of those
people who, in his own words, "either from lack of experience or out of sheer
stupidity, turn away from such phenomena, and strong in their own sanity,
label them either mockingly or pityingly" (215)? For this we have no answer
except to presume that a man as attuned to the social and historical implications of art would have a difficult time ignoring those so obviously inherent
in the curious art of tattooing.

Works Consulted

King, Michael, and Marti Friedlander. *Moko: Maori Tattooing in the Twentieth Century.* Welling-
    ton, NZ: Alister Taylor, 1972.
Nietzsche, Friedrich. "Apollonianism and Dionysianism." *A World of Ideas: Essential Readings for
    College Writers.* Ed. Lee A. Jacobus. New York: Bedford Books of St. Martin's Press, 1983.
Richie, Donald, and Ian Buruma. *The Japanese Tattoo.* New York: John Weatherhill, 1980.
Scutt, Ronald, and Christopher Gutch. *Art, Sex and Symbol.* Cranbury, NJ: A. S. Barnes, 1974.

QUESTIONS FOR READING AND REVISING

1. David Christman talks about the Dionysian and Apollonian aspects of tattooing. How are *Dionysian* and *Apollonian* defined in this essay? How does a
   standard college dictionary definition in each instance differ from those pro-

vided in the essay? What points, if any, would you like to add to the definition supplied by Christman?

2. Outline Christman's analysis of the art of tattooing. Which aspects of tattooing does he consider Dionysian? Which does he think are Apollonian? What evidence does he use to verify each of these points? Do you agree or disagree with his conclusions? Why?

3. One of Christman's goals of this essay, as he tells us, was to contrast "tattooing as both an ancient and modern art and as a personal and cultural phenomenon." Where does he introduce the ancient/modern contrast? Outline the comparison as Christman develops it in the essay. Which version of tattooing does Christman prefer? Why?

4. In presenting this writing exercise, Christman's instructor noted, "Remember, your audience for the piece is not necessarily someone who is totally familiar with the work or event you are analyzing. Some information about the work is necessary." What kind of information does Christman work into the essay? How well does Christman satisfy the requirements of the exercise in this respect? What additional information, if any, would you recommend that he include? Rewrite one paragraph including whatever additional information you think necessary.

5. David Christman's writing course included a good deal of peer editing. (For an explanation of peer editing procedures, see Part V.) Here is Christman's explanation of what happened:

> The original rough draft was read to students in my writing class, where, for the most part, it was not very well received. Most people felt that the historical information drew the reader's attention away from the topic. Others simply could not see any viable connection or validity for the essay's central thesis. A second draft, which was handed in for the grade (an A), made some slight changes. I tried to simplify those passages containing historical data so as to make them more palatable to the reader. At this point, I was already satisfied with the essay.

Reread Christman's essay and focus on his use of historical information. Where and with what effect is historical information used in the essay? What additional changes, if any, would you suggest Christman make in the way he handles it?

6. The peer editors who responded to Christman's rough draft "could not see any viable connection or validity for the essay's central thesis." What is the thesis of this essay? Where is it stated? What specific changes, if any, would you recommend that Christman make to clarify and strengthen his thesis statement?

7. Christman's first draft of this essay did not include what is currently the last

sentence in the opening paragraph. In his second draft, Christman added the following sentence: "It is a discipline which by its permanent nature requires unerring dexterity coupled with an eye for beauty and mystery." Christman later changed the sentence to read: "It is a discipline that requires not only unerring dexterity, but an eye for both the beautiful and the grotesque." List the specific changes in these versions of the same sentence and assess the advantages of each.

8. Reread paragraph 8 of Christman's essay, paying special attention to the sentence: "That these members of nobility would hope for a long and prosperous reign would be no surprise." In Christman's first draft, this sentence is preceded by one that he removed from later drafts, which reads: "If we define existence as the ability to chart progress or changes against some standard then what better standard than a permanent mark." Based on your reading of both these paragraphs and the entire essay, how could you defend or challenge Christman's decision to eliminate this sentence?

9. Review the verbs in this essay. What do you notice about them? What consistency do you recognize among them? How might they be improved? What other consistencies can you identify in Christman's *diction* and *tone?* What are the strengths of these two aspects of his essay? What suggestions, if any, would you offer to reinforce their effectiveness?

10. Analyze Christman's use of personal experience to illustrate points in his essay. What reasons would you offer to support—or challenge—Christman's decision not to invoke personal experience at the end of his essay?

SUGGESTIONS FOR WRITING

1. One of the strengths of David Christman's essay is the *contrast* he draws between ancient and modern tattooing. Consider another activity, one that can trace its origins to ancient times (for example, playing a musical instrument or engaging in sports competition) and write an expository essay contrasting the ancient and modern ways of doing it. Include in your essay a clear sense of the procedures involved in each method and show the superiority of one.

2. Choose some activity in contemporary American experience and write an essay in which you analyze its Dionysian and Apollonian elements. You may choose to work with either a standard dictionary definition of these terms or with Nietzsche's, but be sure to support each of your points with detailed references to the activity you have chosen.

3. Christman's essay raises issues about what constitutes art and whether tattooing can claim for itself the respect due to art. Consider the case of advertising. D. H. Lawrence once observed that "some of the cunningest American literature is to be found in advertisements of soap suds." So too, Aldous Huxley regarded

advertisements as "the most exciting, the most arduous literary form of all, the most difficult to master. . . ." But Thomas Wolfe regarded advertisements as nothing more than "fat, juicy, sugar-coated lies for our great Boob public to swallow." Write an *argumentative* essay in which you argue for—or against— the position that the language of advertising should be regarded as art and ought to command respect comparable to that afforded literature.

RAVENEL BOYKIN CURRY

Yale University
New Haven, Connecticut
Fred Strebeigh, instructor

"Having a good idea is a lot easier than establishing it in an essay. The hardest part is pulling your emotions and impressions together well enough to get the first sentence on the page. From there, you may change your direction many times, but at least you have something in front of you to see, at the very least something to cross out and replace. The most horrible experience has got to be sitting at a desk with forty-three ideas swimming and colliding in your mind while the piece of paper sits there empty, that white sheet just staring back at you," notes Ravenel Boykin Curry.

Born in Charlottesville, Virginia, Curry lived in North Carolina for several years before moving to Summit, New Jersey, where he graduated from Summit High School in 1984. The first teenager to appear on the Common Cause National Governing Board ballot, Curry has also been active in the campaigns of many Democratic candidates in national and local elections. He has traveled a great deal with his family ("to Europe, Asia, and the Soviet Union") and has also worked at a newspaper, a gas station, on a peach farm, and at Bloomingdale's department store. He currently operates a vegetable stand with a friend. About his interests at Yale, Curry notes "I will probably double major in history and economics. . . . I hope to be an investor, but I will maintain a constant involvement in politics. If my writing skills develop, I would love to keep writing."

Asked to write a nonfiction portrayal of a place, Curry chose to focus on "A Small Town" in rural South Carolina where his parents grew up. And from his earliest draft, as he explains, the audience and purpose he had in mind for his essay were intertwined: "not the people of Chesterfield (they would probably find it boring) but people who had grown up in some Eastern suburb and had no understanding about the lives of people living just twelve hours (if you hurry) away. I didn't want them to come away with some saccharine picture of a bucolic paradise where Farmer Brown rides around on his tractor while his wife bakes pies and the kids happily milk the cows. On the other hand, some northerners have mistaken the lack of worldly sophistication among southerners in small towns for shallow naiveté. The popular southern myth that results is a condescending view of the happy, ignorant farmer, oblivious to the important problems of the 'real world.' I tried to break the simplistic stereotype by showing people who are complex, who live lives with important cares and tragedies and successes. I wanted the reader to laugh without condescending. To admire without romanticizing. To understand better that no people can be so simply understood."

A Small Town

Junior Boy is thirty-nine and he has made it. But his is no Horatio Alger 1
story. He was born December 26 in the four-room shack that would be shared
for the next eighteen years with two parents and four sisters. His best friend
was Jay Calvin Rivers until they realized Jay was rich and white and Junior
Boy was poor and black and that all of that meant much more than they had
thought. While Jay went off to Pawley's Island, Junior Boy suffered through
the scorching summers of the South. One especially hot August afternoon
when he was thirteen, Junior Boy made a pledge in the style of Scarlet O'Hara.
"I promised me that no matter what, someday I would have an air-conditioning
box and a telephone to talk to people."

Today, the front of Junior Boy's house, at least the part that isn't a porch 2
with a weight bench, is decked with imitation-brick-pattern linoleum that
suggests a cross between a kitchen floor and a factory wall. Junior Boy is
standing in front of this three bedroom structure next to an old rusty water
pump in the front yard while he discusses his cars. One of them is a dusty
black '79 Buick rested in front of the porch. He is still making payments on
it, but he bought the new, rarely used Thunderbird (bright white) parked just
outside the kitchen because, "If I can't make a payment and they come and
take one of them away, then, tell me, what would I have to ride around in?"

Both cars still have Jimmy Carter bumper stickers on them. "He was such 3
a good man. He was just so *good.*"

Junior Boy's wife Nora comes to the door and calls us inside, interrupting 4
the political discussion. The main room has a black vinyl sofa with white fluff
bursting from a long rip in one arm. A purple shag carpet covers the floor,
and an iron wood stove, taunting us in this hundred-degree heat, stands waiting
for the winter next to the wall on our right.

The door to the bedroom is open and Junior Boy sees me looking inside. 5
There are no windows, so it is very dark, but everything is neat. "Nora keeps
this place clean," he says, and in a time when many sneer at the labors of
"just a housewife," Nora restrains a breaking smile and pokes at Junior Boy
for making it so hard. "By the time I get one room straight, Junior Boy and
the kids've all gone and destroyed another one. If they didn't go to sleep, I'd
never be caught up."

One thing Junior Boy likes is his comfort, so when the telephone man came 6
to install his first phone, Junior Boy had to think about where he wanted it.
He finally walked over to his bed, lay down, reached his right hand up, and
asked for the phone to be installed where his hand was. And there it is.

Junior Boy and his house and his two cars are all in Chesterfield, a tiny,   7
semidusty farm town in the state of South Carolina. The land is sandy, but
the workers who live on the unyielding ground wrench what they can from it.
The buildings on the four blocks that make up downtown Chesterfield are too
new to be quaint and too old to be fresh. Architecture is mid-1950s-Cement
Block, and the flashiest it ever gets is when they put up the plastic Christmas
trees on the street lights in late October.

On one of these blocks, twenty-five years ago, Lee Davis and his wife Dell   8
used to run the Chesterfield Theater where they showed Westerns and serials,
fourteen cents for kids, twenty-five cents for adults. Blacks in the balcony only
please. Dell would take the money as kids filed in and Lee would yell at them
and kick out anyone who talked during the movie.

Now the building is the ultra-up-to-date, air-conditioned Da-Le Discount   9
Drugs and Cosmetics, the biggest store in town. Dell is very pale, pretty fat,
and a little crippled now. She sits behind the register and Mr. Davis shoos out
any kids who are reading the comic books without buying them. There is no
soda fountain in the back yet, but just inside the door is a machine that spits
out cold sandwiches for seventy-five cents and lukewarm hotdogs for a dollar.
Junior Boy is one of their best customers and today he's buying plastic flowers
for Lizzie's funeral.

Lizzie would be seventy-one today if she still lived on the farm in her little   10
home. A fence surrounds the yard to hold all the chickens who scratch around
outside—and occasionally inside—the house, and a screen porch with too
many holes to discourage any kind of insect dominates the facade. She had
lots of chickens and thirteen children. When my mom was four, Lizzie had
her last child, and a few weeks later my mom came by to see him. Lizzie said
she had run out of names, and asked the girl what name *she* liked. Thinking
of a song she had just learned, my mom said that Billy Boy sounded best to
her. Billy Boy is thirty-eight now and he's in Chesterfield for the funeral with
his son, Billy Boy, Jr.

Lizzie locked herself up in her house and shut her windows for three days   11
and suffocated in the heat.

Chesterfield is not a thriving center of commerce and it rarely makes even   12
the South Carolina papers. The nearest major city is Atlanta, two hours away
in a plane, five by pickup (though most people in Chesterfield have never
gone beyond Cheraw, the nearest town with a movie screen). People driving
through on the way to Myrtle Beach to the east or the Blue Ridge Mountains
in the west probably think it seems like a pretty boring place, if they notice
it at all. But before they glibly conclude that this small town builds small

minds, they should talk to Junior Boy, who wonders what kind of minds come from kids who have to play in crowded city streets instead of ponds and fields and giant silos. What comes from men and women who type the same boring letters and listen to the same boring customers for eight hours every single day. Who build the same houses, read the same magazines, and discuss the same topics over cocktails with the same identical neighbors every single night.

Junior boy's family has tomatoes to pick and one of the mother pigs won't 13 feed her six piglets and a teacher says one of the kids might get a college scholarship if they push him a little harder and one of the little tractors has to be fixed and it's looking like fall might be too wet for the pecans and now Elizabeth is saying she wants to get married before she's finished with high school.

There is a lot of humor and a lot of drama in a tiny town in the sandhills 14 of South Carolina. People say New York has a rhythm, and you can feel the pulsing, blasting, pounding movement as soon as you enter. Well, Chesterfield has a rhythm too, and if you listen, you can hear.

QUESTIONS FOR READING AND REVISING

1. Ravenel Boykin Curry explains that "inspiring me to write this essay was a combination of desires: to solidify some impressions of my mother's farm, to show friends that small towns aren't mindless, and to get a paper finished for my English class before the 5:00 deadline. It started out as a character portrayal—a local color type essay of something I knew well. But as I explained each character and the way they interrelated, I began to discover other themes which in turn helped me to organize the mini-vignettes in a specific way." As you reread Curry's essay, what do you regard to be the central theme? Where is that theme stated? What other themes emerge as you read, and how does each help organize the essay?

2. What do you think Curry means when he talks about "mini-vignettes"? Examine each carefully. What does each contribute to the overall success of the essay? How does Curry manage to unify them into a portrait of "A Small Town?" How does his essay demonstrate that his portrayals of the town and its inhabitants are "interrelated"? What function does Curry's portrait of Junior Boy serve in the essay? What purpose is served by Curry's returning to Junior Boy in paragraphs 13 and 14?

3. Consider the organization of Curry's essay. Does he follow a pattern of moving from the general to the particular? from the particular to the general? some

other pattern of organization? Explain. Several of Curry's paragraphs (see, for example, paragraph three) are one sentence long. Identify these paragraphs and comment on their effectiveness. Why—or why isn't—the length of these paragraphs appropriate to the effect Curry tries to create?

4. When asked how he would like readers of his essay to respond to what he had written, Curry noted:

> I would ask the reader to let his mind wander a little. There are nineteen different scenes (changes in time or place) in a very small space, and each of them can do something different. Do you think Junior Boy's ambitions were inspiring or pathetic? Is Nora a woman oppressed by sexism, or does she have a responsibility to maintain a traditional role to keep the family going? Were Lee and Dell evil when they were racist? Could you say the same thing if you were the one being put in the balcony? Let ideas bubble around and try to make some concrete conclusions.

Sketch out the "nineteen different scenes (changes in time or place)" Curry refers to here. How does each illustrate his overriding point? Answer the questions Curry poses to his readers, supporting your responses with a detailed study of specific sentences.

5. *Compare and contrast* the rhythm of the sentences used to describe this small town and its inhabitants with the cadences of the sentences characterizing urban life. Show how Curry uses the verbal rhythms of his sentence structure to evoke and then reject the city dwellers who might drive through Chesterfield "on the way to Myrtle Beach to the east or the Blue Ridge Mountains in the west." How does the rhythm of his sentences underscore the controlling idea of his essay?

6. One of the most successful aspects of Curry's essay is his ability to use specific details to evoke particular responses in his readers. Consider, for example, the "imitation-brick-pattern linoleum that suggests a cross between a kitchen floor and a factory wall . . ." in paragraph 2. Point to other equally evocative specific details that make his description of Chesterfield and its inhabitants so vivid and memorable. Consider the effectiveness of Curry's verb choices. What makes them effective? Do the same for his adjectives.

7. How does Curry prevent his depiction of Chesterfield and its inhabitants from being "condescending"? Recall Curry's depiction of the lives of urban dwellers and of "kids who have to play in crowded city streets instead of ponds and fields and giant silos." In this section of his essay, how does Curry succeed in avoiding lapsing into the kind of condescending tone that he criticizes city residents for adopting in their view of the rural South? Support your response with a detailed examination of specific sentences.

8. Curry wrote several drafts of this essay. Here is an earlier version of his ending:

> Chesterfield is not the epicenter of any megalopolis, and the nearest major city is Atlanta, two hours away in a plane, five by pick-up (though most people in Chesterfield have never gone beyond Cheraw, the nearest town with a movie screen). But there is a lot of humor in a tiny Southern town that you might think looks like Sinclair Lewis's *Main Street.* You might also think this town builds small minds, but Junior Boy probably wonders what kind of minds come from kids who have to play in some crowded city streets instead of ponds and fields and giant silos. What comes from men and women who type the same boring letters, and listen to the same boring customers for eight hours every single day, who build the same boring houses, read the same boring magazines and discuss the same boring topics over cocktails with the same boring neighbors every single night.
>
> They have tomatoes to pick, and one of the mother pigs won't feed her six piglets and one of the teachers says Alexander might get a college scholarship if they push him a little harder and one of the tractors had to be fixed and the fall might be too wet for pecans. And Elizabeth wants to get married before she's finished with school.
>
> They have things to do in Chesterfield.

What specific differences do you notice between this draft and Curry's final version? Comment on the effectiveness of each change. If Curry had yet another opportunity to revise these paragraphs, what specific changes would you suggest he make? Why?

9. Compare Curry's depiction of the rural South with Ann Louise Field's of the rural West (see "The Sound of Angels") and Julie Reardon's of the rural Midwest (see "The Unmarked Road"). What specific strengths do these essays seem to have in common? What distinguishes each—thematically and stylistically—from the others? How, for example, does each writer handle his or her character's recognition of poverty? Which essay do you find most successful and memorable? Why?

SUGGESTIONS FOR WRITING

1. One of Ravenel Boykin Curry's *purposes* in writing this essay is to use his *description* of Chesterfield and its inhabitants to break simplistic stereotypes.

Write an essay using Curry's essay as a model to "break" some stereotype about the people around you that you find condescending and offensive. As you develop your essay, try to include a detailed description of the nature of the stereotype and the specific ways in which the people you have chosen to write about defeat it with the complex richness of their lives.

2. The success of Curry's essay depends on his sense, which is not made explicit, of what the word *home* means. How would you define this term? What would you regard as the essential and distinguishing feature of a home. Bret Harte, the late-nineteenth century American writer of local color stories, once had this to say about a related subject: "Nobody shoulders a rifle in defense of a boarding house." Write an essay in which you use your own experience to illustrate Harte's point. As you proceed, try to work in your own definition of a *home* and contrast it to your definition of a *boarding house*.

3. Observe a place in your hometown or neighborhood—a street corner, a park, a bar, a convenience store—where people tend to congregate. What is there about this place that encourages people to gather there? Write an essay *describing* it. As you write, try to make each of the specific points of your description support some overriding and more general idea about that place.

BEVERLY P. DIPO

Utah State University
Logan, Utah
Joyce Kinkead, instructor

Beverly Dipo can recall with remarkable detail and winsome irony the first day she worked on cursive writing:

> I was in the third grade. My wooden desk was, even then, ancient and bore the history of previous academic scholars and shirkers. The glossy surface had acquired its glow more from the sweaty palms of test takers and greasy elbows of second-base sliders than from wood polish. The dark embedded pencil scratches attested to the fact that Shirley had once sat here; Patrick was a lousy speller; J. K. did unspeakable things to S. D.; and much to my relief, someone had kindly left me the seven times table.

With her feet wrapped around what she describes as the desk's "de-painted metal legs," Beverly Dipo spent hours practicing large, wire-thin, continuous circles, impelled by her teacher's well-intentioned cautioning: " 'Be sure to use your whole arm to glide evenly over the paper; do not use just your wrist,' she warned, 'or you will have a sloppy slinky'." Born in Hayward, California and a 1984 graduate of Sky View High School in Smithfield, Utah, Beverly Dipo writes these days on an old, water-stained bathroom door that has "no pencil marks or times tables to entertain or inform me." It is cluttered, she reports, "with books, cans of pencils and colored pens, paint brushes, a vase of ugly brown and yellow flowers, a recipe file, a clock, a basket of scissors, tape, paper clips, and other assorted junk, all of which I pay little attention to until they come up missing." Such painstakingly careful observations reflect the strength of her work both as a licensed practical nurse and as a writer at Utah State University, where she is pursuing a degree as a registered nurse.

Asked to write a narrative that focuses on an experience in which she gained some insight, Beverly Dipo responded with what is at once an incisive description and a moving account of the personal and clinical routines that attend the quietly dignified death of an elderly victim of cancer. "Death happens in my profession," Beverly Dipo observes, "it is not uncommon. I think it is difficult for nurses to remember sometimes that these experiences are special and that we need to cherish them more than we do."

For a more detailed discussion of Dipo's essay, see Part IV.

No Rainbows, No Roses

I have never seen Mrs. Trane before, but I know by the report I received 1
from the previous shift that tonight she will die. Making my rounds, I go from
room to room, checking other patients first and saving Mrs. Trane for last,
not to avoid her, but because she will require the most time to care for.
Everyone else seems to be all right for the time being; they have had their
medications, backrubs and are easily settled for the night.

At the door to 309, I pause, adjusting my eyes to the darkness. The only 2
light in the room is coming from an infusion pump, which is flashing its red
beacon as if in warning, and the dim hall light that barely confirms the room's
furnishings and the shapeless form on the bed. As I stand there, the smell hits
my nostrils, and I close my eyes as I remember the stench of rot and decay
from past experience. In my mouth I taste the bitter bile churning in the pit
of my stomach. I swallow uneasily and cross the room in the dark, reaching
for the light switch above the sink, and as it silently illuminates the scene, I
return to the bed to observe the patient with a detached, medical routineness.

Mrs. Trane lies motionless: the head seems unusually large on a skeleton 3
frame, and except for a few fine wisps of grey hair around the ears, is bald
from the chemotherapy that had offered brief hope; the skin is dark yellow
and sags loosely around exaggerated long bones that not even a gown and
bedding can disguise; the right arm lies straight out at the side, taped cruelly
to a board to secure the IV fluid its access; the left arm is across the sunken
chest, which rises and falls in the uneven waves of Cheyne-Stokes respirations;
a catheter hanging on the side of the bed is draining thick brown urine from
the bladder, the source of the deathly smell.

I reach for the long, thin fingers that are lying on the chest. They are ice 4
cold, and I quickly move to the wrist and feel for the weak, thready pulse.
Mrs. Trane's eyes flutter open as her head turns toward me slightly. As she
tries to form a word on her dry, parched lips, I bend close to her and scarcely
hear as she whispers, "water." Taking a glass of water from the bedside table,
I put my finger over the end of the straw and allow a few droplets of the cool
moisture to slide into her mouth. She makes no attempt to swallow; there is
just not enough strength. "More," the raspy voice says, and we repeat the
procedure. This time she does manage to swallow and weakly says, "thank
you." I touch her gently in response. She is too weak for conversation, so
without asking, I go about providing for her needs, explaining to her in hushed
tones each move I make. Picking her up in my arms like a child, I turn her
on her side. She is so very small and light. Carefully, I rub lotion into the
yellow skin, which rolls freely over the bones, feeling perfectly the outline of

each vertebrae in the back and the round smoothness of the ileac crest. Placing a pillow between her legs, I notice that these too are ice cold, and not until I run my hand up over her knees do I feel any of the life-giving warmth of blood coursing through fragile veins. I find myself in awe of the life force which continues despite such a state of decomposition.

When I am finished, I pull a chair up beside the bed to face her and taking   5
her free hand between mine, again notice the long, thin fingers. Graceful. There is no jewelry; it would have fallen off long ago. I wonder briefly if she has any family, and then I see that there are neither bouquets of flowers, nor pretty plants on the shelves, no brightly crayon-colored posters of rainbows, nor boastful self-portraits from grandchildren on the walls. There is no hint in the room anywhere, that this is a person who is loved. As though she has been reading my mind, Mrs. Trane answers my thoughts and quietly tells me, "I sent . . . my family . . . home . . . tonight . . . didn't want . . . . them . . . to see. . . ." She cannot go on, but knowingly, I have understood what it is she has done. I lower my eyes, not knowing what to say, so I say nothing. Again she seems to sense my unease, "you . . . stay. . . ." Time seems to have come to a standstill. In the total silence, I noticeably feel my own heartbeat quicken and hear my breathing as it begins to match hers, stride for uneven stride. Our eyes meet and somehow, together, we become aware that this is a special moment between us, a moment when two human beings are so close we feel as if our souls touch. Her long fingers curl easily around my hand and I nod my head slowly, smiling. Wordlessly, through yellowed eyes, I receive my thank you and her eyes slowly close.

Some unknown amount of time passes before her eyes open again, only this   6
time there is no response in them, just a blank stare. Without warning, her breathing stops, and within a few moments, the faint pulse is also gone. One single tear flows from her left eye, across the cheekbone and down onto the pillow. I begin to cry quietly. There is a tug of emotion within me for this stranger who so quickly came into and went from my life. Her suffering is done, yet so is the life. Slowly, still holding her hand, I become aware that I do not mind this emotional tug of war, that in fact, it was a privilege she has allowed me, and I would do it again, gladly. Mrs. Thane spared her family an episode that perhaps they were not equipped to handle and instead, shared it with me, knowing somehow that I would handle it and indeed, needed it to grow, both privately and professionally. She had not wanted to have her family see her die, yet she did not want to die alone. No one should die alone, and I am glad I was there for her.

Two days later, I read Mrs. Trane's obituary in the paper. She had been a   7
widow for five years, was the mother of seven, grandmother of eighteen, an

active member of her church, a leader of volunteer organizations in her community, college-educated in music, a concert pianist and a piano teacher for
over thirty years.

Yes, they were long and graceful fingers.   8

QUESTIONS FOR READING AND REVISING

1. Beverly Dipo reports that in writing this essay, "I just sat down and typed up
   a rough draft, made some minor wording changes, typed a second draft and
   turned in that." This second draft was "critiqued" by the peer editors in her
   class: "I was worried about its needing some sort of introduction, like 'I'm a
   nurse and I work the night shift,' or something like that. I couldn't come up
   with anything that didn't sound like Jack Webb, so I left it out." Reread the
   opening paragraph of the essay carefully. When—and how—do we know in
   unequivocal terms that the speaker is a nurse? Comment on the alternative she
   chooses to sounding like Jack Webb of *Dragnet* fame ("I'm a nurse and I work
   the night shift"). What choices does Dipo make to increase the effectiveness
   of her opening paragraph?

2. "No Rainbows, No Roses" begins with the first person pronoun. When—and
   how—does that *point of view* shift in the first paragraph? Reread each of the
   subsequent paragraphs. Is the emphasis in each personal? impersonal? some
   blend of the two? Support your response with specific examples. Dipo notes
   that one of her readers suggested she revise paragraph 3 by adding personal
   pronouns. As a writer, however, she exercised her authority over her own work
   and resisted, explaining: "As a nurse I frequently observe *things* before I ever
   speak to a patient or get to know them as human beings. Right or wrong, it's
   the way we are trained." What do you think are the "things" Dipo has in mind
   here? What reasons would you offer to support—or to challenge—her decision
   that her essay ought "to remain impersonal at that point"?

3. Dipo describes outlining in her head as the most effective method of getting
   started: "I sit down at the typewriter and start typing my thoughts on paper.
   I'm a pretty organized person, so my first thoughts seem to organize themselves;
   sentences fall into paragraphs for me." Which paragraphs in this essay strike
   you as well organized? Why? Less well organized? Why? What would you suggest
   that she do to strengthen those you judged less effective?

4. How does Dipo's careful attention to detail in the first two paragraphs reinforce
   the atmosphere she seeks to create in her *narrative*? At the end of the second
   paragraph, she announces that she will "observe the patient with a detached,
   medical routineness." Point to specific examples of her "detached" *point of view.*
   What is the effect in each instance?

5. In the final sentence of paragraph 4, Dipo shifts the focus of her essay from the woman to her own reaction to rubbing lotion on this woman's frail body: "I find myself in awe of the life force which continues despite such a state of decomposition." Comment on the effectiveness of this sentence. How does it either add to or distract from the overall point of this paragraph and of the essay as a whole.

6. One of the appreciable strengths of Dipo's essay is its use of evocative *diction*. Identify at least three instances where the writer chooses an especially effective word or phrase to underscore the effect she aims to create. Explain why each is so effective.

7. Identify the contending forces in the "emotional tug of war" the writer describes in paragraph 6. Why does Dipo note that she "needed" this experience "to grow, both privately and professionally"? Our familiarity with superficially similar movie scenes and soap operas threatens to reduce the painful intensity and emotional integrity of this woman's dignified death. At what moments does the essay come closest to melodrama, and how does Dipo prevent her essay from slipping into it?

8. Dipo explains that she knew her essay was finished "when I remembered [Mrs. Trane's] obituary and recalled thinking then how appropriate that she had played the piano; her hands were the hands of a piano player." When—and how—does she introduce the detail of Mrs. Trane's hands in the essay? with what effect? Explain whether or not you think she should have given more attention to Mrs. Trane's hands throughout her essay. Explain whether you think her title ought to reflect this controlling image.

SUGGESTIONS FOR WRITING

1. Beverly Dipo's account of Mrs. Trane's death exemplifies the medical profession at its best: well-trained people who can display both rigorous objectivity and generous compassion. Consider other careers that require such seemingly paradoxical qualities as objectivity and compassion. Choose one and write an expository essay using concrete examples to explain why such qualities are necessary in that particular line of work, and how one can create a proper balance between them. You may find it useful to explore not only the external but also the psychological aspects of the job.

2. Part of the success of Dipo's essay depends on the element of surprise—both at how Mrs. Trane responds to her own impending death and the reaction this elicits from the professional who cares for her. Write a *narrative* essay recounting in detail how someone you know behaved in ways that defeated the expectations of those around him or her.

3. As a nurse, Dipo notes that she sees "human suffering, weaknesses, triumphs,

and tragedies on a daily basis." Write an essay describing the ways in which someone you know has had to deal with a serious illness, a family member's death, or an awareness of his or her own impending death. What changes has this knowledge brought about in both the person most directly affected and in those around him or her? What insight have you gleaned from this experience? Recalling what Beverly Dipo has accomplished in her essay, include as many evocative details as possible.

ANN LOUISE FIELD

University of Iowa
Iowa City, Iowa
Nancy Jones, instructor

"When I was about three, I packed all of my clothes in a paper sack and informed my parents that I was running away to an alligator farm and could they please tell me where to find one. Ever since then I've been making up all kinds of stories in my head. Many of the stories were based on things that my brother Brett and I had done or wanted to do. Those stories never left my head or ended up on paper until after Brett died in 1977. It was in remembering all that Brett and I had shared that I realized the stories in my head about our youth were interesting even without the parts I made up. I felt as if I had something to say that others might be interested in reading."

Asked to write an essay on some aspect of her hometown or childhood, Field reports that she knew she would write about Brett and herself. "Brett was my childhood. We spent every minute together. He taught me how to climb trees, how to peel an orange in one continuous piece, how to spit, how to throw dirt clods, and how to shoot rubberbands across the room."

Ann Louise Field was born in Ukiah, California, spent the first sixteen years of her life in Redlands, and now calls Bellingham, Washington her hometown. She is studying nursing at the University of Iowa and plans to become a nurse-midwife. Field has worked as a manager for McDonald's, a seamstress in a drapery business, and as a maid in a motel in order to help pay for her college education.

The Sound of Angels

When I was nine I lived in Southern California. Redlands was a small town, as California towns go, and not an exciting place to live. My life in Redlands was as predictable as the fact that we always had tacos for dinner on Saturday, chili on Sunday, and tamale pie on Monday. Every day was a carbon copy of all the previous days. Nothing ever seemed to change. But in spite of this sameness I wasn't unhappy. My brother Brett and the orange groves at the top of our street were both a big part of the sameness and the source of happiness.

Brett had an afternoon paper route in the summer of 1969. The route and the money he earned were something that he and I shared. Every afternoon at two he'd deliver *The Daily Facts* to 107 paying customers and I would ride with him on the last half of the route. I didn't really help deliver any of the papers on the paper route. I was still too new at riding a bike to hold the bike steady with one hand and heave a rolled-up paper onto the porch of a house

76

with the other, but I don't think Brett wanted the help—he wanted the company. Brett never let me go with him to the newspaper office to pick up the papers because some of the other boys would say nasty things to me. He didn't want me to hear the things these boys would say, and he was concerned that the long uphill ride home would be too much for me, so Brett did the first half of the route alone. And I would wait, in the front yard if it wasn't too hot, for Brett to come riding around the corner on his new orange ten-speed.

Brett's bike was the most beautiful bike I had ever seen. It was much too 3 expensive for Mom and Dad to buy so Brett had helped pay for it by selling greeting cards. It was nicer than my bike. My bike was blue and it didn't have any speeds, just stop and go. It was the first bike I had ever owned and I had finally gotten it for Christmas when I was eight after having wished for a bike since I was six. The bike was used and had been painted over and the purple basket on the handlebars was faded, but I didn't care. Brett liked my bike almost as much as I liked his. He never treated my bike as if it were any less valuable than the one he had. He took good care of his own bike, washing and waxing it on the weekends, and he helped me do the same to mine.

Brett bought things for the two of us with the money he made from his 4 paper route. He bought things that we never seemed to get enough of at home; a dozen doughnuts that we didn't have to share with anyone, plastic vampire teeth and fake blood at Halloween, toys from the five- and ten-cent machines just inside the door of the store, and a note pad of pink paper with matching envelopes that he had seen me admiring. When I saw these things in the store I never asked Brett to buy them for me. He just did. Whenever he chose something for himself he chose one for me too. But the doughnuts were the best of all. I can remember getting up early on cool Saturday mornings in the fall or spring and riding with Brett two miles to the Winchell's doughnut house. We would spend thirty minutes just looking in the window at all the different shapes and sizes and kinds of doughnuts. Then, when we had decided which twelve we wanted, Brett would buy them. We would bicycle two blocks over to the high school and eat them there on the lawn in front of one of the buildings. I would eat four and he would eat the rest. They were just for us. If we decided that we didn't like one of the doughnuts that we chose we just left it there for the birds. They were our doughnuts and we could do with them whatever we pleased.

Brett and I also spent a lot of time in the orange groves at the top of our 5 street. Running through these groves were sankies, open drainage ditches that caught the runoff from the groves. When the groves ended the sankies went underground and continued, for miles sometimes, until they reached the next grove. The sankies were lined on the sides and bottom with rock and cement. Sometimes they had a few inches of water in the bottom and sometimes they were dry. We weren't supposed to play in the orange groves but we did anyway. The orange groves supplied us with rotten oranges that we liked to throw at passing cars. It was into the sankies that we dove for cover when an angry motorist stopped to locate the source of the rotten orange, but not even the most ardent pursuer could catch us once we went underground.

The orange groves were always a pleasant place, winter or summer. In summer we had the shade of the trees and the dust rising from the dry dirt to fill our nostrils and stick to our sweaty skin. We could sit in the sankies with our feet in the water and feel the coolness of the rock wall against our backs as we ate sweet, stolen oranges. In the winter the wind whispered through the leaves bringing with it the pungent odor of oil from the smudge pots burning nearby to keep the trees and their fruit warm. There was a crispness to the cold that could carry the smell of a chimney fire a mile away and bring the stars in the sky within reach. 6

It was in this cold that Brett and I would steal Christmas lights off of houses. We would go out after dark for a walk to look at the houses decorated for the holiday and we would steal the lights. Never very many though. Only one or two from each house and never more than a handful each trip. It was a challenge for Brett to sneak up to the front of a well-lit house and take the bulbs without getting caught. I was too chicken to leave the safety of the shadows so I was always the lookout. Once we had the bulbs we would return to the orange grove at the top of our street and break them. As they struck the ground there was a hollow POP! followed by the tinkling of colored glass. It was such a pretty sound. Brett said it was the sound of angels. That sound put me at peace and made me happy in a way I had never known. By the smile in his eyes and the way he held my hand as we walked home, I knew it made Brett feel the same way. 7

We loved our orange groves, our bicycles, the dozens of doughnuts we shared, and the carefree life they gave us. It was the only side of life we knew. I figured that one morning I would wake up and find that I had grown up during the night, but I didn't think that it would change things. Nothing could possibly matter more than paper routes, climbing trees, eating oranges, and crawling around on our bellies in the sankies under the streets. 8

It was sometime during the latter half of 1969 that I realized we were poor. It was 6:15 one fall evening and the sun would be setting in about an hour. I was standing on a footstool in front of the kitchen sink doing the dinner dishes and I could see Dad and Brett out of the window. Dad was talking and Brett was shaking his head and saying "no" with an intensity I had never seen before. 9

I thought Brett might be crying. After a few moments they both came in the house and my dad handed Brett two empty grocery sacks.

"Go with your brother, please," was all my dad said. 10

Something in his voice frightened me so I went without asking why. Word- 11 lessly, Brett and I left the house and climbed over the back fence. We crossed the dirt field of the junior high school and passed the buildings until we came to an orange grove on the other side of the school. We climbed this fence too and went back into the trees. I wondered what we were doing there because we never played in this orange grove. Brett opened his sack and began picking oranges and dropping them into it.

"What are you doing?" I screeched. "Dad will kill us if we steal oranges!" 12

Brett looked at me with tears running down his cheeks. "Dad said to take 13 them."

"Why? Dad would never let us steal." 14

"Just shut up and do it!" Brett yelled at me. 15

I stomped my foot. "Not until you tell me why." 16

"Because we're poor!" he shouted. "If we don't steal these oranges we won't 17 have anything for lunch tomorrow." With that he threw the two oranges in his hands at me. They hit me on the head and the arm and I gave a startled cry. Brett wiped his eyes and nose with the sleeve of his shirt and said more quietly, "Just pick the damn oranges."

As our house came into view on the walk home I saw it as if for the first 18 time. The paint was peeling and the yard was overgrown with bushes and ivy. The run-down condition embarrassed me. From inside the house I could hear two people yelling at each other. I saw my whole life in that frame; my hand-me-down clothes that had been Brett's before mine and somebody else's before his, and my used and shabby bike with rust and dents under the cheap blue paint. I remembered a time when I was six and we had "camped out" in front of the fireplace for a week. It had been fun sleeping on the floor, pretending we were pioneers and cooking over the fire. I also remember trying to turn the bathroom light on and my mother's strange look when I asked her why it wouldn't work. I knew now why it wouldn't—the electricity had been shut off. That same year a box of food and some presents appeared on the front porch Christmas morning. My mother cried when I scolded her for not leaving the door unlocked for Santa.

We were poor. I had three oranges as my lunch the next day to remind me. 19

The days went on and so did Brett and I. We continued to play the way 20 we always had, but I think it was easier for me than for him. Sometimes I felt that he was simply going through the motions of play for my sake. At times he would grow tired of our games and want to just sit quietly in one of the trees. I sensed that things weren't the same because the more we did the things we once loved to do, the more withdrawn Brett became. I didn't like seeing him this way so I was glad when we drifted away from the orange grove. I knew that something had taken the fun out of our orange grove, but I wasn't sure what it was or what it meant.

I'm not sure exactly when it happened, but my brother and I drifted apart. 21 We occasionally went for doughnuts on Saturdays and stole Christmas lights each year, but we weren't as close as we had been. And then puberty came along and gave Brett longer legs and me wider hips and I could no longer wear his old clothes and that somehow set us farther apart. The unpleasant memories associated with that day in the orange grove faded and were almost forgotten until I was fourteen and in the ninth grade. I came home one afternoon to find that my mother had tried to kill herself. I was angry at her for doing it. Not so much because she had almost died but because she had brought reality back into my life once and for all. I didn't want to see what reality had to show me. I didn't want to see the shabbiness of the blue bike or the hand-me-down clothes that filled my closet. I didn't want to grow up if it was going to be so complicated that it made some people want to die so bad that they could cut their own wrists. I wanted camping in front of the fireplace to be just camping, not keeping warm because the electricity had been shut off. I wanted to eat an orange without remembering that week when they were all we had to eat. I wanted to share a dozen doughnuts with Brett on a Saturday morning and disappear laughingly into the sankies where reality, like the angry motorist, wouldn't follow. I wanted to close my eyes and hear the hollow POP! and the tinkling of colored glass. I wanted the sound of angels to mask the fact that life wasn't always as easy as orange groves and sankies and a dozen doughnuts.

But the sound of angels couldn't help me anymore. As my mother lay in 22 the hospital and my life went on I said goodbye to the magic, the predictability and the simplicity of a life filled with paper routes, colored Christmas lights, and a dozen doughnuts to share with Brett. These things were gone, and with their going came the knowledge that they could never return.

QUESTIONS FOR READING AND REVISING

1. Ann Louise Field tells us that when she was nine her life was as predictable as the fact that "we always had tacos for dinner on Saturday, chili on Sunday, and tamale pie on Monday. Every day was a carbon copy of all the previous days. Nothing ever seemed to change. But in spite of this sameness I wasn't

unhappy." What are the happy memories that Field remembers about this time in her life? How did she think of these events as a child? How does she think of these events now?

2. What was the major event that caused Field to see her life differently? How did this event change her life?

3. What do we learn about Brett in paragraph 2? How is this impression of him maintained throughout the rest of the essay? How did he react to the stealing of oranges?

4. How many different stories does Field tell us about her childhood? Why does Field choose to tell a number of stories and present a number of memories to her readers instead of just one? How does this strategy serve her *purpose*?

5. Field writes with tremendous care and detail in describing her relationship with Brett: "Brett bought things for the two of us with the money he made from his paper route. He bought things that we never seemed to get enough of at home; a dozen doughnuts that we didn't have to share with anyone, plastic vampire teeth and fake blood at Halloween, toys from the five- and ten-cent machines just inside the door of the store, and a note pad of pink paper with matching envelopes that he had seen me admiring." Identify details that you found vivid and evocative in the essay. How does Field use these details to create the picture we have of her younger self and her relationship with Brett?

6. Field presents a number of recurring *images*—the orange groves, the paper route, eating doughnuts, the sound of angels. What strategies does Field use to keep these images with her readers throughout the essay? How do these images change in meaning for a reader as Field's understanding changes? Why are these images repeated in the last two paragraphs?

7. Field does not indulge in self-pity or sentimentality in writing about her childhood. Describe her *tone*. How does she achieve this tone? What effect does her tone have on your reading of this essay?

8. In Field's first draft, her essay began this way:

> I grew up in southern California. When I tell this to people their next comment is always along the lines of how nice it must have been to live near a beach. Redlands, California, was far enough away from any beach for adults to say "inconvenient" or "too much driving involved" whenever we asked to go. Sun and sand and surfers were not a part of my life. Nor was much of anything else in the summer of 1969.

Why do you think Field deleted this paragraph as her introduction? Why is her revised introduction a more effective one?

9. Field reports: "The biggest problem I had in writing this essay was cutting

unnecessary parts out of the essay. To me everything belonged in the essay and I wanted to find some way to work it all in. Normally I can revise essays with no problems, but revising this paper was like cutting off bits of my arms and legs."

Field wrote and revised her conclusion many times before she was satisfied with it. Here are two earlier versions:

> From draft 1:
> I was growing up, but not overnight. It had been happening little by little for I didn't know how long. The sameness of my life that I hoped to leave behind was partly responsible for my maturity. And as my mother lay in the hospital and my life went on I was comforted in knowing that the sameness would never leave me completely.

> From draft 2:
> Five years before I had tried to leave the orange groves because everything Brett and I did there seemed to remind us that we were poor. The sameness and the peace that I knew there had been everything to me once. That sameness that I had hoped to forget was now what I wanted most. As my mother lay in the hospital and my life went on I was comforted in knowing that the sameness would never leave me completely.

Compare these two conclusions with the conclusion in the final draft. What are the differences between these rough draft conclusions and the final draft conclusion? How does the revised conclusion more successfully tie together the various ideas in the essay?

SUGGESTIONS FOR WRITING

1. Write an essay about some aspect of life in the town where you grew up. You may decide to tell a number of stories as Field has done, or you may decide to write at length about a single memory. Whatever strategy you choose, try to give your readers a sense of your younger self and of the particular town, city, or rural area you called home.

2. Field successfully writes about the vivid edges of experience that children know and the small pleasures that give childhood its meaning. Select an experience— or a series of experiences—from your childhood and reflect on its meaning.

3. Field's essay illustrates the idea that life looks a lot different to a child than to an adult. Do you think that Field's parents should have told her that she was poor and explained to her what that meant? Should children be protected and sheltered from the realities of life? Write an essay to illustrate your point of view on this issue.

ERIK FIELD

Iowa State University
Ames, Iowa
Patricia L. Cagwin, instructor

"There really is nothing easy about writing an essay," Erik Field observes, even when the subject is as familiar as popular music. In describing his own writing process, Field notes: "I usually freewrite the body of the paper first. I let the body dictate what I am going to write in the introduction and the conclusion rather than beginning with the introduction and running into a dead end." Most often he prepares for writing by "lying in bed with all the lights turned off. It would be one o'clock in the morning. I do my best thinking under these conditions. I am more creative when I am on the verge of sleep. . . . Nearly all of the essays that I write are conceived immediately before, or during, sleep, and then written the following morning." Field spends much of the rest of his day avoiding writing, if he can. "I avoid writing letters by making phone calls. I avoid writing essays by enrolling in a minimal number of composition courses. I write well when I have to. I prefer not to have to." With a major in statistics, Erik Field plans to pursue a career as an actuary.

Born in Poughkeepsie, New York, Field graduated from Wheaton Central High School in Wheaton, Illinois. Both his parents are Iowa State graduates and, as Field notes, have "had the greatest influence on me. . . . They have always emphasized hard work, honesty, and the importance of a good education." Field's extracurricular interests and hobbies include intramural sports, the statistics clubs, baseball cards, music, and reading (Joseph Heller, John Irving, Dave Marsh, Ken Follett, and Stephen King).

Given a wide range of subjects and structures to work with, one of which was an essay classifying the people and experiences that comprise much of ordinary life in contemporary America, Field chose "to categorize the phonograph records that I own." Setting out "to make my readers realize that there are such things as good and bad rock music," he creates a strikingly fresh analogy for grading the latest cuts from the world of rock and roll.

Rock Around the World

On my tenth birthday I received a transistor radio as a gift from my parents. Ever since that day I have been truly enamored with rock and roll music. I started out as just a casual listener, but I soon became a rabid rock fanatic. However, as my knowledge and my appreciation of good rock increased, so did my contempt for truly awful rock. If that makes me a snob then so be it, but I honestly believe that there are such things as good rock and bad rock. I believe that there is such a thing as good taste and that good taste comes with education. Just as surely as a wine connoisseur would refuse to drink muscatel, and as a gourmet chef would refuse to serve Spam, I refuse to listen to low-grade rock.

However, in recent years the radio airwaves have been flooded with Spam.   2
Personally, I am more partial to filet mignon than to Spam so I have been relegated to listening to my own records rather than to the radio. Through the years I have accumulated several hundred records which encompass a vast musical spectrum. Certainly any attempt to classify every one of these albums would prove to be futile, so I have decided to concentrate on what I feel are the six most musically prolific geographical regions, all of which have a definitive rock and roll style. The music from these areas has had a profound influence on me, and I feel that by sharing my musical views with you I am revealing my character as well as my musical tastes, or if you prefer, my B-side as well as my A-side.

The first, and undoubtedly the largest, geographical segment of my record   3
collection falls under the heading "British Invasion" music. The British Invasion era began in early 1964 with the arrival of the Beatles and is considered to have ended by about 1966. During this relatively short period of time, literally dozens of British musical acts found success in the United States. These artists, most notably the Beatles, the Rolling Stones, the Kinks, the Yardbirds, the Who, and the Animals, are well represented in my album library, and deservedly so. The hallmarks of British Invasion rocks are jangly guitars, remarkably tight vocal harmonies, and a general air of adolescent innocence (the Rolling Stones notwithstanding). This was arguably the golden age of rock and roll.

Throughout the 1960s, Detroit was virtually a musical assembly line, pro-   4
ducing one hit record after another. Motown, a Detroit-based record company, continually produced records that were equally irresistible to black and white listeners alike. The Motown recipe consisted of relatively simple lyrics and intense rhythm and blues backing music seasoned with slick pop craftsmanship. The end result was a mile-long list of gold records which included some of the finest dance and party music ever preserved on wax. Detroit musicians employed by Motown include such superstars as Marvin Gaye, Diana Ross and the Supremes, the Four Tops, Smokey Robinson and the Miracles, the Temptations, and Stevie Wonder. Any comprehensive record collection should be well marbled with records by these legends. Mine is.

As segregated as the southern United States were in the late 1950s and   5
early 1960s, it seems only fitting that Memphis, the music capital of the South, should have two entirely different sounds; one white and one black. The white

Memphis sound was a combination of southern rhythm and blues and country made famous in the late 1950s by rock's founding fathers (e.g., Elvis Presley, Roy Orbison, Jerry Lee Lewis). The black Memphis sound, on the other hand, was beautifully soulful. Otis Redding, Sam and Dave, Booker T and the MGs, Aretha Franklin, and Wilson Pickett are but a few of the performers who helped to define the Memphis soul sound of the sixties. No music collection should be lean on Memphis representation. A sizable portion of my collection is devoted to these gems.

Prior to the mid-1960s the city of Los Angeles had no definitive rock and 6 roll sound. However, as the folk rock style became increasingly popular throughout the United States, the city of Los Angeles seemed to adopt this mode. Artists such as the Byrds, the Mamas and the Papas, Buffalo Springfield, and in later years Randy Newman and Jackson Browne combined traditional folk and country with mainstream rock to create a sound that revolutionized folk rock and also contributed heavily to the cultural revolution that was the 1960s. My album collection is peppered with choice cuts by these rock heroes.

As was the case with Los Angeles, San Francisco also became a major rock 7 and roll center in the mid-1960s. However, while the Los Angeles sound was purely folk rock, the San Francisco sound consisted more of psychedelic experimentalism and eclecticism. San Francisco rock heavily influenced (and was influenced by) the hippie subculture of the middle and late 1960s. While this music all seems quite dated today, the raw talent of such San Franciscans as Janis Joplin, the Jefferson Airplane, Steve Miller, the Grateful Dead, the Quicksilver Messenger Service, and Country Joe and the Fish is undeniable. My rock library is thick with psychedelic flavor.

As the 1960s came to a close, a new era in rock music dawned. Psychedelia 8 and hippiedom had become passé. A new generation of rock and rollers had emerged, and they were hungry for a new sound. This new sound was punk, and the pioneers of this style came from New York City. The music that came out of New York in the late 1960s and the early 1970s has proven to be remarkably influential. The sound and stance of artists such as the Velvet Underground, the Ramones, the New York Dolls, and Patti Smith were of seminal importance to modern day and new wave and punk acts. New York rock of this era was dominated by hard-driving guitar work and vocals that were abrasive and often offensive. This music is about as stripped down as rock can get. That may not sound like much of a recommendation; however, what these precursors of punk lacked in talent, they more than made up for in spirit and energy. These rough-edged rockers also displayed a keen sense of social and political awareness that in the "Me Decade" of the 1970s was quite refreshing. These prime New York cuts are some of my most prized possessions.

These are the artists and the sounds that I feel are the filet mignon of rock   9
and roll. They are the living embodiment of all that rock and roll should be.
This is music performed with enthusiasm, sincerity, and intelligence, but without pretension, pomposity, or patronization. So whenever someone asks me,
"How do you like your rock and roll," I reply with a smile, "Well done."

QUESTIONS FOR READING AND REVISING

1. According to what principle does Erik Field classify his record collection? What
   other methods can you think of to classify records? Where and how does Field
   introduce his analogy into the essay? With what effect? How consistently does
   he maintain analogy throughout the essay? In which sections might it be
   strengthened?

2. In commenting on his method of writing this essay, Field explains:

   > First, I made a list of all the geographical areas that have
   > a definitive rock and roll style. Then I wrote a mini-essay
   > about each region, explaining each style and citing ex-
   > amples of musicians who helped to popularize these styles.
   > Next, I decided on the order in which I was going to present
   > these mini-essays. After that, I wrote an introduction and
   > a conclusion. These were the most difficult parts. Then I
   > converted these mini-essays into one long, continuous es-
   > say by adding transitional devices.

   How many geographical mini-essays can you identify in Field's essay? Comment
   on the structure and coherence within each of these mini-essays. How well is
   each organized? What "transitional devices" does Field rely on to link them.

3. How would you characterize Field's *tone* in the opening paragraph? How consistently is this tone maintained throughout the essay? Point to specific words
   and phrases to support your response. Which region of the country—which
   form of rock and roll—does the language of Field's essay suggest he favors?
   Why?

4. Reread carefully the introduction to this essay. Field notes that "writing the
   introduction to an essay is the most difficult aspect of writing for me. I usually
   save that for last." Point to specific words and phrases that suggest Field wrote
   his opening paragraph last.

5. What does Field assume about his audience's knowledge of his subject? Where
   and how does he provide his readers with information that they might not be
   likely to know, but that they need to understand the points he makes? Char-

acterize Field's attitude toward his audience. Does he, for example, regard himself as superior to his readers? inferior? at the same level? Point to specific words and phrases to support your responses.

6. In what ways does the *purpose* of this essay extend beyond *classifying* and *illustrating* the essential features of rock and roll music in this country? When and how do larger points about the general appeal of rock and roll music emerge? about the audience for such music? What are the cultural implications of Field's essay?

7. In the first draft of his essay, Field cast the fourth sentence of paragraph 4 as follows: "The end result was to create records that are among the best dance and party music ever made." What revisions does Field make in the final draft of this sentence? Which version do you prefer? Why?

8. Consider the revisions Field makes at the end of paragraph 8. His first draft reads:

> This music is about as stripped down as rock can get. How-ever, what these prime precursors lacked in talent, they more than made up for in spirit and energy. What makes this music so great is that it is so completely unpretentious and it is never boring. These prime New York cuts are some of my most prized possessions.

Identify the changes in the second version. Which do you think is more effective? Why? Point to specific words and phrases in your response.

9. Now that you have worked through this essay carefully, consider its title. Compare "Rock Around the World" to Field's original title: 'A Geographical Look at the Album Library of Erik Field." What problems—both syntactically and thematically—does Field eliminate in changing his title. Can you think of any ways to improve the title further?

SUGGESTIONS FOR WRITING

1. Despite the success of his essay, Erik Field noted "I never was able to complete the essay to my satisfaction. I would have liked to have included a segment about the Philadelphia soul sounds of the early 1970s and a segment about the Greenwich Village folk sounds of the early and middle 1960s." Choose one of these possibilities—or another "area" of popular music—and write an expository essay in which you follow the method of Field's *analogy* between meat and music.

2. How would you *classify* the books you have read or the films you have seen recently? Are they mostly horror stories? spy thrillers? tales of extraterrestrials?

What essential characteristics does each have, and which of these character-istics does each share? Write an essay in which you *define* the essential ingre-dients of one such genre and explain why the books or films in that genre appeal to a particular segment of the American public.

3. The legendary American songwriter Irving Berlin is reported to have advised the equally popular American songwriter Cole Porter: "Listen, kid, take my advice, never hate a song that has sold a half-million copies." While the statistical standard for success in the music world may have increased since the time when Berlin made his remark, the principle implicit in his advice remains the same: success in the music business can be measured in sales. Consider the pros and cons of Berlin's statement. To what extent do sales determine success? Quality? Does commercial success preclude quality? Prepare an essay in which you argue in support of—or against—this proposition.

PETREA GALLOWAY

Yuba College
Marysville, California
Timothy May, Instructor

"I have been writing something as long as I can remember," Petrea Galloway reports, "but I kept my writing private until I was in college." Galloway is a published writer who has had her short stories, poems, and essays printed in her school's literary magazine, the Yuba Review. About her writing process Galloway reports: "I begin with ragged notes and ideas and compose in my head. If I get too much ahead of myself, I hurry to write my ideas down anywhere since I don't want to forget my ideas before I sit down at a typewriter. I have written on the bottom of Kleenex boxes, in matchbooks, on theater tickets, even on my shoes."

Besides writing, Galloway is an accomplished artist who has received prizes for her paintings. She has worked at various jobs—driving a delivery truck, operating a drill press, and waitressing. As she tells us: "I was married, had three sons, and divorced all by the time I was twenty-three years old. This provided me with the unique opportunity to experience the working world in a way most young mothers would never know. I re-married after three years, my sons young enough to adjust well to their stepfather, and I inherited two more sons. My husband and I and our five sons enjoy cross-country skiing, motorcycle riding, and walking in the hills of northern California."

Asked to write a process essay, Galloway reports that she immediately knew what to write about: "The subject for my essay was a natural choice because at the time of the events described within the essay, I remember saying 'Some day I'm going to write a book or an essay, and this is going in it.' I often say this to myself when I see, hear, or experience anything out of the ordinary."

How to Fill a Car or Freezer with Meat

I live with my husband and sons in an old two-story house in the California 1 foothills. The old place is isolated. It is situated like an island in a sea of forest and pasture. The pasture part leads me to my story about filling the freezer. Many hundreds of acres around us are leased to a cattle owner. He lives about fifty miles away so as a neighborly gesture, my family looks out for the cows. Now, this is not a job. We just do simple things. We may chase a cow back through the fence, then call the owner so he can come and repair the barbed wire. Cows are something I have always considered good freezer filler; and we are surrounded by them!

89

One lazy summer morning, I was enjoying sleeping in. My boys were watch- 2
ing television. A man came to the door. He had just seen a cow out in the
road. He said it had been hit by a pickup truck but he didn't think it was
dead.

He left and I could hear one of the boys saying, "Go tell Mom!" 3

When we reached the cow, whoever had hit it was gone. There it was, 4
making frightful sounds, lying on the side of the road. A man was trying in
vain to put it out of its misery. He had a tiny little twenty-five caliber pistol
and was popping the semiconscious beast between the eyes. It kept trying to
get up—up to its knees, then down—down to the blacktop it would roll. Even
I knew that between the eyes is a thick skull bone. I suggested that he shoot
it in the ear. That location had been most effective for the butcher who once
came and killed our pigs. But the anxious man said. "I . . . I don't have any
more time. I'm late for a meeting in town. I have to go!" And go he did—
leaving me in the road with a half-dead cow and two small boys looking on.

"Well," I thought, "I see I shall have to do something myself." I ran back 5
to the house to get my deer rifle. It was a forty-four magnum. I had shot it a
time or two and knew what I was doing . . . well, almost.

Thankfully, I found a highway worker talking to my watchful boys when I 6
returned with my big gun. The dear man took my gun and skillfully, quickly,
laid the cow to rest. Then he was gone. This time I was left standing in the
road with a dead cow and two small boys looking on.

The next step in this whole mess was obvious: phone Fred, the owner of 7
the cows. I did just that and he was not there. His wife said she would send
him up as soon as he came in.

We decided we'd better wait for Fred out by the poor dead cow. We waited 8
and waited and waited. The sun was rising fast. So was the temperature. As
we were waiting in the increasing heat, our local highway patrol officer stopped
to see what had happenned.

"You're going to butcher it aren't you?" He was serious! 9

"Are you kidding?" I asked, knowing that he wasn't kidding. 10

"Hey, it's getting hot. Don't want all that meat to spoil do you?" Actually, 11
I had not yet thought of the poor unfortunate bovine as "meat."

"The owner will be here soon," I said, "He'll take care of it." 12

"Well, you'd better bleed it at least," said the officer. 13

"Why don't you?" I asked hopefully. "I don't know how to." 14

He got out of his vehicle, removed his pocket knife, and knelt down over 15
the poor old charge. Going at the neck with gusto, but no result, he gave up
and announced, "My blade is too dull. You need a good butcher knife. Better

do it or it'll go bad. I've gotta get on down the road." Climbing back into his car he offered, "Good luck!"

Back to the phone. Back to Fred's wife.   16

"What?" I said with disbelief, "He left two hours ago?" He should have 17 been here easily by now! "Yes, he could have gone about some other business first." (I could not imagine anything more pressing than this dead cow.) "Well," I went on, "I was thinking about bleeding it so your meat won't ruin . . . What? . . . go ahead?" Fred's wife seemed to be under the delusion that I knew what I was doing.

What now? A sharp knife. For some reason I decided to take a towel and 18 a bucket of water back with me. As I was loading this equipment into my pickup, a friend drove up my driveway with her daughter. It just took a hurried explanation and I gained valuable reinforcements.

Now it was my turn to kneel down over the cow. As my friend and now 19 three kids watched, I lowered my sharp butcher knife to the animal's neck. I then discovered just how tough the hide of a cow is. I had to stretch the hide taught, then jab. It took all my force to get the tip of the blade started. Then, using both hands, I had to pull upward in order to cut at all. I was sweating. I was working so hard I forgot all about the poor cow, but my friend hadn't. Although she was turning green, her moral support never wavered. She did ask if we could use the towel to cover the cow's eyes because it was looking at her. Towel in place, I went back to the bloody mess and groped around in the wound I'd made searching for a main vein. My friend closed her own eyes and tried to help by pulling hide out of the way. This was done with two fingers. I continued to probe. I couldn't believe I was doing this. The helpful children pointed out that it was "gross." I had already figured out that part, what with the blood all over my jeans and hands, not to mention the sight of it all.

A low gurgle from deep within the gut of the cow rolled up and became a 20 mighty roar that sent us all back several feet. With all our vast experience, we thought the cow had come vengefully to life! When the panic subsided from our thumping hearts we realized that we had met success. The vein had been cut. Proof poured out of the cow's neck. Somehow, this had caused the loud rumble. We thought there must be more blood inside that would need the aid of gravity to bring it out. We decided to get a rope, tie it to the cow's hind legs, throw it over a tree, tie the other end to my pickup, and haul the cow upside down.

While I was back at the house trying to find a good, strong rope (we did 21 realize the animal would be heavy), Fred showed up.

Fred was pleased that the cow had been bled but said he wouldn't have a 22
chance to get it to a butcher. He turned to me, just returning with the rope,
"Do you want it? Can you get it to a butcher?"

"Sure," I said. No one had ever offered to give me a cow before.   23

Fred filled out a bill of sale for me so I wouldn't be accused of rustling. From 24
that paper I learned that this was not a cow, it was a steer. A cow is female
and raised for milk or breeding calves. A steer is male and raised strictly for
beef. As Fred and his husky partner proceeded to load my steer, with considerable strain, into the back of my pickup, the remaining blood left the animal.

My pick-up had a cracked radiator. It was useless for a trip to town, where 25
a butcher could be found, but I didn't have the heart to tell Fred. Also, I
didn't want to risk not getting the meat, so I kept quiet until the men were
gone. Then I told my friend about the radiator.

"Whatever are you going to do about this animal?"   26

"We'll just have to move it into the back of my Pinto station wagon," I   27
said with confidence. I did not realize what I was asking of the Pinto or of
ourselves.

We parked the pickup in my sloped driveway facing up the hill. Then I   28
opened the back of the Pinto and backed it up until it was just about to touch
the open tailgate of the pickup. We folded the back seats and the front pas-
senger seat of the pinto down and spread an old tarp inside. Now, I thought,
we'll simply roll the steer out of one vehicle into the other. Wrong! Six
hundred pounds of dead weight, cushioned in fat, does not roll. It doesn't
even slide, scoot, or otherwise move. We tied the rope to the steer's leg. We
then passed the rope through the open Pinto and out the driver window where
my friend grasped its frayed end. I was in the back of the pickup with my back
against the cab and my boots planted firmly upon the black, hairy hide. One,
two, three, heave! Again! Our faces were red. We gained two inches. Again,
and again. Finally it slid but the head fell into the slight gap between the
tailgate and Pinto. The neck flopped, like a wedge, blocking all efforts. We
called to the kids.

"Lift up the head so it will slide!" The girl wasn't about to touch the dead 29
cow's head, and it was too heavy for the little boys. I got down from the back
of the pickup and told the kids to slide a shovel under the head as I gingerly
lifted it—by the ear. Now it was looking at me!

With the kids stationed at either end of the shovel holding the head up, I 30
got back to my post. My friend, Janice, was still on the end of the rope. All
together, kids lifted, I pushed, and Janice pulled. We got most of it into the
little station wagon. We did have one problem with a stiff leg. It was pre-

venting the back of the car from shutting. We pulled and tugged and were just considering the chainsaw when it bent enough for the car to close. That was lucky because I don't think any of us knew how to start the chainsaw.

There was only room left in my car for the driver. The boys rode into town 31 with Janice and her daughter. If you have never ridden with a dead steer and about five thousand flies on a hot day, you can't imagine the unpleasantness of the trip. The smell was outrageous. One hind leg hung over my shoulder; a reminder of my grisly deeds, and the flies buzzed incessantly! The thirty-five miles to town seemed a year's journey.

At the butcher shop in town I explained that I had a steer in my car and 32 asked if they could take care of it for me. The man, dressed in a blood-stained white apron, accompanied me to my car.

"If you could back over to the rear door, we have a hoist to unload it with," 33 he explained. He quietly went about his business, throwing strange glances at me from time to time. I'm not very large, about five foot three and one hundred fifteen pounds. Finally, his grin broke through his composure and he blurted out, "Lady, how the hell did you get it in the car?"

After a few days I went back to the butcher shop and picked up over seventy 34 packages of hamburger, steaks, and roasts. The butcher got about fifty dollars for his trouble and I went home and filled my freezer, the hard way.

So you see, there are only four simple steps to filling a freezer. First, obtain 35 a steer. (If this is not possible, you may have to purchase a live one and have it killed. Some butcher shops have them already dead. You will usually get a better price buying them in volume from a butcher than you would at a supermarket.) Second, have a butcher prepare it. Third, pay the butcher, and fourth, take the meat home and fill your freezer. It's as simple as one, two, three—four.

QUESTIONS FOR READING AND REVISING

1. Petrea Galloway succeeds in writing a lively piece about a dead cow. She reports that her *purpose* was "to write something that will inform and entertain."How does she achieve this purpose?

2. Galloway writes: "Cows are something I have always considered good freezer filler; and we are surrounded by them!" What effect does Galloway achieve by

telling us this in her introduction? What is Galloway's attitude toward killing the cow? Does her attitude remain consistent throughout the essay?

3. What does Galloway assume about her reader's knowledge and assumptions about the processes of killing a cow or filling a freezer? Does she give her readers adequate information to understand the *process* she describes?

4. What do we learn about Galloway from reading her essay? What kind of person is she? She entertains her readers with her humor, but what do we learn about her in watching her response to being left "in the road with a half-dead cow and two small boys looking on"?

5. Into what stages has Galloway divided the *process* of filling a freezer?

6. Galloway tells us: "I would love to get to the feelings of the reader, without being overly sentimental, but with real truth, with real life." What details make the essay taste of "real life"? Find the details that are most effective and vivid. Explain how these details work in the essay to establish Galloway's purpose.

7. Galloway uses dialogue in telling her story. What does she achieve by using so much dialogue? Find instances of effective dialogue and explain their function in the essay.

8. In her rough draft, Galloway wrote her introduction this way:

> Everything is expensive today. Meat is something Americans are learning to cut down on for health reasons and because of the cost. But I believe most red-blooded Americans still enjoy good red meat and are willing to pay for it.
>
> In order to fill your freezer with meat, you could just go to your local supermarket and invest a large sum of money for it. It will cost from one dollar and eighty-nine cents to about four dollars a pound. It depends upon the cut. The way I filled my freezer took a good deal more effort but was easier on the budget.

Why do you think Galloway dropped these paragraphs? What does she gain by beginning her essay without them?

SUGGESTIONS FOR WRITING

1. By killing a cow, Galloway filled her freezer in a way she had never done so before. Think of a *process* that you completed in an unusual way. Write an essay detailing this process for your readers that assumes your readers' unfamiliarity with your way of completing this process.

2. Using a humorous *tone*, write an essay in which you offer advice to someone. Some possible topics might include: how to get rich; how to write an "A" paper; how to raise a child; how to lose weight; how to read a poem.

3. Galloway narrates how a disaster (the dead cow) had its good side (a full freezer). Narrate an event that similarly seemed dire at the time but turned out to have valuable consequences. Use dialogue and try to make the story as realistic as Galloway's.

PAMELA GARRETTSON

University of Maryland Baltimore County
Baltimore, Maryland
Wallace Shugg, instructor

Pamela Garrettson was born in Washington, D.C., and has lived in Owings Mills, a semi-rural area of Maryland, all her life. "I have lived a stable, if not sheltered life. I was adopted, which means that I tend to ponder some things, such as my family, that most people take for granted. I am a Christian and my religious beliefs greatly influence my writing."

About her writing process, Garrettson reports: "If someone were to walk in and to observe me writing, she would see a mound of notes sitting on my desk, phrases hastily scribbled on napkins, on the back of a chemistry exam, even in the middle of a math notebook. Amid all the clutter, I sit, trying to make sense of it all. I write a few sentences, frown, scratch out some words, and replace them with others, I shuffle my notes and write a few more sentences. Then I sigh, fling my pencil down, and consult a rough outline. I jump up, pace the floor, grin broadly, and rush back to my desk and write furiously."

Pamela Garrettson reports that she never thought much about writing and considered it a chore until high school. "I was a stereotypical, bespectacled bookworm who was always in the library and who even read the encyclopedia for fun. My reading background eventually made me a writer. I learned to write through reading, much as a small child learns to speak by listening to others." Besides reading and writing, Garrettson enjoys listening to music, running, and being outdoors. She is on the cross-country and track teams, writes for her school's newspaper, and is majoring in biochemistry.

Asked to write a persuasive essay arguing for or against some type of government control, Garrettson reports: "I chose public school prayer as my topic because I felt very strongly about the issue. I wanted my readers to put themselves in the place of school children and to realize how uncomfortable many public school students would feel if spoken prayer were instituted in their classrooms."

Prayer in America's Public Schools: Let's Not Start a Religious War

Separation of church and state has been a hotly contested issue in the United States during the past year (1984). Much of the debate has centered on the role of prayer in public schools. President Reagan is said to favor legislation authorizing organized, spoken prayer in public schools, a proposal which is clearly an example of government meddling.

Proponents of organized, spoken prayer in public schools have argued that   2
its prohibition suppressed students' rights to express their religious faith freely.
However, the laws of the United States are based upon the principle that
freedom should not be exercised to the point that others' rights are violated.
Organized, spoken prayer in public schools would infringe on people's rights.

It is impossible to prove a particular religion "right" or "wrong." A Christian   3
might state that Christ was the Messiah, while a Jew might counter that he
was not. The debate ends right there, with mere assertion. Although a believer
will often attempt to use logic to support his views, one's religious beliefs are
only a matter of faith. The founders of the world's major religions emphasized
that abiding by their teachings was a matter of free choice. Jesus, for example,
did not pressure people into joining him; he invited them to "Follow me."
And even within neighborhood congregations everyone interprets his faith a
bit differently than his brethren.

With religious tolerance in mind, America's founders tried to ensure that   4
its citizens could practice their respective religions without interference. Organized, spoken prayer in our public schools would only serve to undermine
this noble ideal. When one is a member of a minority religion, it is all too
easy to feel uncomfortable in the midst of people who are practicing a religion
in which one does not believe. While attending a Hindu service—so radically
different in both theological content and style from my cozy Lutheran church—
I was quite disconcerted. I felt stupid just standing there and almost compelled
to participate. But I believed not a word of what they were saying. It seemed
to me that if I had joined in, it would have been almost blasphemous. The
same would be true, I suspect, for a member of that church visiting mine.

I was so discomfited, yet I attended the service by choice, and the wor-   5
shippers there tried to make me feel welcome. And, too, I was a seventeen-
year-old with firmly established beliefs. Imagine the distress and confusion that
a younger student might feel if most of his classmates are saying a prayer he
does not believe in. Should he mouth words he does not believe or understand?
Should he just stand there, or perhaps leave the room? Should he have to
make that choice? To adults, this may seem a small matter, but children and
adolescents are generally more sensitive about being "different," and their peers
can be notoriously cruel in taunting them.

Why is organized, spoken prayer needed in our public schools, anyway?   6
According to *Time* magazine (19 March 1984: 12–15), when Congress was
debating this issue in March of 1984, several proponents of school prayer linked
the lack of it with the increase in sexual promiscuity and drug abuse. Virginia
representative Frank Wolf went further, stating that the rate of teenage suicides
"began to climb at approximately the same time that the schools were with-

drawn from prayer two decades ago" (12). These arguments seem illogical, for drug abuse and sexual promiscuity are nothing new, and most psychologists attribute the rise in teenage suicides to America's increasingly mobile, fast-paced society, which pressures young people to "grow up" before they are ready. Representative Wolf attempted to establish a cause-and-effect relationship without concrete evidence connecting the two events.

The question concerning a student's right to express his religious faith in   7
school remains, however. The First Amendment to the Constitution states that "Congress shall make no law establishing a religion or prohibiting free exercise thereof." Clearly, a balance between these two declarations is intended.

The 1963 Supreme Court decisions on the *Abington School District* v. *Schempp*   8
and *Murray* v. *Currlett* cases did not rule against all prayers, just those organized and led by teachers or school officials. The court saw this as "establishing a religion." Clearly, then, a student should be free to pray any time he wants. America's three major religions (according to membership) all hold that silent prayers are heard as well as spoken ones. In fact, most Protestant and Jewish national organizations are opposed to the proposed school prayer amendment, and the Roman Catholic Church in the United States takes a neutral position. A student wishing to pray can do so silently without risk of disturbing or offending anyone. Therefore, the "minute of silence" compromise also proposed by Congress last spring is redundant.

A few months ago, a federal law was passed that addressed students' rights   9
to exercise religious beliefs freely. The law states that if a school provides students with "non-instructional time" to pursue subjects not directly related to curriculum (clubs, for example), then it may not discriminate against student-initiated groups "on the basis of the religious, political, philosophical or other content of the speech at such meetings," and must provide equal access to school facilities for both secular and religious groups. Because this law is qualified by the phrase "student-initiated," it does not violate the Supreme Court rulings banning school-organized religious activity. It was supported by both backers and opponents of the prayer amendments that were proposed, but not passed in the Senate last March.

Since students are not forbidden to pray or to discuss religious matters among   10
themselves while at school, it is obvious that their right to exercise their religious beliefs remains unviolated. Therefore, the authorization of organized, spoken prayer in public schools is not only potentially offensive to students (and their parents and teachers), but also unnecessary.

Aside from the legal quagmire created by the issue of organized prayer in   11
schools, there are practical considerations as well. For example, how and to

whom would the students pray? My mother was a librarian at a Baltimore County public high school during the 1950s. She recalls that the Lord's Prayer was recited as part of morning opening exercises, even though about a third of the school's population was Jewish. Though the Lord's Prayer has fairly universal wording, some Jews might object to its being called the Lord's Prayer when it was authored by a man who was not *their* lord. My mother also said that the prayer exercises "very often turned out being irreverent. You know, kids giggling through it." Wouldn't a devout Christian be offended too, by lack of respect accorded to the recital of "his" prayer?

Jerry Falwell, a leading backer of school prayer, proposes instead that each 12 morning, a different student might lead a prayer from his own faith, with other pupils free to join in or abstain as they wish. This idea avoids none of the problems of the 1950s version of school prayer; it just gives "equal time" to all faiths represented.

Government interference in a matter as personal as prayer only serves to 13 infringe upon the rights of its citizens. In many countries where religion and government are closely meshed, the result is dissension and even bloodshed.

Our public schools should impress upon students their common goals as 14 human beings, not alienate them in a battle over their religious faiths.

QUESTIONS FOR READING AND REVISING

1. Pamela Garrettson tells us: "As a Christian, I realize all too well that devout people of all religions can be intolerant or inadvertently insensitive to others' feelings in their fervor." Where in the essay do we see Garrettson's strong feelings about the issue of school prayer? How do her acknowledged religious views make her arguments more or less convincing? How do her views influence the *tone* of her essay?

2. What is Garrettson's *thesis*? Where in the essay does Garrettson state her thesis?

3. Identify the points Garrettson uses to support her thesis. Which are the most convincing and least convincing arguments? What does her use of evidence contribute in each case?

4. *Classify* the different types of evidence Garrettson uses in her essay. Discuss the effectiveness of each piece of evidence.

5. In paragraph 2, Garrettson makes the point: "Organized, spoken prayer in public schools would infringe on people's rights." What are these rights as she defines them in the essay? How does the argument about people's rights con-

nect to the argument about government interference? Does Garrettson establish the connection in a persuasive way?

6. What opposing *arguments* does Garrettson present? Why, in general, is this an effective strategy for arguing? Does this strategy work in Garrettson's essay?

7. In paragraphs 4, 5, and 11 Garrettson uses personal experience as evidence. How could an opponent argue with this evidence?

8. What is Garrettson's strategy for arguing? Does she move from her weakest argument to her strongest, her strongest to weakest, or does she use some other organization? Can you suggest ways to structure her essay more effectively?

9. Garrettson tells us that her "readers could be anyone." What assumptions does she make about her readers' beliefs? Find specific instances in her essay to support your answer.

10. Reread the last two paragraphs of the essay. Do these paragraphs provide an effective *conclusion?* Suggest ways to revise these paragraphs to make them more effective.

SUGGESTIONS FOR WRITING

1. Garrettson presents a strong *point of view* on the issue of school prayer. What is your point of view on this issue? Write an essay in which you illustrate your point of view using personal experience as evidence.

2. Garrettson uses the issue of school prayer as an example of an area in which she feels there should be no government interference. Consider another issue that influences our public, personal, and political lives (e.g., gun control, abortion, speed limits, food stamps, etc.) Write a *persuasive* essay in which you *argue* why there should or should not be government interference in this area.

3. Find an article in a newspaper or magazine arguing one side of an issue. Write an essay in which you argue for the other side of this issue. Use some of your opponent's arguments as support for your position.

MATTHEW J. HOLICEK

The University of Texas at Austin
Austin, Texas
John Ruszkiewicz, instructor

"When I write I like to have everything I need within arm's reach. The telephone, my bag of Fritos or Oreos, a cold drink, paper, and of course my Walkman. I hate silence when I study and writing isn't any different. I sit at my desk with my typewriter, or sit on my bed with my pillow in my lap, a book to write on, and my blank piece of paper. Sometimes I even have the television going. Sounds like impossible working conditions, but they have been working perfectly fine so far."

Matthew Holicek was born in New Berlin, Wisconsin, and moved to Houston, Texas, when he was twelve years old. He cites this move as one of the biggest influences on his life and reports that "living in two different cultures, Wisconsin and Texas, has given me many different ideas for my writing." Holicek has long been interested in both writing and making films. He was feature editor for his high school newspaper and received a journalism award for his articles. Holicek credits his father, a writer for an advertising agency, with encouraging his writing and for allowing him to use the family's 8-mm movie camera to make his own films. Holicek plans to major in radio-TV-film and make a career out of writing and filmmaking.

Asked to write an extended definition, Holicek reports: "I noticed that one of the choices was to define a particular type of movie, and the idea to write about slasher movies hit me immediately. I have seen so many of these films from working at a movie theater and from renting and watching them on my VCR. Seeing so many of these films has made me, I think, somewhat of an expert on horror movies. These slasher movies are forever imprinted in my mind, which actually might not be such a great thing to have in my memory."

For a more detailed study of Holicek's essay and the drafts that led to it, see Part III.

Look Out Behind You!

Most people get upset if they are told how a suspense or horror movie ends. 1 After all, there's no point in seeing a "who-done-it" film if you already know who did it. But when it comes to a genre of horror films know as "slashers," people seem willing to make an exception. Even though they know that one slasher movie is apt to be just like all the others, audiences enjoy them anyway—perhaps because these stories of people being sliced to death by maniacs are so predictable. John Carpenter's masterful *Halloween*, which premiered in 1978, is widely regarded as the original slasher film. It was soon followed by a rash of inferior imitations which audiences nevertheless flocked to see, uncon-cerned that these totally predictable cinematic clones focused more on high death tolls and gory violence than on developing interesting characters or coherent plots.

Since teenagers are the target audiences for slasher films, the victims in 2 them are almost always independent, fun-loving, just-out-of-high school partyers. Could it be that the filmmakers believe that the teenage audience somehow identifies with other youths being decapitated, knifed, and electrocuted? But the kids portrayed in the movies die so quickly that viewers don't get much chance to learn about them, much less identify with them. The girls all love to take late-night strolls alone through the woods or skinny-dip at midnight in a murky lake. The boys, eager to impress these girls, prove their manhood by descending alone into musty cellars to restart broken generators or chasing psychotic killers into haylofts and attics. Entering dark and gloomy houses, men and women alike decide suddenly that now's a good time to save a few bucks on the end-of-the-month electric bill—so they leave the lights off. After hearing a noise within the house, they always foolishly decide to investigate, thinking it's one of their many missing friends or pets. Disregarding the "safety in numbers" theory, they branch off in separate directions, never to see each other again. Or the teenagers fall into the common slasher-movie habit of walking backwards, which naturally leads them right into you-know-who. Con-fronted by the axe-wielding maniac, the senseless youths lose their will to survive, close their eyes, and scream.

In short, whatever the logical thing to do is, the characters don't do it. Or 3 what they try to do fails. Calling the police is almost always out of the question. However, if they do decide to call the cops, the phone is dead. Or the lights don't work. If the victims try to get into another room, the door is jammed. If the characters manage to escape from the house, they always make the mistake of heading for the car. Sometimes the doors are locked and, naturally, the kids are without keys. But if they are lucky enough to have keys, the car won't start. Couldn't even rely on a new BMW in these movies. Then, looking at the fuel gauge, they realize they should have stopped at the village gas station on the way home from the 7–11 the night before. If the fumes are enough to get the car going, the next obstacle will be four deflated tires. The mad killer doesn't miss a trick!

Of course, it's always easy to tell exactly who his next victim will be. If a 4 girl goes off alone, she'll be murdered. If a guy walks backwards . . . instant death. Car won't start? Expect company in the back seat. An unlit room? It's lights out, forever. All hope is lost when characters come face to face with The Slasher.

The mad slasher is a once-ordinary person transformed into an indestructible, unstoppable, superhuman menace. In the opening scene of the movie, through what appears to be the hazy view of someone afflicted with cataracts, we see a horrifying incident—a burning, a decapitation, a drowning, a lynching, or a car accident—that causes the death or disfiguration of one or more innocent outcasts. Then we are transported ten years forward, to the present time. The plot unfolds. We learn that our happy group of teens—or a similar bunch of kids—is responsible for the incident that maimed or disfigured the maniac on that day ten years earlier (it was Halloween, or Valentine's Day, or Friday the 13th or some other special occasion—a prom, a wedding, a loss of virginity). Or the slasher has seen the teens cause the death of someone dear to him. He is hot for revenge, but he has decided to wait exactly one decade (no more, no less) before exacting his vengeance.

We rarely see where these slashers live, but they obviously don't have the sense to get a comfortable apartment. They seem to prefer dismal, rotting shacks where they dine on furry animals and Chicken McNuggets. They never take off their masks or change their wardrobe—which consists of flak jackets, army boots, and institutional pajamas. They don't talk; they just breathe heavily. Slashers do have the uncanny ability to predict exactly where their victims will be next: teenagers are sure to back right into their killers or open that very door behind which the madman patiently lurks. When a slasher ends up having to chase his victims, he doesn't run. Instead, he just plods on zombielike after his victims who, despite their youthful vigor, are unable to evade him. He enjoys waiting for the teenagers, girls especially, to trip. Or he waits to catch them off guard. That's when he makes his move.

When he murders his victims, he puts his imagination into it. To assure the best and most gruesome results, he selects his tools carefully: knives, machetes, axes, arrows, hot pokers, and sometimes just his bare hands. To save a little time, he'll occasionally put a single spear or pitchfork through two teens making love—killing two birds with one stone. Or he'll cunningly lure his victims to death by slamming doors, snapping branches, or turning off the power in the fuse box.

After the killing spree, the one surviving teenager, usually a hysterical girl, discovers the dead bodies of all of her friends placed neatly and sequentially in her path—leading her directly to The Slasher. But, of course, she doesn't see him until he lunges for her. Fortunately for her, this time his knife (or poker or pitchfork) somehow misses its mark. She escapes and he chases her (zombielike) through the house or the woods. Then, after endless screaming, running, and tripping, the heroine cleverly thinks to defend herself and manages to skewer his eye with a sewing needle, split his skull with an axe, or hang him. He falls to the ground, dead, or so she thinks. The audience groans as the woman stupidly turns around and walks away. The moment she relaxes to catch her breath, this superhuman monster lunges from the darkness again and tackles her. They struggle, and the slasher's true identity is revealed as she strips away his mask.

As the slasher raises his knife for a life-ending blow, two outcomes are   9 possible. One is that, from nowhere, a male hero appears and kills the slasher, saving the girl. The other and more prevalent outcome has the girl discover a butcher knife or machete lying nearby. Just in time, she avoids the maniac's blow and thrusts the knife into his stomach, killing him for good this time— she thinks. In neither ending do the teens actually check to be certain that the slasher is dead. (None of the kids in these slasher movies are destined for careers as coroners; they're all too eager to pronounce anything that doesn't move *dead*.) But the audience knows better. A simple lack of vital signs won't prevent this killer from rising up again, pulling the knife from his stomach (or the axe from his skull, or the machete from his neck), and killing those surviving teens with even greater enthusiasm and ingenuity in the inevitable, and even more dreadful slasher sequel coming soon to your local theater.

QUESTIONS FOR READING AND REVISING

1. Why, according to Matthew Holicek, do audiences enjoy slasher movies?

2. What is Holicek's attitude toward slasher movies? How does he reveal his attitude?

3. Holicek is writing an extended *definition* of slasher movies. What is his definition? What are the essential features of these movies?

4. What techniques does Holicek use in his introduction to bring his readers into the world of his essay?

5. Why do you think Holicek concludes his essay by promising an "even more dreadful slasher sequel coming soon to your local theater"? Why is this an effective *conclusion*?

6. Holicek advises fellow writers: "Details, details, details. Writers need to use as many details as possible so that readers will know that the writer knows what he is talking about." Does Holicek follow his own advice? Find details that you think are vivid and memorable. How does Holicek use these details to support his purpose?

7. In his third paragraph, Holicek has fun with language as he plays with sentence structure, length, repetition, and rhythm. Which sentences do you find especially effective? Why?

8. For whom is Holicek writing this essay? Can you understand the essay if you have never seen a slasher film? Why? What are Holicek's assumptions about his readers familiarity with the slasher genre?

9. Holicek tells us: "I tried to appeal to my readers through subtle humor in poking fun at slasher movies. I hoped people would laugh a little yet also realize at the same time the truth of the points I made." Did you find Holicek's essay humorous? Cite specific instances in the essay to support your answer. Why is Holicek's humorous tone an effective way to express his point of view?

10. In his first draft, Holicek began his essay this way:

> The slasher movie is a specific type of horror film which
> concentrates more on the death toll and body count than
> on developing characters or plot.

Why do you think Holicek dropped this simple and direct definition as his introductory sentence?

SUGGESTIONS FOR WRITING

1. Holicek explains to his readers the popularity of slasher movies. Using a humorous *tone*, write an essay in which you illustrate the popularity of romance novels, soap operas, award ceremonies, etc.

2. Write an essay defining the essential ingredients of one genre of books or films—spy thrillers, mysteries, tales of extraterrestrials, etc.

BRENDA JACOBS

Mississippi Gulf Coast Junior College
Perkinson, Mississippi
Nelda J. Lott, instructor

Brenda Jacobs describes herself as the only child of middle-income divorced parents. "Being the only child of two working parents shaped me most," she explains. "As such, I was often alone, both physically and emotionally. Reading and daydreaming were my refuge and my consolation. . . . I had a dog-eared library card of which I was extremely proud, and by the age of eight, a used typewriter. Mother taught me the correct finger placement, and I supplied the words. My love for words goes back as far as my memory of learning to read." The power of words has remained a central interest in her life. Born in Quitman, Mississippi, Jacobs spent her childhood years in Wiggins, Mississippi, before moving to Sonora, California, where she graduated from Sonora High School. An English major at Mississippi Gulf Coast Junior College with as yet undefined career goals, Jacobs participates in numerous extracurricular activities. She serves as a college yearbook photographer, a production assistant for the college theater, and a "reluctant editor of the college newspaper, now defunct." She is also the author of two plays for children produced by the college's "Perk Players" and presented to more than twenty-four thousand elementary school children during a recent tour of southern Mississippi. Jacobs's accomplishments are recognized in Mississippi Gulf Coast Junior College's Outstanding Achievement Awards in English, photography, and philosophy.

Brenda Jacobs's goal in "Handing Down Grace" is, as she explains, "to convey the sense of fun in word play—to illustrate that the nature of the English language is widely adaptable to the inventive imagery of the individual." Writing with an audience of both southerners and "nonnatives" in mind, Jacobs seeks to celebrate "the wonderful speech patterns which are as richly diverse as the people who make up our country."

Handing Down Grace

The unpaved road, a worn ribbon of white sand and red clay, bisects the 1
heart of Five Mile, a narrow stretch of land which bears the name of the small
creek running through the surrounding woods. Since my grandparents returned
"down home" from California, a portion of the lanky pines and kudzu-entangled underbrush has given way to a plowed field where purple hulls and crowders grow in season. Adjoining the field is the "old place," Grandmother's first
home, now a dilapidated, ghost-grey structure veiled in wild flowers and tall
grasses. Up the road vestiges of a long-abandoned oil well scar the wooded
hill; and a bit farther, ruins of the old frame schoolhouse, where Mother

received her education, mark the end of this rural Mississippi road. Though somewhat familiar from early childhood visits and family reminiscences, Five Mile is, none the less, far from my western roots. But here I was, a California transplant having dinner in post-Confederate territory, where standard English is shunned like the carpetbagger of old. As family members gathered around the table and bowed their heads, Grandma singled out one to ask the blessing or, as she phrased it, to "hand down grace." Although my ear had already become accustomed to many regional expressions, this one had a decidedly different ring. Irreverently, I began to ponder the "handing down" aspect of grace while grace was still being "handed down." I searched for some common denominator in order to leap logically from the conventional "saying" or "asking" of grace to Grandma's variation and failed miserably. To my mind came the possibility of quasi-literal translation, a connection between "handing down" and passing—say, from one person to another. Yet, there was an upside-downness to the expression that struck a discordant note. Between mouthfuls of butter beans, I mused upon the paradoxical term; reason dictated that if grace were to be "handed" anywhere, surely it would be sent in an upward direction.

Such linguistic oddities, bound by neither logic nor reason, are inherent in 2 the colorful, inventive vernacular of the rural South, teasing the unseasoned, transplanted mind with homegrown fabrications and abstractions. To the westerner nurtured on bland euphemisms and commonplace nouns, the separate ingredients that compose the rich diet of southern colloquialisms are oftentimes difficult to fathom and to digest. Family reunions with three and four generations present are guaranteed to provide a dialectal feast. "Other-mothers" and "mammaws," better known in other parts of the country as grandmothers, happily go about their business of collecting "sugar" and hugs from assorted "chilluns," "chaps," or "younguns." While swapping hunting tales, the men of the family talk of "squarehills" and "hillbillies"—squirrels and rabbits, to the uninitiated. And, on occasion, at least one of the kinfolk is certain to "holler" for the "flyflap," for use on either insects or "younguns."

In a southern setting standard words, familiar even to the westerner, some- 3 times assume entirely new functions and meanings. A community gathering where music, usually gospel music, is played and sung is to the participants a "sang." "Wet" and "dry," when associated with alcoholic beverages, translate as "to have" or "to have not." Though somewhat clarified by the accompanying actions, expressions such as "pitchin' a fit," "fixin' to go." and "raisin' cane," throw the nonnative off balance, if only for the length of time it takes to sigh for the apparent demise of the "-ing" ending. Equally jarring are the vowel sounds that undergo a metamorphosis when uttered by a native speaker. Taken

out of context, "tire" and "tar," as well as, "fire" and "far," are often indistinguishable by sound alone. Similarily, the substitution of "ah" for "i" in
"wire" and "hire" forms a sort of verbal mutation. Plainly, southerners just
don't put much store in the long "i" sound.

Southernese, in all its conglomerate forms, enhances the cultural shock   4
experienced by the westerner who finds herself "to home" in Dixie. Not long
after my arrival in Mississippi, I was introduced to "gardens" and "patches,"
southern style. Since the few gardens on the West Coast are scarcely larger
than graveyard plots, it was a revelation to me to come face to face with the
enormous "patches" owned and operated by a single family outfitted with
ordinary hoes. My education in the ways and words of the South had barely
begun when one evening I accepted an invitation to dig potatoes. Not wanting
to appear naive, I did not question the notable absence of a shovel, even
though "dig" and "shovel" are hitched together in my vocabulary like "salt"
and "pepper," and it is my conviction that such words are not lightly separated.
Nor did I give voice to what was uppermost in my mind, that is, what dig had
to do with potatoes in the first place. But by then I was growing accustomed
to words and phrases not quite fitting my preconceived notions. Perhaps, I
reflected, we were off to observe the potatoes doing whatever they do before
winding up at the local market—as in "wow, dig those spuds." However, on
second thought I was confident that, even though outdated, the expression
must have bypassed the South completely. It was simple logic that guided me
to assume that our true mission was to harvest potatoes, and logic seemed to
indicate that "pick" and "dig" were synonyms of a sort. Needless to say, I was
in error on all counts. Mother has always contended that the obvious has a
way of eluding me.

It was then and there, among the potatoes, that my name became linked   5
to "poor thing." A "poor thing," I learned, was not to be confused with being
poor, as penniless, or with being in a poor state of health. "Poor" of body, or
skinny, I was very definitely not; nor was I ailing, as in "doin' poorly." No,
"poor thing" in my case denoted an overall state of mind, implying either
stupidity or ignorance, depending upon the kindness of the speaker.

The southerner's usage of "sister" and "brother" for those related geneal-   6
ogically, by marriage and otherwise, can perplex even the most astute outsider.
In those early days, when my mouth stubbornly refused to form the word,
"ya'll," it seemed that everyone in the entire South belonged to one extended
family. It was a while before dawn broke over the cloudy linguistic horizon to
reveal the true meaning of these fraternal terms. It became evident that, as
long as the gender matched, anyone qualified as a "sister" or "brother," even
if she or he were an only child. Additionally, I had the suspicion that the

given name of every eldest son, who was invariably called Brother, had been long forgotten. Then too, there was Brother Bill, the Baptist preacher, and Brother Bob, the deacon who married Sister Mattie, adding to the confusion. Although Sister Mattie was also known as Miss Mattie, both before and after her marriage, her husband, Brother Bob, quite sensibly called her "Mama." In time I learned to disregard reason and to stick to hunches while attempting to sort and recatalogue definitions in accordance with the southern tradition.

Now that I have at least one foot firmly rooted in Mississippi soil, large 7 portions of the linguistic puzzle, including those seemingly misrepresentative titles, have fallen into their illogical places. It seems perfectly natural that ladies below the Mason-Dixon line "glow" rather than sweat, and that "pot liquor" is a legal substance in both "wet" and "dry" counties. In fact, I've acquired a fondness for the regional expressions annexed, by bits and pieces, to my word store—enough pieces, I'd like to think, to have at last annulled my "poor thing" image.

QUESTIONS FOR READING AND REVISING

1. Brenda Jacobs's essay uses details and *examples* effectively. Reread her opening paragraph and point out the important details and examples she introduces. Explain how each reinforces the overall effect of this paragraph and the essay as a whole. What is the effect of including the phrase "between mouthfuls of butter becans" in the last sentence? Reread the remainder of Jacobs's essay and prepare a list of her most effective details and examples. How well does each reinforce the overall effect she hopes to create in the essay?

2. Jacobs notes that her essay should be "read with a sense of humor." Where—and how—is this humorous attitude toward her subject first revealed? Show how this attitude remains consistent or changes as her essay proceeds. How does the *contrast* between western and southern expressions reinforce her humorous attitude? What is the nature of her comparison between southern and western expressions and how does she introduce—and sustain—it?

3. Jacobs reports on some of the aims of her essay:

   > I hoped that the southern reader might "see" the language habits that by virtue of familiarity go unnoticed. (Interestingly, many southerners are not aware of their particular speech habits, only of the "funny" way everyone outside the South talks.) The typical "Yankee" response was expected to be one of instant recognition and empathy. By

> playing up the confusion, difficulty, and downright igno-
> rance of the city-bred Yankee, I hoped to balance the scales
> of fair play, and to counter any notion that any slight was
> intended.

As you reread her essay, weigh carefully—and explain specifically—how Jacobs does or does not "balance the scales of fair play" in her essay with humor. Support your response with references to particular words and phrases.

4. Based on the way Jacobs presents herself in this essay, what do we learn about her as the essay proceeds? What impression does she create of herself in the opening paragraph? In paragraph 4? In the final paragraph? Explain how her image remains consistent throughout the essay or where and how it changes. In what respects does Jacobs poke good-humored fun at herself?

5. How familiar does Jacobs assume her audience is with southern expressions? Examine paragraph 1 for words and phrases that reveal Jacob's assumptions. How much background information does she provide her readers? Where in the essay does she include it?

6. Jacobs reports that she began working on her essay by "making a list of words or phrases that seemed particularly southern, as well as noting possible inter-pretations. The catch phrase 'handing down grace' seemed a good opening which would set the tone or mood and the stage for the linguistic oddities to follow. Because I felt more interested in and better suited to a light-hearted approach, I decided to include several facets of southern colloquialisms rather than dwell on one particular thing—say, pronunciation." What central idea controls Jacobs's arrangement of these southern expressions and the examples she chooses to include? Where is it introduced? How is it developed? Does Jacobs organize her essay, for example, by moving from general statement(s) to particular examples? From particular example to general statement(s)? Some combination of the two? Something else? Explain. What prevents her essay from slipping into a "catalogue" of southern expressions?

7. Reread paragraphs 4 and 5 and consider the purpose of the anecdote about digging potatoes. What is there in the phrase, "wow, dig those spuds," that might prompt her to say that "the expression must have bypassed the South completely"? Jacobs explains her inclusion of the potato-digging section in these terms: "The action of the potato-digging episode was included to offset a drift toward 'listing,' and to dramatize the subject matter." How effective is this "episode?" How does Jacobs connect it to the overall aim of her essay? If Jacobs had the opportunity to revise her essay, what would you suggest she do to strengthen her handling of this "episode"?

8. Jacobs observes that "the most difficult aspect of revising is throwing out that which may sound good, but which actually lends nothing to the paper as a whole." Which parts of Jacobs's essay might at first seem to illustrate her point?

Reread these sections carefully and explain why each does or does not warrant retention in the final draft. Consider the title of her essay. Her previous draft was called "Southernese." Which title do you prefer? Why?

9. Brenda Jacobs wrote numerous drafts of her essay. In her first draft, the final paragraph reads:

> With at least one foot now firmly rooted in Mississippi soil, a large portion of the linguistic puzzle, including misrepresentative titles, has fallen into its illogical place. After sixteen years, it seems perfectly natural that women below the Mason-Dixon line "glow" rather than sweat, and that "pot liquor" is a legal substance in both wet and dry counties. In fact, I've acquired a real fondness for the regional expressions annexed, by bits and pieces, to my vocabulary storehouse—enough pieces, I'd like to think, have at last annulled my "poor thing" image.

What differences do you notice between her first and final drafts? Which version do you prefer? Why? How does the version you prefer tie together the most important points of this essay?

SUGGESTIONS FOR WRITING

1. Brenda Jacobs's essay is based on her discovery of what she calls "linguistic oddities" (curious regional expressions) when she returned to rural Mississippi after living in California for many years. Consider your own travels. Write an essay in which you re-create your first encounter with a way of talking that you had some difficulty understanding. For example, you may have been visiting a foreign country or simply another part of the United States. (If you are uncomfortable writing about differences in language, you might want to focus on differences in items of clothing, a particular mannerism, or a kind of food.) *Compare and contrast* the differences between your own way of talking and the one you encountered. What did you infer about this foreign or regional culture as a result of this encounter? Contrast these inferences with what you know about your own national or regional culture.

2. Select some aspect of daily life in your hometown—a place, an event, a person, a way of talking—that represents the special regional spirit and texture of day-to-day life. Write an *expository* essay in which you use a detailed *description* of this person, place, or event to explain that texture.

3. The popular media (television shows, films, songs) often profit from projecting images of how people from different areas of the United States talk and behave. (What image does a television serial like "Dallas," which is seen in more than

fifty countries worldwide, create of wealthy Texans?) When these images are repeated week after week, do they harden into stereotypes? What are the consequences of projecting such images across the country? Around the world? Write an *expository* essay in which you *analyze* the regional stereotypes of Americans as they are presented in one such television serial, one American film, or a popular song.

JUDY JENNINGS

Richland College
Dallas, Texas
Rica Garcia, instructor

"My life affects my writing more than anything. I am twenty-nine years old, married
to Les Jennings, and have one son, Christopher. Les and I have a design firm specializing
in large aircraft interiors. I have been attending college on a part-time basis. I tend to
write about things that happen in everyday living—my child, husband, the plight of the
average housewife. It is important for writers to write about things they know about."

Judy Jennings has always lived in Texas; born in Fort Worth, growing up in Greenville, and now living in Plano. Her major hobby is reading, and her favorite authors
include Danielle Steele, Jackie Collins, and Thomas Thompson.

Asked to write an essay in which she explained a situation in her life, Jennings decided
to write about her situation as a stepmother. "My husband's two children live with us
and I feel very strongly about the injustices of stepparenting. I wanted to clarify a
misunderstood role."

Second-Class Mom

On March 22, 1980, I married Leslie Floyd Jennings, Jr. On that same clear 1
spring evening, I also married Daniel Brian Jennings (age seventeen), Lesley
Nicole Jennings (age six), and Phillip Timothy Jennings (age two), Les's children by two previous marital failures. I had been warned by everyone I knew
about the pitfalls of marrying a man with two failed marriages and three children in tow. But marry him I did, and in that dubious deed, settled upon my
youthfully naive shoulders the burdens of the label of "stepmother" that history, mythology, ignorance, and misunderstanding allows our society to dictate.

During the first months of our marriage, I wrestled with having to rearrange 2
our schedules to accommodate weekend visits as well as with my resentment
of the amount of child support my husband was paying and the hardships it
imposed on our already stretched-to-the-limit budget. These factors (and others)
made me often wonder if we would ever be able to have a child of our own
because of these financial and emotional commitments to my husband's children. Yes, I had considered all these things before making a permanent com-

113

mitment to this man, but day-to-day reality is quite different, I found, from the dreams we spin when we are blinded by love's passions.

After only five short months of marriage, Les's two younger children came   3 to live with us, and within thirty days, I was expecting a child of my own. Learning about the trials of motherhood from both Les's children and my own child virtually at the same time, has certainly proven to be a unique and unpredictable experience. I feel that in the last four years, I have learned more about patience, compromise, sacrifice, and endurance than I ever thought possible.

I have never wanted to give anyone the impression that I dislike my step-   4 children, or even that I have no feelings for them at all, but they are not mine. There are times when I want to grab Les by the knot of his tie, pulling him down to my level until the tips of our noses touch and we're looking each other straight in the eye, and then snarl at him through clenched teeth, "THEY'RE NOT MINE." Everyone understands the theories of how difficult it would be to live with someone else's children, but they really never do understand the realities of it. Les's mother is always spouting endless streams of well-meant advice on "raising and disciplining Les's children just like they were my own." Yet, even though she will sit nodding her head in approval while I criticize and correct my own child, she will purse her lips and sometimes burst into tears if I get into a shouting match with one of her grandchildren who is not mine. Even after almost five years, I have never ceased to be amazed and appalled at the injustice of it all. I am expected to perform with perfect precision, but without a single trace of prejudice or partiality, all the mothering rituals, but I am also expected to stop just short of throwing any stones at their characters or past disciplinary guidelines. I'm not supposed to show the slightest bit of distaste or nausea or even say "Yuk" when cleaning up the bathroom after a "didn't-quite-make-it-to-the-toilet" bout of diarrhea or vom-iting, but heaven forbid that I should criticize their clothes or hairstyles or friends, a privilege, I presume, reserved for "real" mothers.

One of the things that makes stepmothering somewhat less a joy than   5 mothering your "children by choice" is that it is such a thankless job. Even after I've spent an endless day in unfruitful toilet training sessions or sore throat crankiness, my own child will make it up to me by climbing onto my lap and snuggling his baby head up underneath my chin, making goose bumps run up and down my arms. I've endured countless times, after days of driving car pools, organizing school bake sales and carnivals, soccer practices, ballet les-sons, and dental appointments, having one of my stepchildren run out to get in the car holding up some crudely fashioned trinket made in school and saying, "Look! Look what I made for Mommy." "Mommy" being their "real" mother.

The mother they see maybe four or five times a year, and who rarely so much as buys them a pair of shoes.

The role of a stepmother is unlike that of any other kind of mother, whether 6
it be foster mother, adoptive mother, or birth mother. Stepmothering is the only type of mothering we do without choice. All children, certainly, are not "planned" children, but even with an unwanted pregnancy, the mother *chooses* not to abort the baby, or give it up for adoption, or something. And certainly, adoptive mothers and foster mothers have a definite choice in the decision to mother or not. The stepmother does not choose the children, she chooses the father. He just comes as a package deal.

Stepchildren also come with an uncanny radar or sixth sense that enables 7
them to zero in with pinpoint accuracy on our vulnerabilities and fire torpedos with deadly insensitivity. Every year, when our whole family assembles to decorate the family Christmas tree, one of my stepchildren will take this one certain ornament out of the box and hold it up for all the rest to see. This particular ornament came with them when they came to live with us. I have always presumed that it was a gift from their natural mother, so I suppose that's why I've never found it in me to throw it away. This ornament is a small pair of very ugly gorillas with toboggans and neck scarves with their arms around each other looking at a book of Christmas carols. They hold it up to everyone in the room (including me) and then announce triumphantly, "This is Mommy and Daddy." Every year I tell myself that they're only children and that they don't know what they're saying, but my face still gets hot and my stomach still flipflops. I don't like being reminded of the "Mommy and Daddy" that used to be. These children are reminder enough. Their very presence seems to almost be a rubber stamp that says, "Your husband used to be in love with someone else," and some things are better left unthought.

I have a very deep sense of responsibility toward these children and a great 8
deal of affection. I will probably never love them the way I love my own son— sometimes I don't love them at all, but they are as much a part of my life as their father or my own child. Just as I am sure about the way I feel about them, I am quite certain that they feel pretty much the same way about me. We have been thrown together by virtue of the mistakes of other people. I can't help the fact that their mother and father couldn't make a go of their marriage, and neither can they, but here we are. We have grown to accept our lives together, and even to depend upon each other somewhat. I am really the only mother they know, and neither I nor they can change that fact.

I would lay down my own life for *any* of my children. For Christopher, I 9
would do it without a backward glance and probably even with a smile on my face. For Nikki and Philip, I would gripe all the way.

QUESTIONS FOR READING AND REVISING

1. Jennings writes with honesty about a subject many people are unwilling to discuss openly. She tells us that she and her stepchildren "have been thrown together by virtue of the mistakes of other people." What does Jennings see as the injustices of being a stepmother?

2. What is Jennings's *thesis?* Does she state her thesis directly? How does she make her ideas clear and convincing?

3. As readers, we have a strong sense of a writer who cares deeply about her subject and who has taken great care to make her essay lively. What strategies does Jennings use to make her ideas interesting to her readers?

4. Jennings writes: "I am expected to perform with perfect precision, but without a single trace of prejudice or partiality, all the mothering rituals, but I am also expected to stop just short of throwing any stones at their characters or past disciplinary guidelines." What details of the mothering ritual does Jennings present to illustrate her thesis? Select details you found effective and explain how these details are used in the essay.

5. Jennings begins her essay in a very direct way: "On March 22, 1980, I married Leslie Floyd Jennings, Jr. On that same clear spring evening, I also married Daniel Brian Jennings (age seventeen), Lesley Nicole Jennings (age six), and Phillip Timothy Jennings (age two), Les's children by two previous marital failures." Do you find this an effective hook for pulling you, the reader, into the world of her essay? Why?

6. In her *conclusion*, Jennings tells us of her willingness to sacrifice herself for any of her children, but that she would be "griping all the way" for her stepchildren. How does her conclusion effectively tie together all the various ideas in her essay?

7. Jennings reports that she envisions her readers as "stepmothers/persons about to become stepmothers." What evidence is there that she is writing for this *audience?* What evidence is there that she is writing for a more general audience? How would paragraphs 4 and 5, for instance, differ if they were written for a different group of readers?

8. We like Jennings even though she confesses to resenting her stepchildren. How do the examples in paragraphs 5 and 7 influence our attitude toward her?

9. Jennings *generalizes* about the role of the stepmother from her own experience. In paragraph 6, for instance, she tells us, "Stepmothering is the only type of mothering we do without choice." Why does Jennings choose to generalize about the role of the stepmother? How does this strategy help to strengthen her essay?

10. In an early draft, Jennings's title was "Number Two Mom." How does her revised title better introduce the essay?

SUGGESTIONS FOR WRITING

1. Jennings illustrates the burdens of the label *stepmother*. Consider a role you have chosen for yourself or have been thrust into and write an essay in which you illustrate what it is like to be cast in the role.

2. Write an essay in which you explain your attitude toward an event or situation in your life that might surprise your readers.

3. Write an essay responding to Jennings's complaints from the stepchild's *point of view*.

MONIKA JERABEK

Harvard University
Cambridge, Massachusetts
Sven Birkerts, instructor

Monika Jerabek regards her immigration to the United States at the age of three as one of the central facts in her life. Born in Prague, Czechoslovakia, Jerabek grew up in California's Silicon Valley and graduated from Henry H. Gunn High School in Palo Alto. "Since immigrating to the United States, I have realized the importance of independence and self-sufficiency while watching my parents create a new life for us and adapt and change to their new-found circumstances." Jerabek has developed her intellectual independence and self-sufficiency in her studies both in high school, where she received an Arthritis Foundation Summer Science Fellowship to work in a DNA lab at Stanford University, and in college, where she serves on the Harvard Advocate Poetry Board and plans to major in philosophy.

Jerabek describes herself as a writer who likes to finish a paper "at one sitting, with a few short breaks," so "that I do not lose the direction and tone of my thoughts." Along with many other student and professional writers, Jerabek finds it most difficult "to strike a balance between a clear, concise approach and a creative flavor." Planning carefully, she feels, makes it easier to balance clarity and originality and increases the likelihood that her essays will succeed. Not surprisingly, her characteristic method of writing involves a good deal of preliminary note-taking and outlining:

> When I start writing I usually write down several general ideas on the topic and try to think of relevant subcategories that would expand on the subject. I further expand these ideas (in my notes and outline) with concrete evidence and examples. That process then leads me to a more obvious focus or thesis for the paper, the explanation of which I include in the opening or closing remarks. After I have completed these preliminaries, I think of the way I want to present the content of the paper—formally, informally, from what perspective, what kind of language—and begin writing, following the guidelines of my notes.

In preparing her essay on Sylvia Plath's poetry, Jerabek set out not only to analyze the father image in Plath's verse but also "to incorporate elements of Plath's life and creative style. I wanted to communicate some of the passion and turmoil in Plath's life as expressed through her poetry."

Sylvia Plath: Electra Inspired

The poet, Sylvia Plath, wrote from a reservoir of experience, motivation, 1
and ambition. One of her main themes, the portrayal of the father figure,
permeates her work and incorporates the autobiographical with other themes—
nature, childhood, death, and suicide. The untimely death of Plath's own
father when she was nine years old left a wound that festered for the poet's
entire life. From the early stages of her writing to the last months before her
death, Plath refers to the father figure, trying to assimilate her reaction to her
father's death.

During her childhood, Sylvia Plath worshipped her father, Otto Plath, a 2
professor of biology and an authority on bees. He took pride in teaching her
science and language, nurturing a close relationship (Salop 10). When he died
after a long illness, Plath's world ripped in two: As she later said, "those nine
first years of my life sealed themselves off like a ship in a bottle—beautiful,
inaccessible, obsolete, a fine white, flying myth" (Aird 4–5). The tragic experience formed a conflict in Plath's mind between feelings of love and feelings
of abandonment, rejection, and guilt, as if her love were somehow responsible
for her father's death. Plath's suicide attempt at twenty—by taking fifty sleeping
pills after visiting her father's grave—illustrates just how intensely she felt the
pain of loss (Salop 13). In her poetry, Plath uses paternal imagery to try to
resolve her inner turmoil.

Her early work not only shows Plath's attempt to define her perceptions of 3
the external world and the relationship of the individual to the outside world
(Aird 5), but includes several poems involving the father-image theme. The
title poem of *The Colossus*, the only collection of poetry published during
Plath's lifetime, creates an encompassing metaphor for Plath's image of her
father after his death: the ruins of an immense statue, representing her shattered image of God-like father, that she can never "put together entirely, /
Pieced, glued, and properly jointed." Searching for the guiding words of a dead
father, she "[labors] / To dredge the silt from your throat" and symbolically
tries to reconstruct the overwhelming figure of her father by uncovering and
rebuilding the statue in "The Colossus." At the end of the poem, however,
Plath concludes that the task is fruitless, that her "hours are married to shadow,"
not only the shadow of defeat, but the shadow of her father. She pictures
herself married to her father—a sign of Freud's Electra complex. Similarly, in
"The Beekeeper's Daughter," the daughter worships her father the beekeeper:
"You move among the many-breasted hives, / My heart under your foot, sister
of a stone." She compares herself to the queen bee, a figure overpowering to
a mere mother, saying, "Here is a queenship no mother can contest." The

autobiographical implications are evident in this case, as Otto Plath was an expert in beekeeping, and Sylvia identified with her mother while loving her father—the pattern of Freud's Electra complex (Salop 11).

Plath further develops the idea of her Electra complex in "Electra on Azalea   4 Path." She describes the aftermath of her father's death: "I went into the dirt, / Into the lightless hibernaculum / Where bees . . . sleep out the blizzard." For twenty years she endures "that wintering," still considering her father God. The scene in which she awakens to reality, on Azalea Path in the graveyard, "a cramped necropolis," parallels her own visit to the graveyard before her first suicide attempt, a result of depression catalyzed by her warring feelings for her father. Depicting her birth as "ill-starred," Plath then tries to blame her mother for "[dreaming] you down in the sea," but at the end of the poem, she blames herself: "your hound-bitch, daughter, friend. / It was my love that did us both to death." Feeling responsible and guilty, just as she felt responsible and guilty as a child, Plath blames his death and her trauma on her love.

Examining the paternal theme in Plath's poetry uncovers other prevalent   5 subjects—nature, for example. In "The Colossus," Plath refers to the "weedy acres" of the statue's brow and the "hill of black cypress," images that not only suggest vivid pictures in the mind but that enhance the metaphor of the statue as her father. The "black cypress" reflects the images of shadows and darkness, while "acres" suggests the vastness of the reconstruction Plath wishes to achieve. The images of nature in "The Beekeeper's Daughter," on the other hand, relate to the sexuality implicit in the Electra complex. With phrases such as "garden of mouthings," "many-breasted hives," and "dark flesh, dark parings," Sylvia Plath subtly illustrates a latent sexual attraction to her father. Similarly, in "Electra on Azalea Path," she speaks of bees like "hieratic stones"— a phrase hinting of the God-like perception of her father. The petals near his grave "drip red" and connect the reader with the blood and death so vividly evident to Plath.

Other related themes emerge in Crossing the Water, the collection of poems   6 judged as the starting point of Sylvia Plath's final development (Aird 39). She continues writing about nature but relates it to more internal experiences. This transitional period finds her fascinated with the trappings of disease and illness and personal isolation, perhaps recalling her hospitalization for psychotherapy and shock treatment after her first suicide attempt the summer of her junior year at Smith College. In "The Surgeon at 2 A.M." Plath compares the intricacies of the inner human body to the multicolored nature. The surgeon finds "the lung tree," the "red-bell bloom" of the heart, and the "sunset" and "hot spring" of the blood, and she senses her power over the "sleepers in gauze sarcophagi," mere "gray faces." She remains completely stoic, almost mesmerized by the clinical specimen of the body in which she can "worm and hack in a purple wilderness." The patient floats alone in a blue haze to which the "angels of morphia have born him up." One feels as though Plath strongly identifies with the sensations she describes. Her images in *Crossing the Water* are "a powerful expression of the constant feeling of a lack of reality, a sub-stancelessness which pervades [her] later work (Aird 43).

While Plath's early work concentrates on visual descriptions and outer per-ception, her later works *Winter Trees* and *Ariel* plunge into "the inner world of pain and alienation" (Aird 69); a journey into self-examination and peru-sal—of childhood, men, marriage, death, suicide, and, of course, the father. Here we see a blossoming of Sylvia Plath's craft and creativity. Her husband, Ted Hughes, has written that "Tulips" was "the first sign of what was on the way. She wrote this poem without her usual studies over the Thesaurus, and at top speed, as one might write an urgent letter" (Ames 291). In "Tulips" Plath presents herself in the inanimate, "flat, ridiculous" substancelessness of a "cut-paper shadow" that the intensely red tulips disturb with their reminder of vigorous life. As she lies in a hospital bed, she learns quiet, pleasant peace-fulness. Everything around her is white, "snowed-in." Nurses tend her as "water / Tends to the pebbles it must run over," and in this passivity she finds an emptiness and a purity similar to "what the dead close on." In contrast to her inanimation, the "excitable" tulips she has received are so starkly red that they hurt her. The same color as blood, they "talk to my wound" and "eat my oxygen." The air "snags and eddies" around them, forcing her to concentrate her attention upon them instead of remaining uncommitted. The tulips make her realize the infirmity of her body—and mind—as far from health as she is from a happy, vigorous childhood by the sea.

Some poems in *Ariel* return to the personal distress related to Plath's dead father, but they also include a more public, political side regarding Nazis and concentration camps. These last poems, written not long before her death, represent a kind of catharsis for Sylvia Plath as she vents her anger and am-bivalence. "Daddy" depicts an attempt to work through the distress connected with a dead father by comparing him to a Nazi. In a reading for BBC radio, Sylvia Plath said of this poem:

> Here is a poem spoken by a girl with an Electra complex. Her father died while she thought he was God. Her case is complicated by the fact that her father was also a Nazi and her mother very possibly Jewish. In the daughter the two strains marry and paralyse each other—she has to act out the awful little allegory once over before she is free of it. (*Collected Poems* 293).

Although the plot is not strictly autobiographical, for Otto Plath could not have been a Nazi soldier since he came from Prussia as an adolescent (Aird 78), the poem effectively incorporates the poet's emotions by using the comparison.

At the beginning of "Daddy" the girl describes the life she has led for thirty 9 years, existing "like a foot" in a "black shoe." Addressing the father as "Daddy" throughout the poem, Plath hearkens back to her childhood by the sea, where she had, instead of a bag of marbles, a "bag full of God" in her father, a giant statue that she associates with the beautiful, "freakish Atlantic." The untimely death of her father while the girl adored and depended on him prompts the girl to try to "recover" the essence of her father and the identity she has lost as a result.

Plath relates this search using descriptions of war, Nazis, and concentration 10 camps to parallel personal feelings of pain, loss, and entrapment. The girl searches "in the German tongue, in the Polish town" for traces of her father; Plath's own father came from the German sector of Poland. The "name of the town is common," however, and like her soul racked by "wars, wars, wars." She feels severed from her background, denied communication with her father, and ultimately trapped in her private hell:

> So I never could tell where you
> Put your foot, your root,
> I never could talk to you.
> The tongue stuck in my jaw.

By using German words and phrases, such as *Ach, du,* or "Oh you," and the repeated *ich,* Plath enhances her parallel of the Nazi and the father. The "barb wire snare" preventing her from speaking becomes the barb wire of the concentration camp. Thinking every German her father and eventually finding "the language obscene," she gets pulled further into the allegory. "An engine, an engine / Chuffing me off like a Jew" brings to mind her role as the victim of persecution just as the Jews were the victims of the Nazis' persecution.

Returning to the idea of the Electra complex, Plath hints that the girl's 11 impurity may be due to a partially Jewish mother or a gypsy ancestress, and that her "weird luck" and her "Taroc pack," intimations of chance and fate, really place the blame for her troubles on herself. She lapses again into ambivalence, saying, "I have always been scared of you," while describing the "neat mustache / And your Aryan eye, bright blue," and pining, "Oh You." Her father at once represents perfection and abomination. Now compared to the symbol of cruelty, a swastika "so black no sky could squeak through," his image tortures the child, who cannot reconcile her love with his cruelty or her hate with his perfection. In a sexual context, Plath intertwines adoration with violence: the "boot in the face" from the "brute heart." Plath flashes again to childhood when "the black man" "at the blackboard," referring to him as a teacher, "Bit [her] pretty red heart in two."

In a final attempt to join her father, the girl remembers how she tried to 12 commit suicide at twenty, another familiar theme for the poet. Unsuccessful, and with the broken pieces of her mind "stuck . . . together with glue," the daughter tries to escape by marrying a model of her father, a husband "who has been chosen for his similarity to the father in the hope that his presence will exorcise the daughter's obsession" (Aird 81). The marriage does not work: she says she has killed "the vampire who said he was you / And drank my blood for a year, / Seven years." Plath's inclusion of the failed marriage could reflect her own separation from her husband around October of 1962, when she wrote "Daddy." Nevertheless, the girl in the poem, having worked through her anguish, concludes that she is "finally through." With passionate persistence, she insists that "There's a stake in your fat black heart." She figuratively dances and stamps on his image with her mind and calls him a bastard, almost as if she doubts that she is free of his memory—as if she is trying to convince herself of it.

The imagery and word usage emphasize the sensual aspects of the poem and 13 bring it to life for the reader. Plath's use of assonance, for example, not only adds cohesiveness to "Daddy," but also highlights recurrent images, such as "boot," "root," "you" (Daddy). In line 1 Plath has "You do not do," followed by "shoe" and "Achoo." Later she continually repeats "you," rhyming it with "gobbledygoo," "blue," "through," "who," "two," "do," and "glue" (stanzas 9–13). By repeating key words, such as "wars, wars, wars" (line 18), "ich, ich, ich, ich" (line 27), "brute" in lines 49 and 50, and "back" in line 59, Plath directs the reader's attention toward the meaning of the poem. Thus, we can notice the double meaning of boot: "an effective image for the obsessional nature of the daughter's neurosis" and "carrying suggestions of the brutality associated with the father as a Nazi officer" (Aird 80). Moreover, Plath chooses words that convey distinct visual or auditory association. For instance, "barb wire snare" (line 26) connotes the entrapment and pain of the mind and in the camps with its harsh *r* sounds. Similarly, "Chuffing me off" (line 32) sounds like trains chugging away to the concentration camps, and "gobbledygoo" sounds like confusion and garbled language. The "rack and the screw" (line 66) immediately draw up visions of torture, while "drank my blood" (line 73) implies the sapping of strength and life force—both adding to the inner turmoil of the daughter. The frequent use of black in "Daddy" to describe the father and his effects conjures a powerful feeling of evil, darkness, and cruelty; we encounter a black shoe, a black swastika, a black man (the devil), a black telephone, and a fat black heart. Furthermore, images of the grave, the devil, the vampire, and worms all relate to the theme of death and the otherworld. In essence, the extended metaphor of the poem incorporates many of Sylvia Plath's dominant themes enhanced by potent imagery.

Sylvia Plath molded the content of "Daddy" into sixteen, five-line stanzas. 14 Plath herself called it a piece of "light verse," a term which "becomes clearer if we consider the theory of light verse held by W. H. Auden (Aird 81). Auden sees light verse as an attribute of form, not subject matter. In this way, the choppy, conversational swing of the poem, with its direct address to "Daddy" and its simple, sometimes colloquial vocabulary, earns the poem the label "light verse" (Aird 83). The tone changes with the ebb and flow of the daughter's passion. In the beginning she is sentimental about childhood and distraught at her abandoned state. In the middle she wavers between love and hate of her father. At the end she assumes an almost amused, angry sarcasm as she repudiates the father's image. However, throughout the piece, Plath maintains a certain impersonality, since the girl in the poem is struggling to rid herself of these paralyzing emotions. Thus "Daddy" contains the detached attitude of self-examination found in many of Sylvia Plath's other poems.

"Lady Lazarus," another *Ariel* poem written shortly after "Daddy," has that 15 same impersonality of tone set against dramatic content. Plath paints a picture of a woman who is reborn after death and to whom "dying / Is an art like everything else." In the words of Eileen Aird, "the poet again equates her suffering with the experiences of the tortured Jews." Her fascination with death includes images of Nazis, doctors, and power—a curious power over the watching spectators and over men: "I rise with my red hair / And I eat men like air."

Several of the last poems dwell on the subject of death, but in the last week 16 of her life, Sylvia Plath "moved away from an anguished contemplation of the suffering of living to a concentration on the peace of death" (Aird 86). In "Edge," for instance, the woman attains peace with nature and herself by stepping over the edge into death: "The woman is perfected. / Her dead / Body wears the smile of accomplishment." She gathers her dead children "into her body as petals / Of a rose close" when night falls onto the garden like death falls onto the woman. Perhaps in her own life, Plath used similar reasoning to resolve her problems with depression, paternal obsession, and daily pressures. She resolved her situation in favor of death by placing her head in a gas oven in February of 1963.

Although Sylvia Plath's life ended in an expression of desperation, her 17 creative expression during life showed a wealth of experience, emotion, and energy directed at discovering the mysteries of the outer world and the inner self. Through her craft, she created something fresh and original to add to the world—something many wish to accomplish. Even though her problems overcame her, she endures in her poetry, in its riveting subject matter and intricate imagery. Sylvia Plath would be glad to know that she did not live in vain.

Works Cited

Aird, Eileen M. *Sylvia Plath*. New York: Harper, 1973.
Ames, Lois. Biographical Note. *The Bell Jar*. By Sylvia Plath. New York: Harper, 1971.
Plath, Sylvia. *The Collected Poems*. Ed. Ted Hughes. New York: Harper, 1981.
Plath, Sylvia. *The Journals of Sylvia Plath*. New York: Dial Press, 1982.
Salop, Lynne. *Suisong*. New York: Vantage Press, 1978.

QUESTIONS FOR READING AND REVISING

1. What is the *thesis*—the controlling idea—of Monika Jerabek's essay? Where does she state it most explicitly?

2. What assumptions does Jerabek make about her readers' familiarity with Sylvia Plath's poetry? In this respect, approximately what percentage of Jerabek's essay is devoted to paraphrase? To direct quotation?

3. Outline the major points of Jerabek's analysis. Show how each paragraph supports and extends her thesis. What principal themes in Plath's poetry does Jerabek analyze? Where—and how—is each principal theme introduced into the essay? Consider, for example, the theme of nature in paragraph 5. How does Jerabek connect her discussion of this theme to the controlling idea of her father's image? Could the section on nature be eliminated from the essay? Why? Why not? Consider paragraph 8 on her father's "more public, political side." Explain how this paragraph is related to the controlling idea in the essay and why it should/should not be retained in any new draft Jerabek might write.

4. How does Jerabek organize ideas about Plath's poetry: From simple to complex? From Plath's first book of poems to her last? According to some other principle of organization? Explain with specific examples.

5. Jerabek notes that in preparing this essay, "I had to work out transitional problems—between specific points and their relevance to the central topic. . . . Throughout the writing of my paper, I tried to aim for cohesiveness and a flow of ideas." Examine carefully the *transitions* Jerabek develops from one major point to the next and from one paragraph to the next. What specific compositional devices does she use to create effective transitions?

6. Identify the strengths of Jerabek's literary analysis. Where does she draw on evidence from Plath's poems most effectively to support the points she makes? What other strategies does she use? Where—and how—for example, does Jerabek effectively work into her paragraphs the response of other readers of Plath's poetry?

7. Monika Jerabek effectively blends informative biographical details into her essay. Consider paragraph 2 where she notes that Plath's father was "a professor of biology and an authority on bees," that "he died after a long illness," and that Plath tried to commit suicide at twenty "by taking fifty sleeping pills after visiting her father's grave." Point to other examples of Jerabek's inclusion of useful biographical information to support her reading of Plath's poems.

8. In what specific ways does Jerabek reveal her own attitude toward Plath's poetry? Where does she state it, either directly or indirectly? Which part of speech—verbs, adjectives, or adverbs—does she rely on to express her attitude and to voice her own response to Plath's poems?

9. Monika Jerabek reports that she prepared two drafts of her essay. Here are the opening sentences of the first draft:

> In the quest for self-expression, few people have had the intensity of motivation and ambition of Sylvia Plath. As a poet, she examines life through the windows of nature, personal experience, and dramatic situations, seeking to satisfy the senses and vent her emotions. Most would find her poetry rather graphic, blunt or morbid, but in the interweaving of words and images, comparison and metaphor, her central themes of death, nature, childhood, and suicide, for example, come alive to the reader in new perspectives. One of Sylvia Plath's main themes, the portrayal of the father figure, extends throughout her work and incorporates the autobiographical with the other themes.

What specific differences in Jerabek's opening do you notice between the first and second drafts? What specific qualities make one version more effective than the other? Explain.

SUGGESTIONS FOR WRITING

1. A teenager's perception of his or her father can often be quite complex, fluctuating greatly from one year to the next and from one situation to the next. Consider, for example, Mark Twain's comic remark about his relationship with his father: "When I was a boy of fourteen, my father was so ignorant I could hardly stand to have the old man around. But when I got to be twenty-one, I

was astonished at how much he had learned in seven years." Consider your relationship with your father. Write an essay in which you contrast your understanding of your father when you were a child to your current perception of him. Specifically, how has your perception changed? With what effects? Support your thesis with specific examples.

2. In her essay, Monika Jerabek analyzes the image of the father in Sylvia Plath's poetry. In his essay "Of the Affection of Fathers for Their Children," Michel de Montaigne (1533–1592) offers another view of the relationship between fathers and children. Read carefully the following passage from Montaigne's essay:

> A true and well-regulated affection should be born and increase with the knowledge children give us of themselves; and then, if they are worthy of it, the natural propensity going along with reason, we should cherish them with a truly paternal love; and we should likewise pass judgment on them if they are otherwise, always submitting to reason, notwithstanding the force of nature. It is very often the reverse, and most commonly we feel more excited over the stamping, the games, and the infantile tricks of our children than we do later over their grown-up actions, as if we loved them for our pastime, like monkeys, not like men.

After you have read the passage and feel that you understand its meaning, prepare an essay in which you draw on your own experience with your father to support—or challenge—the wisdom and the accuracy of Montaigne's observation.

EARNESTINE JOHNSON

George Mason University
Fairfax, Virginia
Lois Cucullu, instructor

Earnestine Johnson's advice to first-year students interested in improving their writing is to "read as much and as often as possible." Her earliest recollections of her own childhood reading include "my mother's telling me stories at bedtime about Brer Rabbit and Brer Fox. Even though my mother never went beyond the second grade, I never tired of listening to her versions of those stories. I remember to this day the way she made those stories real for me. As a result of that enjoyment I read as much as possible." Johnson was born in Williamsburg, South Carolina, and raised in Philadelphia, where she worked as a volunteer in a local hospital (including reading to patients) while studying at John Bartram High School. After graduating, she settled in Woodbridge, Virginia, and enrolled at George Mason University. Her academic interests include the humanities and the social sciences. She plans to pursue a career in social work, her college major.

Asked to write a three- to five-page paper responding to Alice Walker's The Color Purple, Johnson discovered in that book "an example of the influence my mother had on my writing." Johnson recognized similarities to the circumstances of her own childhood in the characters and life styles depicted in The Color Purple. "The guidance and interpretations of my mother taught me to rise above the circumstances of our life then and now, in my personal life. I wrote the paper because I knew those characters, and it awoke my own lessons of survival."

Thank You Miss Alice Walker: The Color Purple

I was required to read the book, *The Color Purple*, by my English course professor. I enjoy reading and therefore I did not mind the assignment. I read the first page and closed the book. I was ashamed of the ignorant definitions given to the parts of the body. I was embarrassed by the explicitness of the sex act. I opened and closed the book many times before I could go beyond the first page. But I did read beyond the first page. I understood the lack of communication between Celie and her mother. Celie was fourteen years old and did not understand or appear to know the functions of her body.

A few days after starting to read this book, I was listening to a news report and heard, ". . . ten-year-old mother and baby both doing fine. The young girl and her family did not know she was pregnant until she was ready to give birth, after complaining of severe stomach pains." The newscaster went on to

128

say the authorities were questioning two male acquaintances of the family. Celie's circumstance, like that of the child-mother's, is ageless. Miss Walker, you brought the situation out into the open, awakening my senses. I did not want to see it, read it, feel it, or be a part of it. This was no longer "just a reading assignment." I was enthralled. I had to read on. How else would you shock me, embarrass me, and shame me?

My class is comprised of a mixture of nationalities, but only four of us are   3 black and female. I, embarrassingly, thought of all of them reading the lines of shame and ignorance of my people. I listened as one male classmate disassociated himself from the males in the story. I wondered if it was because the characters were black, or was he so naive that he believed such things did not happen? As a contemporary black female, I have buried the Celies of my past. Then why, Miss Walker, do you awaken those emotions? What do you expect to accomplish by telling me how it was, or is? Why, of all the subjects to write about, do you choose one which hurts me so deeply? I am furious with you.

I knew a lot of Celies in my teenage years. I met a few Sofias. I heard about   4 one or two Shug Averys too. I left them behind along with the old neighborhood. Those encounters were during an impoverished and ignorant period of growth. I chose to forget them. I have grown and expanded from the narrowness of my childhood and developed through the heritage passed on to me. I have also risen through the classes of the ruling society. I speak like them, dress like them, yet I know that I am but a shadow of them.

Miss Walker, I was compelled to go on with the reading of *The Color Purple*.   5 It was the language usage you gave your characters that held my interest this time. My mind's voice spoke the words by Celie so clearly that I could hear Mrs. Brown, from my youth, "Baby, run across to the store. . . ." Sofia became Mama Liz, big boned, dark complected, mammoth breasted, and as stubborn as the day was long, but oh what a heart. She was full of compassion and empathy for all who encountered her. It's the wonderful memories like those that made the reading of your book painful. Celie and Sofia's language was so familiar to me that in spite of the pain, I settled into the good memories the dialogues conjured up. I was also interested in what Nettie had to say, but Nettie's dialogue had connotations of my own language, educated and refined. I heard it every day. It catalyzed no images. But the other characters' dialect brought memories of faces and voices that had long ceased to exist. Those faces had diminished to just a flicker until your book revived them. Those good memories came with the people you portrayed, along with their examples of survival. Some of the people I knew were very much like Shug Avery and many were like Sofia.

Your message was subtle, Miss Walker. Now after the shame, anger, and 6
memories, I continued to read to the end of the story. Your characters came
full circle. They survived. They matured and became wiser from their experiences. You showed me how they accomplished that. Sofia's way was that of
self-reliance and stubbornness. She was not just physically strong, but she had
a strong nature as well. She was also patient and long suffering. I cannot say
that Sofia's way was successful because she lost so much. She lost her husband
and children to another woman. She lost her freedom to the ruling society,
first jail and then to the mayor's family. Shug Avery was independent and
worldly. She learned to stroke the egos of the people she could not easily
maneuver. Shug was a free spirit, her own person. Celie developed and escaped
to a future of her own making by learning another method of survival than
the one she lived. Celie took a portion of Sofia's stubborness and self-reliance
and mixed that with a little of Shug's independence and literally walked with
a survival plan of her own.

I have read your message Miss Walker, and anguished through the learning 7
of it. This teaching of survival will not soon be forgotten because it was too
painful an experience to relearn. It is for the lesson learned that I thank you.

QUESTIONS FOR READING AND REVISING

1. One of the distinguishing features of Earnestine Johnson's essay is her honest
   and intense response to Alice Walker's *The Color Purple.* Reread Johnson's
   essay carefully *aloud.* How would you characterize the sound of her *voice?* Does
   she sound, for example, tough-minded or sentimental, strident or intimidated?
   Young and impetuous, or experienced and worldly? Some combination of these?
   None of them? Do you notice any changes in Johnson's voice as the essay
   proceeds? Support your response with specific words and phrases.

2. At the beginning of paragraphs 6 and 7 Johnson talks about coming to understand Alice Walker's "message" in *The Color Purple.* Based on your reading of
   Johnson's essay only, summarize that "message." With which character in *The
   Color Purple* does she identify? How can you be sure? How did reading Alice
   Walker's novel help Johnson come to terms with—to understand better—her
   own past? What "message" does Johnson's essay offer about the truth of human
   relationships?

3. What recognition prompts Johnson to regard *The Color Purple* as much more
   than "a reading assignment"? What impels her to continue reading the novel
   after her initial reaction to Walker's explicit depiction of sexual experience?

Johnson notes that she "had to read on" and proceeds to address Alice Walker directly: "How else would you shock me, embarrass me, and shame me?" How does the evidence of her essay suggest that Johnson answered her own question? What is "the lesson learned" for which she thanks Alice Walker?

4. Consider Johnson's explanation of the stages in her personal transformation as a result of reading *The Color Purple:* "Upon completing the book, I was able to see the message Ms. Walker conveyed. I found I had a beginning, my anger, a middle, life experiences, and an ending, my expressed gratitude, for my paper." Reread Johnson's essay and identify where each of these three sections begins and ends. List the points Johnson makes in each section.

5. How would you characterize Johnson's relationship with her audience? To what extent does her audience seem to be a presence in her essay? What specific words and phrases can you point to that indicate who Johnson thinks her readers are (their probable level of intelligence, color, age, social and economic class, etc.)? To what extent must Johnson's readers be acquainted with Walker's novel to appreciate each of her points about the book?

6. One of the unusual features of Johnson's essay is her apparent resistance to being specific. She notes that, "being specific . . . was exactly what I was trying to avoid." What do you suspect she hopes to gain by this strategy? What are the advantages and disadvantages of this decision?

7. Johnson explains one of the problems she had writing her essay: "trying to describe the ruling society without actually saying 'white race.' I became so frustrated with the revision of that particular section, I almost gave into being specific. . . . I continued to rework that section until it finally became acceptable to me and with its connotations, understood by others." Reread paragraph 4 and explain with as much detail as possible exactly how Johnson accomplishes her aim. What other moments in the essay can you identify that seem to reflect Johnson's decision to make her points indirectly rather than explicitly? What is the *purpose*—the desired effect—of her resistance to being specific in each instance?

8. Johnson describes the goal of her essay as trying to "induce a sense of empathy with my feelings by the examples I gave." What stylistic strategies does Johnson use to induce empathy in her readers? What exactly are the "examples" she uses? Roughly what percentage of them are drawn from *The Color Purple?* From her own experience?

9. Johnson offers the following advice to her readers: "I would have failed in the writing of my essay if I had to advise the reader how to understand or read what I had written. I will state what I use as a 'rule of thumb': begin reading with an open mind, void of any preconceived ideas. This should allow for the possibility of involvement, and then see what, if anything, has been gained

from the experience." Apply this "rule of thumb" to Johnson's reading of Alice Walker. How well does Johnson's essay satisfy each of the criteria she establishes? Apply this "rule of thumb" to your reading of Johnson's essay. Identify what you have "gained from the experience."

SUGGESTIONS FOR WRITING

1. Discovering books has allowed innumerable readers to explore the life of the mind and discover the self by identifying with the circumstances of literary characters. Richard Wright's autobiography, *Black Boy,* includes the following passage on the transformative power of reading:

   > I read Dreiser's *Jennie Gerhardt* and *Sister Carrie* and they revived in me a vivid sense of my mother's suffering; I was overwhelmed. I grew silent, wondering about the life around me. It would have been impossible for me to have told anyone what I derived from these novels, for it was nothing less than life itself. . . . In buoying me up, reading also cast me down, made me see what was possible, what I had missed. My tension returned, new, terrible, bitter, surging, almost too great to be contained. I no longer *felt* that the world about me was hostile, killing; I *knew* it. . . .

   Consider your own experience as a reader. What books have you read that have had a profound effect on your sense of self-identity? Write an expository essay in which you explain how a particular book helped to transform your own sense of who you are.

2. In *Black Boy,* Richard Wright talks about reading as an addiction: "Reading was like a drug, a dope." Consider the nature of this *comparison.* Track out as fully as possible the analogy between reading and taking a drug and write an expository essay in which you develop this analogy between reading and drug addiction.

3. Consider the differences between reading books and watching television as addictions. In what specific ways are these possible "addictions" similar? Different? Write an expository essay in which you *compare and contrast* reading books and watching television as addictive activities.

AMBER KENNISH

New York University
New York, New York
Claire Gleitman, instructor

"I'll do anything to avoid writing. One of my favorite techniques, especially when avoiding a really difficult assignment, is to tell myself that I shouldn't worry about it because as soon as I really sit down to do some serious writing it will come easily. Sometimes this works; sometimes it doesn't." Asked to write a response to Caroline Bird's frequently reprinted essay, "College Is a Waste of Time and Money," Kennish worked through three drafts, trying "to appeal to my audience through a metaphorical 'boxing match' between my father and me that I thought would be a familiar scene of doubt and anxiety to other people my age."

Born in Lawrence, Kansas, Amber Kennish grew up in Essex, Connecticut, and graduated from Valley Regional High School in Deep River, where she participated in numerous student organizations and clubs, including the school yearbook, the theater group, and the Connecticut High School Bowl team. A contributor to the school newspaper and literary magazine, Kennish also won awards for excellence in English, history, science, language, and math.

Writing well has figured prominently in Kennish's academic success, and she is quite conscious of the environment in which she feels most comfortable working: "I usually listen to music when I write, because silence only makes distracting thoughts louder. I usually don't work at a desk—I feel too much pressure to write well when I'm sitting at a desk or in a library cubicle, and sometimes my best writing comes from my worst drafts. I usually write in pen because the grating graphite pencils make on the paper annoys and distracts me." At this point in her studies at New York University, she is uncertain about her major, although her plans do include study abroad in her junior year.

Three Rounds with Dad

Armed with Caroline Bird's argument against college education presented 1
in her essay, "College Is a Waste of Time and Money," I challenged my father
to three rounds on the issue. He graciously accepted my challenge, and with
Bird providing support from my corner, at the sound of the bell I danced into
the center of the ring, hoping my father was prepared for a quick defeat.

I did a little footwork around the idea of dropping out of New York Uni- 2
versity at the semester break in January, stating that I shouldn't be here because
I hate school. I followed by explaining that the only reason I had always done
so well in high school was because it seemed to me that the only way to "get

back" at school and the nuisance it was to me would be to do really well with whatever they tried to challenge me with. I had hoped this would annoy him into taking a swing at me. Unfortunately, it seemed to have little effect, so I stopped, put my hands on my hips, looked him straight in the eye, and defiantly declared that I wanted to support myself. This stunned him a bit, so I seized this opportunity to hit him hard with the idea that I planned to move to North Carolina, become a waitress in the sleaziest diner I could find, and live happily ever after in a leaky mobile home. Seeing him waver, I followed with Bird's best punch—I was only in college because it was expected of me, having graduated second in my high school class. My father gave the appearance of weakening, but I didn't let up. Next was a blow to the wallet, with which I informed him that I was only wasting his money because I didn't know what I wanted to get out of school.

The bell ending Round 1 sounded, and I, having brought forth every valid 3 point in Bird's essay, retired to my corner and to pats on the back from Bird. I confidently awaited Round 2 and the possibility (slim though it was) of a rebuttal from my father.

Rrrring! My father came out fighting with the premise that while Bird refers 4 to a college degree as an "empty credential," due to the fact that much of a college education may never be utilized, it is still a worthy credential to have. I countered with a quick jab, "Why?" Not fazed by my speed and agility, Dad countered by boxing my ears with the fact that Americans today place an enormous amount of emphasis on a college education, and a degree even in something as "impractical" as a liberal arts subject would grant me the diploma that could make all the difference in the tough competition of today's job market. The realization that an employer, faced with a choice, will hire a person with a college degree over the nondegreed applicant left the taste of blood bubbling in my nose and mouth.

My ears still ringing from this blow to my reason, I felt a sharp pain in my 5 chest. I realized that this pain came from my heart, following my father's paraphrase punch borrowed from essayist Newman, "Knowledge for the sake of knowledge." A series of quick punches to the chest brought home the fact that I needn't necessarily attend college for a practical purpose. Another blow told me that to rush through college in pursuit of the "good job" a diploma is supposed to guarantee is wrong—"Learning is the key"—and I knew he was right, as the red acceptance of his argument trickled from the corner of my mouth.

Suddenly, a blow to the gut knocked the wind out of me. My legs weakened 6 under me as my father hit me with the fact that I may never get another chance to go to college. Bird yelled from outside the ropes, "But college is really just a holding pen for eighteen- to twenty-two-year-olds because society does not know what to do with them!!" I lamely hurled this retort at my father, who said that, while most college freshmen are in this age group, it is often because that it is the only time in their lives in which they are not tied down to a family or job—they are responsible only for themselves—and this gives them the freedom to put the time into college that it needs to pay off. College requires time to do an enormous amount of work, time that might not be so easily found at any other point in life.

Luckily, the bell ending the second round rang, and I retreated to my corner 7 bleeding badly. Bird appeared with a rag to wipe away the sweat and blood from my face, but I pushed her away, preferring to let the blood run out of my mouth and nose and onto the mat, for all to see. Through the sweat streaming into my eyes, I stared intently at my father, who appeared not to be hurting at all. As the bell beginning the third round clanged, I wiped some blood off my face and onto the back of my hand. I went to the center of the ring, bruised and near-beaten, to receive my father's final point.

And a pithy point it was for me. I felt my head throbbing to the rhythm 8 of my father's speech. "College will teach you to inquire, to become a questioning, alert member of society." His words pummeled me as I struggled for support from the ropes. "College offers the serious student the chance to move not only in a linear fashion through life, but to expand himself laterally at the same time by learning about different cultures, art forms, and history." I felt lightheaded, I stumbled. My world began to darken as he spoke of sight. "College offers exposure to many aspects of society that might be otherwise overlooked by less educated people. If nothing else, it is this exposure and sight into human nature and society as a whole that makes higher education worthwhile." I slumped to the mat in defeat. I looked up at my father through eyes filled with sweat and admiration. Out of the corner of my eye I saw Bird sulkily slink into the shadows, out of my sight. My father didn't seem to have a scratch on his body, and when he bent down his words washed over me. The smile on his lips was the last thing I saw as he said, "That hurt me more than it did you." I chuckled, content with my injuries, and closed my swollen eyes.

QUESTIONS FOR READING AND REVISING

1. Amber Kennish creates an *analogy* between boxing and arguing with her father. Identify the major points of her analogy. How well does she introduce—and develop—each of these points? How appropriate do you think this *comparison* is to her subject? Explain.

2. Analyze how Kennish is able to make her essay sound reasonable and believable while developing her analogy. What does Kennish assume is her audience's *point of view* on the issue she argues about?

3. Kennish's essay is based on Caroline Bird's "College Is a Waste of Time and Money." Where in her essay does Kennish rely on Bird's essay to support her own *argument?* How effectively does Kennish draw on Bird's ideas? What specific suggestions would you offer Kennish to strengthen her essay in this respect?

4. Summarize the points Kennish's father makes in rebuttal. What tactic does he use to counter his daughter's argument? Which of his points seems to have the most effect on Kennish? Why? Before the end of the "fight," when does Kennish consider "throwing in the towel?" Why doesn't she?

5. One of the strengths of Kennish's essay is her use of colloquial expressions from the world of boxing to reinforce the points she makes. See, for example, the beginning of paragraph 2, where she reports that she "did a little footwork around the idea of dropping out of New York University." Make a list of other similar words and phrases and comment on how effectively she uses each. What general colloquial expressions does she use in the essay? With what effect?

6. Reread paragraph 7. What is the major point Kennish makes in this paragraph? What is the significance of her refusal to let Caroline Bird help her at the end of the second round? How does this decision reinforce that major point?

7. Reconsider Kennish's final paragraph. What is the liberal significance of her father's final comment: "That hurt me more than it did you?" What is its metaphorical significance? Why does Kennish end her essay by "chuckling?" Why do you think she is "content" with her injuries?

8. In discussing her essay, Kennish noted: "I hope that my audience, after reading my essay, would feel that a college education is a worthwhile investment of both time and money." How would you respond to her statement? What additional points would you make to reinforce—or to challenge—her argument?

SUGGESTIONS FOR WRITING

1. Amber Kennish creates an *analogy* between boxing and debating with her father on the merits of a college education. Write an essay in which you develop a similar analogy to argue about a subject that interests you. This debate could focus, for example, on such issues as banning fraternities and sororities from campus or eliminating scholarships from intercollegiate athletics.

2. Kennish's essay is a response to Caroline Bird's essay, "College Is a Waste of Time and Money." Think of an essay you have read recently whose ideas you would like to refute. Write an argumentative essay in which you present the

essay's ideas and then argue against them. Integrate references from the essay you've read into your essay.

3. Kennish's essay argues for the value of an education. Write an expository essay in which you explain what it means to be educated. Your emphasis in this essay should be on explaining what it means to be educated, not on arguing on behalf of the value of an education.

KAREN L. KRAMER

University of Nebraska—Lincoln
Lincoln, Nebraska
Joan Griffin, instructor

"If someone walked into my room while I was trying to get started, I would probably shut off my typewriter and talk to that person for an hour or so about anything and everything except my paper. But let's suppose the person is invisible, or observing me through a one-way mirror or some such thing. They would see me sit down at the typewriter, turn it on, stare at it for a minute, and then turn it off again, get up, pace around the room, return to the typewriter, turn it back on again, line up the paper, turn the typewriter off, pace around the room, sit back down again, turn it on again, type maybe a paragraph, read it, out loud of course, decide that it stinks, yank the paper out and throw it away, put in a new sheet and then just start typing away."

Karen Kramer's description of her own writing habits seems very much in keeping with her general level of energy and accomplishment. A graduate of Daniel J. Gross High School in Omaha, Nebraska, Kramer's extracurricular activities there included playing in the "concert band, pep band, stage band, musical, and dixieland band," as well as writing copy for the yearbook. In her junior and senior years, she was selected for the All-State Band, ranked fourth in her class academically, was elected salutatorian by her classmates, and was chosen to be a member of the All-State Academic Team. A Regents and National Merit Scholarship winner at the University of Nebraska at Lincoln, Kramer continues to develop her interest in music by playing in various bands both within the university and outside it. She plays the trombone and piano, sings, enjoys drawing, and occasionally works with sculpture and computers. While at school, she has also worked part-time at, among other jobs, her dormitory food service, Ponderosa steakhouses, and a local Burger King. She plans to major in English but is uncertain about her career goals.

Asked by her instructor to write a comparison and contrast essay, Karen Kramer decided to write about her high school band experiences. "My years in band in high school inspired me to write my essay. . . . Music was my life then. I had ample opportunity to observe my fellow musicians. Hence, I wrote about them." As to her purpose in writing "The Little Drummer Boys," Kramer quickly adds: "The goal of my essay was to have fun, pure and simple. No earth-shattering messages here."

The Little Drummer Boys

Quick—what do you call a person who plays the trumpet? A trumpeter, of 1
course. A person who plays the flute is referred to as a flutist, or flautist, if you prefer. Someone who plays a piano is usually known as a pianist, unless of course he plays the player piano, in which case he is known as a player piano

player rather than a player piano pianist. Got the hang of this yet? Okay, then what do you call someone who plays that set of instruments belonging to the percussion family? Why, you call him a percussionist, don't you? Wrong! It's not quite as easy as all that. There are two types of musicians who play percussion instruments, "drummers" and "percussionists," and they are as different as Quiet Riot and the New York Philharmonic.

You can find an initial difference even in the very names of the percussion-playing musicians. If you called a percussionist a drummer, he would be highly insulted. If you called a drummer a percussionist, he wouldn't know what you were talking about. The two don't really think much of each other. Percussionists generally consider drummers to be what can only be described as "the scum of the earth," two million years behind the rest of mankind in the evolutionary process. Drummers, on the other hand, consider percussionists to be weak, boring, effeminate individuals with questionable sexual preferences. The differences don't end there.

Take the drummers, for example. It is their belief that all drums have to come welded together in a set, not unlike Siamese twins. As for other pieces of drum equipment, cymbals are all to come perched atop a stand and are to be smashed with a stick and never hand-held and clashed together. Cymbals do not ever come in pairs, except for the high hat. Triangles, sleigh bells, woodblocks, etc., are for second-grade rhythm bands, not drummers. As for kettle drums, as far as the drummer is concerned, they're used for boiling water. The xylophone is merely a word in an A-B-C book. Nobody actually plays any of those things professionally.

At least, no self-respecting drummer would because after all, drummers are cool. Some drummers are so cool, they act as though they're on drugs. Some drummers are on drugs. Regardless of the latter fact, most drummers are very cool, hep, and laid-back kind of guys, you dig? Except, of course, for when they play. It is then that the drummer lets the rabid, primordial Neanderthal that lurks just beneath the surface take complete control of his very being. When performing, the drummer throws his head around as though he were trying to toss it from his shoulders. Sweating profusely, his face twisted into a veritable mask of anguished, tormentuous pain, he looks not unlike a mother-to-be who has been in labor for over nine hours. By the time a drummer finishes a solo, he looks as though he had just come in last in the Boston Marathon. Yet it is this very selfsame animalistic behavior that gives the drummer his appeal to the masses. Almost everybody loves the drummer. Women love him because sweaty, hirsute, muscular guys in torn T-shirts are macho. Men respect drummers, too. Not-so-scientific research has found that deep down within every male of the human species there is a burning desire to beat the hell out of a trap set, and thus men respect those members of their sex who can do that and get paid besides.

Drummers aren't popular with everyone, however. There are those directors   5 and conductors who expect drummers to play slowly or quietly or even— heaven forbid—with a little class. Needless to say, drummers and conductors do not get along, but this is inevitable. The art of drumming requires a total lack of self-control, whereas the conductor is actually trying to impose behav- ioral controls on the drummer, which naturally leads to confrontation. One simply should not try to rein in a wild, crazy, drugged-out individual who behaves as though he were raised by gorillas.

Percussionist are on the completely opposite end of the spectrum. Percus-   6 sionists always get along with their directors, as they respect them and bend over backward to follow them and cooperate. Percussionists are *not* cool. Rather, they are very clean-cut, square, straightforward individuals. Their hair is always short and neat. Instead of the sweaty muscle T-shirt of the drummer, the percussionist wears a dress shirt, sweater, and sometimes even a tie. Percus- sionists don't even know what drugs are. On the contrary, percussionists don't drink or smoke, and they make a habit of attending church services regularly. They're the basic Oral Roberts type.

Thus, percussionists don't enjoy the wide popularity of drummers. It's not   7 that people particularly dislike them. It's just that they don't particularly like them, either. Percussionists are somewhat lacking in personality. They're rather bland, not unlike oatmeal or unflavored soda water. They only become some- what animated when performing.

Whereas the drummer is merely interested in creating as much noise as   8 possible, music in the true sense of the word is of importance to the percus- sionist. Whether it be a well-placed cymbal crash or a tiny "ting" on the triangle, the percussionist, with utmost precision, makes the most of it without overpowering the ensemble with which he happens to be playing. His face a mask of concentration, the percussionist's eyes bug out as he stares steadily at his lord and master, the conductor. With moves as sharp, quick, and accurate as a frog nabbing flies, the percussionist tings a triangle, whirls to whap a wood block, and with one deft, lightning-swift move, silently drops everything and seizes a pair of mallets with which he gives the tympani a resounding thump to precisely fill the gap in the music. Percussionists, who are able to create the sound illusion of a trotting horse or a babbling brook, are as subtle as a morning breeze blowing across the dew-covered grass, whereas drummers, who do their best to create the illusion of an artillery barrage, are about as subtle as a panzer division smashing through the concert hall. No one notices a percussion sec- tion. They complement the band. Drummers *are* the band as far as they are concerned. Such an attitude would appear egotistical and uncouth to a percussionist but would seem perfectly natural to a drummer.

Drummers and percussionists do have one thing in common. They both are   9
in love with their equipment. Tenderly they fondle the drumheads, cymbals, and all of their sticks, brushes, and mallets; a pair for each day of the week. They let nothing come between themselves and their equipment and woe unto the ambitious unassuming amateur who dares to sacrilegiously set sticks to the "skins" or sets of the devoted drummer or perniciously protective percussionist. Such an act is sure to ruffle the feathers of even the least temperamental drummer or percussionist.

Another sure way to ruffle them is to call a drummer a "percussionist" or a   10
percussionist a "drummer." After all, there should be no excuse for this since it is apparent that the two are as different as a piccolo and a tuba. So when addressing a player of a percussion instrument, be sure to get his name right, or at least apologize profusely for getting it wrong. Then, he'll smile at you— parum-pa-pum-pum. He and his drum.

QUESTIONS FOR READING AND REVISING

1. Karen Kramer was asked to write a *comparison and contrast* essay. List all the points Kramer makes about percussionists. How do percussionists differ from drummers? Show how Kramer organizes these points. Does she proceed point by point? Subject by subject? Some combination of the two? Support your response with detailed references to her essay.

2. Characterize Kramer's *point of view* in this essay. Is she detached and objective? Involved and subjective? Some other combination? Support your response with an analysis of specific words and phrases from the essay. What is her attitude toward percussionists? Toward drummers? When is each attitude first expressed? Which group does Kramer seem to favor by the end of her essay? Why? Having read her essay, explain why you agree or disagree with her conclusions.

3. Karen Kramer explains her *purpose* in writing this essay in the following terms: "What I really want is for the readers to enjoy themselves and have a good laugh or at least a slight chuckle. I'd even settle for a warm smile, or a raise of the eyebrow." How would you describe "the readers" Kramer seems to have in mind here? How familiar does she assume her *audience* is with her subject? How familiar need they be? Describe—specifically—the features of Kramer's humorous essay that make it successful.

4. Make a list of as many of the *similes* and *metaphors* Kramer uses in this essay as you can. Which seem especially effective? Why? When asked to clarify how

she intended to appeal to her readers, Kramer replied: "I appeal to the reader by using incongruous comparisons, such as that of a drummer with a Neanderthal, etc. I exaggerate like crazy, because I feel that one aspect of humor is exaggeration." Identify the moments in her essay that are marked by exaggeration and comment on the effectiveness of each.

5. Kramer has an eye for useful detail. Identify as many details as possible. What does each contribute to the sentence in which it appears? To the essay as a whole? How does Kramer's use of detail support her humorous intentions as well as some purpose beyond being humorous? What, in your judgment, might this larger purpose be? Is this essay finally about naming people? Naming things? Some combination of the two? Explain.

6. How would you describe Kramer's *tone* in this essay? What specific strategies does she use to maintain that tone, or does it change as she proceeds in the essay? Comment on Kramer's *diction.* Is it primarily informal or colloquial? Point to specific examples where Kramer has fun playing with the conventional meaning of words and phrases.

7. When describing her methods as a writer, Kramer noted: "The most difficult thing about writing a first draft is thinking of a beginning and a conclusion. I cannot begin writing from anywhere except the beginning. Some people can write the body and then tack on an intro when they're finished. I cannot. I may have the whole body written word for word in my head, but I haven't thought of a snappy intro yet, I can't type one word of it." Consider Kramer's first draft of her opening paragraph:

> Quick—what do you call someone who plays the trumpet? A trumpeter, of course. A person who plays the flute is referred to as a flutist, or flautist, if you prefer. Someone who plays a piano is usually known as a pianist, unless of course he plays the player piano, in which case he is known as a player piano player rather than a player piano pianist. Got the hang of this yet? Okay, then what do you call someone who plays that set of instruments belonging to the percussion family. Why, you call him a percussionist, don't you? Wrong! It's not quite as easy as all that. There are two types of musicians who play percussion instruments, "drummers" and "percussionists," and they are as different as Quiet Riot and the New York Philharmonic.

What changes did Karen Kramer make as she moved from her first to her final draft? Explain the appropriateness—and the effectiveness—of each.

8. When reviewing the procedures she follows in revising an essay, Kramer observed: "I read the paper *out loud.* This is very important. I could read a paper a hundred times to myself and never catch something, but if I read it out loud,

I'll catch it. Sometimes you have to actually *hear* what you wrote before you realize that it sounds like something a fourth-grader wrote. So, I read it out loud, and I change what doesn't sound right. Clumsily constructed sentences, weak words, questionable modifiers, etc. all come to light when I read it and then I correct them." Keeping in mind the criteria Kramer establishes in the last sentence of this quotation, reread this draft *aloud.* If she had an opportunity to revise her essay, what recommendations for revision would you offer her? Why?

SUGGESTIONS FOR WRITING

1. What kind of music do you most enjoy listening to? Who are some of the most respected artists who compose and/or play that music? Write an essay in which you *compare and contrast* the respective styles of these two musicians in performance. If you most enjoy listening to rock and roll, for example, you might want to compare and contrast the musical styles of Elvis Presley and Bruce Springsteen. If classical music interests you more, you might prefer to look at the styles of violinists such as Itzhak Perlman and Isaac Stern.

2. One of the reasons Kramer's essay is successful is that she takes a relatively familiar experience (listening to a drummer and a percussionist) and exaggerates it, both to make a point and to make a lively, amusing essay. Yet Kramer does not exaggerate the differences beyond recognition. In fact, we appreciate her essay all the more because of her effective control of exaggeration. Consider a familiar experience that might be exaggerated in a similar fashion to make a point: preparing for your first date with someone; studying for final exams as opposed to quizzes; taking the road test for your driver's license. Write an account of what happened, playfully exaggerating to make a point.

3. Musicians are often asked to create *similes* to describe their compositional methods. Here are two rather celebrated, if somewhat indecorous, responses: "I produce music as an apple-tree produces apples"—Camille Saint-Saëns (1835–1921); "I write [music] as a sow piddles"—Wolfgang Amadeus Mozart (1756–1791). Here is another, somewhat more dignified comparison: "[Claude] Debussy is like a painter who looks at his canvas to see what more he can take out; [Richard] Strauss is like a painter who has covered every inch and then takes the point he has left and throws it at the canvas"—Ernest Bloch. Analyze your method of writing and write an essay in which you explain your methods in terms of an analogy.

LINDA LAVELLE

Harrisburg Area Community College
Harrisburg, Pennsylvania
Edward McCarthy, instructor

Linda Lavelle appreciates the patience and effort needed to write well. She also trusts herself as a writer. Assigned a topic, she is confident that "an idea will come to mind immediately. What works best for me is to let that idea rattle around in my head for a few days until a few key phrases or sentences develop. With those few key phrases in mind, I can sit down to write and come up with something that resembles a first draft." Yet, as she explains, moving beyond that first draft proves to be the most frustrating aspect of writing for her: "My first draft usually ends up a chaotic stream of ideas. Organizing this mess into a second draft is the most difficult phase." Given this tendency, Linda Lavelle tries to leave little to chance and prepares for long sessions when she works on her essays. She equips herself with, as she notes, "cigarettes, coffee, crackers, and a favorite pen. I also have my dictionaries, a reference manual, and my notes, which consist mostly of those few key phrases."

Amid what she describes as a "mess" of "books and papers scattered on the table," Linda Lavelle sits "gulping coffee, chain smoking, crumpling papers, and (so I am told) making faces, twirling my hair, and talking to myself." This scene often yields to another, one in which Lavelle can be seen "tapping my pen on the dictionary, staring into space for long stretches of time. This is followed by bouts of frantic writing."

Linda Lavelle works hard at her writing, a skill she has been practicing since childhood. "I started making up stories and poems when I was about three years old. By the time I was nine or ten I had started putting them down on paper and dreaming of being a writer." Lavelle describes herself as having led a rather "unconventional" childhood and adolescence: "As a child I traveled frequently, living in many different places, with many different families, and was therefore exposed to a wide variety of lifestyles and philosophies. As a writer this gives me a great deal of experience to draw on. . . . Yet I believe my writing has been most influenced by the people and places of Philadelphia." Born there, Lavelle graduated from that city's Frankford High School. She has worked as a "gofer" in a playhouse, a waitress, and in electronics. She currently divides her time among her family, her work, and her studies. She plans to major in English or journalism and hopes to write professionally.

Asked to write an essay using personal experience as the basis for a commentary on a contemporary social issue or national problem, Lavelle turned to her "own postponed goals as an example." She set out to "show that blue-collar workers are not necessarily illiterate or lacking in ambition. I wanted the reader to remember to view people as individuals, not write them off as a group. . . . My goal was to show that people who work in factories are not mindless machines, just trapped by them."

Confessions of a Blue-Collar Worker

The large brick building was a factory that made circuit breakers. There 1 were assembly lines, spot welding machines, riveting machines, and hundreds of people handling the same small parts over and over. There were several of us naive eighteen-year-olds who, courtesy of thoughtful relatives, entered the world of concrete and noise that day. This was a place where youth had an advantage. It was bonus work, and we couldn't believe it was possible to earn so much money for performing such simple tasks.

As the weeks passed, and the overwhelming boredom set in, we began to 2 realize what we were really being paid for. Forty hours a week, while our hands moved with lightning speed, our minds were free—to wander, to dwell on problems, to rot. We were being subjected to a form of mental torture—for a paycheck. Still, we were not discouraged because most of us planned to make it a temporary stay. I, for one, had my future mapped out: work for a year, buy a new car, fatten my bank account, then join VISTA (the application was safely tucked away in my desk drawer), and later start college. My plans had not allowed for getting caught in the quicksand of money and machinery.

A year passed, and another, and another. We were all still there, still 3 planning to leave. Only now we looked differently at the young women, always on the verge of divorce, popping their valium, while the life was slowly sucked out of them with each movement of the assembly line. We looked differently too at the old ladies with knotted hands and varicose veins who were struggling to keep pace. It became frightening to realize these stoop-shouldered old ladies with the bitter smiles had once been young and full of dreams. We looked into their empty eyes and saw the ghost of things to come.

I lost my VISTA application, but I did acquire my new car, and another, 4 and a houseful of furniture—not to mention the house and husband. I applied and was hired for more dignified positions, but I always changed my mind. I just couldn't walk away from the high pay and good benefits. So I continued to fill circuit breakers with little parts as the assembly line moved on.

Like many of the others, I tried to continue my formal education. And like 5 those others, in the face of frustration and fatigue, I finally gave up. At the same time my *informal* education flourished beneath the fluorescent lighting, although the knowledge I was acquiring wasn't taught in any classroom or found in any text. I studied business up close. I learned the intricacies of the numbers operations and the going price of stolen goods. I learned how management and unions function on the intimidation of workers, and how to fight for rights against both of them.

I met people who taught me volumes about human behavior. I saw people 6
take amphetamines to keep up with ever-rising production rates. I saw good
friends, and even relatives, physically attack each other over job assignments
that would mean a few cents' difference. I observed women cheating on their
husbands and men cheating on their wives. I watched women hand over their
entire paycheck to a bookie. I saw pregnant women, their feet too swollen for
shoes, come to work in slippers. I saw women with colds stuff pieces of tissue
up their nostrils so they wouldn't have to keep stopping to blow their nose.

I even studied a new language—"Shop Talk"—which consists of insults and 7
profanities shouted by supervisors and workers at each other. Fluency in this
language is essential to blue-collar work, as the need for it occurs frequently.
I had lessons in vocabulary as well. I learned the definitions of obscenities I
had never even heard before. And while the words "self respect" were being
driven from my vocabulary, the definition of dehumanization was being driven
home each day. I learned the meaning of many words, like humiliation, when
I heard two foremen referring to their workers as "the stupid whores."

In time all the vulgarities became part of the scenery, like the peeling paint 8
on the machines or the faded partitions that covered the windows. And when,
six years after that first day, I climbed out of the quagmire to ring out my time
card for the last time, I had learned the value of a good sense of humor. We
had laughed a great deal. We joked about our "prison uniforms" and being
replaced by chimpanzees. We joked that some people pay large sums of money
to have their fingerprints removed while we were having it done for free. We
laughed about our "fringe benefits," like being able to buy "hot items" on our
breaks. We laughed at so many things that weren't funny. We laughed at the
office workers, with their small paychecks, who looked down their prissy noses
at us. We laughed, but we always glanced at our calloused fingers and knew
that we were becoming something less than human beings.

QUESTIONS FOR READING AND REVISING

1. Linda Lavelle's announced *purpose* in writing this essay is "to show that people
who work in factories are not mindless machines, just trapped by them." Reread
her essay carefully. What specific points does she make to *illustrate* and underscore this idea?

2. From what *point of view* does Lavelle recount the events in this essay? Where
is that point of view first established? Show how this point of view remains

consistent—or changes—as the essay proceeds. Lavelle's essay occasionally shifts between "I" and "we." Who are the people Lavelle associates with this "we"? Whom does she exclude?

3. Lavelle observes that "this was a difficult essay for me to write because I was so personally involved with the subject. I knew what I wanted to say, but I just didn't work it out until I used my own experience as the focus—something I really hadn't wanted to do." Consider the way in which Lavelle presents herself and her own experience in this essay. What do we learn about her as the essay develops? What reaction does her self-portrayal elicit in paragraph 4? Does her self-image in this paragraph remain consistent in the paragraphs that follow? If so, what specific writing strategies does she use to sustain it? If not, where and how does the image change?

4. What motivates Lavelle to climb, as she reports in paragraph 8, "out of the quagmire to ring out my time card for the last time"? What is the "mental torture" Lavelle mentions in paragraph 2? What is the significance of the comment in paragraph 8: "I had learned the value of a good sense of humor"?

5. In describing the difficulties she faced in writing this essay, Lavelle notes: "The next problem was to avoid sounding bitter or sarcastic." What specific strategies does Lavelle use to resist lapsing into bitterness and sarcasm? In paragraph 3, she observes: "It became frightening to realize these stoop-shouldered old ladies with the bitter smiles had once been young and full of dreams." How would you characterize the nature of Lavelle's own smiles in this essay?

6. Lavelle takes a fairly familiar topic—the drudgery of working on an assembly line—and offers a reflective view of the limits of that world and her rejection of it. What specific writing strategies does Lavelle use to make her essay fresh? Which paragraph(s) do you find most successful thematically? Stylistically? Why? Point to specific words and phrases to support your response.

7. Reread Lavelle's essay paying special attention to her use of repetition. Consider the verb choices in paragraph 1. What do you notice about them? Show how they strengthen—or undermine—the effect Lavelle aims at creating in this paragraph. Which paragraphs feature repetition of sentence structure? Why? What is the effect of this repetition in each of the paragraphs where it occurs?

8. Lavelle wrote six drafts of her essay. Here is the opening paragraph of her first draft:

> At eighteen, college held no appeal for me, but my marketable skills consisted of youth and a desire to help my fellow man. VISTA was my answer, but before I had completed my application I was told of a job opportunity too good to ignore. My mother, with the best of intentions, pointed out how it would be to my advantage to have a bank account to draw on while I was completing my VISTA

service. Her ideas made sense, so I decided to work for a year before I went off to live with the Indians.

Here is the opening paragraph from her fifth draft:

> I was not alone when I first set foot in that large brick building. There were several of us naive eighteen-year-olds who, courtesy of thoughtful relatives, entered a world of concrete, dust, and noise that day. This was a place where youth had an advantage. It was bonus work, and we couldn't believe it was possible to earn so much money for performing such simple tasks.

Compare and contrast each of these opening paragraphs. Identify the strengths of each. What changes in direction and focus does Lavelle make as she moves from one draft to another? Which version do you prefer? Why? If Lavelle were revising her essay, what recommendations would you offer? Why?

9. In Lavelle's first draft of her final paragraph, she wrote:

> In time all the vulgarities were just part of the scenery, and when, six years after that first day, I rang out my time card for good I had learned the value of a sense of humor. We had laughed a great deal. We joked about our "prison uniforms," and being replaced by chimps. We joked that some people pay a great deal of money to have their fingerprints removed while we were having it done for free. We laughed about our "fringe benefits," like being able to discount shop on our breaks. We laughed at the office workers, with their clean hands and small paychecks, who looked down their prissy noses at us. We laughed, but we would always look down at our calloused fingers and know that we were becoming something less than human beings.

Compare and contrast this ending to Lavelle's final version. What changes has she made in the final draft? Evaluate the effectiveness of each. What additional changes, if any, would you recommend? Why?

SUGGESTIONS FOR WRITING

1. In the fourth and fifth paragraphs of her essay, Linda Lavelle recounts the conflict she faced as a young adult working in a factory between "high pay and good benefits" and the "frustration and fatigue" of the work she faced each day. Write an essay in which you *describe* a serious conflict you faced in your own experience on the job or in school and explain how you did—or did not— succeed in resolving this conflict.

2. Lavelle talks about being humiliated and dehumanized by her experience as a "blue-collar worker" on an assembly line. At the end of her essay, she and her co-workers laugh in ironic awareness of their own calloused fingers. They knew, as Lavelle reports, "that we were becoming something less than human beings." Examine some line of "blue-" or "white-collar" work today that encourages the people who perform it, whether deliberately or not, to regard themselves as "something less than human beings." Write an essay in which you use a detailed *description* of that work to illustrate this idea.

3. The twentieth-century philosopher José Ortega y Gasset once observed that "an unemployed existence is a worse negation of life than death itself. Because to live means to have something definite to do—a mission to fulfill—and in the measure in which we avoid setting our life to something, we make it empty. . . . Human life, by its very nature, has to be dedicated to something." Consider the circumstances of your own life or those of someone whom you know fairly well. Write an essay in which you use that experience to support— or undermine—the validity of Ortega y Gasset's proposition. You might prefer writing an *argumentative* essay in which you endorse—or refute—the accuracy of Ortega y Gasset's proposition. Either way, try to make your personal experience, or that of someone you know, the basic evidence for verifying your contention.

PATRICK KINDER LEWIS

Wheaton College
Wheaton, Illinois
Sharon Ewert, instructor

Patrick Kinder Lewis describes himself as "not a 'reader' in the traditional sense in which writers seem to be. That is not to say I don't read. I read voraciously—I can almost never be caught anywhere without a book in my possession. But the habit is more from a thirst for wisdom than from any learned-pleasure of reading for its own sake. I didn't grow up reading, but thinking and doing instead. . . ." Lewis has spent nearly all of his life on the move. Born in Moses Lake, Washington, Lewis and his twin brother Mike, along with an older and a younger sister, have lived as U.S. Air Force dependents in various parts of the world. A graduate of Kubasaki High School in Okinawa, Japan, Lewis grew up during years of being what he calls a "perennial traveler. I have lived in over a dozen places since I was fifteen and spent two years traveling through the United States."

Lewis's experience on the road prompt him to characterize himself as "a people-oriented philosopher," a phrase he explains in these terms: "My folks have lent me their own brand of stoical toleration mixèd with lots of love. From rather obscure sources, both I and my twin have grown into quixotic convention flouters . . . which has led us to the 'existential edge' of our lives more than once." "Five Minutes North of Redding" recounts one such experience.

In writing this essay on hobos and the saving grace of friendship while riding the rails, Lewis hoped "to create the snapshot which I never took of that epiphanic moment" on board a freight train. The lesson of that experience, Lewis suggests, is that "nothing in this life comes cheaply—nothing of value anyway—but none of us pays anywhere near the face-value for what we get either: what we have, we have been given on loan."

For a revised version of Patrick Kinder Lewis's essay, see Part V.

Five Minutes North of Redding

I rolled out of the weeds into the crisp daylight of that late September 1 morning to catch the north train out of Roseville. The herder had said it would leave about 3:00 A.M. so I had huddled in my coat for at least three hours, wishing in the predawn chill for a cup of hot anything. But the noise and lights of the train yard had filtered through the tall grass and disturbed even those harmless dreams.

Finally she came. Forty cars were in sight before the engines passed me. 2 Moving down to the rail bed, I noticed for the first time that I had not slept alone on this stretch of tracks. Three figures were coming down to claim a rail

150

car 150 yards up the line, and even as I cautiously watched them, two other groups of riders were claiming cars behind me. I bounded onto a flatcar, concerned that the line of empties would soon pass me by—then thought again. A solitary presence on that flat deck, instinct shouted within me warnings about such a vulnerable position. I crossed the ten-foot width and dropped down onto the ground on the other side of the car. This time I watched until everyone was on board before I picked out one of the last empty boxcars. And still there were some fifty closed cars behind mine. This train was surely big enough, I imagined, for all of us.

The line of cars came to its first stop on a siding three hours up the Sac-   3 ramento Valley as we allowed another train to pass. Groves of plum trees lined the track on either side. Even so late in the season, the trees to the train's right were still full of hard purple fruit. I laid down in a splash of sun on the deck of my car. For the first time that morning warm and relaxed, the startling sound of shouts out the east door caused me to retreat into the shadows again. I peered out to find six men playing among the trees like kids as they picked plums only to pelt each other with them. I watched intently, as if it were some elaborate social experiment, until the sound of boots on gravel brought me back around. Looking to the shadow behind me, I suddenly realized that it was too late to conceal myself. The man whose crunching boots had just announced his approach was somehow already at my back door looking me over.

"There you are. I've been lookin' for you. You're travelin' alone ain't you?"   4 All the wrong questions to ask someone who is already scared of you. Luckily the voice betrayed nothing but a desire for friendship.

"That's right, I am. What . . . are you alone, too?" I sized him up coolly   5 as I moved toward my knapsack in the far corner. In its open front pocket I had a knife if I needed it. He had an eight-inch Bowie knife strapped frontier-style to his right shin.

"No. Couple of beaners and me pick up together in Stockton; but they ain't   6 speakin' nothin' but Spanish, man. You want sumpum to eat? They're gettin' some plums. We got cukes and tomatoes still that they picked in the Valley yesterday. And I got a box of saltines in Roseville."

He had a ruddy face that was roughly pocked, probably from adolescence,   7 and a scraggly mustache that only became noticeable when he looked right at you. I had reached my pack, but simply turned toward him in a crouch to look for my next move.

If I planned to turn down his offer, standing four feet up in a boxcar was   8 the time to do it. His bony frame and large hands gave away his height: I

would be at a three- to four-inch disadvantage once down on level ground.
And he just looked tough. Shoulder-length, muddy blond hair he had tied
back with a lace of dark buckskin; it laced the seams of his chamois pants too.
(He was fond of buckskin and wore it well.) Very tough but somehow gentle.
He seemed all in all an atavism, a confusing mixture of General Custer with
a sixties flower child. I decided to trust my second inclination.

"Sounds good," I said closing my pack. "What's your name?" I grabbed my   9
jacket and hopped down onto the loose shale bed. The train was just pulling
away with a halting rumble as we neared his car. On quickening our pace, I
noticed he was limping from his hip down. I was in the car before him and
offered him a hand. But he ignored it and managed an agile roll into the car
by catching hold of a break in the floor.

Alex and the Beaners were the first hobos I was to travel with. For the   10
space of a couple days we ate, drank, slept, and fought like brothers. I learned
their pasts and their plans in that short time together and laid awake to think
what it would be like to live their lives. At one point, left behind by our train
somewhere south of Red Bluff, we hiked together most of the way to the next
railhead, ducking many a curious sheriff en route. Finally Alex found us a ride
out of a truck stop with an ex-Harley biker. Ambling over the gunwales of his
pickup, we rode it all the way to Redding.

That night, we caught the last train out still on its dinner break. Ducking   11
into a store nearby, I quickly bought enough sardines, crackers, and canned
sausages for ten men. While the train sat idle we found a boxcar that was open
only on its east side. (For the cold trip into the mountains ahead, warmth was
a more important concern than a view of the scenery to the west.) We had
just finished off the sardines as the train at last began to lumber out of the
yard. Our bodies exhausted, our hunger at last abated, we sat on the dirty floor
of our boxcar enjoying the last warm breath of the evening. We were now at
the northernmost end of California's fertile basin. From here on the land would
climb more steeply. Only the Sacramento River lay between us and the Cascade mountains. As we approached the trestle, the track took only one slow
curve to the northwest. On ahead, I was sure it would begin a series of slow
switchbacks to climb Mt. Shasta's side. But for now, because dead ahead,
Shasta was out of sight.

I leaned tiredly against the back door and watched as the scene in front of   12
me began to change. Low on the horizon, a nearly full moon was rising slowly
to take its place in the center of our stage. Mt. Lassen's distant volcanic head
joined it as we rounded the last turn before the river, showing mutely through
a carpet of velvet green peaks. Inside the car, Alex stood up to blow the smoke
of his cigarette out into the crystal air. He propped himself like a caryatid
supporting the right border of our window on the world. My Mexican com-

padres sat nearly motionless at the door's left side. Mesmerized, I dug blindly into my pack to find the harmonica which I had saved for just such an inspiring moment. I sucked in a chord or two of "This Train Is Bound for Glory," laughing inside. Suddenly, another actor entered from stage left and I came up to a squatting position to get a better vantage. The wild Sacramento below us had begun to snake its way into view, illumined only by the bright moon-light.

It was all I could do to keep from walking out our door onto that stage. 13 Like something from a dream, it seemed too fantastically beautiful to be real. And finally, unexpectedly, the train itself emerged as a player. The trestlework not only poised the line of cars two hundred feet above the river's surface but managed as well to bend it into a slow arc midway in the crossing. The sweep of that northward arc turned our view to the south. And just for that instant both the front and rear of the train were visible at once. The engines at our head disappeared slowly into the shadow of Mt. Shasta while the cars that trailed our coach paraded behind us across the massive trestle. And on it all was poured the stark quiet of the moonlight reflected in the river below.

The trestle, from south to north, could not have been over a mile long. 14 The entire panorama played before us for less than two minutes. Yet, in a very real way, it has run in my mind's eye ever since.

As that team of Southern Pacific diesels pulled us out of Redding, eternity 15 sat captive for a moment. Like a stolen glimpse of childbirth, I shared in that peaceful feeling of something both beginning and ending at once. And like a mother smiling at her child born at last, I found myself smiling with a similar relief. It was joy without euphoria. I hunted again for the insights of the moment before but found them fading with the darkness of the mountains ahead. What race had I run to earn such rest? What was born in that moment? I looked to my companions for an answer but found it instead full-formed in the darkness between us. There was the sudden realization of the only bond that we all shared: our passion for life. We were living life moment by moment. That was our race well run. As our moonlight halos began to fade I picked up my harmonica and found myself playing "Bound for Glory" in a different key.

QUESTIONS FOR READING AND REVISING

1. Patrick Kinder Lewis's essay recounts a youthful adventure "on the rails." How does he organize the story he tells? Is it organized, for example, strictly according to chronology? incident? some other principle? explain. What are its major parts? What is the relation of each part to the whole essay?

2. One of the strengths of Lewis's essay is the presence of an engaging *narrative voice*. How would you characterize the narrator? What information are you using to create this characterization? What does the narrator tell us about himself? In discussing his essay, Lewis notes: "I wanted to explain not only what was going on around me but also what was going on inside the narrator as well." How does the narrator change as the essay develops? What is your attitude toward the narrator? At the end of the essay, how has your attitude changed, if at all? Support your answer with examples from the text.

3. Characterize Lewis's *point of view* in telling this story. Is he involved and sub-jective or detached and objective at the beginning of his essay? Where—and how—does his point of view change as the essay proceeds? Where does Lewis restrict himself to reporting his observations of incidents and where does he allow himself to draw inferences based on those observations? With what effect? Point to specific words and phrases to support your response.

4. In explaining his *purpose* in writing this essay, Patrick Lewis notes: "The ex-perience about which I wrote was a brief but meaningful excerpt from a much longer story I hope to write about learning from life-lived-on-the-edge. 'Five Minutes North of Redding' was in a way the fulfillment of a youthful dream and the beginning of a more mature vision." Locate the moments in this essay that illustrate this point. In the final paragraph when Lewis states: "I hunted again for the insights of the moment before," what, exactly, are the insights he refers to? How does the final paragraph amplify each of them?

5. This essay is rich in detail. Readers can sense the presence of a writer working hard—and consciously so—at *description*. One distinguishing feature of effective description is the use of *concrete*, sensory details. List the instances where Lewis appeals to each of his reader's senses. Another characteristic of effective de-scription is its specificity. Consider paragraph 9, and more particularly, the last three sentences in it. How does the final sentence in the paragraph extend and develop the point made about Alex's "limping from the hip down"? How is Lewis's use of detail in action in this paragraph reinforced at other moments in the essay?

6. In paragraph 12 Lewis develops a compelling image of a "stage." Identify each of the "actors" who play on this "stage." In addition to the individuals and groups you have listed, what additional "actors" does Lewis's drama depend on? Show how the *metaphor* of the stage controls the last several paragraphs of Lewis's essay. What other metaphors can you point to in the essay that further his *purpose*? Support your response with specific words and phrases.

7. Reread the final paragraph of this essay. What does Lewis mean, when he talks about "the sudden realization . . . that we all shared: our passion for life." How does the final paragraph serve to clarify this "passion"? How has it been dra-matized in each of the preceding paragraphs? If you had an opportunity to suggest revisions for improving Lewis's essay, what specific changes, if any,

would you encourage Lewis to make in his final paragraph? Would you, for example, recommend that he delete it? Why? Why not?

8. When discussing how he wrote his essay, Lewis noted: "I seem to like writing introductions . . . which lead to several different beginnings. . . . I must have written six or more openings before settling on picking up in the middle of one version. Then I reworked that much shorter approach at least another six times." Here is Lewis's first draft of his opening paragraph:

> There are some memories which you need to recall on cold stormy nights. When a chilling blast begins to whisper the worst sort of misgivings about life, their inner glows can throw dark doubts in the cellar where they belong. And if ever you are sure human beings are simply perpetual self-centered trouble, it may take a real warm memory to shake free from the acid experiences with the more ignoble among us. Someone has said, "Everyone needs certain works of the literary arts to guide them through troubled times." I have expanded the rule. We can create our own art within us to carry us through storms.

Here is a much later draft of the opening paragraph:

> There are memories that chew at your insides and shorten your life. They wake you up on chilly nights and rip the blankets off. Like the time your favorite jacket was stolen from the closet at the high school dance: you shivered all the way home, convinced that the only answer to injustice was to be just as nasty and brutish as everyone else. You shivered, shook, and wanted to cry out, and none of it did any good—the doubts had been planted deep. At such times we need to recall the "angels unawares" and warm puppies in our lives. Like waking up from a bad dream, our only answer may be to hope for a good dream to warm us again from such cold memories—from the inside out. That is when I remember Alex.

Consider Lewis's final draft of his opening. What specific differences do you notice among these three drafts? What does each emphasize? What are the connections among the three? Which version do you prefer? Why?

9. In an earlier draft of his essay, Lewis included several paragraphs recounting the "story" of Alex's life. Here, for example, is one such paragraph:

> Somewhere south of Red Bluff I confessed how new I was at running the rails. Alex wasn't running anymore. He was "tired of all that" and he was simply headed home to

help out his mother. He joked that he might even settle down with a waitress who had been chasing him for some time. In any case he had begun to feel at thirty-eight that the years were wearing him away little by little. Like the Snake River near his home, he could feel time cutting its own sort of canyon. And if he was going to lay down roots, it might as well be near where he began. His father was long since dead and his mother was getting to a point where she really needed him, he said. Still, I remember thinking there was something missing from his story. It just made too much sense.

Consider the gains—and the losses—of Lewis's decision to delete this paragraph. How would Lewis's essay be strengthened and weakened by adding more information about Alex?

SUGGESTIONS FOR WRITING

1. Patrick Lewis's first draft of his opening paragraph ends on this point: "Someone has said, 'Everyone needs certain works of the literary arts to guide them through troubled times.' I have expanded the rule. We can create our own art within us to carry us through storms." Examine your own experience carefully, and write an essay in which you recount an experience to *illustrate* either of Lewis's "rules."

2. At the end of his essay, Lewis notes: "As that team of Southern Pacific diesels pulled us out of Redding, eternity sat captive for a moment. Like a stolen glimpse of childbirth, I shared in that peaceful feeling of something both beginning and ending at once." We have all had experiences that have changed our perceptions so that we develop a new way of understanding something. Write an essay in which you recount such an experience to show how your perception changed and what this change in perception meant to you.

3. Lewis's essay raises questions about the nature of friendship. Montesquieu, one of the most accomplished essayists in literature, once gave the following definition: "Friendship is an arrangement by which we undertake to exchange small favors for big ones." Write an expository essay in which you relate an *anecdote* that serves to verify or challenge Montesquieu's definition.

WILLIAM G. MALLEY

Harvard University
Cambridge, Massachusetts
Holly Weeks, instructor

"*I rely on self-discipline when I write,*" *reports William Malley. "Writing is hard work that requires concentration and effort. For this reason, I never eat, listen to music, or carry on a conversation while writing. The first draft is never easy. I must say that I have not found any short cuts to a good paper.*"

William Malley was born in Buffalo, New York, and graduated from Canisius High School. His father writes for the Buffalo News *and has always encouraged Malley's writing efforts. Malley believes that his own extensive reading has given him a subconscious understanding of how words should look on the printed page and an instinctive feel for language. At Harvard, Malley writes for the* Crimson, *the school's daily newspaper, and plans to major in history or government.*

Asked to write an argumentative essay on a topic of his choice, Malley explains his choice this way: "I had just read The Making of the President 1960 *and was interested in the religious issue in the 1960 campaign. I started by going to the library and reading a wide range of periodicals from 1959 and 1960: popular mass-circulation magazines, Catholic magazines, Protestant magazines, and political journals. I wanted to read articles from a broad spectrum of viewpoints. After weeding out a few of the less useful pieces, I began taking notes from the ones that were left. At first, I took notes on just about everything, because I didn't really know what I was looking for. Later, after reviewing my notes, I began to get a better understanding of the whole debate; at that point, I began to read with a more critical eye.*"

An American Catharsis: The Debate Surrounding the Issue of Religion During the 1960 Presidential Campaign

We tend to remember a presidential campaign in terms of a particular issue   1
that dominated it, and indeed we should, for it is often this dominant issue
that determines the character—or even the outcome—of the campaign. More
often than not, this issue is political in nature; the issues of recovering from
Watergate in 1976, of the impending war in 1940, and of the Great Depression
in 1932 are typical. Each of these issues derives its importance not so much
from the attitudes of the particular candidates as from the state of the country

as a whole at the time. Certainly, the positions of the candidates affect the development of the issues, but each of these issues would have been important even if other men had run. The campaign of 1960, however, did not fit this pattern. In that campaign, the issue of whether a Catholic should be president played a dominant role; if John Kennedy had not run, this issue would not have come up. But he did run, and in doing so he forced the nation to face a unique issue, one that differed greatly from the political issues of other elections.

Veterans of presidential campaigns had seen these issues come and go. Every   2
four years, a few new ones arose, and a few old ones died out. These issues were by no means unimportant or insignificant; in fact, they had played pivotal roles in every campaign. But they were manageable. For the most part, they were debated in the context of the campaign and lost much of their importance after the election; those few that lingered on were generally confined to the political arena. The religious issue, however, had a life of its own. It had existed for hundreds of years and had been debated at one time or another or nearly every level of society. It transcended politics. By running for president, John Kennedy brought this old issue out into the open and made it a topic of popular debate. He didn't create the issue—he simply made it relevant. And once he had done that, he was powerless to make it irrelevant. He couldn't push the issue off the stage or out of the spotlight. The situation was further complicated by the fact that this was, after all, an issue of religion. Religious beliefs are not rooted in reason but in faith. The unreason that is a necessary part of religion instills in religious believers an unreasonable bias, prejudice, and fear that often runs nearly as deep as the faith itself. These unfortunate byproducts of religion color the perceptions of any believer and render reasonable argument ineffective as a method of debate.

In terms of politics, then, this debate was nothing but trouble. It hurt both   3
candidates, it divided the American people, and it raised difficult questions that simple political slogans could not put to rest. In another sense, however, the debate was more than a troublesome campaign issue. Religious bias, prejudice, and fear had existed in America for centuries, rarely out in the open but never forgotten entirely; they were chronic, malignant, festering sores on the American subconscious. The debate brought these sores out into the open, compelling Americans to recognize that they existed and to deal with them. The process was one of national catharsis which, though painful, was both necessary and good.

The religious prejudice that Americans confronted in 1960 grew out of a   4
religious division that began centuries before. Protestants, not Catholics, had founded America. Protestants had led the war for independence, drawn up the

Constitution, and passed the first Laws; Protestants had chosen the principles upon which the nation was built. Among the most important of these principles was the one that guaranteed separation of church and state and gave each man the right to worship—or not to worship—as he chose. For the early Protestants, the very antithesis of this idea was the church of Rome, which sought secular as well as religious power (White 284–85). For Protestants in 1960 the situation had changed little. The tradition of suspicion of the Catholic church had become ingrained in the Protestant consciousness; whether the suspicion was still justified had little bearing on the matter. For many Protestants, Roman Catholicism remained synonymous with intolerance and bigotry.

These Protestant feelings were far from unfounded. Even Protestants who 5 supported the right of a Catholic to be president found certain papal statements extremely difficult to digest. These statements could not have been less ambiguous: in 1832, Pope Gregory XVI condemned "the mad belief that every individual must be allowed and guaranteed freedom of conscience"; in 1864, Pius IX supported the view that "the Catholic religion should be considered the only religion of the state to the exclusion of all other forms of worship"; and in 1888, Leo XIII declared that "the state cannot adopt the same attitude toward all religions and grant them the same rights without discrimination" (Andrews 1241). From these statements it was hard to draw any conclusion except that the Catholic church had repeatedly rejected the idea of separation of church and state. Furthermore, as if to erase any hope that teachings had changed since the nineteenth century, the Vatican newspaper *L'Osservatore Romano* published an editorial on May 17, 1960 that budged not an inch from the established church position:

> The church . . . has full powers of true jurisdiction over
> all the faithful and therefore has the duty and the right to
> guide, direct, and correct them on the level of ideas and
> the level of action . . . The Catholic can never overlook
> the teaching and instruction of the church; in every field
> of his life he must base his private and public behavior on
> the guidance and instruction of the hierarchy. ("Vatican
> Paper" 73)

The position of the Catholic church on the religious freedom of its members 6 seemed just as threatening as its position on the religious freedom of those of different faiths. This willingness on the part of the church to intrude so boldly into the secular world was made unmistakeably clear by the bishops of Puerto Rico just a few weeks before the election. These bishops issued a pastoral letter forbidding their parishioners to vote for a certain party, the Popular Democrats, in the uncoming Puerto Rican elections. For speaking out against the letter, the mayor of San Juan was threatened with excommunication, as was any Catholic who chose to disobey the injunction ("Biggest Issue" 36–37).

Even at the beginning of the campaign, before the L'Osservatore editorial   7 or the pronouncements of the Puerto Rican bishops, the odds—and the experts—were against John Kennedy. It was a standard political rule of thumb that Catholicism and presidential politics did not mix; the 1928 candidacy of Al Smith was proof of that. Even the Democratic party, whose constituency and leadership were both substantially Catholic, would not hear of a Catholic candidate (White 228). Still, Kennedy had the minimum of support necessary to get a campaign under way. When, on January 2, 1960, he officially declared his candidacy, the first phase of this American catharsis had begun.

Kennedy's route to the presidency led through the Democratic primaries,   8 so it was in the individual states that the issue was first tentatively raised. As the primaries got under way, the issue grew in importance, but it was not until the West Virginia vote in early May that it became a dominant factor. The predominantly Protestant West Virginians had favored John Kennedy by a 70–30 margin over his opponent, Hubert Humphrey, in polls taken in December of 1959; just three weeks before the primary, however, they had reversed their position of 60–40 in favor of Humphrey. When Kennedy asked his advisers for an explanation, they said simply, "No one knew you were a Catholic in December. Now they know" (White 121).

For the Kennedy campaign, this reversal of opinion was certainly disap-   9 pointing but not altogether unexpected. They realized that the campaign had just gotten under way and that neither the candidates nor the issues were very well known; the fact that John Kennedy was a Catholic was one of the few hard bits of information available to the West Virginian voters. Thus, when pollsters asked them to choose between two candidates, the voters chose not between Kennedy and Humphrey but between a Catholic and a Protestant. In a country in which a Catholic had never been president, this could hardly even be called a choice, so it could not have been a surprise when the people picked the Protestant. In rejecting the Catholic, the voters were merely following a centuries-old tradition. And up until this point, Kennedy had given them no reason not to.

The anti-Catholic opposition in West Virginia was not an organized polit-   10 ical effort but rather a gut-level reaction on the part of individual voters. Clearly, this reaction was powerful, but Kennedy realized that it could be manipulated. The reaction was based on the justifiable assumption that a vote for a Catholic was a vote against separation of church and state. To win, Kennedy had to turn this assumption on its head; he had to show that a vote

for a Catholic was a vote against intolerance and against those who sought to
deny public office to forty million Americans simply because of their religion.
Once the decision became a matter of tolerance or intolerance, the voter could
only prove his tolerance by voting for Kennedy (White 127).

To effect a massive reversal of public opinion is never easy; to do so in a 11
matter of weeks is almost never possible. Poor odds, however, meant little to
the well-oiled Kennedy machine, which now moved briskly into battle. Thousands of Kennedy volunteers flooded the state to provide a broad base of
support. Each of the eight area commanders paid his first call to the district
leader in the local county courthouse. And Kennedy himself was everywhere.
In speeches, in parades, and on television, he relentlessly drove his message
home. There was Kennedy the war hero, Kennedy the young father, Kennedy
the strong leader—and, above all, Kennedy the believer in separation of church
and state (White 127–29). Against this awesome tide of men and money,
Humphrey was helpless. On May 10, Kennedy won easily, forcing Humphrey
to withdraw. John Kennedy was now the front-runner in the race for the
nomination.

Politically, Kennedy's campaign in West Virginia had been a success. His 12
strategists had been able to manipulate the religious issue for political advantages, and it almost seemed possible that this could be done throughout the
campaign. This, however, was not to be. In West Virginia the debate was in
its first, formative stages. For the most part, it was confined to the level of the
individual, and it could be controlled by political game playing. Ultimately,
however, all the attention in West Virginia served to fuel the debate rather
than to control it. Within weeks, the debate had spread beyond the limits of
the political arena, and it soon reached every sector of society.

Both Kennedy and his opponent in the general election, Richard Nixon, 13
quickly realized the difficulties inherent in the religious issue and attempted
to avoid it as much as possible. But while the two candidates did their best to
ignore it, the debate among the American people grew faster than ever. Up
to this point, the debate had taken place mostly in private conversations. The
majority of public figures had refrained from taking a stand on the issue; they
feared that even an honest attempt to criticize Roman Catholic doctrine would
be condemned as bigotry. But now the debate took a new turn. In the last
week of May, the annual meeting of the Southern Baptists was held in Miami.
Not once in the course of the proceedings was John Kennedy mentioned by
name, but the references to him were unmistakable. Dr. Ramsey Pollard of
Memphis, reelected president of the group, opened with a harsh attack on the
Catholic church. "Roman Catholicism," he declared, "must come to us with
clean hands and admit her own sin in the field of religious persecution and

bigotry before she can raise a finger at us" ("Dogma" 43). The convention then approved a sharply worded resolution that dealt specifically with the election. "When a public official is inescapably bound by the dogma and demands of his church, he cannot consistently separate himself from these. This is especially true when that church maintains a position in open conflict with our established and constituted American pattern of life" ("Dogma" 43).

With the increasingly vocal support of groups like the Southern Baptists, 14 Protestant leaders began to speak out. The press covered each new development with increasing boldness, and Catholic leaders for the first time began to respond publicly. The issue had broken out into the open and was now recognized as a legitimate topic for debate. Once this had happened, the traditional bias, prejudice, and fear were quickly dragged up from the American subconscious to confuse the debate and to be examined by it.

Back and forth, point and counterpoint, the people puzzled and probed. 15 What they found was interesting. The Catholic church that had traditionally been seen as so monolithic, rigid, and unambiguous was proving to be something quite different. It turned out that the papal pronouncements that had seemed so clear were in fact open to interpretation; the authority of the church hierarchy that had seemed so far-reaching and absolute was in fact limited. American theologians and clergy entered the debate to defend and explain their faith with great vigor. In a lengthy interview with *U.S. News and World Report*, Monsignor Francis Lally of Boston articulated the opinions of many modern Catholics. Contrary to the beliefs of some Protestants, he explained, papal encyclicals are meant to be "guides" to help Catholics apply their faith, not "blueprints for action." A Catholic president, he went on, would not be obliged to follow these guides, but only to consider them as he would any document that came from a prestigious source. Citing the leaders of France, Italy, and West Germany as examples, Monsignour Lally said that a Catholic leader of a democratic nation could function independently of the Vatican ("If a Catholic" 66–67). From throughout the Catholic church in America there came a new message: Roman Catholicism was more open, more liberal, and far, far less rigid than was popularly supposed; as far as America's Catholic leaders were concerned, there existed absolutely no religious barriers that would restrict a Catholic president's ability to function.

For many Protestants, this was a welcome revelation, and it confirmed what 16 they had hoped all along. For others, however, including many Protestant theologians, this was not the case. One of those who still remained unconvinced was Dr. John Mackey, a former president of the Princeton Theological Seminary. He outlined the principal questions of many of his fellow Protestant theologians in an essay in *U.S. News* that appeared five weeks after the Monsignor Lally interview. In carefully chosen, unemotional words, he questioned the extent to which a Catholic president would be free to follow his own will and the degree of authority which the church claimed in relation to the state. His feeling, clearly, was that the Catholic president's freedom of conscience was too small and the degree of authority claimed by the church was too great (Mackay 50). He went on to attack what he called "clericalism" and defined as "the pursuit of power, especially political power, by a religious hierarchy carried on by secular methods and for the purposes of social domination" (Mackay 48). This clericalism, Dr. Mackay suggested, was a threat to American institutions, and could only be furthered by the election of a Catholic president.

Throughout the summer, Catholics like Monsignor Lally and Protestants 17 like Dr. Mackay continued the debate. As the weeks passed and the number of participants increased, it became clear that this debate could not be satisfactorily resolved by the time of the election. For this there were several reasons. First, and most obvious, was the fact that a centuries-old conviction cannot be completely reversed in a matter of months even under ideal conditions—and conditions were far from ideal. Protestants who believed that the ultimate aim of the church was control of the state simply would not be persuaded that this was not the case; even when church leaders in America flatly denied all accusations of clericalism, the suspicion persisted. Catholic leaders abroad made the situation even more difficult when they issued orders that seemed to confirm the Protestants' suspicions. Second, and less obvious, is the fact that the question was being debated in the context of politics. Religious beliefs were intimately connected with cultural attitudes and political allegiances. Many people who would have found them difficult to separate in any case found it even more difficult now, as politicians and clergymen alike sought to play upon these connections to influence the outcome of the election. Finally, there is the point which many people probably understood but which few actually brought up. This point is that the only way to know how a Catholic president would act would be through experience. They were debating a question that was, for the time, unanswerable.

So the debate ran on, endlessly, with a momentum of its own, swinging 18 first to one side, then to another. In early September, the Reverend Norman Vincent Peale graced the growing Protestant movement with his prestige, and the anti-Catholic sentiment threatened to crystallize. Kennedy realized that he could not end the debate, but he knew that he had to prevent it from swinging too heavily against him. For Kennedy, the course of action was clear: he had to address the issue directly, and he had to address it soon (White 311).

With this in mind, then, Kennedy accepted an invitation from the Greater   19
Houston Ministerial Association to discuss his religion on September 12 in
Houston. In addressing his Protestant, somewhat hostile audience, Kennedy
spoke powerfully and effectively:

> I believe in an America where the separation of church
> and state is absolute—where no Catholic prelate would tell
> the president, should he be a Catholic, how to act, and
> no Protestant minister would tell his parishioners for whom
> to vote—where no church or church school is granted any
> public funds or political preference—and where no man is
> denied public office merely because his religion differs from
> the president who might appoint him or the people who
> might elect him. ("Both Sides" 74)

In the question-and-answer session that followed, Kennedy addressed all the
areas of Protestant concern over Catholic policy. By the time he had finished,
he had clearly defined the personal doctrine of a modern Catholic in a democratic society and won the respect and friendship of his audience as well
(White 313).

The Houston speech had its intended effect on the debate. It reversed the   20
growing tide of support for the anti-Catholic Protestants and threw the debate
back into a state of relative equilibrium. By the end of September, most American figures, both lay and clergy, had spoken on the issue; the media had made
sure that the basic questions were clear to the American people. During the
last month of the campaign, then, the debate returned to the level of the
individual. Across the country, outside the view of the television camera,
individual Americans made up their minds. Over the course of the campaign,
most of these people had, at one time or another, been forced to face the
difficult issue of religion. They had seen, with varying degrees of clarity, their
own prejudice, bias, and fear, as well as that of others. As election day approached, they were forced to make a decision: would John Kennedy's religion
be a factor or wouldn't it? As each individual voter made that decision, he
helped bring the process of national catharsis to an end.

On November 15, the American people chose John Kennedy, for reasons   21
neither the pollsters, nor the politicians, nor even the people themselves knew
for sure. It could have been a vote for a Catholic, or a vote against bigotry,
but it just as easily could have been a vote that in the end had very little to
do with religion. In spite of all the talk and speculation, in spite of all the
intense feeling and deep emotion, the decision could have rested on what John
Kennedy called the real issues: the issues of the Communist threat in Cuba,

of hunger and poverty in America, of education, and of outer space. Or maybe it rested not on the issues but on the images of the two candidates, who had met for five debates on that new and powerful medium, television.

In one sense, however, the reasons and even the decisions themselves were 22 insignificant. Regardless of how they eventually voted, the American people had accomplished something. As a society and as individuals, they had confronted issues that generations of Americans had tried to ignore. They had engaged in a divisive, painful, but ultimately necessary debate. Their success, in any concrete sense, was difficult to measure, but that, too, was somehow insignificant. In the end, it was the process itself that mattered.

Works Cited

Andrews, Charles R. "A Catholic President: Pro." *Christian Century* 26 Oct. 1960: 1241–43.
"The Biggest Issue." *Newsweek* 7 Nov. 1960: 36–37.
"Both Sides of the Catholic Issue." *U.S. News and World Report.* 26 Sept. 1960: 74–81.
"Dogma and Politics." *Time* 30 May 1960: 43.
"If a Catholic is President." *U.S. News and World Report.* 30 May 1960: 64–69.
Mackay, John A. "The Other Side of the Catholic Issue." *U.S. News and World Report* 4 July 1960: 48–51.
"A Vatican Paper Tells When Church Has Role in Politics." *U.S. News and World Report.* 30 May 1960: 73–74.
White, Theodore H. *The Making of the President 1960.* New York: Pocket Books, 1964.

QUESTIONS FOR READING AND REVISING

1. William Malley explains that "the first few paragraphs were extremely important in setting up the rest of the paper. I had to communicate to my reader my own sense of the wonderful uniqueness and complexity of the religious issue in the 1960 campaign." How does Malley "set up the rest of the paper"? How does he invite his reader into the world of his essay? How did he succeed in communicating to you his own sense of the "wonderful uniqueness and complexity" of his topic?

2. Why does Malley provide the historical background to the religious conflict in paragraphs 4 to 7? Why does a reader need this information? How does this information advance his *argument* and help establish his *purpose*?

3. Malley chose to unfold the story of the religious debate through the democratic primary and general election. His strategy was to provide his interpretation of this debate within the context of the events he *narrates*. Why do you think Malley chose this strategy? What does this strategy offer him as a writer?

4. What is Malley's *thesis*? Classify the various types of *evidence* Malley advances to support his thesis. For instance, in paragraphs 15 and 16, he quotes a monsignor and a Protestant theologian. Did you find these questions effective pieces of evidence?

5. Malley relies heavily on three magazines—*Time, Newsweek,* and *U.S. News and World Report.* Does he rely too heavily on these sources? What other kinds of sources could he have used to document his essay? What would these additional sources have contributed to the essay?

6. Malley reports: "My essay can be read by a fairly wide audience. Any reader with even the slightest knowledge of the campaign should be perfectly able to grasp the ideas presented in the essay." What assumptions does Malley make about his *audience*? How does he provide his readers with information they are unlikely to know, but which they need to understand his essay?

7. Describe Malley's *tone*. What does his tone contribute to the impact of his essay?

8. What is the significance of the first part of Malley's title, *An American Catharsis*?

9. Malley writes: "Regardless of how they eventually voted, the American people had accomplished something. As a society and as individuals, they had confronted issues that generations of Americans had tried to ignore. They had engaged in a divisive, painful, but ultimately necessary debate. . . . In the end, it was the process itself that mattered." How does Malley prepare a reader for this *conclusion*? Do you agree with his conclusion?

SUGGESTIONS FOR WRITING

1. Malley demonstrates that the religious issue in 1960 had "a life of its own . . . it transcended politics." What issues interested you in the 1984 Reagan-Mondale campaign? Was there any issue (for instance, women, taxes, the nuclear freeze) that had a life of its own? Select one issue, research it, and write an *argumentative* essay in which you use your research to present your *point of view* on the issue.

2. Malley writes about the changes in attitude that took place during the 1960 presidential campaign. Select and research a political issue such as Watergate or the Teapot Dome Scandal. What was the background to this issue? What were the dominant attitudes about it? How have attitudes changed?

JOHN E. MASON, JR.

Central Connecticut State University
New Britain, Connecticut
Patricia Lynch, instructor

Like many students, John E. Mason, Jr. has had to work while attending college. Managing the schedules of both can sometimes prove difficult, as Mason's own memorable experience attests: "I was trying to juggle college with work, and I had to work [installing linoleum] before I went to school on that particular day. I thought I could make it home after the job in order to shower and get a change of clothes, but because the job ran over, I was placed in a rather awkward position. The customer, who had gone shopping, wouldn't be home for an hour. I figured since I couldn't make it home to get cleaned up, maybe I could take a shower at the lady's house before she came back. In any case, I got caught in the act when she arrived home early for some reason. There I was, drying myself off."

Charming anecdotes about family, school, and work punctuate John E. Mason's account of his childhood and adolescence. Born in Hartford, Connecticut, Mason attended elementary school in South Windsor, Connecticut, where, in Mrs. Sullivan's second-grade class, he was considered "the king of the 'once upon a time' stories. . . . I don't think anyone knew that I had an interest in writing when I was younger, except for Mrs. Sullivan, who loved my fairy tales." He graduated from South Windsor High School and enrolled in his first writing course in college.

John Mason's goal as a writer is "to write something good enough to be possibly published in the Northeast Magazine [local city paper] so all my friends could go around saying, 'That can't be the same guy'. . . . I usually write so friends and relatives can get a thrill out of seeing their name in print. One measure of my writing success would be to have my best buddy, Groove, call me yelling about why I didn't use his first name!"

Asked to write an essay describing a person in his or her setting, Mason chose to focus on Mrs. Sullivan, his second-grade teacher. In the course of his essay, Mason recalls his trip to Mrs. Sullivan's funeral and the wealth of memories she inspired.

Shared Birthdays

As usual he had waited until the last minute. Route 5 wasn't a very direct 1
route, but it was free of stop lights and he was already late for the funeral. On
the other hand, Ellington Road was more direct, but it was a back road littered
with stop lights. He knew he couldn't make as good time on Route 5 and from
a distance he saw the miniature golf range, which signaled the fork in the
road. At the last possible moment he swerved right, just narrowly missing the
curb, but managing to cause his wheels to squeal nicely. In spite of the fact

167

that it was the middle of June, the golf course was closed as usual. He momentarily wondered how people could possibly support themselves on such a seasonal business. He quickly remembered from his own experience that, when night rolled around, the place would be packed with teenagers competing for each other's attention. He chuckled as he read the sign on Lucian's Restaurant, which used to be called Lou's Drive-In. He could just imagine the steady customers, mostly truckers, calling Lou by his new name. He wondered if building a new addition, acquiring a liquor license, and widening the parking lot had changed his personality the way it did his name.

He checked his watch and realized that no matter how fast he drove, he would be late as usual. After all, it was his trademark. He was blessed at being able to wait until the last possible moment to do anything. This habit, practiced throughout his life and constantly corrected by his mother, had caused her to patent the saying, "Someday you're going to give yourself an ulcer." But now he couldn't really decide whether he wanted to go to the funeral at all. Mrs. Sullivan, his second-grade teacher, his favorite teacher, had died, and he was going to pay his respects. But he couldn't for the life of him remember what she looked like. It had only been twenty-five years. 2

He whipped around a truck that was traveling thirty-five in the thirty-five mile an hour zone. He looked across the field and even from the road he noticed that the drive-in movie screen was in desperate need of a paint job. He shot back to the days as a thirteen-year-old when he and his gang spent many a summer night sneaking in through the back for the pleasure of watching the movie standing outside the concession stand. But the main reason wasn't to watch the movie; the passionate lovers in the back row were their feature attraction. Pounding on the steamy back windows of young neckers' cars, only to be chased through the potato field, was at that time a thrill and a half. The perilous excitement of being chased through a wet and sticky potato field was comparable to the times when Groove and he would bomb cars with snowballs. It was a systematic process of a snowball crushing against the side of a car, brakes squealing, and swear words filling the winter dark, only to be drowned out by the laughter of kids. 3

He thought ahead to who would be at the funeral today. Would any of his fellow second graders show? He'd have to run into someone he knew. It was inevitable. "I remember you . . . what are you doing with yourself?" He didn't rehearse what he would say, as he usually did. Instead, he again tried to imagine Mrs. Sullivan, a woman he remembered as nice and kind and sweet . . . everything a girl scout would envy. But he knew there was something more— why else would he take a day off from work and drive thirty miles? Reading the obituary the night before, he racked his brain trying to remember if her 4 first name was Mary. There are so many Sullivans. She seemed so old, even then. Could this be the same Mrs. Sullivan who was his second grade teacher? The same Mrs. Sullivan who shared the same birthday as he?

He slowed down for the newly installed light in front of Elmore's. Although it was not actually Elmore's since a glass company bought it out, he still insisted on calling it Elmore's. In the same way he called Jerry Z's Restaurant, Dell's, after its original owners. He always felt a twinge of guilt on driving past Elmore's. As a fifteen-year-old it became customary for him, after playing basketball, to walk down from the school and steal ice cream sandwiches. It was a cold and calculated ordeal which sometimes caused him to nearly freeze his private parts. This was mainly because Mr. Elmore, who loved kids, loved to talk. Years later when he found Elmore's had gone out of business, he envisioned poor old Mr. Elmore broke with no place to go, mainly because of the loss of his ice cream sales.

"Today is a very special day and we have some special birthdays to cele-brate." Everyone knew it was Mrs. Sullivan's, and he'd tried to tell as many people as possible that it was his. But Al Jankowski's? There Al sat, like a fat cat, purring in the lap of Mrs. Sullivan. He knew that he, and *not* Al, should have been nestled in that warm and secure lap. Thank God for Al's neighbor who finked that Al's birthday was in September and not in March. In the dignified manner in which she seemed to do everything, she kindly asked Al to return to his seat and not to fib in the future. Seeing fat little Al get caught in the act, he quickly promoted himself to the best seat in the house. From the lap of Mrs. Sullivan, he was able to look down on all the little eyes jealously looking at him. He was also able to shoot Al a "better luck next time" smirk. He crossed his arms, resting his head on her breast, and listened as Mrs. Sullivan explained that even though we're all very different, on our birthdays we're that much more unique, because that's the day that God made us spe-cially. The bell rang telling them that lunch was ready, but he would have gladly missed it for a few more moments of playing king.

He tried to imagine what she would have looked like today. He combined what he remembered of the faces of all his old teachers to construct some sort of imaginary face. Even the sight of Pleasant Valley School, the school where she taught, didn't jog his memory; Pleasant Valley School . . . Pigsville . . . as it was so affectionately called by its devoted students. He slowed down just enough to notice that they had built an addition to the back of the school covering the basketball court. The old blacktop . . . it was on that blacktop that he perfected the dying art of chasing a girl to pull her braids. And of course, there was . . . Kathy . . . his first love. He had had his eyes on her, along with half the boys in school, since they went to kindergarten together at the Little Red School House. The blacktop served as his stage to entertain and amuse Kathy. His antics, long forgotten by most, were filed away in his memory bank, always to be relived when passing "Pigsville." The climactic moment of belting a home run, aided by six errors, crossing the plate to have Kathy tell him she liked him more than Graham . . . Even though it only lasted the length of the recess period, it didn't matter. She liked him! Deliberately tripping and falling, getting his new pants dirty was well worth it to see Kathy laughing. Despite the scoldings by his mother, he loved every minute of it. Probably the deciding factor for his crush on Kathy was the head maintenance man in charge of the whole school. He was her grandfather. Everybody wanted to be on a first name basis with the janitor. Two dreams he had had during those early years were to marry Kathy and to be on the safety patrol . . . "Single file under the lights. . . ."

He stopped abruptly for another damn light. The car before him could have   8 made it. He knew he'd definitely be late and decided to drive straight to the church. It's funny, but it was at this specific light that he set the record for the longest kiss in town. It was mostly caused by peer pressure from his eighth-grade friends who seemed to think there was something wrong if you didn't kiss a girl after going with her for eight months. But he loved Anita, he respected her, and what if she slapped his face? On that day, standing at the light waiting for it to change, he again struggled to find a way to say good-bye. "I'll see you in school . . . Call you tonight . . . Going to church tomorrow?" But for some reason unknown to him, he just turned and kissed her. It was a hot and sticky summer day and the sun seemed to melt their lips together. Despite the honking of the passing cars, they managed to stay glued together for three changings of the light. He couldn't even look her in the face as he went to leave, too embarrassed that someone he knew might have seen him. But as he bounced away, had never felt so good about being embarrassed.

What would he talk about if he did run into anybody he knew? He always   9 felt uncomfortable about returning to his home town. If only they didn't ask the same basic and boring questions. "What are you doing now? Are you still working for your father?" He'd always dreaded that twofold question. He couldn't exactly figure out why. Maybe it was because he didn't enjoy the work he inherited from his father; maybe because he didn't enjoy only being his father's son; or maybe because he just didn't enjoy himself. In any case, he was there to pay tribute to a special teacher; so special he couldn't remember what she looked like. If anyone inquired about how he knew the deceased, he could always say they shared the same birthday. He pulled into the church parking lot, scanning the faces of the few people to see if he knew anyone. He was surprised, even relieved, to see the familiar face of his good friend, Nurse Files, the high school nurse. Through the years after high school they had kept in touch. It was only today he was to learn that she was Mrs. Sullivan's sister-in-law.

He took a seat in the last pew, separated from the rest of the mourners. 10 This assured that if he did have to cry, he wouldn't be heard by the others. The preacher in the middle of his eulogy expounded on the fact that through the years, Mrs. Sullivan dedicated her life to not only teaching youngsters, but more importantly, showing love and compassion to people in all walks of life, including the needy and the less fortunate. As the pastor rattled off the list of her finer attributes, he wondered to himself what the difference between teaching youngsters and helping the needy was. For some reason, the way the reverend worded the differences between youngsters and the needy and less fortunate struck him as funny. What would he classify himself as? The only substantial memories he had of her were ones of love that she showed not only for him, but for all her children (including Al). With each story of accomplishments being recited by the proud preacher, he felt tears burning a path down his face. He didn't make an effort to wipe his face, even though people slowly began filing out past him. Farewell tears, because he would miss her, grateful tears for her being a part of his life, tears because he no longer had the need to remember what she looked like.

As the weary family members lined up to receive their condolences, Nurse 11 Files made it a point to introduce him to the family—"This boy was a favorite of your mother's." She was cut short by the pressing line of friends who wanted their say in the matter. He shook hands with the daughter, dying to say her mother's birthday was the same as his, but judging by the look in her eyes, she too wanted to keep the line moving. He kissed Nurse Files goodbye, promising to keep in touch, knowing he wouldn't. The cold air chilled his face where the tears had covered. He felt a strange sense of accomplishment, the way he felt whenever he pushed himself to do something he didn't want to do. He was happy, not only for having attended the funeral, but for having taken the back road, even if as usual he had waited until the last minute.

QUESTIONS FOR READING AND REVISING

1. John E. Mason, Jr. explains one of his purposes in writing this essay: "I wanted people to know that Mrs. Sullivan was a special woman, not just to me, but to everyone who was a part of her life." How does he describe Mrs. Sullivan?

What does he tell us about her life and her teaching? What memories does thinking about her evoke? Based on what he says in this essay, why do you think Mason regards Mrs. Sullivan as "a special woman"?

2. Reflecting on why he wrote this essay, Mason notes: "As we get older, each of us has a tendency to forget special people who helped us along the way. I originally had questioned my motives for attending the funeral of a teacher I'd known so long ago. But the more I wrote, the clearer I saw our relationship." What explanation does Mason offer for attending Mrs. Sullivan's funeral? What does he describe as the nature of their relationship?

3. Mason explains that in writing his essay, "I wanted people to be able to relate, to be able to remember doing the same thing, to say, 'I felt the same way about that,' to just share feelings about growing up in a small town. I wanted people to feel good about themselves." What specific strategies as a writer does Mason use to elicit this response from his readers? Support your response with detailed references to particular paragraphs and sentences. What do you think he means when he reports: "I think I was saying that the things I seem to find the hardest to do in life are usually the most gratifying"?

4. Characterize Mason's *point of view* in this essay. Is he, for example, detached and objective? Involved and subjective? Some other combination? Support your response with an analysis of specific words and phrases. Consider the way Mason presents the "he" in this essay. Why is—or isn't—using the third person point of view here appropriate to his overall purpose? How is this person introduced? Show how his character remains consistent—or changes—as the essay unfolds.

5. What is the primary function of the series of *anecdotes* about the past? What do these anecdotes have in common? What is the effect of each on the overall success of the essay?

6. Mason's essay seems to be divided into two parts: the driver's reflections as he travels to Mrs. Sullivan's funeral and his thoughts while attending the funeral service in church. Outline the major points Mason makes in each section. How does each contribute to the overall effect of the essay? How does Mason unify these two parts of the essay? What frame or overall structure does Mason create for his essay?

7. Mason's essay makes skillful use of *irony*. See, for example, paragraph 1, where he ponders the effects of the change in the name of "Lou's Drive-In" to "Lucian's Restaurant." Find other instances of irony in Mason's essay and comment on their effectiveness. How does irony add to—or detract from—the success of Mason's essay?

8. Mason wrote several drafts of his essay. In discussing the first draft, he observes: "The difficult part about writing the first draft is getting tangled up in how to phrase the lead sentence. Should I have a delayed lead?" What do you think

he means here by a "delayed lead"? What advice would you offer Mason on this question? Consider the first sentence of Mason's first draft: "Like everything in his life, he was waiting until the last minute." Evaluate the effectiveness of this opening sentence. What specific changes does he make in the final draft? Which version is more effective? Why?

9. Here is the complete opening paragraph of Mason's first draft:

> Like everything in his life, he was waiting until the last minute. Route 5 wasn't a very direct route, but it was free of stop lights and he was already late for the funeral. On the other hand Ellington Road was more direct, but was a back road that was littered with stop lights. He knew he couldn't make as good time and from a distance he saw the miniature golf range, which signaled the fork in the road. At the last possible moment he swerved right, just narrowly missing the curb, but managed to cause his wheels to squeal. Despite being the middle of June the miniature golf range was closed as usual. He momentarily wondered how anyone could support themselves on such a seasonal business. But he knew from personal experience that when night rolled around that place would be packed with teenagers competing for each other's attention. He chuckled as he read the sign of Lucian's Restaurant which used to be called Lou's Drive-In. He could just imagine the faithful customers of truckers calling Lou by his new name. He wondered if adding a new addition, acquiring a liquor license and widening the parking lot would change his personality the way it did his name.

Contrast this version to Mason's final draft. What specific differences do you recognize? Which version established a more effective *tone* and direction for the essay?

SUGGESTIONS FOR WRITING

1. In writing his essay, Mason wanted people "to know that Mrs. Sullivan was a special woman, not just to me, but to everyone who was a part of her life." Recall your own elementary, secondary school, and college teachers. Whom among them could you describe as special? Write an essay in which you explain and *illustrate* this teacher's "specialness." You might want to include a detailed *description* of the teacher and recount one or more *anecdotes* to illustrate the points you make.

2. Mason observes near the end of the first paragraph that "Lou's Drive-In" has been changed to "Lucian's Restaurant." Describe a similar change in some business establishment you know about. Write an expository essay in which you *compare and contrast* the old place of business with the new, reborn version. How have the physical appearance, the products or services, the staff, and the management changed since the place assumed a new look and identity?

3. You have accumulated more than enough classroom experience by now to warrant speaking and writing publicly about the qualities that distinguish outstanding teachers. Read the following quotations on teachers and teaching:

> A teacher affects eternity; no one can tell where [a teacher's] influence stops. (Henry Adams)

> The mediocre teacher tells. The good teacher explains. The superior teacher demonstrates. The great teacher inspires. (William Arthur Ward)

> The art of teaching is the art of assisting discoveries. (Mark Van Doren)

> In teaching it is the method and not the content that is the message . . . the drawing out, not the pumping in. (Ashley Montagu)

Choose one of these statements and make it the focus of an essay in which you use your own experience and that of others to verify or refute it.

NELSY MASSOUD

Hunter College
New York, New York
Rebecca Mlynarczyk, instructor

"I used to think about my readers when getting started. It became so confusing that I would give up writing, convinced that I wouldn't be understood, or that my writing was not formal or clear. Then, three months ago, a ninety-five-year-old friend said to me: 'Say it the way you want it, the way it pleases you, the way you see and hear it. It must reflect you. The rest is not your problem, but up to your readers.' Isn't she wonderful."

Born in Damascus, Syria, Nelsy Massoud grew up in Beirut, Lebanon. She reports that she writes "anywhere—a bomb shelter, a car, a bar—and at any time—four in the morning or three in the afternoon, whenever the feeling is there." She always carries a small notebook and pen with her. First drafts are most difficult for her because "my ideas seem so disorganized at this point, they seem to say to me: 'If you don't catch me, you'll lose me.' And they all seem so important at this point. But then I know which ideas are really important. I revise and revise, but I never feel that an essay is finished. The end of one essay is a beginning to another essay."

Asked to describe a personal experience, Massoud reports: "About a month before I wrote my essay, I spent a whole day talking to a friend who had been pushing me to write about the war in Lebanon. It started as a political discussion but then became personal. It was the first time I had shared this experience with someone. I knew I had to write about Lebanon and to appeal to my readers by revealing what the war had done to my parents, friends, and compatriots."

War in Paradise

1 The story goes that God created the universe and found it beautiful. He admired it and was proud of it. Then God wanted to create a paradise and . . . there was Lebanon. Lebanon was to become the link between Eastern and Western cultures. In time, the Lebanese society was torn apart, some looking toward the East, others toward the West. With growing stakes on both sides and a very complex situation in the Middle East, civil war became unavoidable.

2 The phases of this war have been so numerous: the Lebanese against the Palestinians; the Christians and the Moslems against each other; the Maronites (a Christian sect) against the government, then against one another; the Left against the Right; the Poor against the Rich; Israel against the Palestinians;

the Syrians first with the Christians, then against them; the Druzes, the Sunnis, and the Shias (three Moslem sects) against the government, then against each other, the Iranians against Imperialism, and the list keeps growing. . . . The Lebanese, civilians, fighters and politicians alike, when asked to sum up nine years of war, explain: "It's an American plot. It's a big game and we are its victims. It's beyond us. The two superpowers, the USA and the USSR, are fighting on our soil. This war should end, but still, do you hear now? What are they bombing? Who are they killing? Us, the civilians. So we say that this war is beyond our comprehension, ala Allah, leave it to God."

I left Lebanon nine months ago, after living through a year and a half of 3 continuous battles. Now I live in New York. Every time I lie down to think about how I can pass along the essence of war to those who are ignorant of it, I can hear the sound of heavy bombs and explosions closing in on me. It's not that I want to share this because it's so awful, but because I hope to do something to stop it. It's been one of my most unrealistic dreams, but the only one that has kept me going.

Several weeks ago, I was riding my bike around Washington Square, en- 4 joying the good weather, when right in front of me a motorcyclist fell under- neath a bus. I didn't blink. It was as if I had no heart. I just kept going. Suddenly I stopped, shocked by my attitude: no feelings? No, just a flashback: a nineteen-year-old girl, back there, tied up between two cars and split in two when her torturers finally decided to end her suffering by driving off in opposite directions. Then, I had been powerless. I had had to suppress my human instincts, knowing from previous experiences that any effort would be in vain and might be fatal to myself and my family. I had asked a man, watching next to me, "Why?" He said in a tone of total conviction: "She is," (was, I thought) "Moslem, and by doing this publicly, we teach those bastards a lesson and pay them back for their atrocities." That was back in 1976.

A very dear friend of mine once came to visit me in 1977, bringing a present 5 created by his own hands—a key ring made from a human ear.

"Whose ear is this?" I stammered. 6

"A Palestinian's," he said. 7

I lost all sense of time. What century was this? Were we both of the same 8 generation? Had we grown up together? Had we held the same beliefs in years past?

My parents, who had not hesitated to beat me in my childhood to teach 9 me honesty, have accepted stolen goods during the war: televisions, tables, lamps, paintings, and other miscellaneous property from houses deserted by non-Christians in their neighborhood. "If we don't accept them, somebody else will and, besides, everybody is doing it." At one time, there were thirteen TV sets in our living room.

War is not only shooting, fighting, and killing. It's much more personal 10 than that. There is no more normalcy in one's life. There is nothing to hold onto anymore. It kills all valuable principles in one's heart and mind. War is the caricature of life because it means death. One might lose everything over-night, and the only refuge is one's friends, family, co-victims—people, in a word. We are killing each other, although every one of us knows that only a human being can understand and help another.

Let me return to the motorcyclist for a second. Normal people would have 11 stopped and tried to help him. I didn't. I have seen worse. I had been im-munized against suffering by living through a war. In Lebanon, children grow up amidst violence. By the time they are nine, their favorite game is war, leadership their dream.

Most of us believe the problem of war is so big and complicated that we 12 choose not to get involved, feeling impotent before it: "It's beyond us," we say. This is the very attitude that has cost Lebanon nine years of unbearable war. I thought for a while that the solution would be to disband all armies by convincing young people everywhere not to serve. But once in the USA, I realized the complexity of the problem. It is much bigger than the war in Lebanon. We all live with the fear and loathing of a nuclear war. We must all change our way of thinking and admit that we are personally contributing to such disasters with our knowledge, fatalism, and money, and in the case of small, bloody wars such as the Lebanese one, with our silence. Nothing that we create should go beyond us, but it will as long as we don't start acting responsibly and feeling concerned. Every one of us is needed, because it is we who will be the victims.

QUESTIONS FOR READING AND REVISING

1. Massoud's assignment was to describe a personal experience and to indicate what she learned from this experience. What do you see as Massoud's true *purpose* in writing her essay? What message is she trying to leave with her readers?

2. How does Massoud portray herself in her essay? What techniques does she use to create this impression of herself?

3. Massoud includes a lot of information about the war in Lebanon. She invites her readers to imagine that they too not only see, but also feel what she is feeling. How does Massoud draw you into the world of her essay? What gives her writing power and authority?

4. What assumptions does Massoud make about her readers? What information does she feel her readers need? For instance, why does she provide a long list of the phases of the war in paragraph 2? Do we need more information to understand the implications of her essay?

5. Why does Massoud give us the *anecdote* about the motorcyclist? How does this anecdote help establish her purpose? Why does she return to this anecdote in paragraph 11?

6. What is Massoud trying to persuade us to believe or to do? What strategies as a writer could she use to make her ideas more persuasive?

7. Massoud presents her *thesis* toward the end of her essay. What is the effect of delaying the thesis? Is this an effective strategy?

8. Massoud uses her personal experience to make a larger statement about the political situation in Lebanon and war in general. How does she move in her essay between personal writing and *exposition*? Is she successful in both?

9. In an earlier draft, Massoud's *conclusion* was written this way:

> However, we are life; we are family, community, society. Something can be done if only everyone is willing to bear a share of the responsibility. The first step would be to disband all armies by convincing our own brothers, friends, and neighbors not to serve. If we really need to fight, let's do it with our bare hands. Let Lebanon be something God and all those who knew it in the past can be proud of again.

Compare this version with Massoud's final conclusion. What are the differences between these two conclusions? How does the revised conclusion more successfully tie together the various ideas in the essay?

SUGGESTIONS FOR WRITING

1. Most of us have not had personal experiences of living in a war-torn country like Nelsy Massoud. However, we have all had powerful experiences that have changed our lives. *Describe* an experience in which you have seen or heard something but did nothing about it, and later regretted your inaction. Why

did you ignore the experience? Why did you later regret it? What have you learned about yourself from this experience?

2. Do you agree or disagree with Massoud's claim: "We must all change our way of thinking and admit that we are personally contributing to such disasters with our knowledge, fatalism, and money, and in the case of small, bloody wars such as the Lebanese one, with our silence." Write a response to Massoud's claim, illustrating your point of view with convincing ideas.

KELLY J. MAYS

Emory University
Atlanta, Georgia
Jerome Beaty, instructor

Kelly J. Mays traces her interest in writing to the encouragement of her fifth-grade teacher: "She pulled me aside after a creative writing assignment and asked me if I wrote a lot, encouraging me to do so because she felt that my paper was interesting. It mattered to me a great deal, and even now I remember the exact assignment. She asked me to write on the blackboard all the words which we thought of in connection with school, and after we had done so, she asked us to write a story about a day at school without using any of these terms. I don't remember what I wrote, but I think that it was a really interesting assignment, and her encouragement made it even more important to me. Since that time I have gotten a lot of encouragement from teachers, professors, and my family."

The third of four children, Mays was born in Decatur, Georgia, which her family still calls home. Writing and reading have always figured prominently in her life, both in and out of school. She attended Decatur's Shamrock High School, where she coedited the school newspaper, served as the sports editor of the yearbook, and graduated with the English Department Award and a National Merit Scholarship. Now a member of Sigma Tau Delta (the English Honor Society) at Emory University, Mays plans to pursue a Ph.D. in English literature and to teach in college. In addition to her interest in literature, she enjoys modern dance, acts in campus productions, and lives "in the S.P.I.C.E. dorm on campus (the Saunders Program for International Cultural Exchange)."

Asked to write a five-page paper analyzing the images and structure of Andrew Marvell's "On a Drop of Dew," Mays reports that "the main thing which I wanted the reader to gain from my paper was the awareness of the depth and complex richness of the poem. Poetry is such a compact form that the true poet must be a concise artist whose word and phrase contributes to the poem's effect. I think that this poem is a good example of the multi-layered quality of the poetic form at its best. I hope that reading my paper might reveal this craftsmanship to the reader, as writing it did for me."

An Analysis of Images and Structure Within Andrew Marvell's "On a Drop of Dew"

Within "On a Drop of Dew," Andrew Marvell uses a single comparison to 1 examine the nature of the soul and the possibility of its salvation. Marvell uses a drop of dew and the natural cycle of which it is a part to illustrate the nature of the soul and its relation both to the heaven which creates it as well as to the earthly body in which it lives. His vision of the soul is one of a pure and complete entity which embodies, at birth, the Heaven which created it. Yet, as a drop of dew is threatened with contamination from its contact with the earth, so, he implies, is the soul threatened by the potentially corruptible elements of an earthly form. He ends by suggesting that salvation comes not only from the natural state of the soul, which tends toward the goodness of its creator, but also from the active grace of God and, perhaps from the actions of man himself. Marvell expresses this idea through this overriding comparison with the dew in addition to other underlying images and finally through the structure of the poem itself.

The poem is based on the metaphysical comparison of a drop of dew to the   2
soul. Marvell begins this image by describing the inherent innocence, youth, and purity of the newly created drop through such references as "orient dew," which suggests its connection to the rising sun, "from the bosom of the morn," which implies a childlike connection with the parent-Heaven, "careless," which suggests its innocence of thought, and "little globe," which, as a diminutive phrase, again emphasizes the dew's childlike state. These descriptions not only vividly portray the natural state of the soul, which is inherently connected to God's goodness, but also set up the contrast between this state and the earthly. This contrast is furthered by the darker, more active descriptions of the earth implied by "blowing roses," "purple flow'rs," and the soul's subsequent, "trembling," and "restless" and "unsecure" "roll[ing]." By achieving such a great contrast Marvell points up the fear of the the dew or soul for its own contamination. The image of the drop continues within the second verse paragraph as it is "exhal[ed]" back to its birthplace and so provides the transition within the poem to a more direct comparison between it and the soul. This transition is aided also by the connection between the images of the human flower to the images of the actual flowers in the beginning. The dew image again returns within the last section in active references to manna, and within the first three phrases which connect the characteristics of the soul to those of the dew. That is, "loose" and "easy" refer back to "restless" and "unsecure," "girt" to "round in itself incloses," and finally "moving but on a point below" to "scarce touching where it lies," so that with this last paragraph Marvell rounds off the comparison between the soul and the dew, strengthening both images with the support of the other. This support relies not only on the actively described characteristics but also on the natural cycle of which the dew is known to be a part. By using the cyclical falling-evaporating of the moisture, he emphasizes the transitory and similarly cyclical nature of the soul's states.

In addition, this idea of a perpetuated cycle connects with a second prev-   3
alent image of the poem, which is the circular or round ideal. Marvell presents images of the circular throughout his poem. From the beginning he uses such terms as "round," "incloses," "globe," "sphere," "circling," "wound," and "girt," which emphasize this image of roundness. He ties this image, both through

implication and active association within the poem, to the heavenly, especially its virtues of purity, eternity, wholeness, and harmony. This idea connects not only with the underlying cycles within the poem but also with the images of the drop, the world and the soul. As a circle or globe, all of these are connected, able to face every way and yet to turn away and so connect both the purity to heaven with the earth, goodness with sin, and disdain with love. Further, this image of the sphere refers not only to the general heavenly sphere but ties in more specifically with the sun at its center.

The sun becomes almost an embodiment or symbol for God's power within   4 the poem. Marvell achieves this powerful image through both the implied power of the sun within the water cycle but also through its active presentation within the action of the poem itself. The first time it is mentioned explicitly it is presented as the powerful body which "pit[ies]" the "pain" of the drop/ soul and "exhal[es]" it back to the sky. Thus it is presented in a Godlike way through its mercy and its ability to bring the drop/soul back to its original state of grace. This idea seems to connect the sun to the "sphere" (line 14) of the dew's actual origin. Further, the sun becomes an active participant again within the last paragraph in Marvell's reference to Manna as well as in his ending, which emphasizes the power of the "almighty sun" to dissolve the body and reclaim the soul. This image is also supported within the poem by the references of "shed" (radiate), "shines with a mournful light," "that ray," and "eternal day."

Many other images also lend richness to the poem. The drop of dew is in   5 some ways compared to a tear since it is "shed" and "shines . . . like its own tear." But it also seems to be compared to a drop of blood in the same references to "shed" and the later phrase "congealed." In these two comparisons, then, Marvell ties the poem to the biblical not only through reference to manna but in this allusion to the blood and tears of Christ. Through these images of active grace and Christ's suffering, in conjunction with the strong and active portrayal of the "almighty sun," Marvell seems to suggest the action of grace within the idea of salvation. To this idea however, he seems to add the suggestion that there is some action necessary on man's part. This idea seems to come through his reference to the drop's "pain," its action of "shun[ning]" and "moving," as well as the idea of "climbing" inherent in the word "ascend." In addition, there may be some connection within the idea of "piety" in the root of "pity."

Connecting images of warmth and light, cold and darkness also play a major   6 role within the poem. Largely, they serve to emphasize the contrast between heaven and earth, good and evil, and yet their ultimate connection. To this and the author uses such phrases as "orient" (shining), "clear region," "shines," "its own light," "warm sun," "bright above," and "white" to refer to the heavenly nature of the soul/drop. These images of light and warmth emphasize the purity of heaven, its goodness and its compassion, and by implication the holy light, the good. Contrasting these images are the dark, colder ones of the earth. These images are found not only in the flower descriptions but also in the phrases "dark beneath" and "congealed and chilled." These images again emphasize the contrast between the qualities of heaven/earth, soul/body through their active portrayal within the poem and through traditional connections between light and dark with goodness and evil. These images also, however, point to the ultimate connection of these forces. Marvell achieves this connection through yet another cycle, that of night-day (where the sun is again the chief power), and through the circular image of the world, which may both reflect and accept light just as the soul connects both good and evil.

Through these images, Marvell has moved the reader from a basic description of a dewdrop, to an active comparison between it and the soul, and finally, to his conclusion of both the comparison and of his vision of the soul. The structure clearly follows and aids the movement of Marvell's ideas by its three verse-paragraph form. Within these paragraphs too, Marvell's structuring mirrors and supports his ideas. As the drop of dew exists in a "restless," "unsecure," and "trembling" state, so the poem begins with an erratic meter and rhyme scheme. As the drop becomes "inclosed" and assumes its "coy figure," so does the poem tighten in form. Within lines 27–32, Marvell increases the regularity of the length and meter of his lines as well as the rhyme scheme so that they, too, move toward harmony and balance with the soul's movement. This regularly also emphasizes the culmination of his active comparison, which occurs within this section. In the third verse paragraph, the same rhyme scheme is retained so that regularity is still apparent, but Marvell uses, too, the somewhat looser, flowing and yet highly regulated iambic lines to emphasize the contrasting description of the soul as being "loose" yet "girt." At the last, the poem again seems to largely lose its regularity perhaps reflecting the dissolution of the soul; yet, there are also many heavy stresses, caesuras, and strong couplet rhyme, which emphasize the summation of his poem, the power of the almighty and the salvation of the soul itself.

Through the strong, basic image of the dew, underlying images of the sun, the cycles of water and light, the suffering of Christ, and the eternal circle, in addition to the structure of the poem, Andrew Marvell creates a complex vision of the soul. Through the opposing and yet connecting nature of his images and structures, he creates the portrait of a soul which is similarly divided and whole. He stresses, especially with contrasting imagery, the inherent goodness of the soul and suggests this inherent connection with the good, Heaven, as the essential element in its salvation. He also, however, hints at the importance of God's active grace and the soul's own attempts (at reconnecting with its good) in the process of salvation. Thus Marvell ends by creating a hopeful vision of life, which is by nature transient and yet eventually connected to the pure and whole of God by its fall from, and eventual return to, grace.

Andrew Marvell
"On a Drop of Dew"

See how the orient dew,
Shed from the bosom of the morn
   Into the blowing roses,
Yet careless of its mansion new,
For the clear region where 'twas born
   Round in itself incloses,
     And in its little globe's extent
Frames as it can its native element;
   How it the purple flow'r does slight,
   Scarce touching where it lies,   10
But gazing back upon the skies,
   Shines with a mournful light
     Like its own tear,
Because so long divided from the sphere.
   Restless it rolls and unsecure,
     Trembling lest it grow impure,
   Till the warm sun pity its pain,
And to the skies exhale it back again.
     So the soul, that drop, that ray
Of the clear fountain of eternal day,   20
Could it within the human flower be seen,
   Rememb'ring still its former height,
   Shuns the sweet leaves and blossoms green;
   And recollecting its own light,
Does, in its pure and circling thoughts, express
The greater heaven in an heaven less.
   In how coy a figure wound,
   Every way it turns away;
   So the world excluding round,
   Yet receiving in the day;   30
   Dark beneath but bright above,
   Her disdaining, there in love;
   How loose and easy hence to go,
   How girt and ready to ascend;

Moving but on a point below,
It all about does upwards bend.
Such did the manna's sacred dew distill,
White and entire, though congealed and chill;
Congealed on earth, but does, dissolving, run
Into the glories of th' almighty sun.   40

QUESTIONS FOR READING AND REVISING

1. In describing how she intended to appeal to her readers, Kelly Mays notes: "I think that the best appeal to any reader is a sense of clarity, control, and purpose within the paper. It is important to gain the reader's interest with a clear and interesting statement of purpose, which then should be heightened and fulfilled by careful and organized evidence within the body of the paper." As you reread Mays's essay, identify this "clear and interesting statement of purpose." Explain how it is "heightened and fulfilled" by her "careful and organized evidence."

2. Outline the major points of Mays's literary analysis. On behalf of what *thesis*— what governing or controlling idea—does she make points? Make a list of each of the images Mays analyzes. Which does she deal with most convincingly? What points does she make about the structure of "On a Drop of Dew"?

3. Mays's announced goal in this essay is "to analyze the metaphysical conceit on which the poem is based, the underlying imagery, and the structure (especially rhyme and meter) to see how the poet utilized these three elements to express his ideas." Consult a dictionary or a handbook of literary terms for the meaning of "metaphysical conceit." With this *definition* in mind, reconstruct Mays's analysis of the extended *comparison* in Marvell's poem between a drop of dew and the soul. Evaluate the effectiveness of her analysis. How thorough has Mays been in covering each point of comparison?

4. What are the specific strengths of Mays's literary analysis? Where in her essay does she examine *diction*—words and phrases from Marvell's poem—most effectively? What other aspects of the poem does she attend to with unusual skill? Given her announced *purpose*, which aspects of the poem, if any, might Mays have devoted more attention to?

5. In organizing her essay, what pattern of sequence does Mays use to control the presentation of her ideas? Does she move from the simple to the complex? From the general to the specific? From the specific to the general? From the beginning to the end of the poem? According to some other pattern of principle? Verify your response with examples.

6. What specific strategies as a writer does Mays use to present her analysis? What

assumptions does she make about her readers' familiarity with Marvell's poem? How does she introduce the poem to her readers in the first paragraph, and what does she have to say about it? What percentage of her essay does she devote to paraphrasing the poem's ideas? To literary analysis?

7. One of the difficulties the writer of a such a detailed literary analysis faces is creating effective *transitions* between one major point and another, between one paragraph and another. What particular devices does Mays use to create graceful transitions? Which transitions, if any, do you think could be strengthened further?

8. Mays wrote three drafts of this essay. Here is the first draft of her opening paragraph:

> Within "On a Drop of Dew," Andrew Marvell uses a single metaphor to illustrate the nature of the soul and its possible salvation. Marvell uses a drop of dew, and the natural cycle of which it is a part, to illustrate the nature of the soul and its relation to heaven which creates it as well as the earthly body wherein it resides. His vision of the soul is of a pure and whole entity which embodies at birth the heaven which creates it. Yet, as a drop of dew is threatened by adulteration from the earth it contacts so he implies is the soul in danger of this impurification. Marvell suggests in his second verse paragraph that it is not only the soul's innate form but also the grace of God symbolized within the tree which helps the soul return to its heavenly state. Marvell uses not only this overriding metaphor but also underlying and implicit images, as well as structure to express this idea.

Compare and contrast this rough draft to the opening paragraph of Mays's final draft. What specific changes has she made? With what effect? Which version do you prefer? Why? If Mays were revising her essay, what additional changes would you recommend? Why?

SUGGESTIONS FOR WRITING

1. Mays obviously admires Andrew Marvell's ability to create a compelling *analogy* for the concept of the soul. Choose some *abstract* word or phrase and write an expository essay in which you create an analogy to define the term and how it functions in our lives.

2. When asked to offer first-year college students some general advice to help

them improve their writing, Mays responded most generously, although not in essay form:

> First, I do think it is really important to approach your reading as if you were going to have to write on the work. This approach might mean slower and more careful reading as well as underlining or jotting down notes to yourself. Listen in class to what the professor has to say about the work and try to expand on these ideas in your own mind. Pay careful attention to the assignment and be sure that you really do understand what the teacher expects from your paper. If you don't understand or don't really know where to begin, ask for help. I used to be really afraid to do this, but professors would probably rather help now than wade through a horrible paper. Everyone will tell you not to procrastinate and that is probably the best as well as the least followed advice in the world. I rarely can follow it myself, so if you do procrastinate on a paper, try not to panic. Instead, spend as much time as you can thinking about the text, the professor's comments, and your own ideas rather than in trying to write blindly. When you do start, it is much easier if you have a clear idea of where you want to begin, where you want to end, and how you're going to get there. It is important to remember that you have to prove what you are contending; you can't expect your reader to read your mind or to understand what you're trying to say if that is not what your writing is saying. It also helps if you pick a topic that you want to write on rather than whatever is the easiest; but don't try to answer the questions of the universe either. For me, a sense of routine is also helpful when I write as is the realization— although I want to write well—that I am not Shakespeare.

Consider Mays's advice on writing. How consistent is what she says with the advice you would offer other first-year students of writing? Write an *expository* essay in which you present, in as much detail as possible, your own composing process. Based on your own writing process, what advice would you offer to other first-year students of writing?

THU HONG NGUYEN

Palomar College
San Marcos, California
Donald S. Pratt, instructor

Thu Hong Nguyen was born in Vietnam, the youngest child in a large family and now lives in Escondido, California. She reports that having lived in two countries is an advantage to her writing; she has learned from the two different cultures and expresses her observations through her writing. Nguyen began writing for herself at the age of nine but reports that her family, most of whom are accomplished writers, did not think much of her writing then. Her teachers, on the other hand, had faith in her writing, encouraged her, and used her short stories as examples. Besides writing, Nguyen enjoys reading and drawing. She plans to study engineering.

About the conditions necessary for writing, Nguyen reports: "I first put on my favorite record of Handel's 'Water Music.' Once the music begins, I walk stealthily to my desk, afraid to awake the peaceful world in my small room."

Asked to write an essay in which she defined a subject, Nguyen decided she wanted to offer a picture of the life that a woman in Vietnam is likely to lead. The model for such a Vietnamese woman is Nguyen's mother—a widow who devoted her life to serving her family.

For an extended discussion of Nguyen's work, see Part VI.

A Good Woman

A good woman means an industrious daughter, a devoted wife, and a loving mother. Thus is the saying that has been a collective belief for many centuries in Viet Nam. As soon as a female infant is born, it is given the middle name Thi—meaning female—to emphasize its role as a woman in later years. Then, in growing up, this child receives lessons about a woman's duties and must practice what she learns. Parents wholeheartedly train their daughters to achieve the qualities expected of a woman. Should they forget, their neighbors promptly remind them. In a Vietnamese village, the entire community helps, by words of praise and by punishment, to bring up a female child to be a good woman, whose service, obedience, and generosity bring much comfort to those around her. With the fear of retribution, the child grows into a woman who follows loyally the instructions of virtue which determines her fate. From the moment her mind is mature enough to understand commands, to the day she is married off, to the time when she bears her own children, a Vietnamese woman continuously tries to establish a good name as a diligent daughter, a submissive wife, and an altruistic mother.

In order to be approved by everyone, a Vietnamese woman must first be 2 industrious. This begins with her services at the house of her parents who keep her from idling with endless housework. Already at the age of nine, she is the babysitter of her younger siblings. Carrying a baby on her back, she spends the day sweeping the house, carrying messages, and doing errands. As she grows older, she shares more of the housework with her mother. Upon the first crow of the rooster, she rises to brew tea and prepare breakfast. Afterward, she does the laundry by the river bank. At noon she cooks lunch and has just enough time to tidy up the house before she prepares dinner. In the evening she goes to bed, but only after having fixed the shirts or pants that were torn or missing a button. In keeping busy, she has no time to wonder and to dream, which often result from idleness.

Besides working diligently, a good Vietnamese woman must also submit to 3 her husband. She is expected to revere the man whom her parents have chosen for her after they have accepted his valuable gifts. Once married, she must show that she is unequal to her husband. When husband and wife are seen together in the street, she usually keeps a respectful distance behind him. She also has to acknowledge her inferior position in her speech. When addressed by her husband, she always answers in a well-modulated tone. In talking to him, she uses formal address. Even in the most intimate moments, she still cannot use the familiar form of address. If she has permission from her husband, she may speak aloud her opinions but should not try to make the decision. Whatever her husband says, she will listen and not contradict. Remaining silent is usually the most encouraged means for her to be respectful.

Finally, to be recognized favorably, a Vietnamese woman must try to sac- 4 rifice herself for the benefit of the children which are her duty to bear. At mealtimes, she eats little, repressing her hunger with the gratifying consolation that her children are growing taller and stronger. She must not dream of any kind of luxuries. Plain clothing gives her an air of modesty and thriftiness. Wearing perfume or lipstick may lead other people to condemn her as wanton and irresponsible. Instead of beautifying herself, she should give her children more food to eat and better clothes to wear. She must also refrain from any kind of pleasure. She spends her evening hours at home looking after the children rather than at a nightclub or theater. A pack of cigarettes, a bottle of beer, or a few piasters lost at the casino can deprive her children of their right to be fed more. A Vietnamese mother does everything for the sake of her children.

In trying to be what one expects of her, a Vietnamese woman continues to   5
serve if not her parents and siblings, then the husband and children of her
own. Year after year, she humbles herself to make her husband happy as a
proud superior, from his youthful days of good health to his time of age and
sickness. Day after day, she dedicates herself to the welfare of her children
even after they grow up. In this lifetime of striving to be a good woman, she
sets herself as an illustrious example to other women who are also trying to
achieve the same desired qualities. Realizing her goal, she is the pride of her
parents, husband, and children. People around her are satisfied with her. They
feel proud and sure of their lasting tradition in bringing up a good woman. In
any generation, they will always have a good Vietnamese woman to admire.
In any century, they will always have a slave to praise.

QUESTIONS FOR READING AND REVISING

1. Thu Hong Nguyen sets boundaries in her essay and tells her readers how Vietnamese culture *defines* a good woman. According to Nguyen, what are the
   essential traits of a good woman? What is she and what is she not?

2. What did you learn about a woman's life in Vietnam? What did you learn
   about life in general in Vietnam? In what way does Nguyen's purpose extend
   beyond defining and illustrating the life of a Vietnamese woman? What are the
   cultural implications of this essay? What is Nguyen's unstated *purpose?*

3. What does Nguyen assume about her readers' attitudes toward women's roles
   in society? What reaction, as a reader, did she intend for you to have toward
   her essay?

4. Analyze the *introduction* to Nguyen's essay. What function does paragraph 1
   serve? Besides telling us the traits of a good woman, Nguyen also tells us about
   her training. Does she provide too much information in her introduction.

5. What is Nguyen's *thesis?* Where does she state her thesis? How does she use it
   to organize her essay?

6. How would you characterize Nguyen's *tone?* Find instances in her essay to
   support your answer. How does her tone serve her *purpose?*

7. Nguyen concludes her essay with these lines: "In any generation, they will
   always have a good Vietnamese woman to admire. In any century, they will
   always have a slave to praise." Did you suspect such a *conclusion?* How did
   Nguyen marshall her information toward this conclusion? Is it satisfying?

SUGGESTIONS FOR WRITING

1. Nguyen writes about the role of the good woman. Consider a role you now fill—daughter, son, wife, student, friend, worker, etc.—and write an essay defining this role as you see it.

2. Nguyen writes about the "good woman" as defined by Vietnamese culture. Write an essay in which you *define* and illustrate the "good woman" or the "good man" as defined by American culture.

3. Here are three statements from Nguyen's essay:

   > A good woman means an industrious daughter, a devoted wife, and a loving mother.

   > [A woman] must try to sacrifice herself for the benefit of the children which are her duty to bear.

   > [A woman] must show that she is unequal to her husband.

   Choose one of these statements and consider how American culture views a woman's role. Does the culture, in general, agree or disagree with these statements? Use examples from television shows and commercials, advertising, and your own experiences and observations to support your thesis.

CAROL A. OBERHAUS

Auburn University at Montgomery
Montgomery, Alabama
Gerald W. Morton, instructor

"Writing is an emotional and intellectual catharsis for me," reports Carol Oberhaus. "I become very excited when I write, squirming and shifting in my chair, crossing then uncrossing my legs, scratching my arms, and chewing on my lower lip. I sit at my kitchen table consuming large quantities of popcorn and wearing loose-fitting clothes. I need to be physically comfortable and to have complete silence when I write."

Oberhaus says that for her, the easiest part of writing is getting all the ideas down on paper. She first brainstorms, "emptying her mind onto the paper," and then outlines. An outline gives her a framework yet allows her the "freedom to think in a disciplined way." Then she writes a draft and "revises and revises until it is just right. For me, revising means removing myself from the role of the writer and stepping into the role of the reader. I read what I have written and decide if I have actually communicated what I intended to say."

Oberhaus reports that until she reached college she was primarily influenced by her conservative rural education, which cast the machines of writing "in concrete." Born and raised in Muscatine, Iowa, Oberhaus moved to Montgomery, Alabama, to live with relatives and go to college. She has worked as a nurse for nine years and is now studying to become a veterinarian.

Asked to write a definition essay, Oberhaus reports: "We were told to have fun with our writing. I had recently had a conversation with my cousin's husband in which we were discussing southern men, and he had used the word Yahoo to describe a certain type. I knew I had my subject; that was all I needed to get started."

For Ladies Only

I have always been envied by other women for my ability to find unique 1
boyfriends. I know this is true because every time I introduce a boyfriend to
my friends, they say, "Boy, she really knows how to pick 'em." Well, I may
be skilled, but I'm not selfish. Therefore, I will give you ladies my no-fail
method of finding the most unique and desirable type of male, the Yah-Hoo.
There are many men who try unsuccessfully to imitate Yah-Hoos. Consequently, you must be able to quickly decide if he is a real Yah-Hoo, or a cheap
imitation. Your success will depend on your ability to remember that above
all, a Yah-Hoo is characterized by his special dialect, style of clothing, vehicle,
restaurant etiquette, and choice of music.

A Yah-Hoo's dialect will distinguish him from other men. His speech is an 2 exciting blend of a southern accent plus the sounds of a mating call of a pair of corduroy jeans. Certain words will be substituted for others, such as "barn" for born, "balkx" for box, "far" for fire, and "bode" for board. If you're lucky, he may "ax" you for a date, but do not be so "far-ward" as to ask *him* for a date, because he will tell you to mind your own "bidness." Yah-Hoos do not like women who, "caw-wull" them on the phone or have their own "chorge" cards. And ladies, do NOT show your ignorance by blushing when a Yah-Hoo talks about a "wang"; he simply means a wing. Understanding a Yah-Hoo's speech is definitely a science, which explains "wah" they date only the most intelligent of women.

A Yah-Hoo can also be identified by his clothing. He will usually be wearing 3 a baseball cap bearing the monogram of either Jack Daniels whiskey or Skoal Bandits. Incidentally, don't forget to look for the sweat stains around the headband of the cap. They are a unique characteristic of the Yah-Hoos. Long-sleeved plaid shirts seem to be popular with Yah-Hoos, even during hot summer months. Yah-Hoos *never* wear pink shirts. When a Yah-Hoo is out looking for a date, he will unbutton his shirt just far enough to give you a peek at his undershirt. Most women find the exposed undershirt a real "turn on." Pressing on, you must skillfully judge a man's pants. This category requires the most skill of all because you must be completely inconspicuous. If the man sees you performing your evaluation, he could misinterpret your intentions, or think that you are from New York. In either case you would surely offend him if he were a real Yah-Hoo. Look for jeans that are baggy in the seat with a white ring on the back pocket where the snuff can has worn through. The white ring on a real Yah-Hoo's pants is permanent and cannot be ironed out. Yah-Hoos successfully obtain an element of mystery by obscuring the shape of their thighs and buttocks with baggy jeans. However, the lower legs of the jeans must be very tight and too long in order to get their famous punched up look at the calves. Last, but not least, a Yah-Hoo will always wear boots with worn-down heels. The worn heels cause a very characteristic rocking, bowlegged walk that only Yah-Hoos do well.

If your potential Yah-Hoo is still in the running after you've assessed his 4 clothing and dialect, then you must note the characteristics of his vehicle. A man that does not drive a pickup truck is a counterfeit Yah-Hoo. A Yah-Hoo's truck will always have all-terrain tires and be jacked up more than any others. A Yah-Hoo never has to worry about remembering where he parked his truck in a K-Mart lot because the truck is conspicuously taller than any other vehicle in the lot and very easy to locate. If you are fortunate enough to be asked to ride in a Yah-Hoo's truck, *don't panic* because you have to climb four feet.

Resist the temptation to ask for a stepladder, a "leg-up," or any other assist-ance. Yah-Hoos really detest "whiners," but they love athletic women, so be thinking in advance of a method that allows you to bound effortlessly into the cab. (Hints: Boosting yourself by holding onto a street sign works, but may ruin your panty hose and get rust on your hands. A curb will give you a six-inch advantage that, with a running start, enables you to vault your way into the cab.) Yah-Hoos like to drive fast; therefore you must maintain good balance on your seat to avoid catching your hair on the gun rack behind your head. No matter how muddy the exterior of the Yah-Hoo's truck may be, the front license plate will always be wiped clean. The plate will usually say "American by birth, Southern by the grace of God," or look like a Confederate flag. Yah-Hoos never have FM radios in their trucks, but they do have CBs with whip antennas.

Another way to tell if a man is a real Yah-Hoo is by his etiquette in a   5 restaurant. The first hurdle, of course, is locating the kind of restaurant in which you might find a Yah-Hoo. Yah-Hoos can usually be found in restaurants that specialize in home-cooked meals twenty-four hours a day. Even more, Yah-Hoos are attached to establishments that possess a particular ambience, such as waitresses with beehive hairdos and a missing front tooth, red squirt bottles for ketchup, small and very thin paper napkins in metal dispensers, and booths upholstered in solid orange or turquoise vinyl. The musical amen-ities will be provided by an AM radio on the counter top that is tuned into the local country-western station. Once you are inside the *truck stop,* you may begin your assessment for potential Yah-Hoos. Try to sit in a booth where the upholstery tears have been patched with silver duct tape because trying to sit on a upholstery tear may cause you to giggle or squeal, and that would attract too much attention to yourself. In your assessment, you will notice that others in the restaurant very clumsily refer to the waitress as "Miss" or "Ma'am." Meanwhile, a real Yah-Hoo has his situation completely under control by calling the waitress "Darlin'." A Yah-Hoo always knows exactly how to order food, too. He will always order his prime rib well done. After all, it doesn't make much sense to put ketchup on your prime rib if all those meat juices are going to mix with it and dilute it! A real Yah-Hoo's etiquette is more creative than most peoples'. He isn't satisfied when the waitress asks "How is your coffee?" to simply answer her, "Fine" or "Good." Instead, he will demonstrate real flair by saying, "Boy! This stuff will make you want to slap your granny!"

You can always tell an authentic Yah-Hoo by his choice of music. Music is   6 a category that will serve many purposes for you in your search for a Yah-Hoo. You will be able to readily identify a Yah-Hoo, and if you're smart, you can use this information to endear yourself to the Yah-Hoo. Let me give you an example. A man who looks and acts just like a Yah-Hoo, but who is listening to Mantovani, is not only a bogus Yah-Hoo, he is the kind of man that Yah-Hoos hate most—a sissy. One of the quickest ways to score points with a Yah-Hoo is to tell him when you see a sissy in Yah-Hoo clothing. This lets him know that you are his kind of woman. Hippie freaks with new haircuts like to dress like Yah-Hoos too, but you can easily spot one if he's listening to rock music. Yah-Hoos often refer to soft mood music as "elevator" music because that's where they were the first time they heard it. Elevator music is favored by doctors and lawyers but not Yah-Hoos. And God forbid that a real Yah-Hoo, while tuning in his radio, should accidently tune in soul music! I don't know exactly what soul music does to Yah-Hoos except that it seems to be like Mexican food—"bad for yer system." The kind of music that Yah-Hoos claim as theirs is music that is sung by other Yah-Hoos. The more sophisticated Yah-Hoos listen to Charlie Daniels or Hank Williams, Jr. However, the majority of Yah-Hoos aren't particular about *who* is doing the singing as long as the song is country-western style and concerns itself with "drinkin' and cheatin'." Examples of their favorites are songs with lyrics such as, "Your Cheatin' Heart," "Who's Been Makin' Love to Your Old Lady, While You Were Out Makin' Love?," "Colorado Kool-Aid," and "Take This Job and Shove It!" Ladies, you may want to go out and purchase a few of these songs just in case you get the chance to entertain a Yah-Hoo in your home. I must warn you, though "drinkin' and cheatin' " music has been known to have an aphrodisiac effect on Yah-Hoos, so *be prepared!*

Any man who is characterized by my descriptions of dialect, clothing, vehicle, restaurant etiquette, and choice of music is a genuine Yah-Hoo. You must move quickly before another woman catches him. And practice makes perfect, so don't be afraid to try several Yah-Hoo boyfriends. You will know that you've really perfected your selection process when people say, "Boy, you really know how to pick 'em." 7

QUESTIONS FOR READING AND REVISING

1. According to Carol Oberhaus, what are the essential traits of a Yah-Hoo? Which details do you find particularly vivid or memorable? Does Oberhaus make you want to know a Yah-Hoo?

2. Oberhaus uses a good deal of sarcasm, a form of *irony*, in her essay. What is her attitude toward Yah-Hoos? Find instances of sarcasm in her essay and

evaluate their ineffectiveness. How does sarcasm add to or detract from the success of Oberhaus's essay?

3. For whom is Oberhaus writing this essay? Is she writing for Southerners? How much does she assume her readers already know about this type of man? What are her assumptions about her *audience*?

4. How did you react to Oberhaus's *description* of Yah-Hoos? Did you find her essay humorous, persuasive, offensive, etc.? Describe your reaction.

5. Oberhaus is writing an extended *definition* of Yah-Hoos. How has she organized her definition? How does each part of her essay contribute to her definition?

6. Oberhaus has a good ear for dialect, capturing the language of Yah-Hoos and using dialogue to help define the man. Why do you think she chose to present so much of the Yah-Hoos' dialect? Point out instances you found effective.

7. Oberhaus reports: "Even though I really could have written an entire book about Yah-Hoos, I felt the essay was complete when that type of man became recognizable to any woman." Did Oberhaus succeed? Is the Yah-Hoo recognizable? What else might she have added to make the character more recognizable?

SUGGESTIONS FOR WRITING

1. Oberhaus *defines* one kind of stereotyped character—the Yah-Hoo. Write an essay in which you define another kind of stereotyped character. Give your readers those characteristics which represent this character's appearance, manners, speech, etc.

2. Select several popular magazines and study the advertisements directed to male and female readers. How are these ads similar? How are they different? How do these ads stereotype males and females? Write an essay in which you analyze the nature of these ads by *comparing and contrasting* the stereotypes advertisers have created.

MAX RAMSEY

University of Richmond
Richmond, Virginia
Joy M. Barnes, instructor

*Max Ramsey reports that he comes from a very average lower-middle-class family.
"My father is a minister, which meant we moved around a great deal. I never really
achieved anything in high school. I guess one could say I was an undermotivated over-
achiever."*

*Born in St. Louis, Missouri, Ramsey graduated from St. Stephen's School in Alex-
andria, Virginia, and now lives in Richmond. He credits his family with encouraging him
to write even though his first memory of writing is when, at the age of three, he wrote
his name on the living room wall and got spanked for it (he figures he received the
spanking because he must have spelled his name wrong). About his writing process,
Ramsey tells us: "When I write I try to remember everything exactly as it happened by
forming a mental picture. I close my eyes and picture events, re-create feelings, and then
jot them down in jumbled words and half-sentences. The paper is done in the rewrite."*

*Asked to write a personal narrative, Ramsey reports: "After high school I joined the
army and trained with the Special Forces. In September 1983 we were sent to Lebanon.
I have had a very difficult readjustment to civilian life and an especially hard time dealing
with my experience in Lebanon. I wrote the essay, as the title suggests, for myself. It
started out as a journal entry. I just scratched down what was in my mind. Later, after
rereading it, I decided to flesh it out. I rewrote it four times before I was finished. I knew
it was finished because it felt right."*

For Myself

Every night I see her face etched upon my dreams. An endless nightmare 1
that wracks my brain and jolts me awake like a slap in the face, her image
returns to haunt me. I sometimes wonder if she will ever fade away.

She was like gold on a charcoal background, a flower in a desert of death 2
and deprivation. Her eyes were big and chocolate brown and peered right into
your soul. And when she smiled, it was as if the sky opened up and a ray of
light poked through and illuminated everything around her.

For me, the war in Lebanon really began three months before I met her. I 3
was a member of a Special Forces advisory team assigned to the beleaguered
Lebanese Army in their seemingly endless war for stability. My war began one
Sunday morning in late October with the sound of an enormous explosion,
crumbling cement, and twisting steel. It was my first taste of death, so close

you had to peel its fingers from around your throat. Since that day, I saw life in nothing but black and white. Nothing was in color. My senses had been numbed by the smell of death, an unmistakable stench that consumes and overwhelms your senses and hangs heavily in the air like humidity. It clings to you, and it won't wash off. Somewhere along the line, I had lost that esthetic part of me that gave me the gift of feeling. Death had not come for me yet, but it had left its mark on my heart. A sheet of thick, cold ice coated my emotions.

Then, one hazy day in late December, my unit was engaged in a firefight   4 across Rue Damur, a rubbled street in Moslem-held West Beirut. Out of the corner of my eye, I saw a ball roll out into our cross fire. Right behind it was a little girl in a dirty white linen dress.

"Shit, she's gonna get blown away," I thought, and I gave the order to   5 cease fire. Apparently, so did the Shi'ite militia leader. We just sat and stared through the thick, sulfurous smoke as this dirty-faced little wisp of a girl picked up her ball, held it to her stomach loosely with both hands, cocked her head to the side, and looked at us, her piercing eyes clearly visible through the silver haze. She turned and looked at the Moslems across the street and then ran off out of sight.

I called my men off, as did the militia leader, and we all went home. I   6 don't know why, but her intervention caused a calm to fall over our private little war, and suddenly nobody wanted to fight any more.

I found her playing in the street the next day while I was on a security   7 patrol through the Shatila refugee camp, about three blocks from where we had been fighting the day before.

Shatila. The land of lost souls. Empty shells of human beings who have   8 nowhere left to go scurry through the muddy, rubbled streets, afraid someone will come to send them away again. The crumbling, blown-out buildings are their homes, the garbage heaps their clothing stores, and the gutters their toilets.

But this little girl glowed in all of Shatila's gloom, playing, oblivious to her   9 surroundings. I walked up and sat down next to where she was bouncing her precious ball. I took out a chocolate bar and handed it to her. She smiled that toothy smile of hers and a warmth fell over me like a blanket. It must have melted part of that ice, because I felt something, admiration I guess you'd call it, for this little twelve-year-old girl with the big brown eyes. How those frail shoulders could hold up under all the shells, disease, fighting, and dying that engulfs that stinkhole of a country was beyond me.

I made patrols through Shatila at least three times a week just to see her,   10 in the hope that some of her warmth would rub off on me. I felt alive inside myself when she and I would talk. I loved to hear her tell stories in her broken English of how she was going to come to America and be a beautiful movie star like Linda Evans. God, she made me feel good again about what I was doing in Lebanon. She was what it was all about.

In mid-February—it was the second Wednesday night of the month is all I 11 remember—the Druze shelled Shatila in an attempt to hit the government positions there. They shelled it for seven straight nerve-racking hours. There was an empty feeling inside me that told me she was dead before I even left the bunker the next morning to help dig out the camp.

I remember the exact feeling I had when I found her body among the dead 12 that were laid out in the street for identification and burial. Her tiny legs were off at the knees and her abdominal cavity was exposed. But what cut right through me were her big brown eyes staring blindly at me and a look frozen on her blood-caked face that asked accusingly, "Why?"

My knees felt weak. My bowels felt loose. I felt as if my heart weighed ten 13 pounds and was pushing down on my stomach. I wanted to throw up and I wanted to cry. I fought back the tears: "A soldier never cries and he never asks questions."

I staggered off to a sandbagged barricade across the street. There I puked 14 up six months of hate, of disillusionment, of betrayal, of fear, and with them the last remnants of my youth.

By the time I'd finished retching, I was raging. It was a white-hot, out-of- 15 control anger that builds and builds and can't be turned off or toned down.

"Fuck this place. Where the hell are all the goddamned liberals who think 16 we shouldn't be here? Why aren't they here now, huh? Fuck this place and the government that sent me here. Why doesn't the rest of the wise and mighty United States have to see this shit? And why the hell is it that the innocent have to pay for these people's fucking ignorance? Tell me that, you bastards. You answer the girl. It's your fucking country. It's your fucking war. You tell her why."

I was screaming at everybody and everything. As I felt the last bit of strength 17 drain out of me, I slumped down against the sandbags.

And then I felt something unfamiliar rolling down my cheek. Tears. I cried 18 like a baby that day. Sitting against the sandbags on the mud-covered street, I cried like a damn baby. I cried for the soul of that blindly innocent little girl that was going to be a movie star. And I cried for a dying Lebanon and its hopeless questions without answers. But most of all, I cried for myself. I cried for the death of a part of me. I cried for the shattering of ideals. And I cried because her death meant to me that life really was in black and white, and emotions and colors were just illusions for somebody else to experience.

They say that time heals all wounds, but some wounds are deeper than   19
others. In time, I'm sure her face will fade from my dreams. But there will
always be that unanswerable and yet inevitable question engraved in my
memory—Why?

QUESTIONS FOR READING AND REVISING

1. Max Ramsey tells a powerful story and succeeds in holding our attention
   throughout his *narrative*. What *purpose* other than offering a personal narrative
   do you find in Ramsey's essay? What messages is Ramsey trying to leave with
   his readers?

2. What gives Ramsey's writing authority and credibility? Find specific details to
   support your answer.

3. As readers, we feel the strong presence of the writer in this essay; we hear
   him and feel we know him through his writing. What strategies does Ramsey
   use in his essay to give us this sense of himself?

4. What *details* does Ramsey use to make the little girl memorable to his readers?
   What do these details reveal about the little girl? About Ramsey himself? Why
   does the little girl remain nameless?

5. Look closely at the selection of events and the dramatic sequence Ramsey
   gives us. How does this organization serve his *purpose*? Determine the purpose
   of each scene. What has he deliberately left out?

6. The title of the essay is "For Myself." For whom does Ramsey seem to be
   writing? To what extent does his sense of *audience* influence his writing? Why
   do you think he gave this title to his essay?

7. Ramsey's narrative is about the little girl, but although she dies in paragraph
   12, the essay continues for another seven paragraphs. Why?

8. Do you find the *introduction* effective? Does it succeed in bringing you into
   the world of this essay? Could you suggest to Ramsey any way in which he
   might revise his introduction to make it more effective?

9. Ramsey sometimes uses phrases such as "Death had not come for me yet" and
   "I felt alive inside myself," which might be classified as *clichés*. Does the
   overfamiliarity of these phrases make them ineffective? Identify these *clichés*
   and explain what feeling Ramsey is trying to create. How else might he have
   expressed these feelings?

10. Ramsey reports: "The only problem I had in rereading and revising my paper
    was the harsh language I used. I didn't know if it was acceptable in college.
    I had no intention of taking it out. I finally said the hell with it and turned

it in. I guess it worked out okay." Do you agree with Ramsey's conclusion that his language "worked out okay"? In what way does his "harsh" *diction* help him achieve his purpose? How would it have changed his essay if he had tried to soften his language?

11. Ramsey tells us that the hardest part of revising is "deciding what needs changing and omitting. It is hard to throw out a memory even if it doesn't fit the paper. What is meaningful to me is not necessarily meaningful to someone else." Was Ramsey successful in revising? Has he included any details of memories that are extraneous? Is there anything in his essay that doesn't fit or advance his purpose?

SUGGESTIONS FOR WRITING

1. About his Lebanese experience Ramsey writes: "There will always be that unanswerable and yet inevitable question engraved in my memory—Why?" Write a personal *narrative* about a powerful experience in your life which you asked, "Why?"

2. Ramsey writes about his disillusionment and the loss of his youth. Select an incident in your life that led to disillusionment and shattered your ideals. Write a *narrative* essay in which you show your readers how this experience affected you.

3. Both Max Ramsey and Nelsy Massoud wrote about the Lebanese War. How do their differing positions—Ramsey as an American soldier and Massoud as a Lebanese civilian—influence their *point of view*? Write a summary-response essay in which you first summarize Ramsey and Massoud's points of view on war and then respond by showing how you agree or disagree with them.

JULIE REARDON

Normandale Community College
Bloomington, Minnesota
Mary Beth Lake, instructor

"Chocolate is necessary to the writing process," reports Julie Reardon, "as is caffeine-free diet Coke. A black-tip magic marker and lined pad complete my required list of items to work with. I have a special writing spot—the couch. I wear a fuzzy blue robe, pink slippers, and keep my cat close at hand during Minnesota's eleven months of winter. If my writing is going well, other people are allowed in the room to watch TV or listen to the stereo. If I am having difficulty, though, my husband and son retreat to their alternate areas—basement or bedroom. Only the cat is brave enough to stay during all phases of the writing process."

Born and raised in Mason City, Iowa, Julie Reardon now lives in Shakopee, Minnesota. She credits her uncle with stimulating her interest in writing. At the age of ten, she began writing letters to him and they maintained a twenty-year correspondence. In addition, Reardon has a close friend, an aspiring writer, to whom she sends examples of her writing for criticism and encouragement.

About her prize-winning essay, Reardon tells us: "My assignment was to illustrate my first encounter with a foreign culture. The life I encountered in a small town in Iowa was like another culture. I had strong memories from that experience and had wanted for years to tell other people the story of the lives of my neighbors. I thought of nothing else but this essay for a week after receiving the assignment. I sat down and wrote nonstop for about three hours. As the story emerged, I finally felt able to deal with all the old emotions that resurfaced as I thought and wrote about this experience."

For a more detailed discussion of Reardon's work, see Part IV.

The Unmarked Road

When I was sixteen, I married and moved to a small town to live. My new 1
husband nervously showed me the house he had rented. It was after dark when
we arrived there, and I remember wondering why he seemed so apprehensive
about my reaction to the house. I thought the place seemed shabby but potentially cozy and quite livable inside. The morning sun revealed the reason
for his anxiety by exposing the squalor outdoors. Up to that point, my contact
with any reality but that of my own middle-class childhood had come from
books. I had read extensively on a variety of topics and considered myself
grown-up and fairly aware of the world. The next four years in a small Iowa

town taught me that I was far from adult, and that reading about poverty is a lot different from living with poverty.

Our own house was an appalling sight from the outside. The siding, origi- 2 nally white, sprouted leprous gray patches where the paint was peeling away. Bark hung down from the huge dead elm in the front yard like long, limp scabs. The tree and a doorless garage leaned ominously toward our house. To the north, weeds grew up around a lonely, abandoned shack. To the south, a run-down house covered with rotting, gray asbestos shingles crouched, a weath- ered outhouse several steps from the back door. Farther south along the frozen, muddy road huddled a tiny one-room dwelling isolated in a swampy hollow. Barely glimpsed through a sea of stiffly dried weeds, the roofs of two ramshackle chicken coops rounded out the view from our yard. Our forgotten lane lacked street lamps and house numbers and was denied even the dignity of a street sign at the corner.

Madonna was the first neighbor I met. She and her two illegitimate children 3 occupied the miserable shack in the hollow. Madonna's occupation belied her saintly name. The number of cars risking axle damage by bumping along the rutted path to her house after dark confirmed she was supplementing her wel- fare money with prostitution. Her older son was disfigured with a bulging navel hernia that protruded visibly through his dirty clothing. I tried tactfully on several occasions to persuade Madonna to take Shawn to the doctor and have this repaired. Her dull, moon face stayed expressionless throughout my pleas. Shawn's hernia remained.

My closest neighbor to the south, Fanny, knocked on our door soon after 4 we moved in. She bore a steaming jar of homemade bean soup and a small, dense loaf of homemade bread. After several weeks of my newlywed culinary disasters, the kindness and the delicious aroma brought tears to my eyes. In my gratitude, Fanny's lined, weather-beaten face, sparse gray hair, and missing teeth were quite beautiful. I was already feeling the isolation and loneliness of that unfamiliar town and nearly deserted lane, and I attempted to coax her to come in for a visit. She told me she had to go right home because her husband was there alone. Gradually, I learned the circumstances of her life. Her hus- band, Buck, was blind, incontinent, and as afraid of being left alone in his permanent darkness as a child. Too proud to ask for help and too poor to pay for it, Fanny took total care of him without even the assistance of a washing machine or indoor plumbing. They eked out a bare existence on Buck's tiny disability pension by cutting out all but the most basic necessities. There was no money to style Fanny's limp gray hair or to have her much-needed dental work done. The often laundered and mended sheets she hung out to dry on the line were so thin as to be nearly transparent. Fanny was able to hurry the two blocks to the grocery store for food, but often as not, Buck's plaintive cries of "Fanny, Fanny, where are you?" greeted her return. He was unable to remember for fifteen minutes where she had gone.

One morning I was startled by a grotesque sight. An enormously fat man   5
with a vivid orange tangle of artificially colored and curled hair was slowly pedaling between the ruts down our road. He was so heavy he overflowed the bicycle seat and squashed down the old-fashioned balloon tires. The tires were barely turning as he wobbled past. I walked over to Fanny's house and asked who he was. Fanny pointed at the larger of the two "chicken coops." "That's Louie. He lives in that house." House! I could barely imagine him able to squeeze his immense bulk inside that tiny shack, let alone live there. Fanny continued. "He works part time cleaning up at the meat locker." That was his sole source of income—barely enough to pay taxes on his piece of land and keep himself in cheap, starchy foods. Fanny hesitated a moment, then decided to tell me the rest of his story. "Louie's father caught him when he was a boy, fooling with his sister. His father castrated him with the pig knife." I was stunned. Louie's unhealthy size hinted at a glandular problem, but this was incredible. I made Louie's acquaintance later on, and found him to be a quiet, painfully shy man. I don't know whether incest had actually been in-volved in his past or whether his father had interrupted an innocent game of "doctor."

I thought by now I had discovered all the inhabitants of the neighborhood,   6
but one surprise remained. I had lived in ——— for over a year, and trudging back from the post office one afternoon, I found myself face to face on the path through the tall weeds with a stranger. He was an elderly, stick-thin old man with face and hair so pale he seemed almost albino. I offered him a friendly hello; and was startled to see him start with alarm, nearly fall, and disappear into the weeds. My question to Fanny revealed that he lived in the smaller of the two "chicken coops." This structure was no larger than six feet by six feet. The old man, Sylvan, lived in that metal box winter and summer. Sylvan had been a frail child, and his mother "protected" him by keeping him always at home with her, never letting him go to school or play with other children. The tragic result of this pampering was that Sylvan grew up so frightened of the outside world that he was never able to associate with other human beings. His sister, never subjected to this maternal smothering, grew up able to function. She married and moved to California, leaving Sylvan entirely alone after his mother's death many years earlier. He did trust Fanny, and he signed over his miserable subsistence check he received from the gov-ernment each month. Out of this check, less than fifty dollars, Fanny paid his

fuel oil bill and bought his groceries. Neither Sylvan nor Louie had running water or electricity, and Fanny provided them both with buckets of water from her cold water tap. Sylvan's sister flew in once a year to check on him and take his clothes to the laundromat.

So we lived, each of us isolated from each other and the rest of the world. 7 Fanny was the single thread that sewed together the crazy-quilt patterns of our lives. Ten years ago, I pulled loose the stitches that held me to a failed marriage and that unmarked road. Late at night, I still wonder about the fates of those other unfortunate people. My several letters to Fanny remain unanswered, and my memories are too painful to allow me to ever return there, even for a visit. I never entered those people's lives to any meaningful extent, but they entered mine. I grew up a lot during those four unhappy years, and from the lesson of those wasted lives, I forged a determination not to waste my own.

QUESTIONS FOR READING AND REVISING

1. What overall impression of "the unmarked road" does Julie Reardon create? What is the significance of the fact that "the forgotten land lacked street lamps, house numbers, and was denied even the dignity of a street sign at the corner"?

2. Why does Reardon *describe* the houses on "the unmarked road" before introducing the people? How does paragraph 2 influence the reading of the rest of the essay?

3. What is Reardon's *purpose* in writing this essay? Where in the essay does Reardon state that purpose?

4. What important points does Reardon make about her life on the unmarked road in the small Iowa town? From her essay, what do we learn about the writer herself?

5. Reardon uses *concrete details* very effectively. She tells us, for instance, that her house, "originally white, sprouted leprous gray patches where the paint was peeling away. Bark hung down from the huge dead elm in the front yard like long, limp scabs." Find other instances in the essay where Reardon appeals to each of her readers' five senses. How do these details help Reardon establish her purpose?

6. Reardon reports: "I would advise my readers to read my essay with an open mind; not to let stereotypes of 'welfare mothers' or 'disabled persons' get in the way of seeing these people as individuals." Was Reardon successful? How does she help you to see and understand the lives of Madonna, Fanny, Louie, and Sylvan? What specific *images* and details illustrate how Reardon feels about these individuals?

7. "Fanny was the single thread that sewed together the crazy-quilt patterns of our lives." How does Reardon use the *example* of Fanny to *unify* her essay? Why is this an effective strategy?

8. Why did Reardon save the *example* of Sylvan until last? On what basis did she organize her examples?

9. Reardon reports that she added the *anecdote* in her *introduction* in a final draft. Evaluate the effectiveness of the introductory paragraph. How effective would the last sentence of the introduction be without this anecdote?

SUGGESTIONS FOR WRITING

1. Reardon chose to write about the most foreign culture she has known—the life in a small town in Iowa, a culture which forged her determination not to waste her life. Write an essay in which you illustrate your first encounter with a foreign culture. Explain the assumptions you had about this culture—and, in contrast, about your own—as a result of this encounter. What did you learn about yourself from this encounter?

2. Reardon writes: "The next four years in a small Iowa town taught me that I was far from adult, and that reading about poverty is a lot different from living with poverty." Consider a similar experience you have had in which reading about something has been quite different from the "real" experience. What were your expectations from reading? What was the reality? Develop a *thesis* to explain these differences and write an essay illustrating your thesis through a series of *examples*.

3. Have you known a series of people, like those Reardon knew, who entered your life and taught you something? Write an essay in which you introduce these people and show your readers their importance to you.

4. *Compare and contrast* two towns or two neighborhoods in which you have lived. Is there one person at the center of the town or neighborhood like Reardon's Fanny?

JONATHAN SCHILK

Highline Community College
Midway, Washington
Luke M. Reinsma, instructor

"*My ideal writing environment is a well-lit but not too bright room. I like to have a radio playing classical music. And I don't like people tramping through constantly asking what it is I am doing. First drafts are difficult. There are so many questions and ideas that are passing through my head that I can't write them down fast enough. Sometimes I get confused and lost in my own ideas. No matter how confused I am, I keep on going. I often write for ten hours straight without stopping.*"

Jonathan Schilk joined the Coast Guard in 1980, served aboard a 180-foot buoy-tender out of Grand Haven, Michigan, and also served in Key West, Florida as a small boat crew member during the Cuban-Sealift Operation of 1980. Schilk received a citation for humanitarian duty and advanced to the rank of Quartermaster First Class. He now works in the Coast Guard Rescue Coordination Center in Seattle. Schilk hopes to work for the U.S. Department of Forestry or the Parks Department after graduating from college.

Asked to write a narrative essay about an important event, Schilk chose to use one of his Coast Guard experiences as his subject. He explains: "*The main inspiration of this essay was that my writing had been mostly run-of-the-mill mediocre; technically passable, but uninteresting. I thought that a well-told sea story would entertain my readers and hold their attention.*"

For a more detailed study of Schilk's essay and the drafts that led to it, see Part III.

57 Degrees

At the Coast Guard Training Center in Alameda, California, our instructors stressed that we still had much to learn about the sea's moods and temperaments. Our training, they said, was only inadequate preparation for what could happen to us in open water. "The ocean humbles even the most experienced skipper!" warned one teacher ominously. He often spoke of the *Edmund Fitzgerald*, an ore carrier which had foundered in a winter storm on Lake Superior. Even though the ship was over seven hundred feet from stem to stern and equipped with the latest technology, she went down in less than a sweep of the radar's antenna. But it made no difference to me. After all, those men on the *Fitzgerald* were only civilians; I was a Coast Guardsman. After fifteen weeks at the Center, after long hours delving into the art of navigation and piloting, I could deal with any emergency. Steering—"wheeling" as we called it—was my forte. Several times, in fact, in less-than-perfect conditions, I had brought ships through narrow entrances in the breakwall. I could handle any ship of any tonnage. There was nothing that I couldn't do.

After graduating, I was assigned as a navigator to the *Acacia,* an 180-foot   2 buoy-tender on the eastern shores of Lake Michigan. I've been ordered to an oversized mudpuddle in the Midwest, I thought. It was like giving a man with a Ph.D. in math a grammar-school job. My fears were confirmed when I first saw the lake: it was flat, featureless, unromantic. Then there were the arguments with my shipmates about the storms. It would never get that rough on the lake. If they wanted "rough," if they wanted big storms, I told them, they ought to sail the Gulf of Alaska in autumn or go on a spring patrol on the Caribbean Sea. Besides, the *Acacia* could handle whatever nature could throw at her. She had been fitted with the latest technology—variable ballast tanks, hydroplane stabilizers, and all—to prevent dangerous rolls. The Boatswain never said much; he just nodded and smiled.

One day headquarters ordered us to sail for a point twenty miles northeast   3 of Chicago, where a 23-foot Chris Craft, adrift in bad seas, had radioed an SOS. We loosened the mooring lines at sunset and glided between the piers into open water. Fifty miles to the southwest storm clouds hovered over the horizon like a gigantic bruise. But here, where the ship only rippled the flawless surface of the lake, I fell asleep in my rack, secure in the knowledge that the *Acacia* and I could handle anything—anything short of a tsunami that is.

I awoke to the sound of water crashing and gurgling on the weather deck   4 above me. Lurching to the port, the ship dumped me onto the deck. I sat there, my blankets and mattress draped over me, wondering what had happened. I picked myself up and numbly eyed my shipmates, who had burrowed among their woolly blankets and lashed themselves in—giant cocoons in the dim red light. Clothes on hooks swung like pendulums with each roll, and a figure in the passageway made his way toward me like the proverbial drunken sailor. "What's going on? Where are we?" I asked.

"We're on the edge of a storm front and it's gonna get worse!" he gasped.   5

Before I could reply the ship pitched forward, and he zigzagged down the   6 passageway to the head. A bucket on wheels, loose from its trices, spun across the deck and smashed against the bulkhead, splashing its contents. I glanced to the berths to see if anyone had awakened. The cocoons hadn't budged. The bucket careened into another bulkhead with a crash. The walls closed in and air became putrid. I hoped this was as bad as it would get.

The sailor who had run into the head emerged, swallowed back another   7 retch, and told me I had the next watch in twenty minutes. Even in the passageway's red light, his features had a greenish hue. The ship plunged forward again, and he struggled back to the head.

After dressing, I climbed the ladder to the wheelhouse, leaving the bucket, 8 the messenger from the bridge, the muffled sloshing, coughing, and gagging behind. I fought my way up, sometimes weightlessly as the ship dropped from beneath me, sometimes ponderously as waves forced me to defy gravity. The bulkhead oscillated up and down, back and forth, up and down until I grew dizzy. I opened the wheelhouse door, stepped inside, and saw the helmsman clinging to the large brass wheel and spinning it in an almost futile effort to keep the ship on course. The Boatswain gazed out the porthole nonchalantly puffing on a Dutch Masters. The Skipper had been sitting in his chair forward of the helmsman's wheel. He too was looking out the portholes. Everyone else, including the lookout, the Officer of the Deck, and the Exec, was hanging on to whatever wasn't flying across the deck.

The acrid stench of the Boatswain's cheroot made me queasier than ever. 9 I would have loved to punch him in his smug, self-satisfied face, but I was too ill to bother. All about me, strewn across the deck, were coffee-stained charts, pieces of broken glass, and crockery. Outside, the Quartermaster of the Watch, draped over the bridgewing's edge like a rag doll, finally staggered toward the door and stepped inside. His face was haggard and drawn. Behind him the sea careened toward the gunwales and then receded.

I turned to see what the anemometer read: the needle had pegged out at 10 106 knots. The lake was as I had never seen it before. Even in an ocean storm, the period from the crest of one wave to the next would run at least three hundred feet. But here in the lake the period was seventy-five feet, and the ship was subjected to an endless thrashing, so that it was impossible for her to recover from one wave before confronting the next. Out there waves holding millions of gallons of water broke upon themselves, and the slicing wind sheared off the wave caps. Waves looming above the ship quickly swept on, leaving vast troughs for the ship to fall into—and she did. Many times I felt as if I had left my stomach thirty feet in the air above. Waves of nausea washed over me, and I wished I were dead. I meant it. I would have done anything to stop the misery.

No sooner had I thought this than a rogue wave plowed into our port beam 11 and sent the ship broadside, cork-screwing into a trough. "Brace yourselves!" the Skipper cried. Losing his grip on the wheel, the helmsman catapulted against the radar and landed in a heap. The wheel spun past hard left to a point where it would jam the rudder and leave the ship without steerage control. I jumped for the wheel and brought the rudder to midships and then hard right to bring the port bow into the seas. But before she responded, the ship gave way to the blow of yet another wave that towered above the signal bridge and mast. The *Acacia* heeled wickedly to the starboard—20, 30, then 40, then 50 degrees. At 57 degrees—seven degrees past the point of capsizing—she slowed to a stop. The fo'c'sle disappeared under thousands of tons of water, and the starboard rail dipped into the black waters.

Inside the pilothouse, maps, pencils, and coffee mugs cascaded off the chart 12 table onto the deck. The table lamp swung into the Fathometer, and sparks flew from its shorted circuits and shattered light bulb. And there, through the porthole, past my wild-eyed reflection, the lake boiled at the bridgewing's gunwales. The ship hovered on the edge of eternity. Deep in the ship's heart, rivets and welds strained and groaned, and deck plates jumped from the concussion. This is it! I thought. We're going down!

Slowly at first, almost hesitantly, the *Acacia* recovered, and the clinometer 13 climbed up its scale. Water washed from the fo'c'sle's deck in sheets as the *Acacia* swung past even keel, whipped through an arc of 100 degrees, and settled into a sedate 40-degree roll for the remainder of the trip.

In the corner, wedged between the Skipper's chair and the radar, the Boat- 14 swain still stood, puffing on the stub of a Dutch Masters and grinning quietly at me.

QUESTIONS FOR READING AND REVISING

1. Jonathan Schilk tells us proudly in the first paragraph of his essay: "I was a Coast Guardsman." What was Schilk's attitude about his own abilities during his Coast Guard training? How did his attitude influence him when he was assigned to be the navigator of the *Acacia*? How did his experience with the *Acacia* humble "even the most experienced skipper"?

2. Schilk tells a powerful story and succeeds in holding our attention throughout his *narrative*. Does Schilk's essay have any *purpose* other than personal narrative? Is Schilk trying to give his readers any message about himself? How do the first two paragraphs set up his purpose?

3. We meet the boatswain in paragraph 2: "The Boatswain never said much; he just nodded and smiled." We meet him again at the end of the essay: "The Boatswain still stood, puffing on the stub of a Dutch Masters and grinning quietly at me." What does the Boatswain represent to Schilk? What is his function in the essay? Why did Schilk end the essay with this image?

4. A reader feels the writer's presence in this essay; we know we are reading an

essay by a writer who cares about what he is saying. What strategies does Schilk use to give his readers this sense of commitment to his subject?

5. Schilk uses details effectively: he writes about a coffee cup flying across the room, the bucket careening down the corridor, etc. Find other instances of specific details you found effective and evocative. How does Schilk use his details to show rather than tell his story?

6. Look closely at the selection of events and sequences Schilk gives us. How does he organize his narrative? How does this organization serve his purpose? Evaluate the function of each scene.

7. Schilk's *tone* is almost conversational, like an old salt sitting in front of us recounting his adventures. What strategies does Schilk use to convey this effect? How does his tone establish his *purpose?*

8. Schilk reports: "I tried to get my readers involved with my tale by appealing to the romantic notions of the sea which most people have." In what way does Schilk appeal to these romantic notions? What else does he appeal to?

9. Schilk uses a lot of nautical terminology in his essay. Were you confused by these terms or did they add a sense of realism to the essay?

SUGGESTIONS FOR WRITING

1. Write a *narrative* essay about something that happened to you that made a difference and that has the potential of making a difference to your readers. Look back with your readers. Recapture some significant event or person or place or turning-point in your life. Help your reader to understand its impact on you.

2. Think of a time in your life when you thought you were invincible. What changed this image of yourself? Was there a particular person, experience, turning point? What humbled you? In a *narrative* essay, explain what changed your understanding of yourself and your world.

3. What does maturity mean to you? Write an essay in which you *define* the word maturity. You might want to use a personal *anecdote* as one *example* to support your definition.

BARBARA SEIDEL

Ocean County College
Toms River, New Jersey
Mary Ellen Byrne, instructor

"My upbringing was traditional," reports Barbara Seidel. "We were a close, volatile family and our home was always filled with relatives. I was the oddball from an early age—hot-tempered, rebellious, imaginative. I always loved to listen to the stories of my relatives; who did what, where, and why. I always wanted to understand peoples' motives, to explain their actions. Even today, I want to lift the lids off peoples' heads, peek inside, and explain the undercurrents of emotion and thought I often sense but cannot see. Writing is the best way to understand the world around me."

Born in Newark, New Jersey, Seidel grew up in Hillside and now lives in Toms River. She has always received praise and encouragement for her writing from her family and teachers. She served as the features editor of her high school newspaper and has written a cooking column and a column on humor in daily life for a county newspaper. About the conditions necessary for writing, Seidel tells us: "I want the house to be silent except for the sporadic squawking of my birds. I need to be left alone, without the phone ringing, or without anyone asking me questions or needing me at the moment."

Asked to write an essay of tribute to someone, Seidel immediately knew she would write about her father. "I knew this paper would be a very personal essay. I made a promise to myself that I would be open and vulnerable in my writing, that I would speak plainly about Dad. If I did otherwise, this paper would not work. I decided not to worry about the reaction my dad or other family members would have because otherwise I would have been paralyzed with the attempt to please everybody. I wrote what I felt and thought, and I hope anyone who reads this essay will understand that it was written with love."

For a more detailed study of Seidel's essay and the drafts that led to it, *see Part III.*

A Tribute to My Father

Thirty years ago, when his father was dying, he would leave his wife and two small children asleep in the square Cape Cod style house, then drive in the predawn light through the quiet city streets to take his father for outpatient medical care. Much later in his own life, his daughter puzzled over his devotion to a man who had divorced his mother, then ignored him and his brother. A faint look of surprise flickered in his eyes; then he answered concisely, "He was my father." He has always said that actions speak louder than words. 1

A soft-spoken man with a frequent low chuckle, he is so slow to anger that 2
some people have been fooled into believing him an easy mark for trickery, a
dangerous mistake. He is just as slow and long in remembering anyone who
violates his strict set of values. He has no textbook education, yet he possesses
an abundance of common sense. He is not religious, yet he is a moral man,
consistent in his values on a daily basis, not only on a Sabbath. The inherent
boundaries of his life, given and expected, have been loyalty, respect, tradition. Perhaps it is from the wild young hellion who quit school, whose idea
of fun was joyriding in his older brother's car while that brother chased after
him, that this man of caution and habit emerged.

Yet it was not caution, but sharp, clear instincts that twirled him fast and 3
dizzy after the woman he would marry. He was already engaged; his fiancée
made the fatal mistake of introducing her fair-haired, blue-eyed, slender man
to the dark-haired woman whose first sight caused some inner voice to shout
at him, firmly, "yes!" This woman would need him, would nurture him; he
knew it. He broke his engagement, then immediately proposed, waiting a year
before marrying only because of his future mother-in-law's insistence that he
do so. He may have been impulsive, but he was, after all, respectful of his
elders. And he had clearly chosen not only a wife but a family style. Tradition
and warmth, tangled relationships, and rash tempers all spoke of people connecting to one another. His life became one of stability and constancy, of the
same meat loaf served on the same day of each week, of the same conservative
clothes worn year in and year out, of a man and a woman whose lives revolved
around each other, so unlike his own past.

He spoke little about his past. No bitterness over the second-hand shoes 4
stuffed with newspapers, or the hand-me-down clothing several sizes too large,
pushed him to pursue great wealth to power. His dream, he later said, was to
be able to work hard and just provide. He found the greatest pleasure in the
small things—the ability to buy himself new shoes. Nor did he wield his own
meager childhood as a club to inspire guilt or appreciation in his own more
fortunate, more spoiled children. Instead, they learned of him through passing
comments—or from his mother.

Her divorce came in an era when such an act was brazen. She worked long 5
days caring for her two boys, who ate one meal daily at the corner candy store.
The counterman would wait until they entered, then place a sandwich and a
drink in front of them. "Never more or less, and all ordered and paid for in
advance," he once said, a respectful, wondering tone in his voice at the sheer
order of it all. She passed her stern work ethic on to him. He became very
good at being responsible, dependable, at providing.

And the errant, alcoholic, polo-playing father—the womanizer who once   6
told his ladies that this then-nineteen-year-old younger son was his younger
brother—had a few admirable traits of his own left up his sleeve. To his son,
he passed on a love of animals and a fascination with cars, with their sight
and smell and the gas-powered freedom they gave to a man. His son, as a boy,
would drag home one protesting stray after another to a firmly opposed mother.
Years later, a father himself, he would laugh when his own daughter did the
same. After spending forty years selling the mechanical monsters, his love
affair with cars has only dimmed. It is telling of the man that in a profession
where truth is not always a recognizable commodity, he has a staunch reputation for honesty and a loyal following of customers.

If his honesty attracts them, so must his humor, gentle and chiding. And   7
of course, there are the quirks. There are the Hershey chocolate bars hidden
in the night table drawer, the towels folded and placed exactly so in the linen
closet, the sink faucet wiped shiny dry after dishes are washed. If his past did
not create anger to unbridled ambition, it did give him a legacy of sorts:
hoarded candy bars contrast with the giving parent; an obsession with details
fills him with anxiety. He worries over each decision like a dog gnawing on a
bone. He is still the small boy seeking security, the ultimate peacemaker avoiding confrontations, reconciling and rationalizing the good in people and in
issues to the frustration of his children. They, grown, have at last learned to
laugh gently at the habits that once exasperated them. There is the family
favorite—the phone joke. His son speaks to him, hangs up the phone, then
counts, "5-4-3-2—hello, Dad!" He knows his father will hesitate, then call
again. Is everyone happy? Should we talk more?

It is this son who is one of the brief detours on his well-laid road map of   8
life. With his daughter, loving was an easy goal. They shared a silent similarity
of vision, of loving and letting go. With his son, such love was reached only
after struggle; they spoke a different language. His son needed questions answered, challenges met, baseball and other games which had found no place
in his own childhood; he was a man concerned with providing. By the boy's
adolescence, they were like two bucks, antlers locked in a battle of dominance.
Now they are two men, two fathers, who reach gingerly, but often, across the
once-volatile differences of self to touch the love that always existed.

And now, at age fifty-eight, his hair is streaked with gray; his oval face is   9
heavily lined; he is tired. The habits of his lifetime have been altered, a difficult
task for a man who dislikes change, by the death of the woman who needed
and nurtured him. For years, he had watched her slowly die, her illness chipping away small pieces of his own courage, creating small anxieties, worrisome
habits that still linger with him. But he is not a man to live alone; he has

remarried. With his new wife, he can sometimes be found at the cemetery where their respective first spouses are buried. Flat bronze plaques and high white headstones stretch across the green fields. He bends down to clear her grave of grass and dirt. She was, after all, his wife. Actions do, indeed, speak.

QUESTIONS FOR READING AND REVISING

1. What is the dominant impression we get of Barbara Seidel's father in her essay? How does she create this impression? What kind of man is Seidel's father? How does he *define* the role of a father?

2. It is very easy to be sentimental about our parents, but Seidel writes about her father with controlled emotion and restraint. How does she avoid sentimentality? What is the effect of her control?

3. Why do you think Seidel chose to write her tribute in the third person? What advantage does she gain? What effect does this choice have on your reading of her essay? What would have been the difference if she had written her essay in the first person?

4. Seidel uses details very effectively to catch the nuances of her father's behavior. She tells us about his "second-hand shoes stuffed with newspapers" and "the Hershey chocolate bars hidden in the night table drawer." Select details and images you find effective and explain how they support the dominant impression of him that she conveys in her essay.

5. Seidel reports: "The hardest part of writing this paper was establishing order, organizing it so it made sense and did not jump from subject to subject." How does Seidel organize her tribute? Describe what holds the essay together so that it does not "jump from subject to subject."

6. Seidel urges her readers to "read the essay twice. The first time just let yourself be carried along by the rhythm of the words. The second time read the essay just to understand the man." Seidel plays with sentence structure, length, repetition, and rhythm. Which sentences and word choices do you find especially effective? Why?

7. About her *introduction*, Seidel tells us: "The lead paragraph in my first rough draft was simply part of the process of pouring words onto paper. I knew it would have to catch my attention if it would be able to catch the attention of a reader. I knew it did not work." Here is Seidel's rough-draft introduction:

> Actions speak louder than words, he often said. If so,
> then his actions say much about the man. There was that
> moment, thirty years ago, when his father was dying slowly.

He would arise at dawn, leaving his wife and small children
asleep in the tiny house, and drive the distance on quiet
city streets. Years later, his own daughter, puzzled, would
ask why he showed such devotion to the man who divorced
his mother and abandoned him and his brother. He answered, with a faint look of surprise at the question, "He
was my father."

What are the differences between the rough-draft introduction and the final-
draft introduction? How does the revised introduction more successfully introduce and tie together the various ideas in the essay?

SUGGESTIONS FOR WRITING

1. Select someone about whom you would like to write a tribute. It should of
course be someone with whom you are close. Try to *describe* this person's faults
as well as merits to give your reader's complete impression of what he or she
is like.

2. Americans ritually celebrate the relationship between children and parents on
Mother's Day and Father's Day. Analyze your family's particular way of re-
sponding to and celebrating these holidays. What rituals have you created?
What do they express about your family?

3. Write an essay in which you *explain* what you believe are the biggest mistakes
parents make in raising their children. Illustrate your *point of view* with convincing examples.

JOHN S. SIEGRIST

Florence-Darlington Technical College
Florence, South Carolina
Holly Westcott, instructor

"*I come from a military family which meant frequent changes in my life. I grew up in a very liberated and educationally free environment. My mother had a great deal to do with my education and desire to gain knowledge because of her open-mindedness and career as a teacher. I did average work in school until college, where I have maintained grade level for the Dean's List.*"

Born in Greenville, South Carolina, John Siegerist graduated from high school in Lyndon, Kansas, and now lives in Florence, South Carolina. Siegrist remembers his first piece of writing as a hundred-word theme given to the class as punishment. Since then, he has been writing for himself, with the encouragement of his high school and college teachers. About his writing process, Siegrist reports: "*When I write, I sit at a desk or table in a quiet place and appear to be staring at an object. I tap my pencil or rub my forehead a lot if ideas are not coming to my mind quickly enough. Once a good idea comes to mind, I begin brainstorming and then outlining until I have enough ideas for my essay. I suppose it looks like I am in a trance until an idea strikes and then I am a flurry of continuous writing until my basic ideas are all on paper.*"

Asked to write about a process with which he was familiar, Siegrist decided to write about a subject he enjoyed: eating rattlesnake.

For an extended discussion of John Siegrist's work, see Part VI.

Rattlesnake: A Palatable Experience

People usually alienate themselves from things and experiences which are not customary to their lifestyles. They close their minds to ideas which might prove enjoyable if they would only give themselves the opportunity to try something different. This is the kind of resistance met when one mentions the idea of eating rattlesnake.

There are people throughout the world who eat snake and find it not only palatable, but delicious. People eat snake in sandwiches and soups, fried or barbecued. I was fortunate during my Air Force Service to be stationed only thirty miles from the site of the most famous rattlesnake roundup, held annually in Texas. I was able not only to find out how snake meat tastes, but to learn how to catch, skin, and prepare the snake myself.

The first step in tasting fried rattlesnake is to collect the ingredients. While most of these can be found at any grocery store, the main item, the snake, must be sought out in its own habitat. One thing must be said before anyone goes out to catch a rattlesnake: Be careful. A snake is like any other wild animal. It is timid until concerned, but then it will fight to survive with every ounce of energy.

The best areas to look for rattlesnakes are among rock piles, rock fences, heavy brush piles, and abandoned animal burrows. Since one would not want to reach into these places, a flashlight or mirror to reflect the sun into the darkened areas is a necessity. I have heard of people using hoses to pour gasoline into these places, but I feel that method is unsporting and creates an unnecessary fire hazard.

One should take into account the amount of meat needed when looking for a snake. A snake two feet long would be all right for two people. If a family is larger or guests are invited over, a snake four or five feet in length is required. This will save the hostess the embarrassment of not having enough to go around.

Once the proper snake is found, it must be caught. This is usually accomplished through the use of special poles or hooks. The idea is to pull the snake from its place of refuge, use the pole to hold its head against the ground, then reach down and grab the snake behind his head. This gives the person control of the snake and allows it to be dropped into a burlap sack or other suitable container for transporting back to the house.

I am either too smart or too big a coward to attempt this practice. Since I don't like the idea of coming within inches of an animal that has the potential to kill me, I prefer to shoot the snake from a reasonable distance. Any type of firearm will ensure that the snake is dead before it is picked up; however, I use a small caliber handgun because it destroys less meat. I shoot the snake in the head, as the body is the part to be cooked.

The very first thing to do upon killing the rattlesnake is to remove its head using a knife, machete, axe, or even shovel. The fangs still contain poison and even an accidental scratch from them could result in serious medical problems. Once removed, the head should be buried to keep stray animals from eating it and becoming sick.

The snake is now ready to be skinned and gutted. I remove the tail first and then attempt to cut a straight line from one end of its belly to the other end. This is fairly simple unless the snake's muscles are still contracting; then it can be a moving experience! If you find the snake trying to curl around your arm, either wait a little longer to do the skinning or have a friend hold the body still. This may show you who your friends are. A pair of scissors is much easier to use than a knife, but either is fine. It is important to keep the cut shallow and try not to go into the snake's organs, as that would contaminate the meat.

Once the cut is finished, the skin can easily be peeled back on each side of 10 the snake's body. I accomplish this by placing two fingers between the snake's skin and the meat on the body and running my fingers the entire length on both sides of the body. The skin will peel away just like a banana's. The snake skin is worth saving and can be used to make belts, hatbands, belt buckles, and other attractive items.

The gutting procedure is very similar to that of skinning the snake. Place 11 two fingers between the internal cavity and the meat of the snake's inner body. Running your fingers the entire length will remove the guts in one clean and effortless motion.

We now come to the actual preparation of the meat for cooking. There are 12 numerous ways to prepare any meat, and snake is no different. The seasoning is left up to one's personal taste, as is the style of cooking. Snake can be steamed, fried, baked, broiled, or even eaten raw. I prefer mine fried, although I would like to try it barbecued.

Frying rattlesnake is probably quickest and easiest of all the methods to 13 prepare it. The snake must be cut into portions which are easy to work with. I find two- or three-inch lengths adequate. I use a deep fat fryer, and while the oil is getting warm, I prepare the snake pieces. I combine several ingredients, the amounts of which depend upon the number of pieces to be cooked. I mix beaten eggs, pepper, and a little onion salt in a small bowl. I dip the snake pieces into the mixture and then roll them in flour. This gives them a light covering which becomes crunchy when fried.

The oil should be kept at a medium temperature. Too low a setting can 14 cause the snake to fall apart, and too high a setting can cause the flour crust to harden too much. The meat should be placed in the oil and left there for not more than a few minutes. The snake sections are similar to fillets of fish and fry very quickly. Once done, they should be removed to drain any excess oil. They are now ready to serve, and I guarantee everyone will be waiting in anticipation of their first bite of rattlesnake.

Eating rattlesnake is a rather unique experience. It can be served as the 15 main dish or as an appetizer. It is especially suited when one desires a light meal or a refreshing change from beef, pork, chicken, or fish. Using a fork to eat fried snake is almost useless, and one must rely upon the most basic of eating utensils, the fingers.

The taste of rattlesnake meat has a flavor all its own, close to that of 16 armadillo. Since most people have not tried armadillo, I would describe it as somewhat like turtle meat. I won't lie and say it tastes like chicken because it doesn't. It is a meat with a very mild flavor, possibly just a little sweet. I can only verify that it does taste exceptionally delicious.

I know most people will not have the opportunity or inclination to eat 17 rattlesnake, but if the chance should arise, try it. The taste is surprisingly good, and the experience may open your mind to other culinary delights which you have previously rejected. Forget about those ideas you have of snakes, and think of fried rattlesnake as one more way to experience life's variety of food.

QUESTIONS FOR READING AND REVISING

1. How does John Siegrist make the subject of eating rattlesnake interesting? What specific sentences in his essay help you to understand why this process fascinates him?

2. What does Siegrist assume about his readers knowledge? How does he anticipate and control his readers' expectations? Why, for instance, does he say: "I won't lie and say it tastes like chicken because it doesn't"?

3. Into how many steps does Siegrist break down the *process* he analyzes? What are these steps? Why are they presented in chronological order? How does Siegrist indicate to his readers when one stage of the process stops and the next begins.

4. Could you follow Siegrist's process? Or is this his *purpose* in writing the essay?

5. Describe Siegrist's *tone*. Do you think he is having fun writing about eating rattlesnake? Point out specific words and phrases to support your views.

6. Do you find Siegrist's *introduction* effective? What would be the effect on the essay if this introductory paragraph were deleted?

7. Siegrist shifts from using *one*, to *I*, to *you*. As a reader, does this shift in person bother you? Why? Would complete consistency be desirable? Which person— one, I, or you—seems the most natural?

8. Look at paragraph 13. Rewrite this paragraph to combine sentences, simplify and add greater variety.

SUGGESTIONS FOR WRITING

1. In his essay, Siegrist analyzes the *process* of cooking and eating rattlesnake, an experience most of us are unfamiliar with. Write an essay analyzing a process with which you are familiar but which may not be familiar to most people; for

example, something from your life as a student, a daughter, a parent, etc. or from your work. Detail the process step by step.

2. Using a humorous *tone,* write an essay in which you offer advice to someone. Some possible topics might include how to belly dance, how to write an A paper, how to get rich, how to raise a child, how to lose weight, etc.

3. Write an essay in which you describe in detail the process of preparing and eating a meal (or any ritual) in which every member of the family participates. Describe not only the nature of the process, but also all the sensual and emotional experiences involved.

KIM SPORT

Our Lady of Holy Cross College
New Orleans, Louisiana
Sister Rose Elizabeth Brown, instructor

Kim sport's ideal writing environment is one without distractions. When she writes, she sees no visitors and accepts no phone calls. About her writing, Sport reports: "I used to try to avoid writing, but now I consider it a challenge. Today I have so much to say about so many things that I look forward to sharing my opinions with others. Writing is a fantastic way for me to gather my thoughts together and resolve problems. Learning to write is the most important element of our education. The ability to write is a measure of a person's qualifications. One should always be proud of what and how she writes."

Sport, a nationally registered X-ray and nuclear medicine technologist, plans to graduate with a degree in health sciences and begin law school at Tulane University. Born in New Orleans, Sport grew up in Gretna, Louisiana. Her hobbies include skiing, sailing, and reading.

Asked to write a persuasive essay, Sport says that her personal feelings about capital punishment promoted her to select this subject for her essay.

Capital Punishment

The average American runs a higher risk of being a victim of violent crime 1
than of being hurt in an auto accident. This is the finding of a study done by the Justice Department's Bureau of Justice Statistics (*U.S. News and World Report*, 12 Dec. 1983: 72) It seems as though crime, rape, and murder are becoming ways of life for many people. To deal with crime, America has become a country on the defense. Airports are equipped with weapon scanners; banks are equipped with electronic security devices; individuals carry Mace or guns and equip their homes with security systems and multiple locks. We have started fingerprinting our children because we are afraid someone will kidnap them, and we have started neighborhood watch programs to prevent crime around our homes. The rise in crime can be blamed on many factors, but the main factor is that the punishment for criminal activity has become very lenient. People are not afraid to commit violent crimes. Criminals are comforted by a legal process that is more concerned with their rights than the rights of their victims, life sentences with parole, plea bargaining, and the availability of appellate courts. Criminals deserve punishment for their crimes, and the worst crimes deserve the worst punishment—capital punishment. The act of capital punishment is a point of great controversy in the United States,

and there are those who are pushing for its abolishment. Capital punishment should not be abolished because: it deters crime, unburdens tax payers, prevents overcrowded jails, and provides absolute justice to society in certain cases.

Not everyone feels that capital punishment is necessary. The opponents of capital punishment have raised three major arguments against it. First, opponents consider capital punishment to be cruel and unusual punishment, and therefore, a violation of the Eighth Amendment. Proponents of capital punishment realize that the Constitution forbids cruel and unusual punishment but do not believe that capital punishment falls into this category. The Eighth Amendment was ratified in the eighteenth century to prevent the punishments practiced at that time. These included public hangings, burnings, decapitations, mutilations, torture, and dragging criminals by horses through towns. Nowhere does the Eighth Amendment prohibit the death penalty, which proponents feel is a civilized punishment when compared to the atrocities committed by those sentenced to death. The second argument against capital punishment is that Christianity forbids it in the words "Thou shalt not kill." Proponents of the death penalty feel that the biblical "eye for an eye" is an argument for capital punishment on the grounds that it is fitting and just, and Jesus' dictum, "All who take the sword will perish by the sword," makes clear that the death penalty for murder still stands. Opponents of capital punishment feel, third, that capital punishment is as much a crime as any other reason for taking a human life. The logical argument presented by proponents of the death penalty is that murder is illegal and capital punishment is not. If capital punishment isn't illegal, then it cannot be murder. Clearly, capital punishment is an emotional and moral issue, but to abolish capital punishment will not solve the problems of crime, overcrowded jails, increasing taxes, and those who demand justice for the offenses committed against them.

Capital punishment addresses the crime problem because capital punishment deters crime. Ernest van den Haag of Fordham University believes that "nobody fears prison as much as death." Economist Isaac Ehrlich built a "supply and demand" theory of murder and argued that capital punishment prevents more murders than prison sentences. Because of the 3,411 executions carried out from 1933 to 1967, Ehrlich speculates that enough potential murderers were discouraged that some 27,000 victims lives were saved (*Time*, 24 Jan. 1983: 35). Repeat offenders prove that prison does not deter crime. For example, Charles Manson, who was arrested many times and was convicted of murder, is eligible for parole next year. His cult is waiting for him. Are we to believe that Manson will find a job and settle down with a wife and children? If Manson gets out, is there any reason that he should fear our judicial and criminal systems? I think not. If the death penalty were properly carried out, crime would be deterred even more, but criminals can see that the 1,289 people presently on death row may be alive for a long time (*Time*, 6 Feb. 1984: 56). Criminals must be made to fear the consequences of their actions, and capital punishment, properly carried out, can accomplish this.

While criminals sit on death row or serve life sentences for their offenses   4 to society, society supports them with its tax dollars. A person whose wife and children were murdered pays for the murderer's food, clothing, and shelter. Isn't something wrong here? These criminals are obligated to give nothing back to society. This situation is not only unfair, but it is a waste of precious funds that could be allocated to those in dire need of food, clothing, and shelter. Ted Guest of *U.S. News and World Report* (2 May 1983: 42) says that "the current cost of $20,000 yr. to keep the nearly 500,000 U.S. prisoners locked up is twice as much as the cost to send a child to Stanford University." Also, our judicial system allows for numerous appeals by death row inmates, and last year, the New York State Defenders Association estimated the typical trial costs for death penalty cases to be 1.5 million dollars each (*Time*, 24 Jan. 1983: 39). This money is being wasted on society's worst offenders. Capital punishment would put an end to this travesty of justice.

Capital punishment, while deterring crime, would also prevent jail over-   5 crowding, which has in itself become a serious problem. Opponents of capital punishment favor life sentences at $20,000 a year for criminals over the death penalty, but where are we going to put them? A Justice Department Bureau of Statistics' study concluded that "in actual numbers, prisons held nearly one-half million inmates in mid 1983—more than double [that] of a decade earlier" (*U.S. News and World Report*, 12 Dec. 1983: 72). There is no more room for prisoners; cities have resorted to tents in some cases, and in a terrible situation in New York, a judge ordered the release of 610 prisoners at Attica Institute to relieve prison overcrowding (*Time*, 5 Dec. 1983: 65). To build new prisons is outrageously expensive, with costs approximated at $70 billion for every 100,000 beds. These costs do not even include the costs to operate and staff the prisons. Why should capital offenders be allowed to take up badly needed prison space?

Realistically, capital offenders deserve to die. Their crimes are so horrendous   6 that the only comparable punishment is death. For example, on the night of June 3, 1973, Henry Brisbon, along with three other men, forced a woman off the road. Brisbon ordered her to strip at gun point, then as she begged for mercy, he thrust his gun into her vagina and fired. The woman died after another shot to the throat. As if this were not enough, Brisbon and his friends stopped another car carrying a young engaged couple. He made them lay down on the shoulder of the road and told them to "Kiss your last kiss," then he shot them both in the back. This case, as reported in *Time*'s "An Eye for an Eye" (24 Jan. 1983: 30) was accompanied by another case which should convince even the staunchest opponent of capital punishment to reconsider his position. Lawrence Bittaker is on death row at San Quentin. He and a friend kidnapped, raped, and sodomized five teenage girls for days at a time in front of a camera. Bittacker tortured the girls by using pliers on their nipples and icepicks in their ears; he recorded their screams. He killed all of them, but did something special to the last victim—he strangled her with a coat hanger, mutilated her genitals, then placed her body on a lawn so he could watch the reactions of its discoverers. Repulsively, both Brisbon and Bittaker complain of their prison conditions and think that they do not deserve to die. Regrettably, because of legal red tape, they never will. These men are not insane. They are as sane as the 1,287 others on death row who are guilty of such disgusting acts that the only retribution is their death.

Society should never have to worry that capital offenders such as Manson, Bittaker, and Brisbon are allowed back on the streets, but this is the greatest consequence of the abolishment of capital punishment. Only ten of our fifty states have adopted statutes which abolish parole. This means that in forty states the Bittakers, Mansons, and Brisbons could be freed on parole. If not paroled, capital offenders will continue to be supported by a society at the cost of $20,000 a year each or 257.8 million dollars a year for capital offenders alone. Simply, the abolishment of capital punishment means fear and increased taxes. It is time for innocent Americans to live without fear. Capital punishment is the only way to put fear where it belongs—with those who intend to harm others.

QUESTIONS FOR READING AND REVISING

1. What is Kim Sport's *thesis?* How does she use her thesis to organize her essay? How does she build her *argument?*
2. Do you find Sport's *argument* convincing? Explain by pointing to specific strengths or weaknesses you see in the evidence Sport provides. What issues does she not address?
3. As a reader, how do you know that Sport has a strong opinion on the topic? Describe Sport's *tone.* Does she seem reasonable and believable to you?
4. How does Sport pull you into the world of her essay? Why do you think she refers in her *introduction* to fingerprinting children, burglar alarm systems, and

neighborhood watch programs? What assumptions does she make about her readers' position on capital punishment?

5. In paragraph 3, Sport provides the opinions of two experts who agree with her position. Has she proved her point? How could an opponent refute her? What further evidence does she need?

6. One of Sport's strategies is to present the position of opponents of capital punishment. If she is a proponent of capital punishment, why does she give the opponent's point of view? What does she gain by using this strategy? Is it effective?

7. Why does Sport choose the dramatic examples of Manson, Brisborn, and Bittacker to make her point? What effect did these examples have on you? Why are these effective examples? Why not?

8. Sport reports; "To read my essay, one must separate thoughts on religion from those on law. Even if my readers believe in the 'Thou shalt not kill' commandment, I want them to consider the victims and not the capital offenders themselves." Was Sport successful in achieving her goal?

SUGGESTIONS FOR WRITING

1. Think of an unjust situation that directly affects you in school, in your family or community, or at work. Write a *persuasive* essay in which you present your reasons for believing this situation unjust. Recommend changes to eliminate the injustice.

2. What is your opinion on capital punishment? Do you agree with Sport's ideas? Write a response to Sport's essay in which you either refute her arguments to support them with additional evidence.

3. Write a persuasive essay on a change you would like to see or an opinion you want to defend. Imagine that your readers disagree with your *point of view*.

FRANCES E. TAYLOR

Hunter College
New York, New York
Louise A. DeSalvo, instructor

"My earliest recollections are of writing squiggly lines, and asking my sister if my squiggly lines said anything. She would say, 'What are you trying to say?' And I would say, 'I love you and I'd like to go outside, and can we play with my toys.' She would say, 'You said it!' and then give me a big hug and say 'That's very good Frances.' "

Frances Taylor, born in Brooklyn, New York, describes her background as a working-class Afro-American family. Her interests include composing for guitar, reading, leather work, carpentry, and minority histories. She plans to write, teach, advocate issues relating to disenfranchised people, and pursue a degree in law.

Taylor reports that there were always books in her home from as early as she can remember. From these books she learned to love the written word. Taylor describes writing as "crafting power" and she advises fellow writers: "There is no voice on earth like your own, and that equals power, learn to craft it, and read, read, read."

Taylor's assignment was to write about her first encounter with someone who had made an impact on her life. About her essay, Taylor tells us: "In writing this essay I got in touch with a very important part of my life that I had been trying to write about for years and had not been able to. I wanted my audience to be moved and to think about my experience, even though it was unique and perhaps, to some, bizarre. I ask that my readers bring their humanity to the reading of my essay."

Carol

She had a moustache, shiny and black against her brown skin. Her front 1 teeth were outlined with gold fillings—I later learned she hated that—but it didn't keep her from smiling. She wanted you to know she saw you, felt you, was listening to you.

She made a hissing sound when she laughed—as if in preparation for an 2 explosion; but she always stopped just before the lid flew off or the sound got too loud. Her body was chestnut brown and sensual, yet tense somehow—as if unhappiness, anger, some long-ago buildup of feeling was locked inside. She wore a red tank top tucked in close to her body. I was immediately afraid of her. She seemed so hot skillet sizzly and those eyes sparkled and caught you like a light out for moths.

I was a recluse rescued by a bookmobile librarian who had a head full of 3 Gerard Manley Hopkins and Sara Teasdale and a heart for the odd. I noticed

Carol because I'd just come to my first lesbian dance at a Daughters of Bilitis meeting room cum dance hall in a musty Prince Street warehouse with a peeling facade. A gypsy lady with spangles and rouge kept telling me to be attentive for bells and cymbals and some great shocking quality in the air in case the woman I dreamed of came through the door. But Carol met someone else that night; another firstcomer just as new and intimidated as I.

The loft was dark, filled with cigarette smoke and cheap soda cans bent and   4 used for ashtrays. Soda stains and beer puddles dotted the splintered, gray-dirt planking of the warped wooden floor. Some lone wailing love song for her and her new love to remember each other and the night by—maybe Roberta Flack— poured from the juke. I hid behind the sticky counter selling orange and grape drinks and colas that were tucked down in the melting ice filling the huge green plastic garbage pail. A skinny Caucasian, dressed all in black—hot pants over leotards—with dyed black hair and insect wings growing out of her eyelids, kept offering me bright red kisses in payment for the drinks and flapping the lids and leaning forward on one elbow, tapping on my cheek with thin red talons.

Carol invited me to stay in New York that night, driven to West 46th   5 Street by her new love with the riding habit in the boot of her Volvo station wagon. Her social worker love was a granddaughter of Philadelphia's black elite "who taught me to respect my elders and how to sit at table." A Roller Derby aspirant when in her teens, she'd somehow cooled her heft and swagger by her student travels up the Mediterranean and down some Elysées. "What have we here?" said Carol admiring all this self-sufficiency. "What a prize!" The "prize" moved her tennis racket and riding boots, the black velvet domed hat, crop, training manuals, feminist books, *Woman Sports* magazines—and made room in the back for me—escapee from under a bed in Queens.

In flight from that spirit-corset in Queens, I moved into Carol's tiny two   6 rooms and slept on the floor with a finicky Doberman in the tight space used for storage. Carol always walked around in black lace panties, smoking her cigarettes, sipping strong drink and mud-black coffee and fighting with her memories. Her breasts and the rest of her body were firm and full and her underarms smelled like flowers.

She used to turn her pointing index fingers around each other as though   7 she were outlining a cylinder when she talked intensely—and as she did it that first morning a light came on like the corona over El Greco's *Toledo* and then snapped off. I loved her fully from then on. I can remember the exact moment. "I feel as if life has chipped away at me—that's why I left my job . . . I couldn't work anymore—but there's still some part of who I really am left in the center of my being. I try to keep it safe" (she hunched her shoulders and spoke in a whisper, pointing at her heart) "guarding it here—in the center of my being." I got a flash of the lay of the land of her soul and never saw anything that mattered but that part of her ever again.

Somehow I became a communications link between her and the "prize," 8 like Elmer's glue, I thought. My pride in being needed encouraged them to manipulate each other through me. I convinced myself I was the lover she'd love if she didn't love the lover she had. But as she drifted with the "prize" she tried any port in her storm, any port but me.

Her vacations home from Mary MacCloud Bethune's campus in Georgia 9 she spent ironing, washing, and cooking for the college boys in the family. "And don't you know they laughed and watched the ball games and thought it was their due!" She'd spend hours shifting canvases she's stretched and filled, rearranging her small apartment, putting blue hospital sheets on the two mattresses stacked on the floor. She told me about the husband whom she'd left, who was just like her brothers, and then about the woman in her life and how strong she felt in her Florida beach house with the twin brandy-hued Dobermans and the narrowed-down and hollowed-out blonde and the blonde's two kids, and the shake-up-the-world sex. That lover left her for an importunating older woman, a bigot with a laundromat in a nearby town.

Examining her painting of a nude black woman one day, she said, "She has 10 no life, has she? Look! She's static, dead!" and ripped into it with her palette knife so the head hung down, brown and floppy.

Many months later. She called me from Florida after her breakup with the 11 "prize" and told me she'd been "hexed" out of New York but wanted to come back. She was missing *my* ex this time. I said, "And what about me, Carol? You're like a sorry old voice from the past—with bad news. . . ." She hung-up on me—four o'clock in the morning—all the way from Delray.

Three months later. The "prize" called to tell me Carol had shot herself in 12 a women's commune on the South Side of Chicago. And that's what I can't forget. She's all dead and blown apart someplace with the last words from me bitter ones.

Back in Florida, her father, the landscape gardener, and her mother, the 13 nursing instructor, have become Seventh Day Adventists and made her bedroom into a little shrine. Her paintings, some of her photographs, and maybe fresh-cut flowers are kept there. And maybe it smells just a little bit like Carol.

QUESTIONS FOR READING AND REVISING

1. In writing this essay, Frances Taylor tells us: "I felt that I had cracked a code, and that the code was my own voice. I was connecting my voice with my work in a way that I didn't think was possible." Taylor's voice is authentic and we

feel and hear the presence of the writer in her essay. What effect does her clear, authentic voice have on your reading of her essay? How do you know that she is writing about a subject that is very close to her?

2. What overall impression does Taylor create of Carol? What *unifies* Taylor's description?

3. This essay is rich in detail. As readers, we feel the presence of the writer working hard to describe what Carol meant to her. Select details and images that you find especially effective and show how these details support the writer's *purpose.*

4. Taylor uses dialogue very effectively. What does the dialogue reveal about Carol? About the writer herself?

5. Taylor begins her description immediately without any introductory comments. What is the effect of beginning this way? What is the effect of referring to Carol as "she" and "her" before we know her name? How does Taylor succeed in bringing you into the world of her essay?

6. For what *audience* is Taylor writing her essay? She tells us that she wrote her first draft without thinking about a reader and that is why she was able to write about such personal things withoug being blocked. Does Taylor seem to be aware of her audience in her final draft? Find evidence in the essay to support your answer.

SUGGESTIONS FOR WRITING

1. Write about a person in your own life who has made an impact on you and about whom you feel strongly. Describe your initial encounter with this person.

2. What is friendship? Henry Adams tells us: "One friend in a lifetime is much; two are many; three are hardly possible." And Montesquieu: "Friendship is an arrangement by which we undertake to exchange small favors for big ones." Write an essay in which you *explain* the concept of friendship. You might want to use a dramatic personal experience as one of your *examples* to illustrate your *thesis.*

GREG WEEKES

University of Central Florida
Orlando, Florida
Gerald Schiffhorst, instructor

Life and work at sea have figured prominently in Greg Weekes's life. The son of a Navy captain, Weekes was born in Corpus Christi, Texas, and has lived with his family in Europe and the Middle East: "Being in a Navy family and living almost all over the world has greatly influenced my life." A graduate of Rogers High School in Newport, Rhode Island, where he earned nine varsity letters in track and cross-country, Weekes worked as a deckhand and as chief mate on east coast charter boats before enrolling at the University of Central Florida, where he majors in science education and plans to teach high school biology.

"When I get a good idea my mind just keeps going, and I find I can't write fast enough. I have a hard time writing when the idea isn't there. But when I get a brainstorm on a story, it flows out like water." Weekes wrote only one draft of the following essay, in which he contrasts the tranquility of a whale in calm Alaskan waters to an account of the violent death of a whale "Off the Grand Banks." His essay seeks "to show others the horror of the modern whale hunt and to impress upon my readers that the 'romance' of the eighteenth-century whale hunt is gone."

Off the Grand Banks . . .

Picture, if you can, a dark blue fjord in Alaska. The snowcapped mountains 1
rise high into the sky around the water, and their reflection is clear on the
still surface. Patches of evergreen trees top the shoreline, and all you can hear
is the cold silence of a still spring day. One lone whale suddenly breaks the
glassy surface of the day, coming up for some air. Just the tip of its head shows,
and soon the air is alive with spray. As it dives again you catch a glimpse of
its tail, strong and powerful, speckled with barnacles. The huge fin slips silently
beneath the water, and you think the whale is gone. But it soon comes up
again, this time in an almost perpendicular position with the surface. Its face
has long white scars all under what would be its chin, probably from raking
the muddy bottom searching for food. Or maybe they're reminders of a fierce
battle, long forgotten by both combatants. Its large brown eye reminds you of
a lonely hound dog, and its mouth is curved into what looks like an eternal
grin—a seductive sort of smile. It slides gracefully back into the water the
same way it came, leaving barely a ripple on the mirrorlike surface.

The same whale, the one you had admired so much, the one so free and ₂
happy, could be the same whale in this story—a story not of whales, but of
men.

I had been crew on the selling ship *Valhalla,* and we were about three- ₃
hundred miles offshore in an area called the Grand Banks. The wind was calm
and the sea placid as we made our way east. It was getting late in the day, so
the captain ordered us to take down the jib and reef the main.

In the process I heard what sounded like gunfire in the distance. I wasn't ₄
the only one who had heard it, as a few of the other deckhands cocked their
heads curiously, taking note of the strange booming.

Looking in the direction of the sound, we saw a dark voluminous cloud of ₅
smoke billowing out of a ship, with many smaller waves breaking around its
bow.

"Whaleship—probably Russian," the first mate told me. Very few of us had ₆
ever seen one, and it was nothing like I had expected as it neared our boat.

It was an enormous vessel, painted red with large rust spots dotting the ₇
hull. I grabbed some binoculars from below and saw the gunman; he was aiming
a lethal-looking barbed weapon at the water in front of him. The whales were
running in a panic toward us and as the ship got closer a female humpback,
surfacing to get air, gave its position away by expelling its blowhole. The
harpoon sunk in deep, and the whale suddenly dived. The line connecting
the animal to the ship tightened, and a plume of blood-red water filled the air
above the whale as the grenade-tipped harpoon detonated. The whale surfaced
again, and blew out its blowhole a tall geyser of blood. When she rolled over,
we saw where the explosive had left its mark. Exposed flesh cut a gaping hole
at least ten feet wide above its fin, leaving a huge depression in the side of
the whale. Blood started to rush into the hole and changed it from stark white
to a pool of red. She took one last dive, and when she came up again all the
blood had been washed away. As the sea around the whale was reddening, we
heard a small cry. Then she rolled on her side, never to dive again.

As the ship moved in to process the whale, men with small rifles opened ₈
fire into the water all around it. Sharks from miles away had sensed the blood
and were tearing huge chunks out of the dead whale. The sea around the whale
was soon churning with sharks, all hoping for an easy meal.

Slowly the whale was hauled onto the ship, its carcass limp on the slanted ₉
floor of the processing deck. We could almost smell the stench as the sun
baked the slaughtered animal. The sharks, still crazed with the smell of blood,
had started to attack themselves and were moving away from the area. Some
sharks had remained attached to the whale even onto the deck and were beaten

to bloody pulps by husky crew members, no doubt to end up on that night's dinner table.

The whale doesn't grin as it lies on the deck; the seductive smile is gone. 10 Its sad brown eyes have been plucked out by scavenging seagulls, and its barnacled tail, useless to man, has been thrown back into the water.

Some say that its usefulness to man is just beginning. And some, thinking 11 of a clear blue inlet on a certain spring day, say it has just ended. But the man who killed it will never know for sure. It probably never bothered him before. Because, you see, he knows only one side of the story.

QUESTIONS FOR READING AND REVISING

1. How would you define Greg Weekes's *purpose* in this essay? Is it to highlight the contrast between describing the tranquility of a whale's surfacing in a "fjord in Alaska" and narrating the violence of a whale hunt? Something else? How does Weekes's essay move beyond either *description* or *narration* to express some larger governing idea? What is the idea that governs this essay?

2. In paragraph 2, Weekes notes that this is *not* an account "of whales, but of men." What function does the paragraph serve in the essay? How, specifically, does Weekes's essay fulfill the expectation created in this paragraph? How do the paragraphs that follow demonstrate that this is indeed an account "not of whales, but of men"?

3. Analyze the structure of the essay. Identify its distinct parts. How does Weekes *unify* them? What order does he establish? Specific to general, general to specific, concrete to abstract, abstract to concrete, increasing importance, increasing complexity, step-by-step, something else?

4. What is the effect of Weekes's extended description in paragraph 1? How does the opening paragraph contribute to the overall purpose of his essay? In your judgment, could—or should—the first paragraph be eliminated? Why? Why not?

5. Effective description uses *concrete*, sensory details. List the instances when Weekes appeals to each of his readers's five senses in his *description* of a whale in "a fjord in Alaska" and in his account of the whale hunt off the Grand Banks? Point to specific words and phrases to support your responses.

6. Effective description also uses clear *point of view*, the perspective from which a story is told or a scene is described. Show how Weekes's point of view either

changes or remains consistent as the essay proceeds. Rewrite paragraph 7 (on killing the whale) from the point of view of the "gunman" on board the whaling ship.

7. What assumptions does Weekes make about his audience's familiarity with his setting? With whale hunting? What does Weekes assume about his audience's attitude toward each subject? How much background information is necessary to appreciate the overall point of his essay? How much background information does he provide? What, for example, is the purpose—and the effect—of Weekes's use of the phrase "if you can" in the opening line of the essay?

8. At several points in the essay, Weekes introduces technical details from life at sea ("jib," "reef the main," "wale," etc.). In what specific ways do you think technical *diction* adds to or detracts from the essay? How does Weekes use these terms to increase or diminish his intended effect? How does he make sure that his audience will not be distracted from or put off by unfamiliar language?

9. Show how Weekes's *narrative* of killing the whale does or does not prepare readers for the points he makes in the final two paragraphs of his essay. Suggest how Weekes might revise this narrative to strengthen the overall purpose of his essay.

SUGGESTIONS FOR WRITING

1. One of the reasons for the success of Greg Weekes's essay is the *contrast* he creates between the tranquility of watching the performance of a whale and the violent spectacle of the whale hunt. Choose some aspect of contemporary American life—traveling by train, ship, or plane; attending a Sunday afternoon doubleheader at the ballpark, etc.—and write an essay in which you combine *description* and *narration* to highlight the *contrast* between the pleasure, and at times the serenity, associated with an activity and the possibility that the activity might well be engulfed in violence at any moment.

2. Weekes talks about the "gaping hole" left in the whale's side by the explosion of a "grenade-tipped harpoon"—surely a far different procedure for killing whales than that practiced by, say, Captain Ahab and his crew in Herman Melville's *Moby-Dick*. Consider the process of doing some kind of work that has been transformed in recent years by technology. Write an expository essay *comparing and contrasting* the past and the present processes. Exactly what changes in procedure have occurred, and what are the short-term and long-term consequences.

3. In the opening paragraph of his essay, Weekes depicts a place where the natural

world and people seem to be completely at peace. Do you know such a place, some location in the contemporary world that you feel still reflects such a peaceful relationship? Describe its distinctive characteristics in detail. Then write an essay in which you use your detailed *description* as the basis for making some larger point about preserving such a relationship between people and the natural environment.

STEVE WEST

Columbia University
New York, New York
Laura Novo, instructor

"After I receive an assignment, I often mull it over while doing other things (like jogging) and most of my ideas for my essays come up during this period. Once I get started, I jot down an outline, often in the margin of some other piece of paper, and try to write the introduction. A person who walked in on me during this stage would probably see me with my feet up on the desk, chewing on a pencil or tugging on my hair, and trying to get the paper started. If he looked over my shoulder, he would probably see two or three sentence fragments of introductions that I had abandoned quickly, and probably a doodle or two in the margin. Somewhere near the bottom of the page would begin an introduction that seemed good enough for the moment."

Steve West reports that he enjoys writing analytical pieces and feels that his ability at analytical thought has shaped both his writing and his interest in debate. West was named one of eighteen John Jay Scholars in the Columbia College Class of 1988. He is a reporter for the student newspaper, the Spectator, and spends from fifteen to thirty hours a week writing for the newspaper. West plans to major in history and is thinking about a career in law.

Asked to write an essay in which he analyzed one of the sources he planned to use for his research paper, West chose to analyze Jeane Kirpatrick's speech to the United Nations since "it was the most thorough and well thought out of the Reagan administration's statements on the Grenada invasion." West explains: "Before writing my essay I had already done a considerable amount of research on the Grenada invasion, and I had some idea of what were the disputable facts in Kirkpatrick's speech. A close reading of her speech and an examination of it in light of the other information I had gathered were the bases of my attacks on her reasoning."

Evaluating U.S. Motives
for the Grenada Invasion

Following the U.S. invasion of Grenada in October, 1983, the United 1
Nations General Assembly adopted a resolution condemning the invasion and
calling for the immediate withdrawal of United States troops. The measure
passed, however, before the United States was allowed to present its case, and
in "The U.N. and Grenada: A Speech Never Delivered," U.S. Ambassador
Jeane Kirkpatrick outlines the arguments she had hoped to present in defense
of the invasion. Although her article is probably the most comprehensive

defense of the invasion advanced by any administration official, her arguments suffer from factual distortions and omissions and from their inconsistency with much of United States policy in Central and South America (11–18).

Kirkpatrick provides four different justifications for the invasion. The first 2 (and the one most stressed by administration officials at the time of the invasion) is the possibility that Americans on the island might have been harmed or taken hostage in the upheaval that followed the assassination of Maurice Bishop. She cites the twenty-four-hour shoot-on-sight curfew imposed by the new regime as an example of the threat facing U.S. citizens. She also maintains that the government failed to fulfill its promise to open the airport to foreigners wishing to leave and concludes that the threat facing Americans on the island was "real and imminent."

Kirkpatrick's analysis seems valid on the basis of the evidence she presents, 3 but she ignores a number of facts that suggest that the Americans were in little danger and could have been evacuated without an invasion. The shoot-on-sight curfew, for example, was lifted the day before the invasion, and Americans at the St. George's University Medical School resumed classes the same day (Kenworthy 637). Charles Modica, head of the medical school, was in contact with U.S. officials several times before the invasion and informed them that only 10 percent of his students wished to be evacuated (Kenworthy 637). Furthermore, the airport was not closed, as Kirkpatrick charges; the single commercial airline servicing the island refused to send its aircraft to Grenada, but chartered planes did remove over thirty foreigners (Americans among them) on October 24, and State Department officials were arranging with the government for the evacuation of other Americans (Kenworthy 638). These facts suggest that whatever instability did exist after the October 19 coup had largely abated before the American invasion six days later.

Kirkpatrick's second justification for the invasion is the threat that Grenada 4 posed to other nations in the region and to American security interests. She quotes Jamaican Prime Minister Edward Seaga, who pointed to the presence of Cuban advisors and to the soon-to-be-completed Pt. Salines airstrip as proof of Grenada's threatening military buildup. After the invasion, Kirkpatrick charges, huge stockpiles of weapons and contracts for future arms shipments were discovered, further justifying fears of Grenadian aggression.

One of this justification's major flaws is the fact that much of the evidence 5 on which it is based—evidence about the stockpiles of weapons and the arms transfer agreements—was not discovered until after the invasion and therefore could not have played any role in the initial decision to intervene. In addition, much of the evidence on which the administration did act is not very compelling. Before the invasion, for example, the administration acknowledged in a telegram to Fidel Castro that the Cubans on the island were a mix of poorly armed military advisors and construction workers, hardly a force that posed a significant threat to either U.S. or regional security ("Truth" 678).

And what about the Pt. Salines airstrip? Kirkpatrick insists that it was to 6 have been a military institution but ignores the plausibility of the Grenadian explanation that tourist airliners and not military jets were intended users of the facility. In fact, the latter explanation seems more consistent with the history and design of the facility. The airstrip was not, for example, a primarily Cuban project; funding was provided by the International Monetary fund and by the British, whose contractors also did much of the work (Kenworthy 642). After the invasion, Plessey, one of the British contractors, published a list of eleven features (including military radar and fuel storage tanks) necessary for a military airstrip but lacked by the Pt. Salines facility (Massing 82). Finally, the length of the new airstrip (9,000 feet versus the 4,300-foot runway of the old airport) was a result of the government's desire to accommodate the largest commercial airliners; the shorter length of the old facility required tourists to transfer to smaller planes for the last leg of their trip to Grenada, and the government hoped that direct flights would boost tourism (Massing 82).

Kirkpatrick also justifies the invasion as a legitimate response to requests 7 made by six Caribbean nations and by Grenada's Governor General, Paul Scoon. Arguing that Grenada's military buildup represented a threat to regional security, she concludes that the request of the four members of the Organization of Eastern Caribbean States (Barbados and Jamaica participated in the invasion but are not OECS members) was legal under the OECS charter. In addition, she notes that Scoon's request carried "exceptional moral and legal weight" because he was the only figure of legitimate political authority on the island.

Closer scrutiny of the facts and of international law, however, finds these 8 justifications seriously lacking in credibility. Under the OECS charter, all seven members of the organization must approve any military action undertaken in its name, but only four members sanctioned or participated in the invasion (Joyner 137). Furthermore, the charter allows a military response only in the event of external aggression against a member nation, but the upheaval in Grenada was an internal affair and posed little genuine threat to regional security (Joyner 136). Kirkpatrick also overstates the impact of Scoon's request; the Governor General was stripped of all but ceremonial duties when the country's constitution was rewritten in 1979, and in any event, his request did not reach U.S. officials until thirty-six hours after they had already begun drawing up plans for the invasion (Joyner 139).

Kirkpatrick's final justification for the invasion is the need to restore de- 9 mocracy to the island after the October 19 coup. The ambassador charges that the Grenadians were subjected to a "brutal reign of terror" before the October 25 invasion and that the nation was in danger of becoming a Soviet/Cuban satellite. The invasion, Kirkpatrick says, restored democracy to the island and won the overwhelming support of the Grenadians.

The major flaw in this argument is its inconsistency with much of U.S. 10 policy in Central and South America; the administration seems to have done a rather abrupt about-face from its former insensitivity to regional coups. In the spring of 1982, for example, the administration responded to a right-wing military coup in Guatemala with an offer of a \$4 million arms sale ("Generals" 29), and in a situation remarkably similar to that in Grenada, the United States stood silently by in November, 1982, when a group of Marxist military officials overthrew the legitimate government of Surinam and instituted their own bloody reign of terror (Dew 6). Kirkpatrick's fear that Grenada would have lost its national identity to the Cubans or Soviets seems exaggerrated given the limited extent of their involvement on the island and is somewhat ironic given the administration's much greater involvement in Honduras and El Salvador. Apparently, the administration's concern is not so much with sovereignty per se as with the possibility that a nation might lose its sovereignty to the wrong superpower.

Interestingly, recent Administration statements about Grenada have largely 11 ignored Kirkpatrick's arguments. President Reagan, for example, declared last spring that the invasion marked the end of the "doom and defeatism" of the Vietnam era, and George Bush sounded the same note last fall in his debate with Geraldine Ferraro, describing the invasion as a "proud, proud moment for America and democracy." Such statements, coupled with the inadequacy of Kirkpatrick's justifications, suggest that the real motives of the invasion may have been to boost American morale and to reestablish America's role as a police officer to its southern neighbors. In a sense, the administration's presentation of its motives for the invasion resembles its handling of factual information about the affair; just as the truth about the invasion and the situation on the island emerged slowly, after much of the fighting had ended and public interest had dwindled, so the invasion was initially justified with talk about rights and the threat of violence and aggression, leaving the less honorable but more important motives to be acknowledged only when the act was over and almost forgotten.

Works Cited

Dew, Edward. "Surinam Tar Baby: The Signature of Terror." *Caribbean Review* 12 (Spring 1983): p. 6.
"The Generals Take Over." *Time* 5 April 1982: p. 29.

Joyner, Christopher. "The United States Action in Grenada—Reflections on the Lawfulness of
    the Invasion." *American Journal of International Law* 78 (January 1984): 136–139.
Kenworthy, Eldon. "Grenada as Theater." *World Policy Journal* 1 (Spring 1984): 637.
Kirkpatrick. Jeane. "The U.N. and Grenada: A Speech Never Delivered." *Strategic Review* 12
    (Winter 1984): 11–18.
Massing, Michael. "Grenada Before and After." *Atlantic Monthly* Feb. 1984: 76–87.
"The Truth About Cuba's Role in Grenada." *Intercontinental Press* 28 Nov. 1983: 678.

QUESTIONS FOR READING AND REVISING

1. Steve West's essay is an example of an *argumentative* essay that starts from the
   writer's strong response to an issue. What evidence in the essay shows West's
   strong reaction to Kirkpatrick's speech? What evidence shows West's commitment to his subject?

2. West's strategy is to attack Kirkpatrick's evidence and the assumptions on which
   she bases her speech. Why is this an effective strategy for *arguing*? Cite specific
   instances from West's essay to support your answer.

3. Do you find West's *arguments* convincing? How do you think Kirkpatrick would
   respond to West's points?

4. West turned an assignment that might easily have been just a reaction to
   Kirkpatrick's speech into a real argument. How does West use Kirkpatrick's
   speech to provide the structure of his essay?

5. Analyze how West uses and *introduces* his evidence to support his argument.

6. What assumptions does West make about his readers' familiarity with the Grenada invasion? Does he provide enough background information? Do you feel
   that you need to read Kirkpatrick's speech to understand West's essay?

7. West advises his fellow writers: "The biggest problem young writers have is a
   tendency to try to sound too polished and too artificially intellectual. It's not
   hard for a reader to tell when a writer is trying to adopt a voice he's not
   comfortable with. Writers need to stick to a simple style that is natural for
   them and not try to adopt an artificially pompous style that the reader will spot
   and dislike right away." How does West follow his own advice? Describe his
   voice in the essay. How does West's voice serve his *purpose*? How does his voice
   help to make his ideas more convincing?

8. West reports: "I had a difficult time writing my conclusion. I went through five
   or six versions of the conclusion and never felt satisfied with any of them. In
   the end, I simply used the one that dissatisfied me the least."
     One of the versions of West's conclusion was written this way:

> Recent Reagan administration statements about Grenada
> have largely ignored Kirkpatrick's arguments and have em-
> phasized the resurgence of pride in the American military

that took place after the invasion. These statements suggest that the administration's "real motives" for the invasion were to boost American morale and to flex the country's military muscles. Perhaps, then, it should come as no surprise that Kirkpatrick's arguments are less than convincing; she may have intended them simply as a diplomatic smokescreen to conceal the less honorable objectives of the invasion.

What are the differences between this version and the final draft conclusion? In what ways is the final draft conclusion more successful?

SUGGESTIONS FOR WRITING

1. Choose a newspaper or magazine article dealing with a topic with which you are familiar. Write an essay evaluating this article as a source. Does the writer present evidence accurately and fairly? Does the writer have a bias? How is the writer's *argument* structured?

2. Think of someone whose ideas you have read and would like to *argue* against. Write an essay presenting that writer's assumptions and then argue against them. Use your outside reading as the basis for the essay and integrate the readings into the essay.

3. *Define* an ethical problem related to being a student, such as the ethics of term paper writing services or plagiarism. Define your position on the problem, and then write an essay explaining the reasons for your *point of view*.

THREE STUDENT
WRITERS
AT WORK

Part III

M OST PEOPLE WRITE without consciously thinking about what they are doing. There are as many writing habits as there are writers. Some people can write anywhere — riding on buses, waiting in line, sitting in restaurants — while others need special conditions. Barbara Seidel, for instance, reports: "I want the house to be silent except for the sporadic squawking of my birds. I need to be left alone, without the phone ringing, or without anyone asking me questions or needing me at the moment. I sit at my desk, running my fingers through my hair, reaching for pieces of chocolate, or grabbing for a drink of ice water. I move around a lot in my chair, sigh deeply, and stare at the wall. Finally, I put pen to paper and write."

This chapter observes Barbara Seidel at work — getting started, drafting, and revising — and considers writing from her point of view. Seidel talks about her concerns as she worked through her pile of notes and six drafts to a final, prize-winning essay. Even though all writers need to find the conditions and circumstances that work best for them, we can still learn a great deal about the stages of the writing process by studying how one writer made important decisions and revisions as she progressed through these stages.

Too often when a piece of writing is successful, readers do not have the opportunity to see how it was written; the writing carries them along so that they are not concerned with the writer's process. The writing reads smoothly and logically and readers assume, if anything, that it must have flowed equally smoothly from the writer's pen. What readers don't see are the scratch-outs and the drafts, the decisions and conversations that went on in the writer's mind to produce such writing.

Seidel's notes and drafts show that her carefully conceived and balanced essay required a great deal of work. She began with fragments — notes to herself. Her ideas did not spring full-blown from her mind in clear, coherent prose. Rather, they tumbled out in unformed, fragmented ways that she developed in draft after draft as she made decisions, evaluated those decisions, and adjusted her writing so that the new decisions were consistent with what she had already written. What guided Seidel throughout the process were the concerns of subject, audience, and purpose.

This chapter begins with a detailed look at how Seidel wrote her essay, "A Tribute to My Father." It concludes with Jonathan Schilk's drafts for his essay,

"57 Degrees," and Matthew Holicek's drafts for his essay, "Look Out Behind You!" which are given as exercises. The drafts of these three writers reveal how writing evolves, from tentative beginnings, to become good writing. What comes through is the power and possibility of writing.

GETTING STARTED

In her freshman writing class, Barbara Seidel was given the broad assignment of writing a tribute to someone. She reports that she decided immediately to write about her father: "My first reaction to this assignment, though, was a feeling of slight panic. I knew I wanted to write about my Dad and I thought the assignment would give me a chance to further understand him and our relationship. But I kept thinking this is going to be tough; I will have to be open and vulnerable if I am going to write plainly about Dad. I knew if I did otherwise, the essay would not work."

For a writer, having a subject to write about is only the beginning. Seidel knew her subject—she knew she had a strong interest in writing about her father—but she didn't know specifically what she wanted to say about him. She needed to get her thoughts down on paper to see what she wanted to write. Seidel's method of getting started was brainstorming, a strategy that helps a writer to think as quickly and broadly as possible about a subject by writing down everything about the subject that springs to mind. Brainstorming usually takes the form of an unstructured list with words and phrases written as quickly and as uncritically as possible. Brainstorming helps Seidel to get involved with her subject quickly. "I jot down words, ideas, and images to give me a way of remembering what I know; the more I brainstorm, the more I have to work with."

The following notes are copies of Seidel's brainstorming sheets for her essay, "A Tribute To My Father."

SEIDEL'S BRAINSTORMING NOTES

```
--58 years old

--parents divorced when he was young

--1 older brother, Arthur, mom's favorite

--young--white hair, pale skin, blue eyes
```

--young--brother had darker skin, brown eyes,
   black hair

--grew up--wore hand-me-down clothes and shoes--
   used to fold newspapers into shoes

--Mother worked early morn til after dinner

--went to corner store for meal--Mother paid $ in
   advance to store

--hell-raiser as teen; didn't like school, dropped
   out (car and Uncle Art)

--Navy man during WWII; never overseas

--loved animals; always bringing home strays

--saw little of his father who was alcoholic,
   til age of 19 (father dating)

--great common sense, wise man, folk sayings

--not an intellectual; doesn't read; not "learned"

--patient; calm in crisis; resigned

--very hard worker; in car business since hung
   around father's car lot in late teens

--family man; loyal, devoted, dependable

--instinctive, yet never called it that (marrying Mom)

--extremely honest

--non-confronter: peace within family at all costs,
   sometimes to detriment of people

--not religious

--worrier; drives people crazy (5 countdown humorous
   quirk)

--obsessive about details; perfectionist: towels
   just so, etc.

--5'7"

--sandy blond hair, reddish gold, curly, short

--blue eyes, glasses

--long oval face with slightly square jaw

--conservative dresser

--man of habits; does not like change

--homebody; needs family warmth and love;

  gravitated to Mom's family

--dependable (Uncle Art; Mom--illnesses)

--loves candy (would hide his choc. in night table

  drawer and diet sundae--humorous quirks)

--strong sense of traditional values (his father

  ill, etc.; his mom driving him crazy yet he's

  there; grave)

--slow to anger but doesn't forget; stubborn

--drives around corner in car to cool down

--horseback riding when younger with daughter

--closer to daughter than son thru childhood years;

  able to talk with son when grown

--likes to talk things out

--Mother said he and his daughter very alike

Seidel spent a half-hour brainstorming, letting her mind roam, and generating details and information. Her brainstorming sheets are rich with possibilities; it is clear that she knows her subject well. To an outside observer, these notes might look rather disorganized and idiosyncratic. We might ask: What does "5 countdown humorous quirk" mean or what about "perfectionist: towels just so, etc."? Yet this is how notes at this stage should look. Seidel is writing these notes for herself, an audience of one, and it is important only that she can read and interpret them. What outside observers can see in these notes, however, is that Seidel asked herself important questions as she brainstormed in order to collect her thoughts and to see what she wanted to write.

She asked, for instance, What does Dad look like? What can I say about his family — his background — his growing up poor? What are his values? One thought suggested another.

These brainstorming sheets offered Seidel enough information for writing a first draft. She had collected a stock of materials to work with, and this helped her feel confident that she knew where she was headed. As she reports: "My brainstorming served as a road map, pointing me where I should focus my attention, and helping me to see how I wanted to view my subject."

Getting started is often the most difficult stage for writers. They stare at the blank page, waiting for inspiration, expecting to write a perfect opening sentence. Or they write something down, strike it out, crumple up the paper, mumble to themselves, "This isn't what I wanted to say," and begin again — and again. Having no sense of direction to guide them, they are forced to improvise, attempting to find ideas at the same time they are developing and organizing them. The time spent in getting started is time well spent. Writers write with more confidence and ease if they have developed a focus for their first drafts. Such a focus shows writers where they are headed and leads them to a more developed and organized draft.

Seidel's brainstorming notes offered her numerous details, but these details were unsorted and unfocused. She spent some time thinking about her notes and asking herself: Which details seem most interesting? Which details can be developed? How can these details be grouped to provide a focus? As she reports, "Before I wrote my first draft, I read and reread my notes. They clearly pointed me in the direction of *contrasts, honor,* and *principles.* These were factors about my father I intuitively knew were important to me, but I had never before identified or singled out. I realized these factors could be used as a focus to write about my father with both objectivity and compassion."

DRAFTING

Having reread and thought about her notes, Seidel wrote her first draft. She reports: "As I wrote my first draft, I was excited about my essay. I knew I had something important to say about my father. I just let loose in writing this draft so that I could connect all my notes and the ideas that were still rushing through my head. If I try to be too orderly in the first draft, then I am stymied. A first draft is always an experiment; I am still testing and exploring what I want to write. I was still trying to describe my father, make me see and understand him, so that my readers could. My lead sentence, 'Actions speak louder than words, he often said,' kept jumping into my head. I found it to be a very telling phrase and I knew it gave me a good sentence with which to start writing."

The following is Seidel's first draft.

SEIDEL'S FIRST DRAFT

A Tribute to My Father

Actions speak louder than words, he often said.   1
If so, there are actions that say much about the man.
There was that moment, thirty years ago, when his
father was dying slowly of cancer. In order to take
his father to and from the hospital for medical care,
he would arise at dawn, leaving his wife and small
children asleep in the tiny house, and drive the
distance on deserted city streets. Years later, his
own daughter, puzzled, would ask why he showed such
devotion to the man who had divorced his mother and
almost abandoned him and his brother. He answered,
with a faint look of surprise at the question, "He
was my father."

As though such an answer explains it all . . . he   2
is still not a man to say more when less will do. Soft-
spoken, slow to anger but long in remembering, he has
his own set of values. The towels in the linen closet
were always folded just so. The lights in an unused
room turned off, to the exasperation of children
lectured to do likewise. One's word is one's bond, he
said. Loyalty, respect, tradition, honesty . . . these
were the basic tenets of his life, unspoken but inherent.
Perhaps it is because of the young hellion who quit
school, tired of being caught napping, who trailed after
his older brother while his mother worked, that the
older man of rigid values emerged. Nonreligious,

unschooled by textbooks, he is a man of enormous common
sense, ready folk wisdom, and stubborn, instinctive
notions. He has always been a man of instincts,
though never introspective enough to notice their
presence.

Such instincts propelled him, fast and dizzy,   3
toward his future wife. He was engaged to her friend,
who introduced him to the dark-haired, pale-skinned
woman, about whom his inner voice said, firmly, yes.
He broke the engagement, proposed to Marilyn, then
reluctantly waited a year before marrying at the
insistence of his future mother-in-law. He chose a
family of traditions and closeness, of gnarled inter-
dependencies and rash tempers, so unlike his own past.
He knew this woman would need him, nurture him.

But then, he never shared much about his own   4
past. No bitterness over the shoes stuffed with newspapers, or the hand-me-down clothes several sizes too
large. No club of guilt-inspiring comparisons was
wielded over his more fortunate, and often unappre-
ciative, children. Instead they learned of him in
casual answers to direct queries, or from his mother,
a woman divorced in an era when such action was hardly
respectable. She worked long, tiresome days, leaving
him and his older brother Arthur to fetch a meal at
the corner candy store. The counterman, waiting, would
place a sandwich and a drink before them. "Never more
or less, and all paid for in advance," he once said, a
tone of wonder in his voice just at the sheer order of

it all. She passed her stern work ethic on to him;
he became a good provider, obsessed with being
responsible.

And the errant, alcoholic, polo-playing father--
the womanizer who told girlfriends his then-nineteen-
year-old younger son was a younger brother--passed on
some traits of his own. A love for animals and a love
for cars that would last a lifetime. The former
caused the young boy to drag home a succession of
dirty pets to an emphatically opposed mother, and the
young man to smile when his own daughter did the same
thing to his wife. The latter prompted an affair
with cars that forty years of selling automobiles has
only dimmed, not ended. It is telling of the man
that in a profession where truth is not a known
commodity, he has a reputation of such staunch
honesty that customers return, year after year.

Perhaps it is his subtle humor, his ability to
enjoy people that attracts them as well. Such humor
takes the form of quirks and annoyances in his home.
There is the "diet" dessert of ice milk over bananas
and Hershey chocolate bars, eaten nightly with an
innocent smile. Or the chocolate bars hidden in his
night table drawer. There is the obsession over
details, prompting him to worry over each decision.
And the peacemaker, the small boy within him still
seeking approval and love, who avoids confrontation,
attempting to reconcile people and issues, provoking
frustration in his daughter. And laughter in his son,

5

6

who at the end of a phone conversation over any issue, hangs up the phone, then counts "5-4-3-2-hello, dad," knowing his father will immediately re-call to be certain everyone is pleased.

If there is a failure in his values, it has been, until recently, with this son. It has taken them until now, when the boy is a father himself, to see the love that exists beneath their opposite personalities. With his daughter, being needed and revered was easy; she idolized him. With his son, there were questions, wants, swirling energy and demands. And he, working to provide for his children, had not time for the baseball or other games that were no part of his own childhood. Now, two men, two fathers, they reach across the distance with love.   7

And now, at age fifty-eight, his blond hair has become a gray-brushed reddish gold. His long, oval, square-jawed face is heavily lined. The habits of his lifetime have been altered, a difficult task for a man who dislikes change, by the death of the woman who needed and nurtured him, and bore his children. Years of chronic illness and possible loss of her created little anxieties, worrisome habits that, he admits, remain with him still. But he has remarried, and with his new wife, can often be found walking at the cemetery where their respective spouses are buried. He bends down to clear the grave of grass and dirt. She was, after all, his wife. And his actions continue to speak.   8

There is quite a jump between Seidel's rough, disorganized notes and this rough, but organized first draft. The details are beginning to make sense, and the essay is beginning to take shape. Seidel's strategy in writing her first draft was to refer to her notes and establish her purpose by grouping details from these notes. For instance, she took her brief sketchy notes:

—grew up—wore hand-me-down clothes and shoes—used to fold newspapers into shoes
—Mother worked early morn til after dinner
—went to corner store for meal—Mother paid $ in advance to store

and developed these details about her father's boyhood into paragraph 4 of her first draft. Seidel also combined and grouped details from different places in her notes. Details such as "hell raiser," "slow to anger," "not religious," and "perfectionist," scattered throughout her notes, all are grouped together in paragraph 2 about her father's values.

As she wrote her first draft, Seidel found that she needed to go beyond her notes in order to define her purpose. New ideas came out in writing as one idea stimulated another and new possibilities emerged. She added the details about her Mother in paragraph three, for example, when she realized that she needed this information to illustrate her father's complex set of principles. Seidel was open and receptive, as writers need to be while drafting, discovering new ideas and following her writing where it took her. Because she spent so much time brainstorming and developing her ideas, and because her notes were so well developed, Seidel was able to write a detailed, focused first draft. Her first draft was indeed a very good beginning.

REVISING

Seidel put her draft aside for one day before beginning to revise. With time, she reports, she gains the necessary distance to rethink what she has written and to see her writing more objectively. "Most of my time 'writing' is really revising. I first revise by reading my draft from start to finish. Next, I begin scribbling changes on the draft—additions, deletions, arrows, circles, notes to myself, and ideas for moving paragraphs around. The draft really looks chewed over at this point. Then, I type a new draft, make more changes on the draft, and continue and continue. I have often felt alone and very strange because I write so many drafts, but I can rarely complete even a very short piece of writing without multiple drafts. It is only through revising that I can keep refining my writing and hope to reach my readers."

Seidel's major concern as she read her first draft was that she had not captured her father and achieved her purpose in writing about him. She describes her thinking at this point: "I was very uneasy about my tribute to my father. I saw too many of my opinions of his actions and realized that I had not distanced myself emotionally from my subject. I had to take my emotional likes and dislikes out of my essay and try to see my work more objectively. In the third paragraph of my first draft, for instance, I described my mother's physical appearance, not my father's. I was getting carried away with my memories. I began to ask myself, 'Well, what is it I want to say? What is my purpose in writing this essay?' I knew I was trying to achieve a sense of flowing movement from one idea to another, so the man I was writing about would just seem to 'appear' to be 'real' the way he was in my mind's eye. I wanted my father to tell his own story; I wanted to show that his actions do speak louder than his words. One of my goals in revising was to remove myself from the essay. I shortened my sentences to let simple statements and my father's actions speak for themselves. I recognized that the more I interjected ME into describing HIM, the less of HIM could be seen."

To revise means, literally, "to see again," and that is what Seidel was able to do. While getting started, she could see her writing only as parts and pieces, but having written an entire draft, she could see from the perspective of the whole if her draft was consistent with her purpose. As she moved from draft to draft, Seidel revised by adding, deleting, and reordering. She refined her writing, searching for a precise word or a more descriptive phrase, rearranging sentences, and tightening her writing. As Seidel tells us: "My sentences were just too wordy. The essay, in fact, was so bloated with words that my father's actions could not speak for themselves. Wordiness is always a first draft problem because it is part of the process of pouring out ideas and discovering a purpose. In revising, I work for a rhythm and mood in my writing that is only possible by removing every excess word and phrase.

Seidel maintained the basic structure of her essay throughout her drafts, but the focus on her father's personality, his contrasts, his honor, and his principles, became more vivid. It was the accumulation of small changes from draft to draft, so that each sentence, phrase, and word fit her purpose, that made the difference in Seidel's prize-winning essay. Seidel reports: "I knew my essay was finished when I saw a clear pattern. I had created a logical transition from paragraph to paragraph. It no longer mattered if I wanted to add anything else; I could 'hear' the essay was complete."

It was through revising that Seidel was able to "reach the hearts of her readers" and achieve the essay she wanted — a vivid and memorable tribute to her father. As we learn from her, the best reason for putting anything down on paper is to allow a writer to see it, understand it, and know how to change it. In revising, Seidel patiently brought her ideas and her imagination together.

On the following pages Seidel's final draft appears alongside her first draft so that you can study the major decisions and changes she made. New sentences or phrases in the final draft have been underlined.

SEIDEL'S FIRST DRAFT

A Tribute to My Father

Actions speak louder than words, he often said.   1
If so, there are actions that say much about the man.
There was that moment, thirty years ago, when his
father was dying slowly of cancer. In order to take
his father to and from the hospital for medical care,
he would arise at dawn, leaving his wife and small
children asleep in the tiny house, and drive the
distance on deserted city streets. Years later, his
own daughter, puzzled, would ask why he showed such
devotion to the man who had divorced his mother and
almost abandoned him and his brother. He answered,
with a faint look of surprise at the question, "He
was my father."

As though such an answer explains it all . . . he   2
is still not a man to say more when less will do. Soft-
spoken, slow to anger but long in remembering, he has
his own set of values. The towels in the linen closet
were always folded just so. The lights in an unused
room turned off, to the exasperation of children
lectured to do likewise. One's word is one's bond, he
said. Loyalty, respect, tradition, honesty . . . these
were the basic tenets of his life, unspoken but inherent.

SEIDEL'S FINAL DRAFT

```
            A Tribute to My Father
     Thirty years ago, when his father was dying, he        1
would leave his wife and two small children asleep in
the square Cape Cod style house, then drive in the
predawn light through the quiet city streets to take
his father for outpatient medical care.  Much later
in his own life, his daughter puzzled over his devotion
to a man who had divorced his mother, then ignored him
and his brother.  A faint look of surprise flickered in
his eyes; then he answered concisely, "He was my father."
He has always said that actions speak louder than words.
```

1. The phrase, "actions speak louder than words," functioned as a touchstone for Siedel's ideas, a way of getting at what she wanted to say about her father and finding the words to express her central idea about his values. In revising, Seidel moved this phrase from her lead sentence to the last sentence. She wanted to make her lead sentence more specific, to draw her readers into her essay by showing one of her father's most telling actions. The last sentence of the final draft, "He has always said that actions speak louder than words," unifies the paragraph and summarizes Seidel's dominant impression of her father. In revising, Seidel has also condensed six sentences into four in order to create a more forceful impression of her father.

```
      A soft-spoken man with a frequent low chuckle, he        2
is so slow to anger that some people have been fooled
into believing him an easy mark for trickery, a dan-
gerous mistake.  He is just as slow and long in
remembering anyone who violates his strict set of
values.  He has no textbook education, yet he possesses
an abundance of common sense.  He is not religious, yet
he is a moral man, consistent in his values on a daily
basis, not only on the Sabbath.  The inherent boundaries
```

Perhaps it is because of the young hellion who quit
school, tired of being caught napping, who trailed after
his older brother while his mother worked, that the
older man of rigid values emerged. Nonreligious,
unschooled by textbooks, he is a man of enormous common
sense, ready folk wisdom, and stubborn, instinctive
notions. He has always been a man of instincts,
though never introspective enough to notice their
presence.

Such instincts propelled him, fast and dizzy,   3
toward his future wife. He was engaged to her friend,
who introduced him to the dark-haired, pale-skinned
woman, about whom his inner voice said, firmly, yes.
He broke the engagement, proposed to Marilyn, then
reluctantly waited a year before marrying at the
insistence of his future mother-in-law. He chose a
family of traditions and closeness, of gnarled inter-
dependencies and rash tempers, so unlike his own past.
He knew this woman would need him, nurture him.

of his life, given and expected, have been loyalty, re-

spect, tradition. Perhaps it is from the wild young

hellion who quit school, whose idea of fun was joyriding

in his older brother's car while that brother chased

after him, that this man of caution and habit emerged.

2. In revising, Seidel took what was essentially a list of details from her brainstorming notes that she had strung together into sentences in her first draft, and focused them by reorganizing and deleting. She decided to develop this paragraph around her father's values as a man of caution and habit. Thus, she moved the detail about the towels in the linen closet to paragraph 7 and cut the last sentence of the first draft about instincts and introspection. She deleted the phrase "to the exasperation of his children" to shift the focus of the sentence to her father. She added the important detail that "he is so slow to anger that some people have been fooled into believing him an easy mark for trickery" in order to establish her father's values.

Yet it was not caution, but sharp, clear instinct   3

that twirled him fast and dizzy after the woman he would

marry. He was already engaged; his fiancée made the

fatal mistake of introducing her fair-haired, blue-

eyed, slender man to the dark-haired woman whose first

sight caused some inner voice to shout at him firmly,

"yes!" This woman would need him, would nurture him;

he knew it. He broke his engagement, then immediately

proposed, waiting a year before marrying only because

of his future mother-in-law's insistence that he do

so. He may have been impulsive, but he was, after

all, respectful of his elders. And he had clearly

chosen not only a wife but a family style. Tradition

and warmth, tangled relationships and rash tempers

all spoke of people connecting to one another. His

life became one of stability and constancy, of the

But then, he never shared much about his own   4
past. No bitterness over the shoes stuffed with newspapers, or the hand-me-down clothes several sizes too
large. No club of guilt-inspiring comparisons was
wielded over his more fortunate, and often unappre-
ciative, children. Instead they learned of him in
casual answers to direct queries, or from his mother,
a woman divorced in an era when such action was hardly
respectable. She worked long, tiresome days, leaving
him and his older brother Arthur to fetch a meal at
the corner candy store. The counterman, waiting, would
place a sandwich and a drink before them. "Never more
or less, and all paid for in advance," he once said, a
tone of wonder in his voice just at the sheer order of
it all. She passed her stern work ethic on to him;
he became a good provider, obsessed with being
responsible.

same meat loaf served on the same day of each week,

of the same conservative clothes worn year in and year

out, of a man and a woman whose lives revolved around

each other, so unlike his own past.

3. Seidel realized in revising that she could use the story in this paragraph about her mother to show us more about her father's principles. She shortened her sentences, allowing her father's actions to speak for themselves, and added an effective detail: "his life became one of stability and constancy, of the same meat loaf served on the same day of each week."

He spoke little about his past. No bitterness   4

over the secondhand shoes stuffed with newspapers, or

the hand-me-down clothing several sizes too large,

pushed him to pursue great wealth or power. His

dream, he later said, was to be able to work hard and

just provide. He found the greatest pleasure in the

small things--the ability to buy himself new shoes.

Nor did he wield his own meager childhood as a club to

inspire guilt or appreciation in his own more fortunate,

more spoiled children. Instead, they learned of him

through passing comments--or from his mother.

Her divorce came in an era when such an act was   5

brazen. She worked long days caring for her two boys,

who ate one meal daily at the corner candy store. The

counterman would wait until they entered, then place a

sandwich and a drink in front of them. "Never more or

less, and all ordered and paid for in advance," he once

said, a respectful, wondering tone in his voice at the

sheer order of it all. She passed her stern work ethic

on to him. He became very good at being responsible,

dependable, at providing.

And the errant, alcoholic, polo-playing father--   5
the womanizer who told girlfriends his then-nineteen-
year-old younger son was a younger brother--passed on
some traits of his own. A love for animals and a love
for cars that would last a lifetime. The former
caused the young boy to drag home a succession of
dirty pets to an emphatically opposed mother, and the
young man to smile when his own daughter did the same
thing to his wife. The latter prompted an affair
with cars that forty years of selling automobiles has
only dimmed, not ended. It is telling of the man
that in a profession where truth is not a known
commodity, he has a reputation of such staunch
honesty that customers return, year after year.

4–5. Seidel divided paragraph 4 of her first draft into two paragraphs, giving her father's mother a separate paragraph, which emphasizes her influential role. In paragraph 4 of the final draft, Seidel added the two sentences on her father's adult ambition and his pleasure in buying himself new shoes. These sentences resonate for us, as readers, because we remember the earlier detail about his secondhand shoes stuffed with newspaper. Seidel cut out unnecessary words in her lead sentence in paragraph 4, again allowing her father's actions to speak for themselves. In the new paragraph 5, we see how small changes make the difference, reinforcing Seidel's purpose.

> And the errant, alcoholic, polo-playing father––   6
>
> the womanizer who once told his ladies that this then-
>
> nineteen-year-old younger son was his younger brother––
>
> had a few admirable traits of his own left up his
>
> sleeve. To his son, he passed on a love of animals
>
> and a fascination with cars, with their sight and smell
>
> and the gas-powered freedom they gave to a man. His
>
> son, as a boy, would drag home one protesting stray
>
> after another to a firmly opposed mother. Years later,
>
> a father himself, he would laugh when his own daughter
>
> did the same. After spending forty years selling the
>
> mechanical monsters, his love affair with cars has only
>
> dimmed. It is telling of the man that in a profession
>
> where truth is not always a recognizable commodity, he
>
> has a staunch reputation for honesty and a loyal fol-
>
> lowing of customers.

6. Here it is the small changes—details added, excess words deleted—that make this paragraph more effective. Seidel added the phrase, "with their sight and smell and the gas-powered freedom they gave to a man," to emphasize her father's fascination with cars.

Perhaps it is his subtle humor, his ability to   6
enjoy people that attracts them as well. Such humor
takes the form of quirks and annoyances in his home.
There is the "diet" dessert of ice milk over bananas
and Hershey chocolate bars, eaten nightly with an
innocent smile. Or the chocolate bars hidden in his
night table drawer. There is the obsession over
details, prompting him to worry over each decision.
And the peacemaker, the small boy within him still
seeking approval and love, who avoids confrontation,
attempting to reconcile people and issues, provoking
frustration in his daughter. And laughter in his son,
who at the end of a phone conversation over any issue,
hangs up the phone, then counts "5-4-3-2-hello, dad,"
knowing his father will immediately re-call to be
certain everyone is pleased.

If his honesty attracts them, so must his humor,   7
gentle and chiding. And of course, there are the quirks.

There are the Hershey chocolate bars hidden in the
night table drawer, the towels folded and placed
exactly so in the linen closet, the sink faucet
wiped shiny dry after dishes are washed. If his
past did not create anger or unbridled ambition, it
did give him a legacy of sorts: hoarded candy bars
contrast with the giving parent; an obsession with
details fills him with anxiety. He worries over
each decision like a dog gnawing on a bone. He is
still the small boy seeking security, the ultimate
peacemaker avoiding confrontations, reconciling and
rationalizing the good in people and in issues to the
frustration of his children. They, grown, have at
last learned to laugh gently at the habits that once
exasperated them. There is the family favorite--the
phone joke. His son speaks to him, hangs up the phone,
then counts, "5-4-3-2--hello, Dad!" He knows his
father will hesitate, then call again. Is everyone
happy? Should we talk more?

7. Seidel's skill as a writer is evident in her revisions of this paragraph. She
has revised every sentence, cut out every excess word, and removed every
unnecessary detail so that her father's idiosyncrasies become real to us. Paragraph 7 of her first draft was baggy and lacked a clear focus. In revising, Seidel
shows how her father's quirks have been shaped by the legacy of his childhood:
"hoarded candy bars contrast with the giving parent; an obsession with details
fills him with anxiety. He worries over each decision like a dog gnawing on a
bone." Seidel dropped the detail about the diet dessert because it didn't fit in,
inserted the example from paragraph 2 about the folded towels, and added the

If there is a failure in his values, it has been,   7
until recently, with this son. It has taken them until
now, when the boy is a father himself, to see the love
that exists beneath their opposite personalities. With
his daughter, being needed and revered was easy; she
idolized him. With his son, there were questions,
wants, swirling energy and demands. And he, working
to provide for his children, had not time for the
baseball or other games that were no part of his own
childhood. Now, two men, two fathers, they reach
across the distance with love.

new detail about "the sink faucet wiped shiny dry." Her sentences become much more direct: Instead of writing, "Such humor takes the form of quirks and annoyances in his home." Seidel's revision says, "And, of course, there are the quirks." The phone joke also becomes more concrete as we hear the father's voice saying, "Is everyone happy? Should we talk more?"

> It is this son who is one of the brief detours on   8
> his well-laid road map of life. With his daughter,
> loving was an easy goal. They shared a silent simi-
> larity of vision, of loving and letting go. With his
> son, such love was reached only after struggle; they
> spoke a different language. His son needed questions
> answered, challenges met, baseball and other games
> which had found no place in his own childhood; he was a
> man concerned with providing. By the boy's adolescence,
> they were like two bucks, antlers locked in a battle
> of dominance. Now they are two men, two fathers, who
> reach gingerly, but often, across the once-volatile
> differences of self to touch the love that always
> existed.

8. Seidel developed this paragraph to make the conflict between father and son more real to us. She straightened out the chronology of the paragraph so that she first describes the conflict and then explains its resolution, by moving the second sentence to the end. Her revision of the lead sentence is important. In the first draft, she wrote of the conflict as a "failure in the father's values," but "failure" was inexact, Seidel realized, because the conflict has since been resolved. In her first draft, she described this conflict between father and son in vague language: "With his son, there were questions, wants, swirling energy and demands." In revising, Seidel wrote: "With his son, such love was reached only after struggle; they spoke a different language. . . . By the boy's adolescence, they were like two bucks, antlers locked in a battle of dominance."

And now, at age fifty-eight, his blond hair has   8
become a gray-brushed reddish gold. His long, oval,
square-jawed face is heavily lined. The habits of
his lifetime have been altered, a difficult task for
a man who dislikes change, by the death of the woman
who needed and nurtured him, and bore his children.
Years of chronic illness and possible loss of her
created little anxieties, worrisome habits that, he
admits, remain with him still. But he has remarried,
and with his new wife, can often be found walking at
the cemetery where their respective spouses are buried.
He bends down to clear the grave of grass and dirt. She
was, after all, his wife. And his actions continue
to speak.

```
        And now, at age fifty-eight, his hair is streaked        9

with gray; his oval face is heavily lined; he is tired.

The habits of his lifetime have been altered, a dif-

ficult task for a man who dislikes change, by the

death of the woman who needed and nurtured him.  For

years, he had watched her slowly die, her illness

chipping away small pieces of his own courage, creat-

ing small anxieties, worrisome habits that still

linger with him.  But he is not a man to live alone;

he has remarried.  With his new wife, he can sometimes

be found at the cemetery where their respective first

spouses are buried.  Flat bronze plaques and high white

headstones stretch across the green fields.  He bends

down to clear her grave of grass and dirt.  She was,

after all, his wife.  Actions do, indeed, speak.
```

9. Seidel has removed all excess words from this paragraph so that her father stands before us in his final actions. In the first draft, she wrote about his first wife by saying: "Years of chronic illness and possible loss of her created little anxieties." In the final draft, her father becomes the actor in the sentence: "For years, he had watched her slowly die, her illness chipping away small pieces of his own courage." Finally, we see Seidel's father in the cemetery, bending down to clear the grass and dirt from his first wife's grave, and honoring her memory. In revising, Seidel brings her essay full circle by connecting the beginning and ending.

EXERCISE:
TWO DRAFTS BY JONATHAN SCHILK

This exercise looks at Jonathan Schilk's second and final drafts to understand the decisions and changes Schilk made as he developed his prize-winning essay.

Schilk was given the broad assignment of writing a narrative essay about an important event. He decided to use one of his Coast Guard experiences because, as he reports, "I thought that a well-told sea story would entertain my audience." Schilk's initial idea was to write about his first experience with seasickness, and the focus of his first draft was the psychological effects of seasickness. Schilk tells us: "I realized after reading what I had written that the focus was all wrong. I didn't really want to read a paper about seasickness and I didn't think that my readers would either. I began to ask myself, 'What is the purpose of this essay?' As I reread my first draft, I began to think that the most interesting idea in this draft was the picture of me being seasick, sitting in the corner, holding my gut, surrounded by water, and feeling very small. In fact, it was my first bout with seasickness that humbled me and made me recognize how small and insignificant I was in comparison to the vastness of the sea. I decided to move on to a second draft, entitling this draft, "The Sea and Me," and to tell the tale of my first experience with seasickness and what it taught me about the sea."

The following is Schilk's second draft.

SCHILK'S SECOND DRAFT

The Sea and Me

To those who sail or steam, the sea is something
to be feared and respected. Mariners hold it in the
highest esteem because he knows that his life is
pitifully small and insignificant in relation to its
vastness. The inexperienced person, however, cannot
fathom this basic maritime tenet. The unguided novice
usually goes to sea overestimating his abilities and
underestimating the sea. More times than not, these
jaunts end in disaster. Books are filled with chill-
ing sea-stories about unlucky sailors caught in
whirling maelstroms. They often lost their lives in
the desperate battle against the elements.

Until I went to sea, the idea of my life being
threatened by wind and wave had never occurred to me.
I had never been to sea before and I naively believed
that I had no reason to fear it. Little did I know
that I was about to learn one of the most terrifying
lessons of my life. The following is an account of
that experience that changed my relationship with the
sea for the rest of my life.

Before I graduated from the Coast Guard Training
Center, the instructors told us that we had much more
to learn about the sea and its ways. They said that
we should remember that the ocean humbles even the
most experienced of skippers. Still, I was cocky
and felt I had the world by the tail. I felt very

confident in my abilities to do any task or to deal
with anything that came my way. No problem seemed
too large.

The first time I put to sea, we had been ordered   4
to search for a boat that was flooding twenty miles
northeast of Chicago. We loosened the mooring lines
at sunset and steamed for the distressed craft. As
the ship slowly glided between the pier heads into
open water, her newly painted sides were gently buf-
feted by tiny ripples. Distant storm-clouds splashed
with a hundred brilliant colors filled the horizon.
Later, I lay awake in my bunk and wondered what my
first watch would be like. The seas were calm and
unimportant; they were the last thing on my mind.
Soon, the gentle rolling of the ship rocked me to
sleep. I later awoke to the sound of water crashing
and gurgling on the deck above me. This was the beginning of the end of my delusion of the sea. The
ship violently lunged to the port and I was suddenly
emptied on to the deck. As I gathered myself up, I
saw a seaman making his way down a dimly lit passageway like a drunken sailor. With each wave, the ship
sickeningly heeled to the port and then to the starboard, and in like manner, so did he. I shouted to
him and I asked what was going on. He said that the
ship was on the edge of a gale and things were going
to become worse. A feeling of claustrophobia was
creeping over my slowly crumbling constitution. In

my mind, the creaking walls were sickeningly swaying
back and forth. With every nauseating tilt, I could
hear something in the next compartment as it spun
across the deck and smashed against some bulkhead.
I began to wonder what I had gotten myself into. Not
only was I beginning to experience my first of many
bouts of seasickness, a cold feeling of dread was
also churning in my stomach. On the way to the wheelhouse, I stopped at a porthole to see how bad it
really was. There, I saw mountainous waves pound
into the bow and explode into billowing spray that
engulfed the ship. I continued upwards and pondered
the tremendous energy of that wall of water. When I
stepped into the wheel-house, I noticed someone bent
over the bridgewing, their arching back showed inter-
mittant convulsive wretches. I felt my own stomach
give increasingly wrenching twists as a succession of
waves sent the ship into a dizzying, oscillating roll.
Everyone, including the captain, was clutching and
grabbing at whatever wasn't flying across the compartment. All about me, strewn on the deck, were
coffee-stained charts, pieces of broken glass and
other things I could not make out in the gloom. As
I made my zig-zag way to the man I was relieving, the
ship gave way to what appeared to be the largest wave
yet. But, before she could recover, another hit us.
The skipper shouted, "Brace yourselves!" The helmsman lost his grip on the wheel. Half-stumbling and

half-airborne, he piled into the radar. Deep in the
ship's heart, we could hear a shudder as metal
strained to hold in one piece. The world seemed to
be turning upside down as we came precariously close
to the point of capsizing. The ship's movement
slowed and she hung there, groaning, for what seemed
hours. I really thought that this was it, the ship
was going down and me with it. Hesitatingly and
almost reluctantly, she came back to an even keel.
Although we had no other experiences with waves of
that proportion again, we still took a beating for
the next sixteen hours.

This shaking experience taught me something.   5
The sea was no longer an unimportant detail as I had,
up to then, believed. No longer could I view the
sea with the same attitude. I saw her change from a
placid, restful friend to a distorted furious malev-
olent whirlpool. With all of the intricate machinery,
high technology, that made the ship so advanced in
our sight, we were still belittled by the elements.
I came to the conclusion that no matter how much
knowledge puny man accumulates, he can never come to
the point of mastering the overwhelming vastness and
limitlessness of the sea.

Questions on Schilk's Second Draft

1. Schilk's second draft provided him with a good place to begin developing his ideas. Describe the strengths and weaknesses of this draft.

2. What point is Schilk trying to make about the "Sea and Me"? What lessons did he learn? As a reader, do you feel that Schilk told you what he learned or showed you?

3. Schilk describes the storm in paragraph 4. From this description are you able to see, hear, smell the storm? What additional information would you like Schilk to provide?

4. Paragraph 4 is a rather lengthy paragraph. In fact, it is the heart of the essay. Is there anything confusing or unclear about this paragraph? What changes would you suggest?

5. Schilk's final paragraph begins: "This shaking experience taught me something." He reports that he wrote his conclusion this way because he was always taught to "tell my readers what I want them to know in my conclusion." Do you think this final paragraph is effective? Could you suggest ways to revise it?

Schilk wrote three more drafts, before he wrote his final prize-winning essay. Here is his final draft.

SCHILK'S FINAL DRAFT

57 Degrees

At the Coast Guard Training Center in Alameda,   1
California, our instructors stressed that we still
had much to learn about the sea's moods and temperaments. Our training, they said, was only inadequate
preparation for what could happen to us in open water.
"The ocean humbles even the most experienced skipper!"
warned one teacher ominously. He often spoke of the
Edmund Fitzgerald, an ore carrier which had foundered
in a winter storm on Lake Superior. Even though the
ship was over seven hundred feet from stem to stern
and equipped with the latest technology, she went
down in less than a sweep of the radar's antenna.
But it made no difference to me. After all, those
men on the Fitzgerald were only civilians; I was a
Coast Guardsman. After fifteen weeks at the Center,
after long hours delving into the art of navigation
and piloting, I could deal with any emergency.
Steering--"wheeling" as we called it--was my forte.
Several times, in fact, in less-than-perfect conditions, I had brought ships through narrow entrances
in the breakwall. I could handle any ship of any
tonnage. There was nothing that I couldn't do.

After graduating, I was assigned as a navigator   2
to the Acacia, an 180-foot buoy-tender on the eastern
shores of Lake Michigan. I've been ordered to an
oversized mudpuddle in the Midwest, I thought. It

was like giving a man with a Ph.D. in math a grammar-

school job. My fears were confirmed when I first saw

the lake: it was flat, featureless, unromantic.

Then there were the arguments with my shipmates about

the storms. It would never get that rough on the

lake. If they wanted "rough," if they wanted big

storms, I told them, they ought to sail the Gulf of

Alaska in autumn or go on a spring patrol on the

Caribbean Sea. Besides, the Acacia could handle

whatever nature could throw at her. She had been

fitted with the latest technology--variable ballast

tanks, hydroplane stabilizers, and all--to prevent

dangerous rolls. The Boatswain never said much; he

just nodded and smiled.

One day headquarters ordered us to sail for a   3

point twenty miles northeast of Chicago, where a

23-foot Chris Craft, adrift in bad seas, had radioed

an SOS. We loosened the mooring lines at sunset and

glided between the piers into open water. Fifty

miles to the southwest storm clouds hovered over the

horizon like a gigantic bruise. But here, where the

ship only rippled the flawless surface of the lake,

I fell asleep in my rack, secure in the knowledge

that the Acacia and I could handle anything--anything

short of a tsunami that is.

I awoke to the sound of water crashing and gur-   4

gling on the weather deck above me. Lurching to the

port, the ship dumped me onto the deck. I sat there,

my blankets and mattress draped over me, wondering what
had happened. I picked myself up and numbly eyed my
shipmates, who had burrowed among their woolly blankets and lashed themselves in--giant cocoons in the
dim red light. Clothes on hooks swung like pendulums
with each roll, and a figure in the passageway made
his way towards me like the proverbial drunken sailor.
"What's going on? Where are we?" I asked.

"We're on the edge of a storm front and it's   5
gonna get worse!" he gasped.

Before I could reply the ship pitched forward,   6
and he zigzagged down the passageway to the head.
A bucket on wheels, loose from its trices, spun
across the deck and smashed against the bulkhead,
splashing its contents. I glanced to the berths to
see if anyone had awakened. The cocoons hadn't
budged. The bucket careened into another bulkhead
with a crash. The walls closed in and air became
putrid. I hoped this was as bad as it would get.

The sailor who had run into the head emerged,   7
swallowed back another retch, and told me I had the
next watch in twenty minutes. Even in the passageway's red light, his features had a greenish hue.
The ship plunged forward again, and he struggled
back to the head.

After dressing, I climbed the ladder to the   8
wheelhouse, leaving the bucket, the messenger from
the bridge, the muffled sloshing, coughing, and

gagging behind. I fought my way up, sometimes
weightlessly as the ship dropped from beneath me,
sometimes ponderously as waves forced me to defy
gravity. The bulkhead oscillated up and down, back
and forth, up and down until I grew dizzy. I opened
the wheelhouse door, stepped inside, and saw the
helmsman clinging to the large brass wheel and
spinning it in an almost futile effort to keep the
ship on course. The Boatswain gazed out the porthole nonchalantly puffing on a Dutch Masters. The
Skipper had been sitting in his chair forward of the
helmsman's wheel. He too was looking out the portholes. Everyone else, including the lookout, the
Officer of the Deck, and the Exec, was hanging on
to whatever wasn't flying across the deck.

   The acrid stench of the Boatswain's cheroot   9
made me queasier than ever. I would have loved to
punch him in his smug, self-satisfied face, but I
was too ill to bother. All about me, strewn across
the deck, were coffee-stained charts, pieces of
broken glass, and crockery. Outside, the Quartermaster of the Watch, draped over the bridgewing's
edge like a rag doll, finally staggered toward the
door and stepped inside. His face was haggard and
drawn. Behind him the sea careened toward the gunwales and then receded.

   I turned to see what the anemometer read: the   10
needle had pegged out at 106 knots. The lake was

as I had never seen it before. Even in an ocean
storm, the period from the crest of one wave to the
next would run at least three hundred feet, But
here in the lake the period was seventy-five feet,
and the ship was subjected to an endless thrashing,
so that it was impossible for her to recover from
one wave before confronting the next. Out there
waves holding millions of gallons of water broke
upon themselves, and the slicing wind sheared off
the wave caps. Waves looming above the ship quickly
swept on, leaving vast troughs for the ship to fall
into--and she did. Many times I felt as if I had
left my stomach thirty feet in the air above. Waves
of nausea washed over me, and I wished I were dead.
I meant it. I would have done anything to stop the
misery.

No sooner had I thought this than a rogue wave   11
plowed into our port beam and sent the ship broadside, cork-screwing into a trough. "Brace yourselves!" the Skipper cried. Losing his grip on the
wheel, the helmsman catapulted against the radar and
landed in a heap. The wheel spun past hard left to
a point where it would jam the rudder and leave the
ship without steerage control. I jumped for the
wheel and brought the rudder to midships and then
hard right to bring the port bow into the seas. But
before she responded, the ship gave way to the blow
of yet another wave that towered above the signal

bridge and mast. The <u>Acacia</u> heeled wickedly to the starboard--20, 30, then 40, then 50 degrees. At 57 degrees--seven degrees past the point of capsizing-- she slowed to a stop. The fo'c'sle disappeared under thousands of tons of water, and the starboard rail dipped into the black waters.

Inside the pilothouse, maps, pencils, and coffee mugs cascaded off the chart table onto the deck. The lamp swung into the Fathometer, and sparks flew from its shorted circuits and shattered light bulb. And there, through the porthole, past my wild-eyed re- flection, the lake boiled at the bridgewing's gun- wales. The ship hovered on the edge of eternity. Deep in the ship's heart, rivets and welds strained and groaned, and deck plates jumped from the con- cussion. This is it! I thought. We're going down!

Slowly at first, almost hesitantly, the <u>Acacia</u> recovered, and the clinometer climbed up its scale. Water washed from the fo'c'sle's deck in sheets as the <u>Acacia</u> swung past even keel, whipped through an arc of 100 degrees, and settled into a sedate 40- degree roll for the remainder of the trip.

In the corner, wedged between the Skipper's chair and the radar, the Boatswain still stood, puffing on the stub of a Dutch Masters and grinning quietly at me.

Questions on Schilk's Final Draft

1. Schilk's final draft is polished, interesting, and highly readable. What has Schilk accomplished in his final draft? What has Schilk achieved in revising?

2. In his final draft, Schilk dropped the first two paragraphs from his second draft. As he reports: "I had been taught to tell my readers what I was going to tell them and I was following this formula in these paragraphs." Describe the tone of these two paragraphs? What were their weaknesses?

3. In his final draft, Schilk plunges right in and starts his essay with a picture of himself. Why is this an effective *introduction*? How does this introduction more effectively draw his readers into the world of his essay?

4. In the third paragraph of his second draft, Schilk gives his readers the cliché that he felt he had the world by the tail. He drops this cliché from the final draft and instead *shows* his readers how cocky and confident he was. What information about himself does he add to his essay? How does this information help to set himself up for a fall?

5. In revising, Schilk built up the details of the storm. Why do Schilk's readers need to see the storm? Find specific details that Schilk added that help you to visualize the storm.

6. In revising, Schilk also developed the character of the boatswain. What did he represent to Schilk? What is his function in the essay? How does the boatswain help Schilk to show his readers what he learned?

7. In his final draft, Schilk ends with the image of the boatswain "puffing on the stub of a Dutch Masters and grinning quietly at me." Compare this ending to the final paragraph of the second draft. Why do you think he dropped that paragraph? Why is the image of the boatswain a more effective conclusion?

8. Schilk's original idea to write about seasickness became a minor point in his final draft. What does this suggest to you about the process of revising?

9. Schilk reports: "When I first start writing an essay, the reader is not really that important. I feel that at this stage my subject and *purpose* are most important. When I revise, though, I begin to consider my readers and the readability of my essay. I try to keep in mind as I revise that my natural way of writing is rather stiff, and I pay attention to that problem. In my early drafts of this essay, I wrote as if I had a collar on that was too tight and that itched." In what specific ways has Schilk considered the needs of his readers in his final draft?

10. Summarize what you have learned about revising from studying Schilk's two drafts.

EXERCISE:
TWO DRAFTS BY MATTHEW HOLICEK

This exercise looks at Matthew Holicek's first and final drafts to understand the decisions and changes Holicek made as he developed his prize-winning essay.

Holicek was given the broad assignment of writing an extended definition. As he reports: "My reaction to this assignment was very different from that of other assignments. Most of the time when an assignment is given, I scan it over for a while, and when no ideas come to my mind, I just put it aside so I don't have to think about it until later. This assignment, though, was a little different. An extended definition paper didn't sound too interesting, but one of the topics my professor suggested, a type of movie, interested me. 'Horror Movies,' I thought: 'Perfect.' I have seen so many horror movies, especially slasher movies, that I am somewhat of an expert on them. I went into the writing of my essay with a fairly good idea of what I was going to say and how I was going to say it. I started out with a simple and direct definition of a slasher movie. Then I thought about all of the different categories within horror movies that are common, such as plot, victims, and locale. I used these categories as a focus for writing my first draft. I tried to rethink a couple of memorable slasher movies so I could poke fun at the many actions that are common to almost all these movies. Because these actions themselves are so funny, I decided to appeal to my readers through humor. By poking fun at these movies, I hoped my readers would laugh and see the truth of what I had written."

The following is Holicek's first draft.

HOLICEK'S FIRST DRAFT

Look Out Behind You!

A slasher movie is a specific type of horror film   1
which concentrates more on the death toll and body
count than on developing characters or any form of a
coherent plot.

The victims in these slasher horror movies are   2
almost always teenagers. But they are murdered so
quickly that the audience doesn't even get a chance to
learn about them. The characters are almost all the
same and all act as stupidly as each other. Girls
love to go through late-night strolls alone through
the woods or take a midnight skinnydip in the lake.
All the men want to be heroes and go by themselves to
find out where the strange noise is coming from. Upon
entering dark and gloomy houses, men and women decide
that now is a good time to conserve energy and save a
few extra bucks at the end-of-the-month electric bill;
so they leave the lights off. After hearing a noise
coming from within the house, they always foolishly
decide to investigate, thinking it's one of their
missing friends. Disregarding the "safety in numbers"
theory, they branch off in separate directions, never
to see each other again. Then teenagers fall into the
common habit of walking backwards, which almost always
means certain death. When confronted with the axe-
wielding maniac, the characters lose their will to live,
and just close their eyes and scream, not once making an
effort to get away. Whatever the logical thing to do is,

the characters don't do it. It's hard to believe that
any real person would act the way they do in the
situation they're in. Calling the police is always
out of the question, as is just leaving the place
altogether. It's so easy to tell exactly who will be
the next victim. If the person goes off alone, they'll
be murdered; if they walk backwards . . . death; an
unlit room . . . it's all over. All the characters
just lose any common sense they might have to be a
prime target of the killer.

The mad slasher was once an ordinary person who   3
has somehow been transformed into a superhuman, indestructible and unstoppable menace to whoever crosses
his path. Masks are worn to cover their hideously
deformed faces. Although we usually don't see his
house, we are led to believe that he lives alone in a
secluded shack. (He obviously can't get a job to pay
for a nice apartment, and has to get food on his own.)
Slashers never talk, but rather only breathe heavily.
But these maniacs do have an uncanny gift to predict
exactly what his victim's next moves will be. The
victim walks right in his direction so that he doesn't
have to waste time chasing them around. When he does
chase them, however, he doesn't run after them. He just
walks zombielike after his victims who never seem to be
able to evade him. The slasher seems to have no purpose
in life other than to murder people. But when he murders
them, he puts his imagination into it. Knives, machete,

axes, arrows, hot poker sticks, and sometimes just
his bare hands are used to kill defenseless victims.
Sometimes, when two teenagers are having sex he can
kill two birds with one stone and put a spear or
pitchfork through both of them at the same time.
Otherwise he'll use his cunning and lure his victims
to death, such as by making faint noises or by turning
off the power in the fuse box. By whatever method it
may be, the mad slasher never fails to stop until the
last victim is finally dead, which usually ends up
being himself.

The story most often centers around a certain   4
group of ignorant teenagers being the target of one
mad maniac. Apparently, ten years earlier (commonly
a holiday or other specific day) an unfortunate
incident caused by our teenagers (or a similar bunch
of teenagers) has left an innocent man disfigured
and out for revenge. But he decides to wait until
exactly one decade later to don a mask and purchase an
assortment of sharp instruments through which he intends to exact his vengeance. Luckily for the slasher,
all of his intended victims just happen to still be
together and easy to find. Summer camps and other
isolated wilderness areas are always a good place to
hang out; they also happen to be a favorite spot for
our slasher as well. Night comes around and the fun-
loving teenagers decide to do a little wandering around.
That's when the mad man begins to intentionally make

noises to draw the curiosity of our hapless victims.
As the characters split up, the killer sets each one
up to be butchered. One by one while everyone is
looking for each other, they only find the cold, steel
blade of the slasher's knife. Finally, there's only
one teenager left, aimlessly running around. Suddenly,
the hero (usually a girl) discovers all of her friends'
dead bodies, neatly and sequentially placed leading her
right to the slasher. Somehow, though, the killer
misses in his attempt to kill her. Then, through endless chases, the heroine finally decides to defend herself and stabs the killer. He falls to the ground, dead,
or so she thinks. The audience groans as the woman
stupidly turns around and walks away. The moment she
begins to relax and catch her breath, this superhuman
monster lunges out of the darkness and tackles her. In
the struggle, the slasher's true identity is revealed
as the mask is stripped away. At the moment the
slasher is at his peak for the final kill, there are
two possible outcomes. One possibility is that, from
out of nowhere, a male hero appears and kills the
slasher, saving the girl. The more prevalent outcome
has the girl discover a fairly large knife or machete
just in time to avoid the killer's blow and thrust the
knife into his stomach, killing him for good this time
. . . supposedly. Many times the last shot of the movie
is of the killer's arm or leg moving, or else he is gone
altogether, signifying that another similar dreadful
sequel will soon be out.

Questions on Holicek's First Draft

1. Holicek's first draft provided him with a good place to begin. Describe the strengths of this draft. What are its weaknesses?

2. Holicek's introductory paragraph is a direct *definition*. "A slasher movie is a specific type of horror film which concentrates more on the death toll and body count than on developing characters or any form of a coherent plot." Is this an effective introduction? Does it succeed in pulling you into the world of the essay?

3. Paragraph 2 is lengthy. Is there anything confusing or unclear about this paragraph? How would you advise Holicek to revise it? What needs to be added, deleted, or rearranged?

4. Paragraph 4 is also long. Is there anything confusing or unclear about this paragraph? How would you advise Holicek to revise it?

5. There are no direct references in this first draft to any specific slasher movies. How could such references strengthen this draft?

6. Do you find Holicek's conclusion effective? Could you suggest ways to revise it?

Holicek wrote two more drafts before he wrote his final prize-winning essay. As he tells us: "I always tend to write more than I have to and so when I revise I have to decide what sentences to cut out, trim, or combine so my writing will flow smoothly and coherently. The easiest part of revising for me is reworking individual sentences. When I wrote the introduction, I just thought it should be short, quick, simple, and to the point. But when I reread it I saw the introduction didn't work. I knew that I needed a longer introduction so that the essay didn't just appear from nowhere. I needed to give my readers some background information and slowly prepare them for what they were about to read."

Here is Holicek's final draft.

HOLICEK'S FINAL DRAFT

Look Out Behind You!

Most people get upset if they are told how a
suspense or horror movie ends. After all, there's no
point in seeing a "who-done-it" film if you already
know who did it. But when it comes to a genre of
horror films known as "slashers," people seem willing
to make an exception. Even though they know that one
slasher movie is apt to be just like all the others,
audiences enjoy them anyway--perhaps because these
stories of people being sliced to death by maniacs
are so predictable. John Carpenter's masterful
Halloween, which premiered in 1978, is widely regarded
as the original slasher film. It was soon followed by
a rash of inferior imitations which audiences nevertheless flocked to see, unconcerned that these totally
predictable cinematic clones focused more on high death
tolls and gory violence than on developing interesting
characters or coherent plots.

Since teenagers are the target audience for
slasher films, the victims in them are almost always
independent, fun-loving, just-out-of-high school
partyers. Could it be that the filmmakers believe
that the teenage audience somehow identifies with
other youths being decapitated, knifed, and electrocuted? But the kids portrayed in the movies die so
quickly that viewers don't get much chance to learn
about them, much less identify with them. The girls

all love to take late-night strolls alone through the
woods or skinny-dip at midnight in a murky lake. The
boys, eager to impress these girls, prove their
manhood by descending alone into musty cellars to restart broken generators or chasing psychotic killers
into haylofts and attics. Entering dark and gloomy
houses, men and women alike decide suddenly that now's
a good time to save a few bucks on the end-of-the-month
electric bill--so they leave the lights off. After
hearing a noise within the house, they always foolishly
decide to investigate, thinking it's one of their many
missing friends or pets. Disregarding the "safety in
numbers" theory, they branch off in separate directions,
never to see each other again. Or the teenagers fall
into the common slasher-movie habit of walking backwards, which naturally leads them right into you-know-
who. Confronted by the axe-wielding maniac, the
senseless youths lose their will to survive, close
their eyes, and scream.

     In short, whatever the logical thing to do is, the   3
characters don't do it. Or what they try to do fails.
Calling the police is almost always out of the question.
However, if they do decide to call the cops, the phone
is dead. Or the lights don't work. If the victims try
to get into another room, the door is jammed. If the
characters manage to escape from the house, they always
make the mistake of heading for the car. Sometimes the
doors are locked and, naturally, the kids are without

keys. But if they are lucky enough to have keys, the car won't start. Couldn't even rely on a new BMW in these movies. Then, looking at the fuel gauge, they realize they should have stopped at the village gas station on the way home from the 7-11 the night before. If the fumes are enough to get the car going, the next obstacle will be four deflated tires. The mad killer doesn't miss a trick!

Of course, it's always easy to tell exactly who   4
his next victim will be. If a girl goes off alone, she'll be murdered. If a guy walks backwards . . . instant death. Car won't start? Expect company in the back seat. An unlit room? It's lights out, for- ever. All hope is lost when characters come face to face with The Slasher.

The mad slasher is a once-ordinary person trans-   5
formed into an indestructible, unstoppable, superhuman menace. In the opening scene of the movie, through what appears to be the hazy view of someone afflicted with cataracts, we see a horrifying incident--a burning, a decapitation, a drowning, a lynching, or a car acci- dent--that causes the death or disfiguration of one or more innocent outcasts. Then we are transported ten years forward, to the present time. The plot unfolds. We learn that our happy group of teens--or a similar bunch of kids--is responsible for the incident that maimed or disfigured the maniac on that day ten years earlier (it was Halloween, or Valentine's Day, or

Friday the 13th or some other special occasion--a prom,
a wedding, a loss of virginity). Or the slasher has
seen the teens cause the death of someone dear to him.
He is hot for revenge, but he has decided to wait
exactly one decade (no more, no less) before exacting
his vengeance.

We rarely see where these slashers live, but they   6
obviously don't have the sense to get a comfortable
apartment. They seem to prefer dismal, rotting shacks
where they dine on furry animals and Chicken McNuggets.
They never take off their masks or change their ward-
robe--which consists of flak jackets, army boots, and
institutional pajamas. They don't talk; they just
breathe heavily. Slashers do have the uncanny ability
to predict exactly where their victims will be next:
teenagers are sure to back right into their killers or
open that very door behind which the madman patiently
lurks. When a slasher ends up having to chase his
victims, he doesn't run. Instead, he just plods on
zombielike after his victims who, despite their youthful vigor, are unable to evade him. He enjoys waiting
for the teenagers, girls especially, to trip. Or he
waits to catch them off guard. That's when he makes
his move.

When he murders his victims, he puts his imagi-   7
nation into it. To assure the best and most gruesome
results, he selects his tools carefully: knives,
machetes, axes, arrows, hot pokers, and sometimes just

his bare hands. To save a little time, he'll
occasionally put a single spear or pitchfork through
two teens making love--killing two birds with one
stone. Or he'll cunningly lure his victims to death
by slamming doors, snapping branches, or turning off
the power in the fuse box.

    After the killing spree, the one surviving teen-   8
ager, usually a hysterical girl, discovers the dead
bodies of all her friends placed neatly and sequentially
in her path--leading her directly to The Slasher. But,
of course, she doesn't see him until he lunges for her.
Fortunately for her, this time his knife (or poker or
pitchfork) somehow misses its mark. She escapes and he
chases her (zombielike) through the house or the woods.
Then, after endless screaming, running, and tripping,
the heroine cleverly thinks to defend herself and
manages to skewer his eye with a sewing needle, split
his skull with an axe, or hang him. He falls to the
ground, dead, or so she thinks. The audience groans as
the woman stupidly turns around and walks away. The
moment she relaxes to catch her breath, this superhuman
monster lunges from the darkness again and tackles her.
They struggle, and the slasher's true identity is
revealed as she strips away his mask.

    As the slasher raises his knife for a life-ending   9
blow, two outcomes are possible. One is that, from
nowhere, a male hero appears and kills the slasher,
saving the girl. The other and more prevalent outcome

has the girl discover a butcher knife or machete lying
nearby. Just in time, she avoids the maniac's blow
and thrusts the knife into his stomach, killing him for
good this time--she thinks. In neither ending do the
teens actually check to be certain that the slasher is
dead. (None of the kids in these slasher movies are
destined for careers as coroners; they're all too
eager to pronounce anything that doesn't move dead.)
But the audience knows better. A simple lack of vital
signs won't prevent this killer from rising up again,
pulling the knife from his stomach (or the axe from
his skull, or the machete from his neck), and killing
those surviving teens with even greater enthusiasm and
ingenuity in the inevitable, and even more dreadful
slasher sequel coming soon to your local theater.

Questions on Holicek's Final Draft

1. Holicek's final draft is lively, interesting, and polished. What has Holicek's revision accomplished?

2. Compare the introductory paragraphs from the first and final drafts. Describe the differences between these two paragraphs. How does the revised introduction more effectively draw readers into the world of the essay?

3. Compare the way in which Holicek began his second paragraph in both the first and final drafts and describe the differences. What has Holicek added to make the sentences in the final draft more interesting? Why are these sentences more effective?

4. In paragraph 3 of the final draft, Holicek added these sentences: "However, if they do decide to call the cops, the phone is dead. Or the lights don't work. If the victims try to get into another room, the door is jammed. If the characters manage to escape from the house, they always make the mistake of heading for the car." Why was this information added to the essay? Why does the information make the essay more interesting and effective?

5. Holicek reports: "My paragraphs in my first draft were dreadfully long and an eyesore on the page. They needed to be separated to contain their own ideas while still maintaining the flow of the essay. I took some of the subtopics and created new paragraphs giving these subtopics more emphasis and attention." What has Holicek done with paragraphs 2 and 4 from his first draft? Has he succeeded in giving the subtopics in his essay more emphasis and attention?

6. Holicek tells us: "I had difficulty with the conclusion. The ending in my first draft sounded very awkward. I kept thinking about this paragraph when the coroner idea came to me and everything just seemed to fit together." Compare the conclusions from the first and final drafts. What has Holicek achieved in revising his *conclusion*? How does the revised conclusion more effectively tie together the various threads in the essay?

7. One of Holicek's goals was to entertain his readers. Do you find the final draft more entertaining than the first draft? What specifically is more interesting and humorous in the final draft? Do you feel that Holicek's strategy to poke fun at the slasher movies was effective?

8. Summarize what you have learned about revising from studying Holicek's two drafts.

MOVING FROM PERSONAL EXPERIENCE TO EXPOSITION AND ARGUMENT

Part IV

THE POET ROBERT FROST once observed, "All thought is a feat of association: having what's in front of you bring up something in your mind that you almost didn't know you knew. Putting this and that together. That click." Frost's description of "That click" may well remind you that one of the most appreciable pleasures of writing is recognizing the connections between one of your ideas and another. This recognition usually comes at the most unexpected moments, often after you have struggled for hours trying to express your thoughts clearly in writing. Yet part of the *enduring* satisfaction of writing is precisely that element of surprise, that lifelong pleasure of discovering your own resourcefulness with language, of finding new ways to explore your own intelligence and to contribute in some original and visible way to improving the world of ideas. And as Frost's remark implies, one useful way to approach mastering the art of thinking in writing is to learn how to multiply connections — between the ideas you have, and between the essays you write.

How is one essay connected with another? No paper you write is ever a unique, self-contained task; each is a step in the learning process. Any subject you write about involves two important types of connection: building on what you already know and linking your ideas into a coherent presentation. Suppose you are asked to write an essay for your history class on the post-Civil War South. You may have personal memories of the South or a sense of the post-Civil War era from high school reading that will help you to approach the topic with greater confidence and authority. Once you have written your essay, you may be able to adapt the research and thinking you have already done when you are asked to write, say, an essay on William Faulkner for your English class. Professional writers very often follow this strategy, choosing a single subject — congressional lobbyists, microcomputers, public education budgets — that they can write about from several different angles for different publications. The crucial point, as Robert Frost suggested, is to be attuned to the connections between ideas. The work you do in a freshman composition course can sharpen your awareness of such connections and give you valuable practice at building related ideas into a lucid essay. So too, the effort to recognize and develop productive connections between one essay and another is very much akin to the process of *revising* your ideas within the boundaries of a single essay. In both instances, you *re-see* (re-vise) your thinking from a fresh perspective. More generally, frequent practice in recognizing — and developing — the productive connections between the ideas you generate and the essays you write will also better prepare you to discover the intellectual connections between the courses you take.

We have designed *Student Writers at Work* to encourage you to recognize and develop the abundant resources of your own intelligence by practicing your skills as a writer — one who is able to connect and extend ideas both within an essay and from one essay to another. The discussion questions following each of the thirty-five student essays in this book focus on analyzing how each writer has developed an essay governed by a powerful idea. The ability of these writers to create clear and convincing relationships, both between and among the ideas in the sentences they write in an essay, has earned them the special recognition of a Bedford Prize in Student Writing. Their explanations of the strategies they used to come up with ideas, draft, and revise offer accessible models for *every* student writer, whether practiced or inexperienced. In the previous chapter, three student writers — Barbara Seidel, Jonathan Schilk, and Matthew Holicek — explained in even greater detail the specific strategies they used to plan, draft, and rewrite their essays. Part IV extends those same principles and strategies to a larger issue: how can student writers most successfully connect the ideas in one essay form to the intellectual demands of working in another essay form?

COMPARING THE PERSONAL ESSAY
WITH EXPOSITION AND ARGUMENT

Our correspondence and conversations with teachers and students across the country underscore what we have noticed in our own composition classes: many student writers find it difficult to move from writing personal experience essays to writing expository and argumentative ones. For most first-year students, personal essays seem easier to write because they focus on what we think we know best. Expository and argumentative essays, however, can also focus on what we know. The difference lies less in the subject matter than in the way the writer approaches and organizes it.

All writing fundamentally expresses an idea about a subject, but the purpose, the language and forms used, the evidence summoned, the point of view adopted, and the audience imagined may vary greatly. Personal experience essays most often *narrate* an event (report what occurred) or *describe* a person, place, object (record appearance in sensory terms). For example, you could write an essay in which you describe in detail a favorite hometown hangout that is now gone. Or you could write a narrative essay in which you recount a memorable incident of your adolescence that occurred at that hangout. In both descriptive and narrative essays, the perspective or point of view from which you write is usually first person. The evidence you present to convey a clear sense of that place (description) or a vivid rendition of what happened there (narration) is normally bounded by the limits of your own experience. The audience writers envision for personal experience essays can be either themselves or others as well. And because the emphasis in personal experience essays is usually on narration and description, such writing may not explicitly assert an idea about the subject rendered.

What distinguishes expository and argumentative writing from personal experience essays is the nature of — and the critical prominence given to — asserting an idea about a subject. "Exposition" is a form of nonfiction prose that puts forth facts and ideas about a subject. But more importantly and specifically, expository writing *asserts and explains an idea about a subject.* That subject can be a person, place, object, or an event, or an abstraction such as *justice* or *liberty*. Because it asserts or explains an idea about a subject, exposition often involves generalizing; that is, it requires a greater distance between the speaker and the subject than would occur in a personal essay. And since its purpose is to explain, exposition assumes an audience beyond the speaker.

Consider again the example of the favorite hometown hangout. A descriptive essay about the hangout would emphasize what the place looked like several years ago. A narrative essay might recount a memorable incident that occurred there. In contrast, an expository essay about the hangout might assert the following idea about it: the hangout has changed a great deal in the years since you last spent some time there. Given the fact that the purpose of the exposition is to explain an idea about a subject, you might well want to explain how (comparison and contrast) or why (cause and effect) the hangout has changed. (For a complete list of the forms of exposition, see the Glossary.) The audience imagined by writers of expository essays always includes other readers.

"Argumentation" is another form of nonfiction prose in which the speaker attempts *to convince an audience that a specific claim or proposition is true.* What makes the claim or proposition true is that it is supported by a body of logically connected statements that are true. Argumentation is, in effect, a form of theorizing; proposing that a specific claim or proposition would be true if certain statements proved to be true. When writers move from personal experience essays to exposition and argumentation, they broaden considerably their point of view, their range of evidence, and their conception of the real or imagined audience to whom they are writing.

Return to the example of the hangout once again. An argumentative essay on this subject might address the issue of whether urban redevelopment displaces more people than it helps. Or the writer of an argumentative essay might formulate the following proposition or claim: urban renewal programs destroy the architectural character indigenous to a neighborhood in favor of governmentally sanctioned standards. The purpose of such an essay would be to convince an audience of the validity of the proposition or claim by citing evidence, which might range from personal anecdote to research reports. The writer of an argumentative essay wants to do more than explain an idea; he or she wants to convince an audience of the truth of a proposition or claim.

The purpose of this chapter is to help you apply the range of options available to you as a writer to your own essays and practice your skills in moving from personal experience essays to expository and argumentative ones. As a starting point, let's observe how two student writers—Julie Reardon and Beverly Dipo—discovered ample resources in their original prize-winning essays for writing other papers. Because Reardon's "The Unmarked Road" (p. 202) and Dipo's "No Rainbows, No Roses" (p. 70) are both strongly felt personal accounts of topics with broad implications, each writer was invited to write a second essay, using her original paper as a springboard into a different rhetorical pattern. The following sections trace Reardon's and Dipo's progress—from carefully rereading their personal essays to generating ideas to formulating and ultimately writing a new composition.

JULIE REARDON: FROM DESCRIPTION TO EXPOSITION

In her essay "The Unmarked Road," Julie Reardon responded to an assignment in which she was asked "to relate my reaction to a foreign culture." Her life in the small town she chose to write about was "like being thrust into another country. I had strong memories from that experience, and writing the essay gave me a chance to form my feelings about that period in my life . . . . The goal of my essay was to show the other students in my class how differently and how miserably other people can live in our country, not so far from home. I tried to appeal to these readers by relating the confines of my neighbors' lives. I tried to appeal to the reader's sense of compassion for those less fortunate than themselves. I wanted them to really see the borders of my characters' lives."

As you reread "The Unmarked Road" (p. 202), notice the techniques Reardon uses to accomplish these goals. Watch particularly closely how she organizes her description: the type of language she uses, the evidence she summons, the point of view she adopts, and the ways in which all these elements suit her purposes and her intended audience. These are the tools you will see Reardon using in new ways when she reaches the writing stage of her second essay.

When she first approached the challenge of moving from description to exposition, Reardon's main concern, of course, was to find an appropriate topic. What aspect of "The Unmarked Road" might become the core of a new essay? Here is Reardon's explanation of how she proceeded to generate ideas:

> Step 1: I reread my essay.
>
> Step 2: To generate new topics for an essay, I thought about my original paper and then freewrote about as many new thoughts as I could. Some of the ideas I came up with were:

—How life experiences shape a person's outlook on life.
—Compassion for others.
—How much money is enough? Interview several people. Thesis: "amount of money not as important as person's attitude toward money."
—The importance of friends.
—Neighborliness—once restricted to neighbors but not found at the office.
—Determination to succeed.
—Poverty—compare life of the poor in earlier times with now.
—Isolation—literature is full of people isolated in a strange culture.
—Fanny's influence on me.
—Stereotypes of the poor in literature.
—Teen marriages—why they fail.

> Most of these ideas were quickly discarded. I thought I had covered developing compassion in my original essay, so I also abandoned that idea. Ditto with life experienced affecting a person's life. The idea to interview several people about their attitudes toward money was stymied by a lack of people at the higher end of the income levels for me to interview. Determination to succeed and teen marriages have been done to death already in the media. The idea of neighbors now being found at the office rather than next

door was my favorite idea, but I had read a similar article in *Newsweek* some time earlier, and I was afraid of plagiarism, even unconscious plagiarism. I finally narrowed down my choices to poverty — compare and contrast today with many years ago or examine stereotypes of the poor in literature. Poverty as a subject finally sparked my interest when the thought occurred to me to compare grandmother's hard life with what her life would be like today.

Here is the final draft of Julie Reardon's new essay. Notice how, in addition to moving from description to exposition, she has also moved from autobiography to biography. Her point of view is no longer that of the central character in her essay, but of a narrator writing in the third person. Though her language is not dramatically different, her descriptive passages are focused toward a different purpose. Both her language and the organization of her material are adapted as well to the new kinds of evidence she incorporates. Her intended audience remains the same, but her change in purpose and point of view means a change in the tone with which she addresses her readers. Reardon did not decide these aspects of her essay in advance; they fell into place as she began work.

REARDON'S EXPOSITORY ESSAY

A Woman of the Times

Poverty has always been synonymous with a hard life   1
and deprivation. Just two generations ago, being poor
meant an endless struggle to find work and to obtain
food, clothing, and shelter. My grandmother raised her
family in those days on very little money and coped with
difficulties impossible to imagine today. If she were
raising her family in modern America, her life
would be much easier. Yet she would face new problems
that she never had to deal with in earlier times.

My grandmother, Molly Halvorson, was born on a   2
small farm in Iowa in 1891 (Westcott). Always dis-
pleased with her name, Molly maintained that she was
named after the family cow. Her firm sense of right
and wrong revealed itself in her small, determined
chin and serious blue eyes. She loved growing flowers
and could happily root about in her garden for hours,
amazingly not getting her hands dirty. She protected
her exquisite Nordic coloring from the sun with a wide-
brimmed straw hat, and was somewhat vain about her small,
dainty feet. She began school speaking only Norwegian
but quickly learned English and became an enthusiastic
student. She loved to read, wrote an elegant hand, and
won many school spelling bees. In an era when many farm
children attended only a few semesters of school, Molly
resolved to learn all that she could. She insisted on
staying in school and proudly graduated from the eighth
grade.

Molly's job opportunities were exceedingly limited.   3
As a woman, she was forbidden to even consider a "man's
job." The options available to her were teaching,
nursing, or domestic service. Teaching and nursing required training her family couldn't afford; domestic
labor was her only realistic choice. Throughout her
life, Molly supplemented the family's income by cooking,
cleaning, and ironing for others. At times, she was the
sole support of the family. Her domestic skill was
highly prized by her employers, yet she was paid no more
than the prevailing wage for "hired girls," twenty-five
cents per hour.

She married Leroy Abbott in 1910. They had their   4
first son, Arthur, the following year. My mother, Viola,
was born five years later, Don the next, and Betty in
1924. Leroy supported them with a variety of short-term,
low-paying jobs: horse trader, meat packer, dairy
delivery. Occasionally he could barter a horse meant
for the rendering works to someone for a pound of butter
or perhaps a dollar cash. Depressions in 1907, 1919,
1921, and the Great Depression in the thirties period-
ically terminated Leroy's employment. There was no
unemployment insurance; he was let go without notice,
and until he could find a new job, no money came in.

The family moved often in search of work. Molly   5
sometimes had to sell her few sticks of furniture to
pay for the move and would arrive at the next rented
house without even a bed to set up. Molly loathed dirt

and would immediately dig into scrubbing down the place, which was invariably filthy and sometimes rat infested. Molly brightened the rooms with hand-sewn curtains and rag rugs crocheted from scraps.

At each house, Molly had to carry water indoors 6 from a spring for cooking, cleaning, and washing. This icy water had to be heated in a copper boiler, then carried outside after use to be dumped. Molly kept their home and the family's clothes spotless with the only cleaning and laundry aids available to her: boiling water, harsh lye soap, and sunshine.

Molly kept her big, black stove handsome with stove 7 blacking. Molly had to build the fire in the morning, feed it throughout the day, and bank it at night to heat the house. During World War I, coal and wood for the stove were scarce and very expensive. Molly's house, drafty and cold at best, was even chillier during those years. The same stove was used for cooking and heating water, making the house unbearably hot in summer. Molly grew much of the family's food and spent many long, airless August days over the stove canning shining jars of fruits and vegetables for winter use.

Molly's children never had to feel like "trash," 8 the common term for poor families with numerous, dirty children. Their house and clothes, though shabby, were clean. It was important that their clothes were patched with tiny, invisible stitches, a skill Molly had per- fected early in her life. The family always managed to

scrape by on their meager income without the humil-
iating experience of "going on the county" for money.
Viola and her friend Eloise entertained themselves
with homemade paper dolls cut from the Sears-Roebuck
catalog. Though only a year older than her brother
Don, often Viola was responsible for his care while
Molly was occupied with household duties or out working.

Molly's days and evenings were filled with never-   9
ending tasks and backbreaking chores. It took her hard
work and sacrifice to see her family decently taken
care of. Yet this bleak life was softened by pleasure
in her children, her love of gardening, and her pride
in the family's ability to be self-supporting.

If Molly was raising her four children today,
chances are that she would be doing it alone. Today's   10
welfare system could support the family far more
adequately than Leroy could. The market for his un-
skilled labor is not much better in today's recessions
and uncertain economy than it was back in earlier
depressions. The antifamily bias in the modern welfare code would actually encourage him to abandon his
family. "Even today, there are twenty-nine states in
which a two parent family, no matter how poor, cannot
receive welfare payments or Medicaid. . . . And even in
the more enlightened jurisdictions, the de facto policy
is to aid only the broken family" (Harrington 17). If
Leroy compared what his minimum wage earnings could buy
for his family with the wide range of services available

to them should he desert them, he would conclude it would be foolish to stay.

In addition, the terrible stigma of "going on the county," which led Molly and Leroy to struggle on their own, is today largely gone. "Simply put, poverty is coming to be seen not as the fault of the poor but as a condition imposed on them by society and the economy" (Harrington 198-99). Consider the changes in Molly and her four children's lives if they applied for welfare today in Hennepin County, Minnesota (McNitt).   11

The family of five would qualify for a three-bedroom, subsidized apartment. Rent would be approximately fifty dollars per month. The housing itself would be required to meet strict safety codes. The plumbing, heating system, electricity, and water must be in working order. This housing is often located in desirable suburban locations. This apartment would be a tremendous improvement over Molly's succession of cramped, ill-heated, rented houses in run-down neighborhoods. Molly's passion for cleanliness would be much easier to satisfy with the aid of modern inexpensive and effective cleaning supplies. Water would run at the turn of a faucet, light and heat turn on at the flip of a switch. Though heating fuel is as expensive today as it was in earlier times, a Federal Energy Assistance program would help Molly with the bills. Her family could stay warm despite the high cost of fuel.   12

Molly's respect for education would lead her to   13

continue her schooling. Free tutoring is available to help her prepare for the GED tests. Passing the test would reward Molly with her high school equivalency diploma. Federal grants are then available to pay tuition at a trade school or college. She would no longer be limited to a "woman's job." Her love of reading, beautiful penmanship, and flawless spelling might cause her to choose the traditional field of teaching, or her concern for plants and flowers might encourage her to enter the "man's jobs" of conservation or horticulture. The Minnesota Job Service would then provide her with free assistance in locating employment in her chosen field.

$150 in food stamps, careful shopping, and a monthly   14
grant of $691 would enable Molly to feed and clothe her-
self and the children. They would no longer be dependent
on what Molly could grow in her garden. Her thrifty
nature would doubtless lead her to continue to sew many
of their clothes, but a sewing machine would eliminate
laborous hand sewing and make the task much easier.

Careful saving over several months would enable   15
Molly to purchase a television and join the 97 percent
of American homes that own a set (Rosenberg and Rosenberg
269). Since television is such an inexpensive form of
entertainment, it seems logical that the family would
follow the average viewing pattern of nearly seven hours
daily (Information Please 269). During that time, they
would be bombarded with programs featuring families much

more affluent than their own, and commercial messages
urging them to buy, Buy, BUY! Toys such as "action
figures," for example, "are backed by heavy market
research and cross-promoted by cartoon shows aimed at
young children" (Barol 54). A survey of one five-hour
period of Saturday morning cartoons revealed the following parade of cartoons blatantly pushing related
toys: Snorks, Muppet Babies, Smurfs, Dungeons &
Dragons, Rubik the Amazing Cube, The Littles, Mr. T.,
and Spiderman. With the dazzling array of toys
advertised on their favorite programs, it seems
unlikely that Viola and Eloise would be content with
their homemade paper dolls. More likely, Molly would
be subjected to whiney demands for the items seen on
television and would feel guilty at not being able to
afford them for her children.

Molly's days would still be busy. School during 16
the day, homework, and being both a father and mother
to her children would occupy much of her time. She
would have to substitute pride in continuing her
education for her former pride in being self-supporting.
Freed from grinding daily chores and endless worry about
employment, today's Molly could lead a more enjoyable
life.

A lifetime of hard work and frugality enabled the 17
real Molly to eventually own her own small home with
flowers blooming indoors and out. With the opportunities
for education and the career choices available to her

today, it is likely that her same hard work and thriftiness would lead her to a similar happy ending. Along
the way, modern inventions would greatly ease her daily
routine. She would be able to improve her lot in life,
but the assistance isn't free. The cost she would pay
would be the loss of her husband and of the family's
self-sufficiency. It might be too high a price to pay.

Works Cited

Barol, Bill. "War Toys on the March." Newsweek
    1 July 1985: 54.

Harrington, Michael. The New American Poverty.
    New York: Holt, Rinehart and Winston, 1984.

Information Please Almanac 1985.

McNitt, Michael. Personal interview with caseworker.
    25 July 1985.

Rosenberg, Norman, and Emily Rosenberg. In Our Times.
    2nd ed. Englewood Cliffs, New Jersey: Prentice-
    Hall, 1982.

Westcott, Viola Abbott. Personal interview. 24 July
    1985.

Julie Reardon wrote three drafts of her new essay, her first being "merely an attempt to get started. I just keep on writing until I'm finished, even though I am well aware of the aromatic quality of what I am turning out." In her second draft, she attempted "to smooth the writing a bit . . . and to begin developing a feel for the information I want to use in the final version, along with the wording I want to retain, the length that will feel comfortable, and the sources I wish to use." Then she turned to the final draft:

> Before starting the final draft, I reread carefully my second draft, I list the facts I wish to include, and I decide the order in which I want to present them. This version received an enormous amount of rewriting and editing. I decide to let the opening and closing paragraphs, which I feel are very weak, simmer in my head overnight.
>
> My original thesis was how much easier it is to be poor today than it was in Grandma's day. The first research I did bore out this assertion. And indeed, physically my grandmother did endless, backbreaking labor no longer necessary today. But the cost of public welfare is high in terms of breaking up a family, and television today is a very big influence on everyone, but possibly more so on poor people. The contrast between what they see on the tube and what they have in their life must be numbing. So my final thesis points out that there were both advantages and disadvantages to each era.
>
> I considered my readers when I decided to use a member of my family as an example. I hoped that decision would appeal to a typical college student more than a dry analysis of "Poverty — Then and Now."
>
> I chose the block form of comparison and contrast rather than the point-by-point method because of the awkwardness of switching decades while keeping the same person as the subject in each paragraph. In the final draft, I attempted to give equal weight to both 1910 and 1985 and to compare each point I wanted to make in similar order.
>
> I edited the final version even as I typed. Rereading it aloud before the final typing suggested more changes. I finally know I'm done because I am REALLY sick of the whole thing. I avoid reading it now that the "final" copy is typed because I am always very dissatisfied with it right after I finish. Later I can appreciate it more.

Questions on Reardon's Two Essays

1. Identify the general subject of Julie Reardon's new essay. What specific idea does she assert about that subject? What specific *evidence* does she offer to support her assertion about that subject? What additional evidence might you suggest to help her strengthen her assertion? Where should that additional evidence be placed? Why?

2. What specific differences can you point to between Reardon's strategies—and accomplishments—as the writer of both "The Unmarked Road" and "A Woman of the Times"? In what specific ways do you think she might be able to strengthen the expository qualities of "A Woman of the Times"?

3. What specific thematic connections can you identify between "The Unmarked Road" and "A Woman of the Times"? What stylistic consistencies link these two essays? Analyze the word choice, phrasing, and sentence structure of Reardon's two essays. Point to specific *evidence* that would verify the fact that these two essays were written by the same person.

4. Review Reardon's explanation of her *purpose* in writing this new essay. Explain in detail how she achieved that purpose. What aspects of her new essay do you think would benefit from additional work? Explain why.

5. Reardon reports that she had a great deal of difficulty "narrowing the points to be covered in the essay. There was so much material I wanted to use that this piece could easily have been ten times longer. I tried to pick what was the strongest contrast between then and now, and to include information that the average student wouldn't be aware of. It was very difficult finding information about a woman's life around 1910; the topic isn't covered in most history texts. I was glad that my mother could furnish me with so many recollections." Identify "the strongest contrast between then and now" in Reardon's essay and comment on how effectively she handles it. Discuss her use of the information her mother provided. How successfully does she work this information into her essay? What sources, in addition to "most history texts," might she have consulted for "information about a woman's life around 1910"?

6. In discussing her essay, Reardon observes that "the easiest part was, as usual, the rewriting. I really enjoy revising my essays. It gives me pleasure to sift through words to find the exact one that I want to use, a phrase that reflects what I want to say." With this in mind, observe the changes Reardon makes in the opening paragraphs of each of her three drafts. Here is the opening paragraph in her first draft:

> The life of the poor is never easy, but survival today for a low income family is much easier than it was in my grandma's day.

Here is the opening paragraph in her second draft:

> Survival today is easier for a low-income family than it
> was in my grandmother's day. There is help available to
> her, but at a cost to her family life.

Compare and contrast these opening paragraphs with the final version. What
changes do you notice in each draft? Which version do you prefer? Why?

7. Reardon lists a number of possible subjects that emerged from rereading her
   original essay. What other possibilities for writing a new essay can you identify
   in "The Unmarked Road"?

BEVERLY DIPO:
FROM NARRATION TO ARGUMENT

Beverly Dipo is a licensed practical nurse who enrolled at Utah State University to "try to get my RN." In her work as a nurse, she sees "human suffering,
weaknesses, triumphs, and tragedies on a daily basis. It provides a unique
perspective that many do not have." Asked to write a narrative essay focusing
on a personal experience in which she gained some insight, Dipo responded
with a compelling account of the death of one of her patients, Mrs. Trane. "I
was asked to write about a moving experience, and Mrs. Trane's death was
just that. I felt I could give an accurate account of the situation. . . . As a
nurse, I frequently observe *things* before I ever speak to patients or get to know
them as human beings. Right or wrong, it's the way we are trained. . . . All
I did in this paper was to describe in detail a situation that really happened
and my reactions to it."

When asked to describe herself as a writer, Beverly Dipo observed that "I
am not a 'natural' at anything, including writing. . . . In fact my writing
process may be unique. I can, and have, written an entire outline and the first
paragraphs of a work at night, in bed, in my head. The next time I sit down
at the typewriter, I put my rough draft on paper. I will make a second rough
draft to redo spelling, punctuation, basic structure, and make revisions as
needed. . . . Then I will proceed to thoroughly mess up the rough draft with
slashes, exclamation points, secret codes, doodles, medical shorthand, and
assorted expletives. . . . I will then retype what is left and repeat the procedure
until I produce a whole essay without one single red mark!" In writing her
essay, "No Rainbows, No Roses," Dipo notes that "the final draft practically
ended up word for word the same as my first rough draft"—a testament to the
emotional intensity of her narrative as well as to her own dictum that writers
ought to "keep it simple."

Beverly Dipo's claim that she is not a natural at writing seems overly modest in view of her impressive work in "No Rainbows, No Roses" (p. 70). As you reread that essay, watch how Dipo uses the skills of observation she has developed as a nurse. "All I did in this paper was to describe in detail a situation that really happened and my reactions to it," she says. In writing down her observations, however, Dipo shows a strong sense of what details to include, how to translate sensory images into verbal ones, and how to balance setting, characters, action, and emotion. To do this requires skills that almost every beginning writer finds elusive, but that improve markedly with practice. As Dipo notes, the innate simplicity and intensity of the incident she chose to write about counted heavily in her favor.

Picking a subject for her second essay proved more difficult than Dipo had hoped. She kept track of her efforts to identify and explore ideas for a new essay based on "No Rainbows, No Roses" in the form of journal entries. After rereading her original essay several times, Dipo was able to note little progress: "Somewhere in my mind I have the general idea of what is expected of me. An 'expository or argumentative essay.' They make it sound so easy. Do I make it a more difficult task than it should be? Yes, I do. I want it to be a good paper." After several more readings, Dipo reports: "I'm still stuck for a subject. I've put it aside — thinking it will 'come to me' in a brilliant flash of light. Well I was hoping. Now I must sit down and do some brainstorming." Here is Dipo's record of the results of that effort:

> Possible subjects:
>
> 1. Avoid death; it's too morbid.
> 2. Nursing the terminally ill — good possibility — a subject dear to me, but still too morbid.
> 3. Why do I want to avoid it? Doesn't everybody?
> 4. How about rainbows? That's as far as I can get from death and still be considered part of my original essay. But what on earth could I contribute to the subject?
> 5. Obituaries? Back to the death thing again.
> 6. Am I going to be able to avoid it?
> 7. Families of patients as a subject comes to mind. A possibility. Families of the terminally ill?
> 8. Nursing in general? Too broad!
> 9. Nursing the elderly — a good possibility — something I really love. They can be so special: the gray, thinning hair, a twinkle in the eye, some with such a sense of humor. It's a joy but it can be painful. I find old folks more afraid of living than dying, especially if they're ill. This may be the choice. I will have to think about it.

Several days of preparing for summer school examinations intervened before Dipo could find adequate time to return to thinking about an appropriate subject for a new essay. When she did, her ideas developed quickly:

> I have been studying for exams; had little time to think about writing an essay. At work this morning, I found a patient's chart on which the Dr. had written: 'patient to be allowed to die with dignity, only supportive care to be given at the pt.'s request.' I wondered: how many times have I seen this actually written on a chart? Once, maybe twice before. And, from this same physician. Why are doctors so reluctant to do this? "The God Syndrome" we nurses call it. Doctors do not actually believe that they are God; they just try to act like Him. What is it that is taught in medical school that tells these people that they can *save everybody*?? It is so foolish, because *everybody* dies, sooner or later!! I admire the few who know when they have done enough, the few who are honest enough to give their patients realistic expectations. I remember Judy, whom you will meet in my essay, and I remember Mrs. Trane. They both died of the same disease. And my essay is pouring out into my brain. I sat down and scribbled out the first two pages before being summoned elsewhere and having to put it aside. My subject: Does a patient have the right to die the way *he* chooses? Is he informed enough to be able to choose? If not, why not? Is it the physician's responsibility to give his patient *informed* choices? These are questions my paper should include. So, I have my subject. The paper is started. Some research is needed.

Several days later, Dipo made the following entry in her journal: "I wish writing were easy! I wonder if I'm making myself understood. The essay is developing — my thoughts ramble though. This will take some organization. An outline may have been of some help, but the first five or six paragraphs came so easily; but now I seem stuck. Will plunge onward!"

Later that same day, Dipo made the following notations in her journal:

> —Euthanasia: "A painless *putting* to death of persons having an incurable disease; an easy death. Also mercy killing."
> —Suicide: "One who intentionally *takes* one's own life. The intentional taking of one's own life; to kill oneself."
> —Murder: "The act of unlawfully killing a human being by another human with premeditated malice; to commit murder." (Not applicable.)

—Ethical: "Pertaining to morals or morality; right and wrong in conduct."

The final entry in Dipo's journal, made a few days later, reads: "Received articles from library. Wow! So *many* different arguments—some good, some bad. I will be very limited in how much of the subject I can present. My first draft is done. Think—as time is limited—I will have to stick with what I've already done."

Beverly Dipo eventually wrote three drafts of her new essay. The final version follows. Notice as you read it that although Dipo opens with a specific case, as she did in "No Rainbows, No Roses," her thesis this time is a general one. She uses the concrete examples of Judy and Mr. Syms to illustrate the abstract principle of "dying with dignity." To do this, she gives up (as Julie Reardon did) the central character's point of view for that of a narrator writing mainly in the third person. Dipo thus draws on her nursing experience for illustrations and information rather than for characterization. Her language and organization show that she is less concerned now with setting a mood— appealing to her readers' emotions—and more concerned with building a case based on claims, evidence, and logic. Although the issue itself is highly emotional, and so is some of Dipo's supporting evidence, her tactics are not. She is still writing for a general audience, but her purpose has changed significantly.

DIPO'S ARGUMENTATIVE ESSAY

A Time to Die

Judy had been looking awfully tired recently. 1
Her husband, Clair, had been in and out of the
hospital over the last six months following his
heart attack, and Judy had been naturally concerned
about his failing health. She had managed to continue working at her full-time job as a registered
nurse, but the effort was beginning to show. There
were now creases in her once smooth brow, dark
circles under dull eyes, and an ashen hue seemed to
dim not only her complexion, but her personality as
well. The vigor which she had once applied to all
her tasks was gone. A number of her friends began
encouraging her to get a checkup, but she claimed
she just did not have the time.

Three months passed, and Judy began to lose 2
weight, have bouts of nausea, and back pain. She
finally decided to find the time for a physical
examination. After numerous tests, X-rays, scans,
and an admission to the hospital for a biopsy, Judy's
doctor told her she had pancreatic cancer. He informed her that with chemotherapy and radiation,
the probability of her living another year, maybe
two, was pretty good. As a nurse, Judy was well
informed about her disease, its treatments, and her
prognosis. She knew her doctor was being optimistic
and kind. She talked to Clair at length about what

her future would be, and then weighing her options
carefully, she chose to refuse treatment. Both Clair
and her doctor pleaded with her to accept the treatments, but she remained adamant. She knew she might
have extra time with the help of the drugs and radiation, but she also knew that the extra time would be
a time in and out of the hospital, nausea, vomiting
weakness, emaciation, and to Judy, the worst side
effect of all, the loss of control of her life.
Finally, as a person whose life was spent in concern
for others, typically, her concern was now for Clair.
Since his heart attack, their income and savings had
dwindled, and she seriously doubted Clair's ability,
either physically or emotionally, to handle her pro-
longed illness. It was not the way she wanted to die.
To Judy, her death was the natural and inevitable consequence of living, and she accepted it with grace
and dignity.

Judy went home from the hospital, arranged her   3
affairs, painted her last landscapes, and died within
five months.

Was Judy's decision a right one? Did she have   4
the right to determine how she was going to die?

Her husband never agreed with her but finally   5
came to accept it as her decision. Her doctor, on
the other hand, maintained that she did not have the
right to refuse treatment. As a matter of fact, he
refused to support her choice. Judy, as a nurse,

knew a doctor who would, and it was easy for her to
seek him out. Other patients are not that lucky.
Most patients do whatever is recommended to them by
their doctors, without question and without the knowledge that they do have a right to refuse treatment because the doctor never gives them that option. A
doctor will explain a terminal illness to his patient
by telling him of the medicines and procedures that
are available to combat the disease. Doctors believe,
and it is sometimes true, that this is what the patient
wants to hear and that this is the treatment the
patient expects to receive. Some doctors will explain to the patient that while there are side effects
to the treatments, they can be controlled by changing
the chemotherapy or by giving more medications to
counteract the effects of the chemotherapy. An
occasional physician will tell his patient he has "a
50/50 chance of living another two years or so with
treatment." Rarely is a patient told that, even after
the chemotherapy, radiation, surgery, and the "two
years or so" of extended life, he is going to die
anyway. A doctor is trained to treat illness and
cure the patient. To him, by not acting to prevent
death, he is allowing his patient to die. To a doctor,
death is an enemy and failure. Every measure is taken
to ensure that the patient does not become a "failure."
When his patient dies, the doctor feels personal
failure.

With today's technology, a patient's appointment   6
with death, while still inevitable, can be rescheduled
according to the arbitrary wishes of the physician.
If a patient's lungs fail, put him on a ventilator to
do his breathing for him; if his kidneys fail, start
dialysis; even if his heart fails, he can be maintained mechanically. Here again, patients are rarely
given information about the effects, the costs, or the
benefits of these treatments, let alone informed of
the potential harm they may cause. Often the institution of these treatments by the physician are after-
wards explained to the patient or family as "necessary
to prevent death." Should not the patient be allowed
to decide if and when and which treatments he wants
to have, prior to their use? Some physicians will
argue that their patients do not have sufficient
knowledge to be able to determine whether or not they
need to be put on a respirator or started on dialysis
or receive any other medical treatment that might be
necessary. I will counter that such a physician has
a responsibility to educate his patients in such
matters. The patient does not need a medical degree
to make decisions about his own care. He needs only
the information pertaining to his specific condition,
and all the options that are open to him, including
his right to refuse any or all of those options.

What about the patient who is unable to make in-   7
formed decisions? Is it possible that medical treatment could become medical abuse?

Mr. Syms was a 73-year-old gentleman who, while 8
walking home from visiting his wife at a local nursing
home, was struck by a car. Besides a shattered left
femur, a fractured pelvis and a ruptured bladder, and
fractured ribs and abdominal bleeding, he suffered
head injuries, the extent of which could not be determined on admission. An emergency operation removed
his lacerated spleen and repaired his abdominal injuries and the ruptured bladder. His left leg was
set as best as it could be, but useful function of
the leg would be doubtful. He lay in the intensive
care unit, his leg in a cast from hip to toe; a
catheter drained his still bloody urine from his
bladder out through his abdomen; he had a nasogas-
tric tube draining his stomach contents out through
his nose; two IV lines were running, one in each arm,
to provide him with fluids. He remained comatose and
an electroencephalogram showed only minimal brain
activity. His wife had Alzheimer's disease and was
not even aware that he was missing from her life. He
had no other family.

Mr. Syms remained in critical condition for two 9
days. On the third day after the accident he had a
heart attack, but with resuscitation was revived.
Within twenty-four hours, he had two more heart attacks
and was again revived each time. In the following
three days, he had two more heart attacks and was
twice again revived and placed on a respirator to keep

him alive. Finally, on the tenth day after the accident and after developing pneumonia, he died even
while attempts to resuscitate him continued.

Here was a body trying desperately to die. Who   10
among the medical profession would step up and say
"enough is enough"? None did. Was Mr. Syms's
medical treatment medical abuse?

In my opinion it was. Had efforts to keep Mr.   11
Syms alive succeeded, he would have been eventually
transferred to a nursing home to be "maintained" in a
vegetative state until he died, a silent reminder of
miraculous medicine.

Besides the obvious ethical issues in Mr. Syms's   12
treatment, there are two questions I feel need to be
asked. First, what about the cost of Mr. Syms's care,
not only his hospital care, but what about the care he
would have needed should he have survived? His hospital bill was over $46,000, which was paid for by
Medicare (you and me). Should cost be a factor in
anyone's care? Mr. Syms's early treatment, right
after the accident, was certainly justified, but when
it was known that he would not ever recover, continued
efforts to keep him alive were highly questionable.

What about his age? If Mr. Syms had been a six-   13
year-old hit by a car while playing in the street
would his treatment be justified, even when there was
no hope of recovery? While most children have parents
or guardians to make decisions for them, it is still

the physician who has the responsibility to inform those
decision makers about reasonable expectations of recovery and the options they have concerning treatment,
including the right to stop or refuse treatment.

Physicians are devoted to a moral duty to heal   14
their patients. They are also faced with an ethical
dilemma which invariably involves taking some risks in
making judgments. In making life-or-death decisions,
they must employ wisdom and judgment. They cannot act
on whims or prejudices, and decisions must be support-
able with the desires and well-being of the patient
in the forefront, even when those desires counter the
physician's own beliefs, and even when they may constitute death to his patient. Conflict arises when the
doctor's moral duty to heal impedes the patient's
right to die.

Euthanasia is a term defined by the dictionary as   15
"a painless putting to death of persons having an in-
curable disease; an easy death." The medical profession
has conveniently broken that definition down into two:
"active euthanasia" or the hastening of death by deliberate action, and "passive euthanasia" or the alleviating of symptoms, even though life may be shortened
and nature be allowed to take its course. This was
the course Judy chose. Was Judy's decision a right
one? It was for her. She made her choice based on
a knowledgeable foundation.

There are not any hard and fast rules within the   16

medical community concerning euthanasia. It is a word
never spoken in hospitals even though passive euthanasia
is practiced by some physicians like the one Judy found.
The right to die is basically a decision now made by
doctors based on their own morals and beliefs, even
though it is a decision that should be based on the
patient's morals and beliefs. Some doctors are thoughtful and reasonable about their expectations of a
patient's course of disease. They are considerate of
the desires of the patient and discuss openly all
options open to the patient, including what will
happen should the patient elect to refuse treatment.
That is as it should be. Other physicians, however,
never give in to that old enemy death. These doctors
will frequently confuse patients and families by offering hope through medications and treatments that are
only temporary measures to prolong life. To them, the
quality of life is not even a matter that needs consideration or discussion. They fully believe they are
doing their best for the patient by saving him from
death, even for a short while, even in misery.

The right to die has been slow in being brought   17
forth for open discussion. Gradually, medical schools
are beginning to recognize that the life of a dying
patient becomes steadily less rich and less worth
living, and that as the pain and suffering involved
in maintaining what is left of life are mounting,
there comes a point when decisions must be made.

These decisions must be made by a knowledgeable patient and family, clergy and physician, all together.

There are no absolute rules that will resolve all 18 the questions with the same answer. Each case and each patient are different and need to be considered on an individual basis. I cannot advocate active euthanasia or mercy killing. That involves one person ending the life of another. I do not advocate patients refusing all treatments, when there are certainly patients who can benefit. I am saying that all of us are going to die sooner or later. I am saying that the medical profession has a duty to accept that fact, that it be given to the patient as an alternative to all other treatments he may be asked to consider, and that his wishes in the choices he makes be accepted gracefully. I do hope that in the near future the medical profession allows that to each individual there is a time to die and that that time is the patient's rightful choice.

As it is written in Ecclesiastes: "To everything 19 there is a season, and a time to every purpose under heaven: a time to be born, and a time to die; a time to plant, and a time to pluck up that which is planted."

Amen! 20

When Beverly Dipo completed the final draft of "A Time to Die," she wrote the following commentary on the process of writing the essay:

It's done! It is always a great relief to get something that is difficult finished. I did find writing an argumentative essay difficult. A personal experience essay requires only that you describe something and report your responses to it. An argumentative essay requires some thought and research. Also, I suppose I had some difficulty because I am basically a passive and introverted person. While I may have some strong feelings and opinions, I do not usually publicize them.

Medical abuse is one subject I do have strong feelings about. I work with it daily, and it is so very frustrating. Nurses are somehow caught in the middle of a great dilemma between the medical hierarchy on one side and just wanting to help people on the other. As for my paper, I am not sure I stated that position as well as it could have been. I hope I gave some good examples and expounded on some of the problems that confront the dying patient. But — being my own worst critic — I feel it probably could have been said better by someone else.

The most difficult aspect of the assignment was to restrain and contain the subject. I did do some research on it and found it to be much more involved than I could possibly cover in one paper. My theme could have covered "codes" or the lack of them, "slow codes," living wills, malpractice, families, or hospice care, among other things. I did feel at times a certain limitation and at other times that I had picked a subject which was more than I could handle.

During the process of writing this essay, my mind frequently wandered back to Mrs. Trane and to so many other dying patients I have taken care of over the years. I wonder, had they really known what their remaining time would be like after a terminal diagnosis was made, how many of them would have agreed to treatment? Would they have refused treatment if they had been given all the facts? I remember one man being so angry about not being told what would happen to him that, much against his family's wishes, he ordered that his remains be cremated, without funeral services. He had shunned every friend and all but his closest family. He did not want to have them see him, during his illness or after his death. He not only blamed his doctors, but the nurses as well. He died an angry and hostile man. One of his last remarks to me was, "This disease didn't kill me, my fellow man did." Well, his disease may have killed his body, but it probably was his fellow man who killed his spirit.

It is people like this that I thought about when writing this essay. It is my argument for them and to them. They are the ones who need to be educated about their rights. They are the ones who need to realize that doctors are only humans, not gods, and that medicine cannot keep everyone alive forever. This argumentative essay let me make that point, whereas the one on Mrs. Trane did not.

Thinking about it now, after the essay is done, I find I like the idea of being able to say right out loud how I feel about the issue. It is not such a bad thing to be able to do. That is probably the thing I enjoyed most about this paper.

In my personal experience essay, I suffered Mrs. Trane's death silently and alone. In this argumentative essay, I gave the burden of sharing death over to those who are experiencing it. Maybe someone will learn something from it, or think about death differently than they had before, or discover that they do indeed have control over their own lives — and deaths.

Questions on Dipo's Two Essays

1. Beverly Dipo's journal entries include "some brainstorming." What relation does this brainstorming exercise have to "A Time to Die"? Which notations, if any, provide an early indication of the eventual focus and direction of "A Time to Die"?

2. At what point in her journal entries does Dipo seem to settle on a subject for her new essay? What specific thoughts trigger her decision to write about a patient's "right to die in the way he chooses"?

3. Once Dipo has begun to write her essay, what concerns does she express about finishing it? Based on your reading of her final draft, how did she resolve those "problems"? Support your response by pointing to specific words and phrases.

4. Dipo's journal entries include several *definitions*. In what specific ways does Dipo incorporate these *definitions* — either explicitly or implicitly — in "A Time to Die"? Where and how does she include information from the library research she has done?

5. Reread Dipo's explanation of her goal in writing this essay. Assess as specifically as possible the extent to which she achieves that goal. Outline Dipo's *argument* in "A Time to Die." What are the specific strengths of her argument? In what ways do you think she might strengthen it?

6. What specific thematic connections can you identify between "No Rainbows, No Roses" and "A Time to Die"? What stylistic features link both essays? What evidence can you point to in the word choice, phrasing, sentence structure, and overall organization that would verify Dipo's authorship of both?

7. Review the brainstorming notes and journal entries exploring possible subjects that resulted when Dipo reread her original essay. What other possibilities for writing a new essay can you identify in "No Rainbows, No Roses"?

TURNING A PERSONAL EXPERIENCE ESSAY INTO EXPOSITION OR ARGUMENT

Now that you have observed how two student writers developed new essays —one expository, the other argumentative—from personal experience essays, you can apply the procedures they followed in your own writing. The whole process, from start to finish, consists of five basic steps:

1. Reread your personal experience essay carefully several times and generate as many new subjects as possible.

2. Generate as many ideas about each of these subjects as possible.

3. Decide on a new subject to write about.

4. Assert a specific idea about that subject.

5. Write a new essay in which you explain (exposition) or verify a claim or proposition about that new subject (argumentation).

You have probably noticed that both Julie Reardon and Beverly Dipo devoted a large proportion of their efforts to steps 1 and 2. For these writers, as for many others, steps 3 and 4 happened together as step 2 progressed. That is, once you have come up with a list of subjects and are thinking about how you might approach each of them, you may well find that a thesis—an interesting idea to assert about a workable subject—occurs to you almost spontaneously. Very often steps 1 and 2, generating possible subjects and ideas, are the most daunting and time-consuming steps in the process. Let's look at them closely.

As Beverly Dipo's and Julie Reardon's examples indicate, the personal experience essays you have already written contain rich and ready resources for writing other types of essays. Although Reardon moved from description to exposition, while Dipo moved from narration to argument, it is clear from their freewriting and brainstorming that Reardon's original paper might just as well have led her to an argumentative essay and Dipo's to an expository one. The choice of which kind of essay to write may depend on your assignment, or on the combination of subject and idea that strikes you as the most promising thesis. Keeping an open mind is wise. Recall Beverly Dipo's initial reluctance to write an argumentative essay; once she did it, however, she commented: "I find I like the idea of being able to say right out loud how I feel about the issue. . . . This is probably the thing I enjoyed most about this paper."

Step 1 involves rereading your original personal experience essay carefully, several times, and listing every subject that comes to mind as you think about what you are reading. When you return to your earlier work after a lapse of time, you are better able to see it from a fresh perspective. Ask yourself questions: What made me feel strongly enough about my original topic to write about it? What controversies does it suggest? What broader subjects does it relate to that would allow me to generalize (exposition) or theorize (argumentation) about my experience? Your goal at this point is simply to list as many new subjects to write about as possible.

After completing step 1, you may conclude that only one of your possible subjects is worth pursuing or that one subject is significantly stronger than the others. If so, go on to step 2 and ask yourself: What idea can I assert about this topic? Focus your thinking about the subject — or issue — until you are reasonably confident you can assert a specific idea about it. Now consider what information, what data you can provide to support and clarify your idea about this subject or issue. Explaining that idea will become your new expository essay. Or, when you have narrowed your list of possible topics to one, ask yourself: what claim or proposition can I assert about this topic? Presenting logically related statements in support of your claim or proposition will lead to a new, argumentative essay.

In most cases, more than one subject on your list will have good potential as an essay topic. Step 2, then, is to generate as many ideas as you can about each of your "finalists." Some possible theses or approaches to a thesis probably will have occurred to you while you were considering topics. Even if these do not look promising, write them down; they may suggest other possibilities later. As you did when you thought of subjects, you can try brainstorming, as Beverly Dipo did — let ideas swirl around in your head and write down everything that might lead to a thesis. Or you can freewrite, as Julie Reardon did — go through your original essay again and list all the thoughts it inspires.

Another Bedford Prize winner, Ravenel Boykin Curry, has described the kind of chain of associations from which he gleans ideas. Curry's essay, "A Small Town" (p. 63), is the result of looking at ordinary personal experience from as many angles as possible. Cultivating this kind of "writer's eye" not only generates a continual supply of ideas but suggests ways of asserting those ideas in an essay. As Curry notes:

I have found that the best way to get ideas (and a more interesting way to live your life) is to look for some kind of significance in little things you observe each day. A mother slaps her whining kid on the beach. You can pursue the aesthetic — the sun is shining on thousands of people laughing and playing in the water, but all that fills this kid's being right now are the pain and anger. You can be psychological — is the child a brat because the mother responds with violence? Or could negative incentive help the kid to understand that the world doesn't tolerate a whiner? Take a political angle — should the state be able to intervene in minor family violence? What if the husband slapped the wife? What constitutes child abuse and who should decide? You can expand anything; ideas are endless.

It sometimes happens, however, that even after rereading your original essay and listing possible subjects and ideas, you still have no workable thesis for an expository or an argumentative essay. If so, you may find the following additional questions helpful. Consider all four sets of questions and then choose one set to guide you as you develop your new essay.

1. *Move from the specific to the general.* A narrative or descriptive essay focuses on a specific event, person, place, or object. Beverly Dipo's "No Rainbows, No Roses" related the death of Mrs. Trane; Julie Reardon's "The Unmarked Road" re-created the rural neighborhood where the author spent four years. Every specific case can be viewed as an example of a generality: people dying in hospitals; people living in poverty. To move from the specific subject of your personal experience essay to a more general topic, think about how your experience can be considered representative of many people's experience. The goal here is to broaden your point of view, to extend your thinking to take in that of others besides yourself. Once you have done this, you may want to choose one segment within that general topic, as Beverly Dipo chose "people dying in hospitals *with dignity.*" Or your first generalization may lead you to others: people dying at home; the value of funerals; the importance of making a will.

   Questions: What general topic is implied in your specific personal experience? What general subject does your personal experience exemplify? What general issue or issues does your experience raise? What other general subjects or issues emerge from rereading your original essay and thinking about its larger implications?

2. *Move from autobiography to biography.* Another way to move from personal experience to exposition and argumentation is to shift the focus of your original essay from autobiography to biography, from a first- to third-person point of view. The shift from a subjective to an objective perspective carries you beyond the limitations of your own experience. It also enables you to understand — and participate in — a multiplicity of cultures and life-experiences that, in turn, may well help to illuminate your own life.

Questions: As you reread your personal experience essay, pay special attention to whether you talk about anyone else during the course of your essay. Consider each such person carefully. What aspects of this person's life do you think are worth writing about — consider beliefs, attitudes, accomplishments, or perhaps an incident or an anecdote in which he or she figures prominently? What ideas can you assert about this person? What general concept is this person's life a specific example of? What proposition or claim can you make on the basis of this person's views or behavior?

3. *Move from the concrete to the abstract.* Narrative and descriptive essays are based in large part on concrete information: sensory details about how something looked, felt, or sounded; actions that occurred; the writer's response to those details and actions. In Patrick Kinder Lewis's essay, "Five Minutes North of Redding" (p. 150), we feel the predawn chill of a railway roadbed, and we share the author's tension as he bounds onto a flatcar. But Lewis's essay also alludes to such abstract concepts as freedom, risk-taking, and friendship. As you reread your own personal experience essay, look for the abstractions it suggests.

Questions: What abstract nouns come to mind as you reread your essay? You may very well think of several abstractions that are associated with your specific, concrete experience. Choose one of these and work at developing its potential as the subject of another essay. Why did this particular abstract noun surface in your mind as you reread your essay? What aspects of your essay suggested it? How does it summarize the point of your essay or indicate what your essay is about? What idea, claim, or proposition might you assert that conveys your thoughts regarding this abstract concept?

4. *Move from observation to inference.* Yet another way to find a suitable subject to develop into a new essay is to move from observation to inference. (For our purposes, an "observation" may be defined as a statement about the visible facts in a specific situation, a statement about which there can be no disagreement. An "inference" is a conclusion based on a premise drawn from observations, a statement about what is still uncertain made on the basis of what is certain. For additional information about observations and inferences, see Part V. In one sense, your original essay might well be considered a series of observations about your experience.

Questions: What inferences about experience in general can you draw from your essay? What theory or pattern of behavior seems to govern the experience you wrote about? Consider that theory or pattern carefully and list as many observations as you can about it. Based on your observations, what inferences can you draw about this theory or pattern? To what conclusion about experience, however tentative, do these observations and inferences lead you? Turn this tentative conclusion into the thesis — the controlling idea — for either an expository or an argumentative essay. How can you use the evidence of your own experience, or your inferences about experience in general, to support this thesis?

Having considered these four broad sets of questions aimed at helping you move from writing personal experience essays to expository and argumentative ones, you need next to decide which cluster seems most appropriate to the purpose of your new essay. Once you have made that determination, you might well want to work with the following summary of useful procedures. As you reread your personal experience essay, what new "angles," what new approaches to this subject can you think of? What broader subjects does this essay suggest? Keep track of these subjects in note form and develop each by following your usual methods of developing an idea about a subject: brainstorm, freewrite, and so on. Narrow your list of possible subjects to one and examine it further. Then ask yourself: what idea can I assert about this subject? Explaining that idea will become your new, expository essay. Or, when you've narrowed your list of possible subjects to one, ask yourself: What claim or proposition can I assert about this subject? Presenting logically related statements in support of your claim or proposition will lead to a new argumentative essay.

Discovering and learning how to develop the connections between the ideas in one successful essay and another are important skills to master, especially for writers who are not only respectful of the richness of their own intelligence but also committed to exploring that richness fully. Learning to explore the connections between one idea and another, between one essay and another, and between one course and another also helps every writer to recognize — and strengthen — both the interrelations of writing and reading and the common threads that weave together the seemingly disparate verbal elements of our lives into a practiced, confident, and unique intellectual identity.

Three Exercises for Moving from Personal Experience
to Exposition and Argument

1. Reread Ann Louise Field's essay, "The Sound of Angels" (p. 76). Here are some possible subjects — and ideas asserted about those subjects — that Field prepared after rereading her essay:

—Paper routes
 1. Early jobs build responsibility.
 2. Forcing children to work at too early an age robs them of their youth.

—Sibling relationships
 1. A little bit of rivalry can be a good thing.
 2. Traditions of childhood; experiences common to all kids.
 3. Love-hate feelings between siblings.

—Orange groves
 1. The rise and fall of the Southern California citrus industry.
 2. The pros and cons of growing oranges for Minute Maid.
 3. The art of tree-climbing.
 4. Linus Pauling and the vitamin C/cancer controversy.

—Childhood pranks
 1. Lead to delinquency.
 2. Encourage imagination and creativeness in youth.

—Christmas
 1. Holiday traditions.
 2. The evolution of commercialism at Christmas.

—Loss of innocence
 1. The effects of economic stress on the contemporary American family.
 2. The need for everyone to recognize reality.
 3. The nature of adolescent rebellion.
 4. The increase in teenage suicide — the inability to function in an adult world?

Based on your reading of Field's essay, which of these possible subjects — and assertions — for expository and argumentative essays do you think Field would handle best in a new essay? Why? Point to specific passages in "The Sound of Angels" to verify your response. Which seems to offer the least potential as the subject — and the assertion — for a new essay? Why?

2. Write an expository or argumentative essay based on a personal experience essay you have written. Follow the questions and procedures outlined above.

3. Write as detailed a commentary as possible on how you wrote your new essay. For instance, how did the idea — or claim — you chose to assert about your new subject develop and change as you actually wrote the essay? What particular problems did you have to work out from one draft to the next? What was the goal of your new essay? Whom did you see as the readers of your new essay? How did you try to appeal to these readers? What did you want them to think or feel after they read your essay? What advice would you offer your readers on how to respond to and understand your new essay?

PEER EDITORS
AT WORK

Part V

THE TWO PREVIOUS CHAPTERS examined the composing process from the writer's point of view. In Part III, "Three Student Writers at Work," Barbara Seidel, Jonathan Schilk, and Matthew Holicek reconstructed the different approaches they used to get started, write, and then revise their essays. In Part IV, "Moving from Personal Experience to Exposition and Argument," Beverly Dipo and Julie Reardon explored the personal experience essays they had already written to generate new topics for additional expository and argumentative essays. This chapter studies the composing process from the points of view of both the writer and the reader by focusing on how writers can work with their peers to improve each other's essays. Like their professional counterparts (see Part VI, "The Professional Editor at Work"), peer editors serve as supportive readers, ready to understand a writer's purpose and to assist the writer in achieving that purpose. In such circumstances, a writer can sense the immediacy of an audience — other students who are willing to read his or her work thoughtfully and offer detailed comments on how effectively a particular draft expresses that writer's intentions. As a peer editor you can provide both specific praise and practical advice about how to strengthen the already successful features of an essay and how to revise its weaknesses. And by responding to and evaluating your peers' writing, you will be better able to write, read, revise, and edit your own essays.

Peer editors and writers can work one on one, in small groups, or within the class as a whole to help each other get started, draft, revise, and edit essays that will satisfy themselves and their course requirements. Although the principles and procedures of peer editing can be applied to any stage of the composing process, peer editing usually works best after writers have produced a first draft of an essay, when they can benefit most from detailed and supportive responses to what they have written. By working collaboratively with peer editors, writers are not limited to their own perspective on the composing process; they can see how other writers — the peer editors — would deal with exactly the same circumstances and challenges.

This chapter examines the most effective techniques peer editors can use when responding to the writing of other students. The chapter first presents an example of peer editing: several students offer detailed responses to and recommendations for Patrick Kinder Lewis on how he might improve his essay, "Five Minutes North of Redding." The chapter then considers in general terms how a writer might work most productively with the peer editors' responses to plan more effective revisions based on their comments and recommendations. More specifically, the chapter presents Lewis's explanations of how and why he incorporated, modified, and occasionally rejected the peer editors' suggestions in working on his revision. A newly revised draft of Lewis's essay follows, along with several peer editing exercises in which you can apply the principles and procedures of peer editing, first to Johnna Lynn Benson's "Rotten at the Core" and then to your own writing.

THE PEER EDITOR'S RESPONSE TO WRITING

The most effective peer editor is an interested and sensitive reader. To be a sympathetic and helpful critic of another student's writing, you should be willing to work diligently to understand the writer's purpose and to offer thoughtful and specific advice about how the writer might best achieve that purpose. You need to be interested in helping other students write better — not by suggesting ways to avoid errors but by assisting them in articulating their ideas fully.

When approaching another student's writing, you should think, talk, and write about it seriously and respectfully; any writer will respond more appreciatively and energetically to criticism — be it positive or negative — that has been tactfully worded. Judicious comments also signal that you are genuinely interested in helping another writer improve; the most helpful comments are specific, direct, and encouraging. A peer editor who says simply that he or she "liked" or 'disliked" an essay doesn't help the writer understand either the essay's strengths or weaknesses. But noting, for example, that the writer has emphasized a particular point by developing a striking metaphor in the third sentence of the second paragraph makes that achievement more appreciable — and the skill more repeatable — for both the writer and the peer editor. And it is, after all, the ability to repeat success that can make writing so satisfying and enduring an intellectual enterprise.

As a peer editor, you can respond in innumerable ways to another student's writing. The most typical and widely used strategies for peer editing fall into two categories: specific comments in the margin of the essay and a general statement, usually at the end of the essay. These specific and general comments most often serve two functions: to describe what the writer has actually said in the essay and to evaluate its strengths and weaknesses.

Perhaps the most valuable service that you, as a peer editor, can perform for a writer is to return a clear and, at least initially, nonjudgmental description of what the writer has written. One of the best ways to do that is to write as many specific observations as possible about the essay, either directly on the manuscript or on a separate sheet of paper to be given to the writer. In peer editing, an *observation* is a statement about which there can be no disagreement. In this sense, an observation is concrete, limited, verifiable, and often fairly obvious. It is also nonjudgmental. The purpose of your observations is to help the writer understand and appreciate a reader's perceptions of what he or she has actually written. Your observation might address, for example, fundamental problems in logic and organization: "You mention the same point about the effects of nuclear weapons in paragraphs 4 and 7." A seemingly obvious observation such as, "I notice that you begin the first five sentences in your essay with 'It is' and 'There are,' " may lead the writer to reread the essay with an eye to varying its verbs and sentence structure. But the decision, and in fact the authority, to do so remains where it belongs—solely with the writer.

Evaluative comments shift the emphasis from describing what the essay says to assessing its specific strengths and weaknesses and suggesting particular revisions. In making evaluative comments, the peer editor writes detailed marginal notations about such elements of composition as word choice, tone, use of examples, logic, and organization. You identify both what the writer does well in the essay and what the writer needs to spend more time on. The more honest your assessments are, the more helpful they will be.

A particularly useful kind of evaluation is for the peer editor to summarize as succinctly as possible the thesis of the essay and to note specifically how the writer develops that controlling idea in each paragraph. The aim of this evaluation is to assist the writer in expressing, clarifying, and developing completely the main point of the essay as well as the assertions in each paragraph that support it.

The peer editor usually writes a general evaluation at the end of the essay based on the specific marginal notations made throughout the paper. Your goal in this general evaluation is to give a balanced overview of the essay's strengths and weaknesses, not simply a summary of its flaws. You should also include suggestions to help the writer develop a detailed and achievable plan for revision. These suggestions should be selective rather than exhaustive and should help the writer set clear priorities for revising. These general comments are also the most appropriate place to review the essay with an eye to helping the writer make it as concise, engaging, and elegant as possible. These are also quite likely the last suggestions the writer can draw on before revising the essay and submitting it to the instructor for an additional reading and eventually a grade.

Student writers who serve as peer editors will be both practiced writers and practiced readers, since the skills of writing and reading are truly integrated. What peer editors learn about the interaction between reading and writing will help them a great deal when they turn to their own writing.

PEER EDITING PATRICK KINDER LEWIS'S ESSAY

To demonstrate how a writer can improve an already successful essay with the help of peer editors, this section presents several peer editors' responses to Patrick Kinder Lewis's essay, "Five Minutes North of Redding." We have chosen this essay because of its complexity and ambition. Lewis writes knowledgeably and dramatically about a youthful adventure "riding the rails" in northern California. Aboard a freight train traveling north from Sacramento, Lewis discovers a great deal about himself and his relation to the world around him.

Lewis spent roughly a year on the road, trying "to figure out what made life tick — and whether there was really anything that made one's life worth all the pain. What I came back with was the beginnings of something more than simple self-worth. That was there too. But that year, more than any other, assured me that life is really only as absurd as we choose to make it. . . . I also came back with a new realization of the value God has placed on every human life. The hobos and mixed-up kids I met were no less worthy of the meagre amount of grace that I was able to show them than any others I might meet under other circumstances. Nothing in this life comes cheaply — nothing of value anyway — but none of us pays anywhere near the face value for what we get either: what we have, we have been given on loan. I began to live in the midst of that antinomy, to be liberated by it. The world of others around me continues to be bathed in that strange light for me."

With this recognition in mind, Lewis set out to write an essay about the chain of events that led to his realization about the profound dignity of each human life, "to create the snapshot which I never took of that epiphanic moment. And I wanted to create the peace of that moment. . . . The experience about which I wrote was a brief but meaningful excerpt from a much longer story I hope to write about learning from life-lived-on-the-edge. 'Five Minutes North of Redding' was in a way the fulfillment of a youthful dream and the beginning of a more mature vision."

At the end of the spring 1985 semester, we invited four writing students at Queens College in the City University of New York to respond as peer editors to Patrick Lewis's essay. At that time, the students—Nicholas Balamaci, Jason Eskenazi, Nelson Farias, and Fran Osborne — had accumulated virtually a semester's worth of peer-editing experience. These students read and responded to Lewis's essay as though he were a classmate. Then Lewis responded in writing to their comments and suggestions and planned and wrote a revision based on their recommendations.

Here are both the specific marginal notations the peer editors made on Lewis's essay and their general comments at the end of the essay. Read the essay as it appears on pages 150 – 153 without any comments on it. Then reread it as it appears below, this time considering the peer editors' responses.

LEWIS'S EDITED ESSAY

This title puts the incident in both time and place.

Five Minutes North of Redding

You tell us where we are immediately. (NF)

I rolled out of the weeds into the crisp day-light of that late September morning to catch the

I notice you use a technical term. Is this the language of hobos? Of railroad people? Both? (JE)

north train out of Roseville. The <u>herder</u> had said

Powerful description of your state of mind (FO).

it would leave about 3:00 am; so I had huddled in

Is this necessary? (NF)

my coat for at least three hours, wishing in the

You transform wishes to dreams here. (FO)

predawn chill for a cup of hot anything. But the

You create a strong sense of anticipation at the end of the first paragraph. (NB)

noise and lights of the train yard had filtered through the tall grass and disturbed even those harmless dreams.

I notice that you equate wishing and dreaming here. Your equation is very indirect, however. Make it clearer? (JE)

Finally <u>she</u> came. Forty cars were in sight

Who is this "she"? (NB)

before the engines passed me. <u>Moving down</u> to the

How about: "As I moved down"? I think it reads better that way. (NB)

rail bed, I noticed for the first time that I had

I notice that you use many participial phrases. (JE)

not slept alone on this stretch of tracks. Three figures were coming down to claim a rail car 150 yards up the line, and even as I cautiously watched them, two other groups of riders were claiming cars

What is this other thought? Is it the next sentence? (JE)

behind me. I bounded onto a flatcar, concerned that the line of empties would soon pass me by--<u>then</u> thought again. A <u>solitary presence on that flat</u>

This is a dangling modifier. (NB) (JE) (FO)

How about: "I was a solitary presence on that flat deck, and within me instinct..."? (NB)

You make me feel how sensitive you are to your own vulnerability here. (NB)

deck, instinct shouted within me warnings about such a vulnerable position. I crossed the ten-foot width and dropped down onto the ground on the other side of the car. This time I watched until everyone was

1

2

+   +

on board before I picked out one of the last empty

boxcars. And still there were some fifty closed *All references to*

cars behind mine. This train was surely big enough, *the journey*
between Rockville and Sacramento are
I imagined, for all of us. *left out. Can we assume that you*
got on board, the train started, and you travelled? (FO)
   The line of cars came to its first stop on a   3

siding three hours up the Sacramento Valley as we *I notice that*
you refer to
yourself and
allowed another train to pass. Groves of plum trees *the train*
collectively.
There are
lots of   lined the track on either side. Even so late in the   *(JE)*
details here.
They work season, the trees to the train's right were still
well. (NP)

                full of hard purple fruit. I laid down in a splash

Who was warm
and relaxed? of sun on the deck of my car. For the first time
(FO)(NB)   *I was*
Another   that morning, warm and relaxed, the startling sound
dangling
modifier?   of shouts out the east door caused me to retreat *If they are*
Add:"I was"   *playing, then*
and "but"? into the shadows again. I peered out to find six *this should*
(NB)   *be fun. "Experiments"*
         men playing among the trees like kids as they picked *are for rats.*
There is an   *(NF)*
innocence plums only to pelt each other with them. I watched
here that
fights against intently, as if it were some elaborate social experi- *By whom?*
the alienation   *you seem to*
you say   ment, until the sound of boots on gravel brought me *want to*
you feel.   *generalize*
(NB)   back around. Looking to the (shadow) behind me, I *here. Why?*
                                                                 (JE)
         suddenly realized that it was too late to conceal *Whose*
                                                           shadow? Your
Excellent myself. The man whose crunching boots had just *participial*
aural and   *phrase keeps*
visual   announced his approach was somehow already at my *me guessing.*
description.   *(JE)*
(NB)   back door looking me over. *Is this word necessary?*
                                        What does it add to
                                        your sentence? (NB)
    "There you are. I've been lookin' for you.   4
You make this sound ominous. It works! (NB)

But only one is asked. (JE)

It would be interesting for a reader to know why you would need to carry a knife. It would create tension if the danger was dramatically present. (NF)

Is this necessary? It seems to me that this phrase reduces the relief caused by the discovery. (NF)

I like how you showed friendship with his voice instead of simply telling us about it. (JE)

You give your audience lots of details here. You make it easier for us to see the knife. (NF)

You're travelin' alone ain't you?" All the wrong questions to ask someone who is already scared of you. [Luckily the voice betrayed nothing but a desire for friendship.] "That's right, I am. What . . . are you alone, too?" I sized him up coolly as I moved toward my knapsack in the far corner. In its open front pocket I had a knife if I needed it. He had an eight-inch Bowie knife strapped frontier-style to his right shin.

There's a real sense of voice, of personality here. These lines back up your point that the stranger is friendly. (Fo)(JE)

You separate the dialogue with lines of description. That gives the effect of coolness, of distance, between the speakers. (Fo)

"No. Couple of beaners and me pick up together in Stockton; but they ain't speakin' nothin' but Spanish, man. You want sumpum to eat? They're gettin' some plums. We got cukes and tomatoes that they picked in the Valley yesterday. And I got a box of saltines in Roseville."   5

Is this necessary? It doesn't seem like essential information at this time. What does it add? (NF)

There is excellent control in here. The tension begins to grow, but its reduced by the following sentence. ("If I planned...") (NF)

He had a ruddy face that was roughly pocked, probably from adolescence, and a scraggly mustache that only became noticeable when he looked right at you. I had reached my pack, but simply turned toward him in a crouch to look for my next move.   6

Do we "look out" for our next move? Don't we get "ready" for it? (NF) This is an unusual way of saying this, and the phrase works well. (NB)

Can "standing" be a time? (NB)

If I planned to turn down his offer, standing four feet up in a boxcar was the time to do it. His   7

bony frame and large hands gave away his height: I

This is a concise description. (Fo)

would be at a three- to four-inch disadvantage once _+_ *You repeat this word later. (NF)*

down on level ground. And he just looked (tough.) *Move to beginning of sentence? (NF)*

Shoulder-length, muddy blond hair (he had) tied back *Do you need this? Isn't this understood? (NF)*

This is a sentence fragment. (NF) with a lace of dark buckskin; it laced the seams of

his chamois pants too. (He was (fond) of buckskin and *How do you know this unless he told you? And if he did, then why not let him speak here? (JE)*

How? wore it well.) [Very (tough) but somehow gentle.] He

The contrast needs to be developed. (NF) seemed all in all an atavism, a confusing mixture of

General Custer with a sixties flower child. I de- *I think it's a good idea to let us figure out what that was. It's more fun for your readers. (NB)*

cided to trust my second inclination.

"Sounds good," I said closing my pack. "What's   8

your name?" I grabbed my jacket and hopped down onto

Where else would he limp from? Sounds like he kicked the door! (JE) the loose shale bed. The train was just pulling away *I notice that you use the word "him" here twice in one sentence. (JE)*

with a halting rumble as we neared his car. On

quickening our pace, I noticed he was limping from

his hip down. I was in the car before him and *This is an excellent sentence. You show his experience in action. This is filled with great details! (JE)*

offered him a hand. But he ignored it and managed

an agile roll into the car by catching hold of a

break in the floor.

Use "in" here instead? (JE)   Alex and the Beaners were the first hobos I (was)   9

You need to give some examples here. (NB)(FO) to travel with. (For) the space of a couple days we *Was seems out of place here. It's like looking back on something you're looking back on? (JE)*

ate, drank, slept, and (fought) like brothers. I

I'm not sure that this is the right word. If you meant "fought" literally, then that seems like a cliché. You need to work harder here on your language. (NB) learned (their) pasts and (their) plans in that short

time together and laid awake to think what it would *I notice that you use the word "their" three times in one sentence. (JE)*

be like to live (their) lives. At one point, left

behind by our train somewhere south of Red Bluff, *Same train? New train? (JE)*

This paragraph confuses me. I've lost a clear sense of time and place. (FO)

we hiked together most of the way to the next rail-

head, ducking many a curious sheriff en route.

Finally Alex found us a ride out of a truck stop

with an ex-Harley biker. Ambling over the gunwales

of his pickup, we rode it all the way to Redding.

Which night? (FO) (NB)

That night, we caught the last train out still   10

on its dinner break. Ducking into a store nearby, I

Nearby what? (NB)
Why ducking if you are a legitimate customer? (JE)

This is ambiguous. Can a train be on a dinner break? (JE)

quickly bought enough sardines, crackers, and canned

sausages for ten men. While the train sat idle we

found a boxcar that was open only on its east side.

(For the cold trip into the mountains ahead, warmth

was a more important concern than a view of the

scenery to the west.) We had just finished off the

This implies that you're impatient for it to move. If so, why? (NF)

sardines as the train at last began to lumber out of

Why? (FO) Show us. Don't tell us. (JE)

the yard. Our bodies exhausted, our hunger at last

abated, we sat on the dirty floor of our boxcar en-

joying the last warm breath of the evening. We were

You make me feel this sentence! Well done. (JE)

now at the northernmost end of California's fertile

basin. From here on the land would climb more steeply.

You move back to being more specific here. That's very effective. (FO)

Only the Sacramento River lay between us and the Cas-

cade mountains. As we approached the trestle, the

I notice that you use another technical term. (JE)

track took only one slow curve to the northwest. On

ahead, I was sure it would begin a series of slow

Read this aloud. Doesn't it sound awkward? (NF)

switchbacks to climb Mt. Shasta's side. But for now,

Something missing? (NF)

because dead ahead, Shasta was out of sight.

The naming of places does not fully produce a feeling of movement! This is especially true for readers unfamiliar with the geography of California! (NF)

Why? (FO)

Is there such a word? (NB) I leaned tiredly against the back door and *Your use of this metaphor from drama is very effective.* watched as the scene in front of me began to change.

You shift here from the concrete to a metaphor → (NF) Low on the horizon, a nearly full moon was rising *It's almost poetic!) (FO)* slowly to take its place in the center of our stage.

Mt. Lassen's distant volcanic head joined (it) as we *I'm not sure what "it" refers to. (JE)* rounded the last turn before the river, showing mutely

through a carpet of velvet green peaks. Inside the

I think it would have been more effective to mention their origin earlier. (NF) car, Alex stood up to blow the smoke of his cigarette *This sentence sounds awkward. (JE)* out into the crystal air. He propped himself like a

This simile seems out of place. (FO) caryatid supporting the right border of our window on

Excellent word choice, suggesting oneness with each other and emphasizing the feeling of the paragraph. (FO) the world. My (Mexican) (compadres) sat nearly motion-

Your words grow more affectionate here, and that seems appropriate. (JE) less at the door's left side. Mesmerized, I dug

blindly into my pack to find the harmonica which I

had saved for just such an inspiring moment. I sucked

Why? (JE)(NF) *Are you using this phrase ironically? Talking about pure pleasure? (FO)* in a chord or two of "This Train Is Bound for Glory,"

The Sacramento? (FO) laughing inside. Suddenly, another (actor) entered *But you don't develop the metaphor of the stage until six sentences after it introduced. (NF)*

You make us figure this out for ourselves I like that. (NB) *The river? If not, who? (JE)* from stage left and I came up to a squatting position

to get a better vantage. The wild Sacramento below *Your essay picks up momentum in these past few sentences, and the momentum increases with each new sentence. (JE)*

us had begun to snake its way into view, illumined

only by the bright moonlight.

What is "it"? (JE) (It) was all I could do to keep from walking out

our door onto that stage. Like something from a *This is an overused word, but here you use it effectively. (FO)*

What is "it"? (JE) dream, (it) seemed too (fantastically) beautiful to be

real. And finally, unexpectedly, the train itself

Excellent! You reinforce your metaphor of the stage nicely. (JE) emerged as a player. The trestlework not only poised

This is wonderful! The train has been a silent player all along, and here you finally see it too, and consciously. (FO)

the line of cars two hundred feet above the river's

surface but managed as well to bend it into a slow

arc midway in the crossing. The sweep of that north-

You return here to talking about yourself and the train in collective terms. (JE)

ward arc turned our view to the south. And just for

that instant both the front and rear of the train

were visible at once. The engines at our head dis-

This seems like a peacocky word to use here. (FO)

appeared slowly into the shadow of Mt. Shasta while

the cars that trailed our coach paraded behind us

This verb makes it sound a little melodramatic. (NB)

across the massive trestle. And on it all was poured

the stark quiet of the moonlight reflected in the

I love the idea of quiet being "stark." It's really a good example of how you control your language in the last two paragraphs so that it sounds greeting-card like. (FO)

river below.

The trestle, from south to north, could not have   13

This sounds philosophical and therefore a little risky for some readers.

been over a mile long. The entire panorama played

before us for less than two minutes. Yet, in a very

real way, it has run in my mind's eye ever since.

Would something like "Time stood still" work here? (NB)

As that team of Southern Pacific diesels pulled   14

us out of Redding, eternity sat captive for a moment.

(NB) These are very powerful images. You handle them well! (JE)

Like a stolen glimpse of childbirth, I shared in that

These sentences seem to contrast, if not contradict each other. (JE)

The metaphor of birth doesn't work as well as your others. It seems inappropriate. (FO)(NF)

peaceful feeling of something both beginning and

ending at once. And like a mother smiling at her

child born at last, I found myself smiling with a

similar relief. It was joy without euphoria. I

hunted again for the insights of the moment before

But what were they? (NB) I'm not sure that you explained them clearly. (NF)

but found them fading with the darkness of the

mountains ahead. What race had I run to earn such

rest? What was born in that moment? I looked to my

I don't understand this. How does an appreciation for beauty show a passion for life?

(FO)

companions for an answer but found it instead full-

formed in the darkness between us. There was the

sudden realization of the only bond that we all

shared: <u>our passion for life.</u> We were living life

moment by moment. That was our race well run. As

our halos began to fade I picked up my harmonica

and found myself playing "Bound for Glory" in a

different key.

The problem of this last paragraph is — unlike the rest of your essay — you tell me this. I want you to show me. I want to experience what you're talking about here so that I can also feel it. (JE)

General Comments at the End of the Essay

The four peer editors added these general comments, in addition to their marginal notes, to the end of Lewis's essay.

NICHOLAS BALAMACI —This is even-keeled, controlled writing. It is also vivid; I "saw" the story. Your essay is also philosophical, and because of that, risks being sentimental. Yet I feel that you avoid this problem very well, although there are just a few lapses (for example "tough but gentle," and "ate, drank, slept, and fought like brothers"). You narrate an important experience in your life, and you emphasize the particular with lots of concrete details. You also use those details to make more general and abstract statements. That's why the essay is so well-crafted.

The only part of your essay that seems a little shaky is the ending. Your words there seem mostly abstract, and you run the risk of letting your essay slide off into impor-tant-*sounding* talk. You should think about saying this more simply or less abstractly. Also, there's one repeated me-chanical problem: you allow loose connections at times between your modifiers and their referents and between your subjects and the participial phrases that modify them. But I want to say also that I could have written beside every paragraph: This essay comes ALIVE! It really makes the experience come to life for the reader. I feel as if I had been there. It's vivid and yet matter-of-fact writing. I look forward to reading it again and owning my own copy of it!

JASON ESKENAZI —When writing for others, we sometimes write more elabo-rately than we need to, changing sentences for complexity, for example. I think you need to watch out for this. Some-times you exchange complexity for clarity. I think you should be clear first.

This essay approaches being a short story. You have the main character come to a moment of insight, and that moment seems to change him at the conclusion. Why did you decide to write an essay? What makes this an essay and not a short story?

If you're going to revise this essay, I'd suggest thinking more about the opening paragraphs. You seem to be much more indirect in the opening paragraphs than you are in the final ones. I think you should be more consistent about this.

The momentum of your essay builds up nicely to the conclusion. Your realization about how the train became a "player" is terrific! Your realization became mine! In moments like that you use a good deal of poetic language. I hear you! The chances you've taken are worth it! You've created many intriguing images and ideas, and you make me want to think more about your story and what it means.

NELSON FARIAS —Your story has lots of fine word choices and effective metaphors. And these choices give your essay its tone. In this respect, your word choices are appropriate to the mood you want to create. But your sentences are sometimes incomplete and your metaphors aren't developed fully. The way to improve these weaknesses is to place metaphors and ideas that are connected closer together.

You also seem to use lots of proper nouns in your story. That's both effective and ineffective. It's effective because you really draw the reader into your experience, but it's ineffective when the nouns are obscure or confusing. For example, what is a "herder"? Also much of the terminology of the trains is hard to understand. What and where is the "east door"? Is a "closed' car the opposite of an "empty" car? What are "switchbacks"? How can you be sure that your reader will understand what these terms mean? I think your essay could be improved if you'd concentrate on who your audience is. If these railroad terms aren't essential to the overall point you're making in your essay, then maybe you should eliminate them. They distracted me. I guess they'll distract other readers. How important are these terms to what you really want to say in your paper? Maybe you should write another paper on the technical parts of railroading! I'm just not sure that these terms contribute anything to your essay. Besides, I'm more interested in reading about what happens to you than I am about what happens to the train! I'd suggest eliminating some of what you say about the train and adding more about yourself and your experiences with Alex and the beaners.

FRAN OSBORNE —Up to this point [paragraph 9], there's a real caution in your word choices. (See all the words marked by +.) But when you come to the end of this paragraph, that caution seems to disappear. Did you intend to do that?

This essay has real power to move your audience, power which stems from your ability to communicate "the magic of a moment." It seems to me that paragraphs 12 and 13 capture that moment very effectively. But these paragraphs also contribute much more to your essay. The metaphor of the "stage" that you introduce in paragraph

11 brings all the elements ("the players") of the essay together into a powerful moment of recognition for you. And
you have prepared your audience well for that moment —
even from the very beginning of your essay. You express
the basic idea of your essay in a beautifully understated
way in the title.

If the moment of recognition in your essay is presented
in paragraphs 12 and 13, then I think you should consider
eliminating most, if not all, of your final paragraph in your
revision. The metaphor of the childbirth, for example, seems
inappropriate to the context you have created. Also, your
tone changes in the last paragraph. You seem to want to
summarize, but you do that in a very different voice. Perhaps you should leave out most of the final paragraph and
end by returning to "playing 'Bound for Glory' in a different
key."

The essay needs some "fixing" in a purely technical sense.
I need to understand better the architecture of the train
more clearly (What does it look like?). I also need to understand better the passing of time more clearly (How much
time elapses while you're on the train?). Finally, I also need
to understand better the relationships between you, Alex,
and the beaners more clearly (How much more can you
tell us about them that will strengthen your story?).

All in all, though, I think your essay borders on the
poetic, and it is all the more effective for it. I enjoyed
reading it and thinking about what you accomplished.

Questions on Lewis's Edited Essay

1. Reread the peer editor's statements about Patrick Lewis's essay. On which
aspects of the essay does Nicholas Balamaci focus his attention? Jason Eskenazi?
Nelson Farias? Fran Osborne? What overall advice does each offer? What specific changes in focus, tone, and word choice do you notice between the peer
editors' general concluding statements and their marginal comments? Which
parts of the essay does each regard as most successful? Least successful? Why?

2. Review the peer editors' detailed marginal notations. Which of the comments
are observations (statements about which there can be no disagreement)? Which
are evaluations that try to summarize the main idea of the essay and then show
the relation between specific paragraphs and this idea?

3. Examine Fran Osborne's comments at the end of the essay. What is her response
to the overall structure of Lewis's essay? to his use of *diction* and figurative

language? to the speaker's voice? Which of these aspects of composition does Osborne think Lewis handles best? Why? Point to specific words and phrases to support your response.

4. List the points the peer editors agree on; disagree on. On what points do you agree with them? On what points do you disagree?

5. Reread Nicholas Balamaci's final comments. Sketch out what Lewis would need to do in a revision to respond adequately to what Balamaci says. Then reread Jason Eskenazi's concluding statement. In what specific ways might Lewis's plan for revision be altered by what Eskenazi says?

THE WRITER'S RESPONSE TO PEER EDITING

As a writer, you will benefit most from peer editing when you listen attentively to what your peer editors have to say about your essay and then examine with them the implications of their observations and recommendations. But peer editing—like writing—is a skill that takes time and frequent practice to develop. So you and your peer editor need to remind each other, at least occasionally, that even the most well-intentioned efforts at peer editing—and especially the first few tries at it—may not bring immediate improvement. There are few quick fixes in the world of ideas.

As a writer about to work with peer editors, you can anticipate receiving a good deal of generous and supportive criticism from readers who are familiar with—and sympathetic to—your purpose. And the presence of a real audience, who will read and respond to what you have written, may well be all you need to reassure yourself that writing is worth the effort involved, especially when you face moments, as nearly every writer does, when ideas seem hard to discover and energy and interest falter.

To make the best possible use of the peer editor's responses and advice, you need to listen thoughtfully to their observations and recommendations and take advantage of them when you write a final draft of your essay. By listening purposefully, you are less likely to be distracted from examining the strengths and weaknesses of your essay by what may occasionally be a peer editor's poorly phrased comment or ill-advised judgment.

When done rigorously, peer editing is as much a writing exercise as a reading exercise. When your peer editors are searching quickly for the best way to convey their responses to your essay, they, too, may occasionally slip into awkward or even inappropriate phrasing. But such moments, however uninstructive they may appear at first glance, can be opportunities for you to reciprocate by helping your peer editors express themselves more effectively. Sometimes their comments may not be entirely clear, and in such cases you should not hesitate to press for clarification. This process often results in a dialogue in which you have a chance to explain more fully your purpose or sense of audience, and the peer editors have an opportunity to clarify and develop some of their comments and suggestions. But whatever the particulars of such dialogue, writing is clearly the source—and the result—of productive conversation.

Writing should be at the center of peer editing. You should leave a peer-editing session with more than the impression of your peer editors' response. You should carry away, and later evaluate and act on, their detailed written responses to your essay, responses that have been amplified in your discussion with them. Having all the peer editors' comments in writing not only makes particular points of the discussion recoverable later, it also enables you to evaluate their comments and enumerate your priorities for revision.

With the benefit of peer editors' responses, you should improve—and perhaps dramatically so—your ability to evaluate the reactions of many different readers, each of whom may read your essay in a slightly different way. You ought to pay special attention to any comments about strengths and weaknesses pointed out by more than one peer editor. In each instance, you as the writer must decide what to change and what to retain in your new draft. Although the peer editors can help, the authority and the responsibility for those decisions remain yours, and yours alone as the writer.

Discussing and then evaluating peer editor comments should help you develop a clear sense of how to improve your essay. Your detailed plan for revision should include the peer editor recommendations you have decided to accept and act on and your own ideas about how to reinforce your essay's strengths and eliminate its weaknesses. The peer-editing process encourages you to treat your essay as a work-in-progress, to understand your specific strengths and shortcomings as a writer, and eventually, to produce stronger writing at every phase of the composing process.

ONE WRITER'S RESPONSE TO PEER EDITING

In this section we present Patrick Lewis's response to the peer editing of Nicholas Balamaci, Jason Eskenazi, Nelson Farias, and Fran Osborne. Patrick Lewis's comments explain his decisions to include, adapt, and sometimes reject their recommendations in the revised version of his essay. Lewis's reactions to the peer editors' final general comments and then to their specific marginal notations are followed by his overall response to peer editing itself—its principles and practices and its value in the composing process.

ON THE PEER
EDITORS' FINAL
COMMENTS

The final comments gave me a general idea of the temperament of my audience. Did they like me and the paper, or did they think I was from another planet? I wanted to know about any big gaps that I needed to bridge. I have taken four general guidelines for revision from the peer editors' end notes:

1. Nicholas comments about my tendency to philosophize to the point of sentimentality. I knew exactly the passages in which I made the offenses. The question I had to ask was, "Is that so bad?" After talking things over with my writing teacher, I came away feeling that, whatever I did — as in so many things — it was always going to be better to use silver polish than a sandblaster. A little philosophy never hurt anyone, so long as it isn't overblown — "important-*sounding* talk" as Nicholas calls it. Since some kind of expository essay seems to be my natural mode, I guess I had better learn to do it well if I can.

2. The same question in my mind comes up in Jason's query about whether I hadn't really wanted to write a short story. The truth is that I would have liked to write one, but that was not the assignment. I decided that, if I hope to really "assay" my thoughts on the story I want to tell, then I should do it engagingly, and without resorting to any abrupt mood shifts.

3. Nelson asked for more development of the "I" character. That in fact prompted the most obvious change in the paper, that is, its opening. Nelson made me realize that the central character was the only thing that made the story coherent. So I worked myself into every line in a more conscious way. Enough said! This begins to sound self-aggrandizing, which is not my intent at all.

4. Fran made me see more clearly that it was the "magic of the moment" which needed to be the teleos of the work. I am glad that she liked it, because I was beginning to lose sight of why I felt I *had* to write this paper in the first place. She also agreed with the haunting feeling I had that the last paragraph was somehow overkill.

Fran also raises a very interesting question for me. She wanted to understand better the relationship between me and the other characters. In fact, she went through and marked words [with a + sign] that seemed to indicate my isolation from them up to the point where I met Alex.

In the revision I have tried to make that theme more

consistent and the transition more obvious. I *was* afraid and then resolved not to live in that unfounded fear. So, as to the basics of human friendship, I wanted to show that change as one that was/is evident to even me. But there is another distance that separated us, which is not as central.

It was interesting to find Fran in a marginal note assuming that we (that is, the travelers) were all in the same boat. There is a barely legible note on my "General Directions" outline where I ask myself (to explain) where the ignorant and illiterate fit into my scheme of the world. I see quite a distance separating me from the fellows that I am writing about. But it is not the same sort of distance I mentioned above (fear), nor the sort I mentioned in the paragraph about hobo life (ignorance and uncaring). I am not isolated from them by my choice as much as by "our choice." I feel for and with them, but there is no less a real distance of understanding. But I resolve that it not be a distance of appreciation. My empathy, born in our exposures (and the sometimes palpable misunderstanding that exposure brought), affords them a very special place in my world — perhaps akin to the place which Jesus intimates in the beatitudes (and in fact throughout his teaching ministry). The poor in spirit *are* blessed. Not simply because of their ignorance nor in spite of it. It is for both of these reasons and more. And somehow, it makes them my *superiors*, in a realm that I don't understand well, but respect very much. The uncomfortable distance which I feel between the "ignorant" and the "enlightened" is the result of *our* misunderstanding — both sides are guilty. It is bridged, then by admission of our own ignorance. The bridge seems intensely spiritual.

ON THE PEER
EDITORS' MARGINAL
NOTATIONS

I am not a detail person, so I guess it shouldn't surprise me that the big things worked in my essay, while, often as not, the sentences struggled to make themselves even coherent. I took Jason's comments about "exchanging complexity for clarity" and "writing too elaborately" to heart. I hope that most of the sentences in the new version are at least readable . . . . Let me quickly mention no more than a dozen marginal comments that got me thinking.

What is so mystifying about the relationship between wishing and dreaming? I added the phrase "half-awake" to a sentence from the old paragraph 1 to clarify the point. I hope it works. I think that more than likely, the heavy opposition was due to first paragraph overzealousness. Anyway, it does read better.

I am truly indebted to Nicholas (my tongue is *not* in my cheek this time!) for two very specific suggestions which I think improve paragraph 2 immensely: just the kind of cleaning up that Jason drew to my attention in his general comments—a misplaced participial phrase and a predicate with a (mis)understood subject.

At the end of the same paragraph, I dropped the last two sentences because they were a weak attempt at developing the "fear" theme. The more direct reference two paragraphs above made them superfluous.

Everyone got their wish in paragraph 3 when I interrupted a very difficult sentence (again with a misunderstood subject) to make a detour for Fran and Nelson's benefit. Actually, I had wanted to put more of the hobo's eye-view description in my original, but couldn't seem to make it fit. I hope the addition gives new insights, though I suspect it has a few difficulties of its own.

I was disappointed that everyone seemed to concur with Nelson's remark that "experiments are for rats," a little later in the same paragraph (old number 3). The sense of observer-observed isolation is exactly what I had felt up to that time. And it is what I tried to convey by that word choice.

Again in the same paragraph, Fran made a practical, seemingly obvious, suggestion that vastly improved the feel of the prose. I substituted the simple Anglo-Saxon verb "hide" for a difficult Latin reflexive phrase "conceal myself."

Both Nelson and Jason helped me clean up the next paragraph (that is, number 4 in the original).

I was trying all along to keep Alex down to a "manageable size." Several of the peer editors, in the paragraph describing Alex's appearance, wanted me to somehow expand on "tough but gentle." Though Alex was a real person, I really wanted him, for the purposes of this essay, to stand for a character type: the good guy, gentleman-of-the-rails. Having to develop *two* characters to everyone's satisfaction threatened to diffuse the overall direction of the essay and add an unnecessary dimension.

The old paragraph 10 has a whole new look for the same sort of reason: too much detail with not enough direction.

Both to introduce a paragraph that contains what I consider to be some "important talk" and to satisfy the urgings of Nicholas and Fran (that is, to expand the somewhat sappy line about "fighting like brothers"), I cut out much of that paragraph and some of the next. Most of the next paragraph in the revision (as well as parts of the new introduction and conclusion) came from the material that I cut out from the original for lack of space.

I thought the question about technical terms perplexing. Anyone who has grown up around mountains should have encountered "switchbacks" as the only practical way for a road or a trail (or a railroad track) to climb a steep grade. Words like "herder" and "beaners" I assumed would be obvious by their contexts (who else in California speaks "nothing but Spanish, man"?).

For the rest of the story, I had spent great pains in getting a very difficult picture in my mind's eye on paper. So I felt comfortable about the generally favorable comments and with leaving it much the same. I made one very specific change suggested by Nelson, shifting the first sentence of paragraph 13 with the last one of 12.

ON PEER EDITING
AND WRITING

I certainly hope that the peer editors like the new look and feel of the essay. It took a while to get started after the preliminary notes I made on everyone's ideas. I didn't really hit a groove until a few hours of working on the revision. Then, and only then, did I start to enjoy what I was doing again. The final product seems more focused than before, moving with a kind of concerted effort it didn't have before. And I also came to feel a lot more comfortable with the distinct voice that an essay should have. It just sounds more controlled than before, less rambling and storylike.

When I began the process of this revision, after reading through both the peer editors' final comments and their marginal notes, I was ready to make a broad statement about the greater relative value of the end-type comments. I thought I would reject 90 percent of the marginal stuff. Now that I have finished, I can no longer make that statement. I ended up weighing every comment carefully, and I would guess that 90 percent of them have affected the new essay in some way or other. I hope the peer editors can see the extent of each of their contributions to the new version. And I very much appreciated the strongly personal approach each took. It made their recommendations "stand apart" with much less overlapping than I anticipated. What's more, they wrote very lucidly about rather difficult subjects. All that said, I am glad there were no more than four peer editors — even five would have been overwhleming.

As a new writer, I suppose it is natural that I am a rather unselfconscious writer. I enjoy writing. I suppose that there is a similar feeling in the neophyte painter. If nothing else, writing always seems to sharpen my perception of what I have seen. The peer-editing process has rushed me into the world of the conscious. There is an almost unimaginable benefit in simply the suggestion that someone is taking something I have written seriously enough to respond to it personally. That feeling of "someone watching," if not allowed to dominate our mind, can probably be the greatest single factor in encouraging seminal talent. But you must, I think, enjoy writing first.

I am also, I think, an unassuming preacher/teacher without a pulpit/classroom. Though I have to guard myself against "manufactured solutions," there is probably nothing wrong with sermons which might not sound like sermons, but still contain real value. To a great extent, that is what I had hoped for in "Five Minutes North of Redding." That is also why the last paragraph is so much different. There is nothing I said in the original which I would in any way call false or contrived. I believed every word. But to believe so strongly can be synonymous with robbing the mystery from truth to leave only bare bones. That kind of truth dies a sudden death of exposure. And dead "truth" becomes confused with the worst sort of lie. The message which I have tried to convey by this essay, because it is existential, is bound to be a little obscure. But then so is life! At its best, it is full of mystery — at its worst, it is full of doubt, especially self-doubt and distrust of others.

Now that you have had the opportunity to read Patrick Lewis's responses to the peer editor's observations and recommendations, examine the revised version of his essay, which he prepared after considering their reactions and advice.

LEWIS'S REVISED ESSAY

Five Minutes North of Redding

My twentieth-fifth year was a mixed-up time   1
for me, full up with broken relationships and lost
hope, all-day school and all-night jobs. I was
"living in the shade of a freeway" (as Jackson
Browne so aptly put it) in a worn-out mobile home
with a Siamese cat on loan from a friend, and a
primer gray Datsun 110 with a bad transmission:
the whole thing was rather comical for a while, but
I was slowly becoming more desperate for whatever
was next. And so it was that I began to notice the
routine of a work train that daily came out of a
cement yard over on the other side of the through-
way fence.

"Riding the rails" had wooed me for several   2
years, from the time I had first seen three modern
hobos jump off their "coach" on the outskirts of
Las Vegas. From that moment on, the romance of life
seen from the door of a boxcar had captured my
imagination. I even resurrected an old harmonica
that I had used in high school and began playing
woeful tunes late at night, while the open road sang
along in a familiar voice. The words of the ballad
promised to tell a tale yet untold, but then they
drifted off into the soft stillness outside my door.

I left the L.A. basin with only one change of   3

clothes, a bedroll, and a little bit of money hidden
so well that it took me ten minutes to get to it. I
waited until I heard the train pulling into the cement
plant and locked the door of my trailer behind me as
I ran to meet it. Twenty minutes later I was riding
my first freight. Alone. And that was just fine.
I had heard too many stories about shifty bums who
would kill for a pair of shoes. I stayed wide of
their campfires and always traveled by myself.

Two weeks later found me near Sacramento, waiting for another train on the outskirts of the biggest
rail yard in northern California. This time I was
bound for Seattle. I rolled out of the weeds into
the crisp daylight of that late September morning
to catch the north train out of Roseville. The
herder had said it would be leaving about 3:00 a.m.
So I had huddled half-awake in my coat for at least
three hours, wishing in the predawn chill for a cup
of hot anything. But the noise and lights of the
train yard had filtered through the tall grass and
disturbed even that harmless dream.

Finally she came. Forty cars were in sight
before the engines passed me. As I moved down to
the rail bed, I noticed for the first time that I
had not waited alone on this stretch of tracks.
Three figures were coming down to claim a rail car
150 yards up the line, and even as I cautiously
watched them, two other groups of riders were

claiming cars behind me. With what looked like
seasoned confidence, I bounded onto a flat car,
concerned that the line of empties would soon pass
me by--then thought again. I was a solitary presence
on that flat deck, and, within me, instinct shouted
warnings about such a vulnerable position. I crossed
the ten-foot width of the car and dropped down onto
the ground on the other side. This time I watched
until everyone was on board before I picked out one
of the last empty boxcars.

The line of cars came to its first stop on a   6
siding three hours up the Sacramento Valley as we
allowed another train to pass. Groves of plum
trees lined the track on either side. Even so
late in the season, the trees to the train's right
were still full of hard purple fruit. I lay down
in a splash of sun on the deck of my car. For the
first time that morning, I was warm and relaxed.
The world of the hobo seemed at the moment to be
everything I had hoped for. Maybe more. For one
thing, I hadn't figured on the dust, but there was
plenty of it to go around. My first hour reclining
against the wall of a boxcar left me smudged with
enough soot to convince anyone that I had been
hoboing all my life. Nor had I counted on the
noise. The crashing clatter, especially of start-
ups, made me wish often enough for the luxury of
earplugs. Even the click of the rails inside this

car (with both doors pushed open wide) was less than soothing after an hour or so. Still, all that seemed to make stops like this one the more enjoyable. The view and the solitude of such regular pauses lured me into the kind of romantic reverie that had inspired this adventure. Later, after a nap, I would get out to step away from the train far enough to see what was up ahead. But for now, what I could see through my door was all the world I had wished for.

Suddenly, the startling sound of shouts out the   7
east door caused me to retreat into the shadows again. I peered out to see six men playing among the fruit trees like kids as they picked plums only to pelt each other with them. I watched intently, as if it were some elaborate social experiment, until the sound of boots on gravel out the other door brought me back around. Looking back to the shadows of the car's interior, I suddenly realized that it was too late to hide. The man whose crunching boots had just announced his approach was already at the west door looking me over.

"There you are. I've been lookin' for you.   8
You're travelin' alone ain't you?" The wrong question to ask someone who is already scared of you. Luckily the tone of his voice betrayed only a desire for friendship.

"That's right, I am. What . . . are you alone,   9

too?" I sized him up coolly as I moved toward my
knapsack in the far corner. In its open front
pocket I had a knife if I needed it. He had an
eight-inch Bowie knife strapped frontier-style to
his right shin.

"No. Couple of beaners and me pick up together   10
in Stockton; but they ain't speakin' nothin' but
Spanish, man. You want sumpum to eat? They're
gettin' some plums. We got cukes and tomatoes still
that they picked in the Valley yesterday. And I
got a box of saltines in Roseville."

He had a ruddy face that was roughly pocked,   11
probably from adolescence, and a scraggly mustache
that only became noticeable when he looked right at
you. I had reached my pack, but simply turned
toward him in a crouch to look for my next move.

If I planned to turn down his hospitality,   12
standing there four feet up in a boxcar was the
moment to do it. His bony frame and large hands
gave away his height. He would be three to four
solid inches taller than me on level ground. He
had tied his shoulder-length, muddy blond hair back
with a lace of dark buckskin; it laced the seams of
his chamois pants too. (He was fond of buckskin
and wore it well.) But, tough as he looked, there
was an obvious gentleness to him as well. He
seemed all in all an atavism, a confusing mixture
of General Custer with a sixties flower child. I

decided to trust my second inclination.

"Sounds good," I said closing my pack. "What's 13
your name?" I grabbed my jacket and hopped down
onto the loose shale bed. The train was just pulling away with a halting rumble as we neared his car.
As we quickened our pace, I noticed he was limping
from his hip down. I was in the car before him and
offered him a hand. But he ignored it and managed
an agile roll into the car by catching hold of a
break in the floor.

Alex and the Beaners were the first hobos I 14
was to travel with. Their friendship wore away the
edge of the fear I had felt since hearing my first
hobo story. Over the space of a few days we ate,
drank, slept, and fought like brothers. I shared
my rations, and at one point, even my bedroll, with
my Mexican companions who had come less prepared,
while Alex laughingly looked on and told story after
story. I learned something of their pasts and their
plans in that short time together, and lay awake to
think what it would be like to live their lives.

Life in a downtown rail yard is much farther 15
away from most of us than simple distance suggests.
The bums, drying out from damp nights by fires
built under the bridges, rarely venture into our
world from their environs plaited out of steel and
wood. Sometimes they make the trip to downtown

skid rows for the social interaction offered at
missions and overnight shelters. But hobos are
really in a class by themselves. Not quite as
permanently debilitated as the downtown drunks,
they generally live their private lives without pan-
handling, building a world of their own in the hobo
jungles that spring up among the weeds and ware-
houses surrounding train yards. Few of them have
anything resembling a year-round home. Transience
and seasonal migrations are the more general rule.
Some do venture in and out of institutional life:
missions, dry-out centers, acute psychiatric wards.
Paranoid schizophrenia is surely their most common
syndrome; alcohol is their drug of choice. But
there are also, of course, many exceptions. Alex
and the beaners were three of them.

While the train sat idle in Redding, we found   16
a boxcar that was open only on its east side. (For
the cold trip into the mountains ahead, warmth was
a more important concern than a view of the scenery
to the west.) We had just finished off several tins
of sardines as the train at last began to lumber out
of the yard. Our bodies exhausted, our hunger at
last abated, we sat on the dirty floor of our boxcar, enjoying the last warm breath of the evening.
We were now at the northernmost end of California's
fertile basin. From here on the land would climb

more steeply. Only the Sacramento River lay between us and the Cascade mountains. As we approached the river's trestle, the track took only one slow curve to the northwest. On ahead, it was sure to begin a series of slow switchbacks to climb Mt. Shasta's side. But for now, because dead ahead, Shasta was out of sight.

I leaned tiredly against the back door and 17
watched as the scene in front of me began to change. Low on the horizon, a nearly full moon was rising slowly to take its place in the center of our stage. Mt. Lassen's distant volcanic head joined it as we rounded the last turn before the river, showing mutely through a carpet of velvet green peaks. Inside the car, Alex stood up to blow the smoke of his cigarette out into the crystal air. He propped himself like a caryatid supporting the right border of our window on the world. My Mexican compadres sat nearly motionless at the door's left side. Mesmerized, I dug blindly into my pack to find the harmonica which I had saved for just such an inspiring moment. I sucked in a chord or two of "This Train Is Bound for Glory," laughing inside. Suddenly, another actor entered from stage left and I came up to a squatting position to get a better vantage, as the river below came into view. It was all I could do to keep from walking out our door onto that stage.

The wild Sacramento below us had begun to snake   18
its way into view, illumined only by the bright
moonlight. Like something from a dream, it seemed
too fantastically beautiful to be real. And
finally, unexpectedly, the train itself emerged as
a player. The trestlework not only poised the
line of cars two hundred feet above the river's
surface, but managed as well to bend it into a slow
arc midway in the crossing. The sweep of that
northward arc turned our view to the south. And
just for that instant, both the front and rear of
the train were visible at once. The engines at
our head disappeared slowly into the shadow of
Mt. Shasta while the cars that trailed our coach
paraded behind us across the massive trestle. And
on it all was poured the stark quiet of the moonlight reflected in the river below.

The trestle, from south to north, could not   19
have been over a mile long. The entire panorama
played before us for less than two minutes. Yet,
in a very real way, it has run in my mind's eye
ever since. As that team of Southern-Pacific
diesels pulled us out of Redding, eternity sat
captive for a moment.

Later that night, I found out that Alex wasn't   20
running away as I had supposed. He was "tired of
all that" and thought it was time to head home
and help out his mother. Maybe he would even

settle down with a waitress who had been chasing him for years. At thirty-eight, the traveling seemed to be wearing him away little by little. I wondered what crisis had brought him to his decision, but decided not to ask. For it seemed that a similar moment had just passed in my life--one which no words could explain. The open road had told me its tale, and now I too was ready to walk into whatever was next. I closed my eyes for the night, humming "Bound for Glory" in a different key.

Questions on Lewis's Revision

1. In his responses to the peer editing (pages 358–363), Lewis discusses some of his plans for revising his essay. What did he decide to focus on in his revision? Which points does he accomplish most successfully? Point to specific words and phrases in both his responses and his revision to support your answer.

2. Which of Lewis's responses to the peer editors' comments do you agree with? Which do you disagree with? Why? Which points in his plan for revision would you like to see expanded? dropped? altered slightly? Why?

3. Which aspects of Lewis's essay would benefit from additional attention and revision? Why? Point to specific places where he could make further changes and indicate what those changes might be.

4. Lewis reports that he made substantial revisions in the opening and closing of his essay. How, specifically, has he done this, and with what effect?

5. Write as many observations as you can about the specific differences between Lewis's original essay (pages 150–153) and his revised essay. In what ways is his *purpose* clearer? How does each paragraph relate more clearly to the main point of the essay? How is his handling of Alex and the beaners stronger? How does he consider his audience's knowledge of hobos, trains, and life "on the rails"? How does his choice of words reflect a different consideration for his *audience*? Point to specific words and phrases in the essay to support your responses.

PRACTICING PEER EDITING

In this section you have an opportunity to practice applying the principles and procedures of peer editing, first to Johanna Lynn Benson's "Rotten at the Core" and then to your own writing.

The following checklist points out many of the concerns peer editors keep in mind as they work on an essay. Your instructor may add others.

1. *Purpose.* What is the writer trying to do in the essay? What is the main idea, the essay's thesis or overriding point? What intention or promise does the essay state or imply? Where and how well does the writer act on that intention or promise? What specific examples, ideas, or information would help clarify or reinforce the writer's purpose?

2. *Organization.* How is the essay organized? What is its basic structure? Comment on the logic and effectiveness of the sequence of paragraphs. How well does each paragraph support and develop the essay's main idea? In which paragraphs is the main idea most effectively supported by details and examples?

3. *Choice of Words.* Is the language of the essay primarily abstract or concrete? If it is abstract, do you understand what each abstraction means? Does the writer use special terminology or colloquial terms? How effective is such language? How well does it support the writer's purpose?

4. *Point of View.* Point of view means the point or perspective from which the essay is written or the story is told. From what perspective does the writer approach the subject of the essay? Where is this point of view stated or implied? Does the writer maintain the point of view consistently throughout the essay? Point to those places where the writer's point of view is most clearly stated, where it seems uncertain, and where it is consistent or inconsistent.

5. *Audience.* Characterize the audience the writer seems to have in mind. What does the writer expect the audience to know about the subject? Point to specific words and phrases that reveal the writer's assumptions about the audience's familiarity with the subject.

From your own experience and your study of peer editors at work, what other aspects of composition should peer editors attend to as they read another student's writing? Prepare sets of questions for each aspect.

Exercises in Peer Editing

1. Apply the principles of peer editing to "Rotten at the Core" by Johnna Lynn Benson (pages 31–35), following the peer-editing procedures outlined in this chapter. Read the essay several times and write your observations, evaluations, and recommendations in the margin.

   —Write as many observations as you can about the essay (remember, an observation is a statement about which there can be no disagreement).

   —Summarize the essay's main idea and note how the writer supports and develops that idea in each paragraph.

   —Identify both the strengths and the weaknesses of the essay. In this respect, pay particular attention to Benson's sentence structure and variety, her verb tenses and voice, her paragraph transitions, and her concluding paragraph.

   —Prepare a general final statement noting the essay's overall strengths and weaknesses and offering some specific recommendations for revision.

   After you have completed your work as a peer editor on "Rotten at the Core," write Johnna Benson a letter in which you analyze the strengths and weaknesses of her essay and offer her as much reasonable, practical, and detailed advice as you can about what she might do in another draft to improve her essay.

2. Now that you have completed your peer editing of Benson's essay, you might find it instructive to compare and contrast your marginal notations and final comments with those prepared by Nicholas Balamaci, Jason Eskenazi, Nelson Farias, and Fran Osborne. Here are both the specific marginal notations that these peer editors made on Johnna Benson's essay, along with their general reactions and recommendations for revision at the end of her essay. Reread Benson's essay, which begins on the next page, this time paying special attention to the other peer editors' responses.

BENSON'S EDITED ESSAY

You use a cleaning metaphor to begin with:

Rotten at the Core

Your title seems inconsistent with the outcome of your essay. (JE)

George A. Kelly's <u>Theory of Personality</u> has   1

neat because you're going to clean your self off and start over. (FO)

scrubbed me on a washboard and put me through the

wringer. Discovering what I actually am under the

Cleansing metaphor works well here. (JE)

dirt and debris has been bewildering and has left me

This word repeats "better off," and it can be considered a cliché.) Remove? (NB)

wondering if I would be better off blissfully igno-

Shakespeare! (JE)

rant. I had thought "to know thyself" an admirable

Reference to Keats's "Ode to a Grecian Urn." But are you searching for "beauty"? (JE)

pursuit, especially since I believed <u>truth was beauty</u>.

Now I see I have been <u>beautifully</u> wrong about who I

(Your use of "blissfully" and "beautifully" worries me because you do not explain how your ignorance was either. (FO)

am and who everybody else is.

You personify the colloquium. (FO)

When <u>the colloquium</u> introduced me to <u>Theory of</u>   2

colloquial language) (FO)

<u>Personality</u>, I was sure we would get along great. I

have always loved dabbling in psychology. My friends

But you do try to be "shocking" and "clever." Why not say so? (And they are not necessarily bad habits.) (NF)

and I would make Freudian jokes or play shrink-games,

using those little tests in women's magazines de-

signed to save on psychoanalysis costs. You could

Combine this sentence with the one before it for the sake of clarity. (FO)

say I won those games; my free associations were

always more bizarre than anyone else's. I wasn't

even trying to be <u>shocking</u> or <u>clever</u>. That is just

You change tenses here. (NB)

a bad habit. My only feud with psychology was that

I don't understand your point here. (JE)

I aspired to be more than a product of my environ-

ment, <u>a multiplication of Mormonism by a material-</u>

<u>istic middle-class suburb.</u> <u>Theory of Personality</u>

eliminated that limitation for me.

Your point of view is now clear. (JE)   I loved it instantly. Kelly's treatise holds   3

that people create their own personalities. As a   *I notice that you go to the source*

person tries to make sense of the circus around him,   *for a dab of objectivity*

Do you mean inferences here? (FO)   he picks up on recurring themes in his life and makes   *I like how you work Kelly*

deductions about what is going on. The individual   *in here. (JE)*

creates these explanations, called "constructs,"

for his convenience in anticipating what the world

is going to hit him with next. As a person con-

strues, he builds an inner road map of himself, of

life, and of what he can expect from it. The psy-

chology I had been exposed to before treated man like

an organism poked and prodded into reactions. I

found the concept of deciding for yourself who you

are and what you can expect from life far more pal-

atable. Claiming total responsibility for my out-

look on life filled me with satisfaction.

Theory of Personality created a little (garden

paradise) in the corner for me, but it also (unearthed)   *This is an effective metaphor. (JE)*

something upsetting. As part of our colloquium study

of constructs, we were asked to write about our core   *The essay really seems to get under way here. (FO)*

Your tone changes here. Is that what you intend?   roles, or how we viewed ourselves. I kept putting

the assignment off because every time I started it,

Do you both love and fear the book and what it reveals? (JE)   my query led me down the same path. [If you do not   *Doing anyway shows determination and strength of character. (NF)*

want to go to Rome, finding that all roads go there

is rather dismaying.] Suddenly it was the day to

This is an innovative and pleasant way to turn around the old cliché, and to make a point besides. (NB) hand in the assignment, and I discovered, as I fran-

tically wrote the thing in the Harris Fine Arts

[What a concise way to put this! Excellent! (NB)]

Center an hour before class, that I had spent enough

time trying not to think about it that I knew exactly

what I didn't want to know. *This could be a sentence by itself. (NF)*

You return us here to the idea of shocking and clever in paragraph one. (FB)

With Fresh, Original, and Bizarre as my highest   5

ideals, my core role seems to be that I must be dif- *"Different" is not a quality word.*

ferent. And I am different, which makes me excep- *"Exceptional" implies better than average. (FO)*

I don't see why being different makes you exceptional. (FB)

tional, though not in a way the general population

appreciates. This arrogant idea actuates my every *This way of talking about yourself seems unwarranted. (FO)*

thought and emotion, a realization that makes me

shudder. Exploring the fact that I'm rotten at the

core reduced me to tears. *But you haven't explained how you are "rotten at the core," only slightly arrogant. (NB)*

Yet I can't seem to get around it. I look at   6

how I hate get-acquainted parties. To adhere

You sound a little snobbish and ego-testical in here. (JE)

"Hello, my name is . . ." on my lapel is to assume

common ground exists between these strangers and me. *This is an innovative, clear, and artful way of putting this. (NB)*

But my core role says my lifeline runs geometrically

askew to theirs. Kelly defines guilt as an aware-

ness of contradicting one's core role structure, and

guilty well describes the uncomfortable feeling I

get pretending such parties aren't futile. I forget

that I actually do share significant parallels and *Can parallels be "shared"? Can "inter-sections"? (JE)*

intersections with family and friends. I like the

differences. By the time I was six I introduced

myself by saying, to the consternation of my play-

mates, that I did not like chocolate cake or soda-

pop. For years my favorite color was chartreuse,

sienna, or puce. My favorite number is 3.02875×10^{14}.

I took up origami because I thought no one had heard

of it. In short, anything popular was not worth my

time, while anything obscure or new was mine by right.

This is unclear. Did the three colors alternate as your favorite over the years? Aren't you certain which was your favorite? (NB)

Moreover, I felt unique enough to assume that

although rules were necessary to keep the regulars

in line, they did not apply to me. Because rules

were necessary, I never quite broke them but found

interpretations to suit me. For example, when an

elementary class punishment to copy five pages from

the dictionary was handed down, my paper always in-

cluded a few words outside the assigned alphabetical

range, like "despot," "toupee," or "maltreatment."

Lights-out at camp meant it was dark enough to

leave the cabin unnoticed and go for a moonlight

walk. Going to parties where friends were too drunk

to really notice my abstinence was showing my love

and understanding for people with problems, not to

mention making them aware of the Mormon Church. And

of course, as long as my boyfriend and I didn't go

all the way, whatever we wanted to do was fine. We

were toying with the idea of marriage anyway.

7

These paragraphs enumerate differences but they also enumerate similarities too. You, like most people, do have a favorite color, number, etc. And you do "obey" rules. The "differences" appear to be semantic rather than substantial. (FO)

This paragraph gives examples of how you "break" rules without breaking them! (FO)

Do you see the contradiction here? If friends are "too drunk to really notice," how can you be "showing"? (FO)

The idea about the Mormon Church seems unrelated to the rest of the sentence. It would help if you gave an example of what the Mormons have to offer such troubled people. Of what exactly did you make them aware? (NF)

Other people needed rules. I did not.

I have been carried away with my own indi- 8
viduality enough to hypothesize that when I was a
zygote, some stray cosmic ray zapped my DNA, making
me a daughter of chance and not of Terry and Dianna
Benson. On a similar note, I latched onto the idea

This seems to say "before I was spiritual, I was physical." (FO)

that I have always existed, that <u>before I was a</u>
" <u>spirit I was an entity, an intelligence bobbing out</u>
somewhere like a chartreuse soap bubble. I did not

colloquial (FO)

want to be someone else's creation. I <u>figured</u> God
recognized the special and distinctive thing I was
and handpicked me to be his child.

Without the religious aspect, your essay still makes sense. Is the sole purpose of your talking about religion to account for your differences? I think not. (JE)

Being Mormon has been convenient in other ways. 9

This is a cliché, and judging from your use of language else-where, you can do a lot better than this. (NB)

It is a guaranteed way to <u>stick out like a sore</u>
thumb. I always felt a swell of pride as I
answered astonished cries of "You've never done
such and such?" I could spend hours elaborating

It would be a lot easier on the reader if you simply spelled it out. (NB)

on LDS precepts with the sole intent of blowing an
innocent Protestant mind. I have had so much fun

There is something arrogant in this: 1) in the impli-cation that you are sophisticated (and so can "slow an innocent mind") and 2) in your focus on Protestant rather than other religious sects. (FO)

being Mormon that I have to wonder how much of my
testimony is based on faith and how much on the
attention it garners. I created my outlook on life

You sound like you're condemning yourself in here. (FO)

according to my convenience, says Kelly. My convenient testimony thus becomes as meaningful as my
green argyle earrings; I would probably join any

group that boasted of being a peculiar people.

The problem you elucidate concerning your faith is never resolved. Is it convenient or is it based on something more? (FO)

Yet my testimony of the gospel encapsulates some of my strongest emotions and most important rational convictions. I founded my belief on study, contemplation, and prayer, not whim. If such a testimony is invalid, there is little I think or feel that is valid. But I must consider (I may have) forced my personality to grow in unnatural and indirect ways because I wanted to be different, cultivating a taste for mustard on my french fries and a taste for LDS doctrine. (I have created) my personality and maybe I could have done a better job. Yet the thought of supplanting myself with a new and improved model based on different criteria scares me. It would be personality suicide; although someone would be here named Johnna, I would cease to exist.

How do you make the leap here from Kelly's theory being merely possible to its being true? (NB)

This is the heart of your essay. It is clear, thoughtful, and very meaningful. (NF)

The problem of looking at yourself in a new way begins here. (FO)

And what about all these other people? I always pictured my intelligence as a chartreuse bubble in contrast with their monochromatic assembly of lemon yellow bubbles. If Kelly gives me the right to be self-made, he also extends that right to all those (dumb slobs). Besides, I doubt Kelly (was) lemon yellow. If he and I can be different, then (probably) everyone else is on a slightly different wavelength, can be a slightly different color. This means I (probably) slightly different color.

Is there another way to convey that you looked down on them without resorting to such? coarse words? They seem inappropriate because the rest of your essay is artful and innovative. (FO)(NB)(WE)(NF)

Don't be insecure here. Take a stand! (NF)

Is Kelly dead? (FO)

Is this necessary? I don't see what it adds. Remove? (NB)

You have used the word "probably" several times. (NF)

I like your realization here. Maybe those previous comments made the necessary contrast. (JE)

10

11

don't stand out at all. I have always understood

why people were worried that God might not know them   *Capitalize? (NB)*

specifically. There was no reason for (h)im to bother

when they were all the same. But if everyone is a

This is a very sensitive question to ask! (NF)

unique individual, how does Heavenly Father remember

which fingerprint I am? In my place in the sun, I   *You cannot stand under the sun and see the stars! (NF)*

did not notice all those stars out there, each one

shining bright for someone. I do not feel important

or special while gazing at billions of stars.

For the first time in my life I feel truly   12

lost, an electron carrying practically no weight,

fairly indistinguishable from any other electron,   *What does this phrase mean? (NB)*

whose orbit is an unknown in a probability cloud.

I am looking at life in a new and startling way,

and this is the ultimate test of my taste for the

This is an excellent verb here. (NB)

new and startling. I find myself attempting to   *Yes, and we are not "dumb slobs." It's an inconsistent metaphor, but it's also a strong way to show what you feel. (NF)*

straddle the importance of my uniqueness and the

You have taken the road to Rome! (NF)

existence of 4.5 billion other unique individuals.

I do not like wondering who I am. I could always

tell before by the stark contrast between me and   *Before you were talking about people in general.*

anyone else. I had three dimensions and the other

person only had two. Now I see that I just had no   *Now you're talking about one other person. (Fo)*

depth perception.   *This is very honest. Now you are not afraid to draw definite conclusions. (NF)*

How everyone can be different intimidates and   13

amazes me. Without its former base, my sense of

You use the image of the soap bubble in a new way by reference to

(identity) has become as fragile as the chartreuse *substance rather than color. (FO)*

You use this image soap bubble I imagine as its beginnings. I fear the

well.
It helps to unify your essay.
(NF) existence of all the variegated personalities that

might crowd and pop it. Yet in returning to that

sense of fragile newness, I see the world freshly.

I have bemoaned the fact that no one could appre-

I feel like I've ciate my special outlook. Now I see there are

gone countless other outlooks for me to explore, each a

through hell with world as strange and wonderful as mine. For the

you and come up first time there is an impetus for me to get to

a winner! know people. This potential soothes my battered
(JE)

psyche and fills me with wonder in proportion to

my fear. *The fear is minimized by wonder:*
You have the equipment now with which to
move forward. (FO)

General Comments at the End of the Essay

NICHOLAS BALAMACI —I thought that the overall structure of your essay was excellent. There is a clear beginning, middle, and end. Your paragraphs and transitions flow well. You seem to be in control of what you want to say and how you want to say it.

—Your essay seems tightly reasoned, yet it also seems spontaneous—straight from your mind and heart.

—The title of your essay is clever, (and therefore tempting to use), but it struck me as inappropriate. "Rotten" is too strong a word and is never really shown or proven.

—Your writing is lean and easy to read. Your use of language is innovative and artful.

—This is an honest and mature essay, and it works in a way that most of us, I think, would have a hard time *ever* achieving. I admire it!

JASON ESKENAZI —This is an effective essay, but I feel it needs to go through the same wringer you described in order to get at its core.

—Your essay is filled with understatement, which makes my view of your essay sway. But there is a vitality to it that keeps me on the edge of my seat. I'd almost lost my faith that words (books) could transform people, and then you introduce me to Kelly.

—The core of your essay is great, but I needed to read what you wrote two or three times to get it. I think that was because of its complexity. You fill up your sentences with many complex and tenuous ideas. You need to develop them and make the relationship between the sentences and ideas clearer.

—Please invent a word that's ten times better than "fantastic," and I'll use it. The ideas flow and are inspiring. Your emergence into the human community is glorious! Welcome to your life!

—I think I'll read it again—this time purely for fun.

NELSON FARIAS —You really do take a meaningful conflict in your life and discuss its implications without fear, which is a very difficult thing to do. This essay is at its strongest when you look into yourself.

—Your writing is loaded with colorful metaphors, which are the result of a creative play on words and ideas. However, they are overshadowed by the reality at which the essay arrives.

—Finding that all individuals are unique should not prevent you from experiencing your own individuality. You have accomplished this extremely well in the essay.

FRAN OSBORNE

—The essential idea in this essay seems to me to be about the uniqueness/commonness of each human being. It is an enormous topic, and you deal with it lucidly and intelligently.

—The idea that you are rotten at the core seems incompatible with the honesty that pervades the essay. How can such frankness/honesty be rotten? The title bothers me as a result.

—The religious issues you introduce are so big that they could be looked at again in a separate essay. Is your religion a convenience?

—As for the structure of the essay, I found it to be well organized, with a good, strong beginning, and a strong, optimistic conclusion.

—The introduction seems slightly overdone: you take five paragraphs before getting into the meat of your essay. From there on, the reading is fast, entertaining, and informative. I particularly like the fact that you use specific examples to show how you tried to be different, but I am slightly bothered by the fact that these differences seem superficial.

—I thought the last four paragraphs were particularly strong: you have a core identity (being different), but you are frightened of giving it up (in spite of its arrogance) because such relinquishing might result in a kind of personality suicide. You find a way around this by looking at yourself in a "new and startling way" that straddles individuality and common humanity. Finally, you find in the wonder of looking at—and exploring—yourself a way of overcoming fear.

Exercises in Peer Editing

1. Reread the general statements at the end of Benson's essay. How is each similar to—and different from—the final general comment you have written about her essay? What does each focus on, and how consistent is their overall advice with yours? Review the four peer editors' marginal notations on Benson's essay. Which are observations? Which are evaluations? Which aspects of composition does each focus on? List the points you and the other peer editors agree on; disagree on. Finally, sketch out what Benson would need to do in a revision to respond adequately to what you and the other peer editors have recommended.

2. Your own writing is the focus for this exercise. Prepare a draft of an essay according to your instructor's directions. Then review the various peer-editing activities described on pages 342–344. Bring your own essay to class and present it to your peer editors. After you have received their written observations and recommendations on the essay, their assessment of its specific strengths and weaknesses, and their recommendations for improving it, prepare a detailed plan for revising your essay. Consult with your peer editors about your plans, and then draft a new version of the essay.

3. Review the peer editing process. Write an essay in which you offer a clear sense of what you think you have learned about writing and reading as a result of your experiences with it. How has peer editing helped you improve your writing? In what specific ways has it strengthened your reading? What new insights have you developed about the processes of writing and reading? How will peer editing affect the ways in which you prepare your next essay? What do you see as the limitations of peer editing? How would you suggest improving or extending the peer editing process? Be as specific as possible. The emphasis in your essay should reflect either your reservations about peer editing or your enthusiasm for it.

THE PROFESSIONAL
EDITOR
AT WORK

Part VI

I N PREVIOUS CHAPTERS we have seen how students revise their work, first on their own and then with the help of peer editors. In this chapter we have the opportunity to see a professional editor, Jane Aaron, make suggestions for revisions as she shapes the essays by Thu Hong Nguyen and John Siegrist as if for professional publication.

Observing a professional editor at work teaches several lessons about the place of revision in the composing process. First, all writing, even good writing, can be improved. Good writing takes time, effort, and patience, and often requires further revision, or editing, even after a "final" draft. At this point in the process, the professional editor's goal is to preserve the writer's intentions while suggesting changes to improve the accuracy, emphasis, specificity, and consistency of the text. The process, though, is not predictable, as Jane Aaron tells us, because "each writer's process is unique, and the barriers to clear, effective expression are many."

Second, professional editing provides a model of close and careful reading that we can translate to our reading of our own and other writer's work. The job of the professional editor, like that of a peer editor or an instructor, is to provide an objective view; by standing in for the audience, the editor becomes a collaborator who shows the writer whether he or she has communicated effectively with the intended audience. Aaron's editing of Nguyen's and Siegrist's essays shows how a revised sentence or paragraph, a change in emphasis or tone can allow the writers' intentions to become even clearer to their readers. We see the power and possibility of revising as Nguyen's and Siegrist's essays move from being strong essays to polished pieces.

Third, observing the professional editing process also shows what happens when a piece of writing goes public. For those who publish their work, whether in a commercial magazine or a school paper, editing is the final step in the composing process. As readers, we are not aware of this stage—of the extensive editing that goes on — because the printed page does not reveal how each piece of writing was created. We see only the polished words and are not privy to the suggestions and changes, the additions and deletions that constitute the important work of editing.

Gary Goshgarian, a professor of English at Northeastern University and a novelist, textbook author, and free-lance writer, is one of the many writers with whom Jane Aaron has worked. In the following passage, the fourth paragraph from Goshgarian's essay, "Zeroing in on Science Fiction," we see the suggestions and changes Aaron offered him.

Science Fiction is that [e] branch of literature that imaginatively speculates on the consequences of living in a scientific or technological world.

A closer look at ~~our~~ the definition will help ~~us to~~ outline

OK to include
conditions
here?
It's used
twice below.

~~understand~~ some SF prerequisites. The word "specu-lates" [e] implies the future. Therefore, a writer who "imaginatively speculates" is one who creates exper-

Have not yet
seems more
accurate, given
what you go
on to say. See
also opposite
margin.

iences *and conditions* that ~~may or may not~~ *have not* yet ~~have~~ occurred in the real world. Certainly ~~the~~ human *s* experience *have d* ~~of~~ love, hate, and fear; ~~are real~~ however, the writer may create unreal conditions out of which those experiences

evolve, as H. G. Wells did in his War of the Worlds.

You might con-sider cutting the Wells example here: it may not be familiar enough to readers to make it useful. The intervening points (besides Wells) are really covered in the earlier sentence. Therefore... real world. And Wells is introduced in more detail at the end of the paragraph.

Here, and later,
OK to delete
circumstances,
redundant
with
conditions?

The point is that SF speculates about some tomorrow conditions ~~and circumstances. Such~~ *The same* may be said of ~~to~~ any non-historical fiction that presumes some general future time.

Dashes OK
to help
emphasize
shift in
focus?

But, *—and* this is where ~~the rest of~~ *differs* ~~our definition separates~~ SF from non-SF. ~~Those con-~~ *—the future sentence* experiences and conditions ~~ditions and circumstances~~ are categorically scien-tific or technological ~~by nature.~~ In other words, *more detail* ~~ing~~ SF is about ~~what it is like to~~ be human in ~~a future~~ *the paragraph.* ~~of~~ some imagined technological *future.* ~~advances.~~ *The* ~~Our~~ defini-tion does not specify locale, so SF stories can be set on earth, in space, or on worlds galaxies away.

Note that if
you cut the
earlier Wells
example you
need to add
Wells's name
to this sentence.

Nor does the
~~Likewise, our~~ definition ~~does not~~ specify whose technology. In War of the Worlds, *the* ~~it is Martian~~

Changes OK to simplify / strengthen phrasing?

know how ~~that permits the~~ bug-eyed ~~invaders to~~ Martians
– of

~~journey the~~ *transports them* millions of miles ~~of space~~ to earth
and then
~~which it~~ nearly devastates ∧ *the planet* with deadly gases and
heat rays.

Aaron's specific suggestions show Goshgarian how to strengthen his paragraph so that his message and purpose are clearer. Her editing suggestions help to simplify his sentences, clarify parts of the paragraph that might be confusing to readers, and improve the accuracy and emphasis of his word choice. Because the interaction between a professional editor and writer demonstrates vividly the very process a writer must follow in preparing a final draft, we invited Jane Aaron to edit the essays of Thu Hong Nguyen and John Siegrist in the same way she worked with Gary Goshgarian. In eighteen years as a professional editor, Jane Aaron has worked with authors of magazine articles, of books for general audiences, and of college textbooks in almost every discipline, including freshman composition. She is the editor of *The Compact Reader*, an anthology of essays for composition courses, and a contributing editor to *The Little Brown Handbook*, a best-selling composition textbook.

Our editing procedure was similar to the standard editing process used by most professional publications. Aaron edited Nguyen's and Siegrist's essays by making some changes, suggesting others, and questioning the writers in places about their meaning and intended effect. With the edited versions of their essays, she sent them a covering letter in which she explained her general response to their essays and offered an analysis to support her comments on their manuscripts. The students were asked not only to revise their essays using Aaron's suggestions but also to describe how they felt to have their work professionally edited. As Jane Aaron wrote to Nguyen and Siegrist, she hoped that they would find her suggestions helpful, but they, as writers, had the final word; all decisions on revision were theirs to make. Before reading the edited versions of these essays, read the unedited essays as they appear on pages 188–190 for Nguyen and 217–220 for Siegrist.

We begin this chapter with Jane Aaron's description of an editor at work.

A PROFESSIONAL EDITOR DESCRIBES HER WORK

In their comments on being edited (pages 401 and 414), Thu Hong Nguyen and John Siegrist describe initial feelings of insecurity and indignation that would sound familiar to any editor. Like most writers who have poured themselves into their work, Nguyen and Siegrist had good reason to believe that their essays were successful. And indeed they were. But, like most manuscripts received by publishers, the essays also had the potential to be better—clearer, more convincing, more enjoyable for readers.

An editor is a kind of messenger between writer and reader, representing each to the other. On the one hand, the editor helps the writer state his or her message as effectively as possible. On the other hand, the editor represents the typical reader for whom the piece of writing is intended, anticipating his or her needs for information, clarity, and readability. At the practical level this dual representation works itself out in one process, as the editor helps shape the writer's work for the reader's maximum understanding and enjoyment.

The goal of the editing process is thus to preserve all the strengths of the manuscript while removing whatever impedes communication between writer and reader. Such a broad goal can encompass any feature of the work, including development, organization, emphasis, pace, specificity, conciseness, consistency, and accuracy. The process is not predictable, however, for each writer's purpose is unique, and the barriers to clear, effective expression are many. From one writer's work to another's, or even from one paragraph to the next in the same work, fresh problems arise to demand fresh solutions. And always the solutions must be conceived in the context of the writer's intentions and the reader's needs.

In order to understand the writer's intentions, diagnose the weaknesses of the manuscript, and conceive appropriate solutions, the editor may read the work as closely and as often as the writer has. Usually the first reading is a quick one to get the gist of the author's ideas and the sound of the author's voice. Then slower readings follow, during which the editor notes any problems in organization, gaps in the development of ideas, shifts in tone, or unnecessary repetitions. These readings require a kind of peripheral vision of the mind, an ability to recall the entire work while concentrating on a bit of it in order to see the connection—or lack of connection—between the part and the whole.

The actual editing is the most time-consuming part of the process, as the editor tries to resolve the larger problems and also weighs every sentence against the author's intentions and the reader's likely response. It is during this stage that the dialogue between editor and writer occurs. The writer's part in the dialogue consists of the words on the page. The editor's consists of changes, questions, comments, and suggestions, either on the manuscript, in the margins, or on separate sheets of paper. Sometimes the editor changes the manuscript without explanation if the need for change seems obvious enough; most corrections of grammatical, spelling, and typographical errors fall into this category. Sometimes the editor explains changes that reflect interpretations of the author's meaning. And sometimes the editor relies solely on suggestions or questions if the meaning cannot be safely assumed or if passages seem to require rewriting that the author is best equipped to handle. (All three approaches appear on Ms. Nguyen's and Mr. Siegrist's essays.) The explanations and suggestions may be lengthy, seemingly out of proportion to the problem being addressed, so that the author will understand why the manuscript is not clear or what impairs its readability. An editor quickly learns that a simple comment like "Not clear" usually prompts the natural response "It's clear to me"—and no revision.

When the editing is completed, the editor returns to the author with a covering letter that includes a general response to the piece—both strengths and any overall weaknesses that will provide some context for the specific comments on the manuscript. (See the letters on pages 396 and 407.) Usually the author's revision is the final round in the process, as it was with Ms. Nguyen's and Mr. Siegrist's essays. But occasionally the editor may negotiate last-minute changes with the author before the manuscript is set in type.

Editing requires a certain amount of mind-reading, to discern the writer's intentions, as well as a sense of the possible solutions, an ear for language, and a firm grounding in the conventions of grammar, punctuation, mechanics, and spelling. It also requires an ability to work "silently," suspending one's own ideas instead of pushing them on the author. Of course, editors sometimes overstep their bounds. Beyond grammer and spelling, few matters in writing are clear-cut: almost everything is a question of choice, of judgment, and judgment calls are endlessly debatable. Although authors have the final word, the good ones, from an editor's standpoint, will always suspend their initial feelings of insecurity and indignation to engage in the debate. By that criterion alone, Ms. Nguyen and Mr. Siegrist are excellent authors.

THU HONG NGUYEN, "A GOOD WOMAN"

What follows is Jane Aaron's editing of Thu Hong Nguyen's essay. We begin with Aaron's letter to Nguyen and her editing of the essay. We then see Nguyen's comments on Aaron's editing and the essay as she revised it in response to Aaron's comments.

EDITOR TO AUTHOR:
JANE AARON'S LETTER TO THU HONG NGUYEN

Dear Ms. Nguyen:

Your essay is affecting and well controlled. You create a clear picture of the life of a Vietnamese woman, eliciting both the respect and sympathy of the reader. Your three-part organization (reinforced by the echoing introductory and concluding sentences of each body paragraph) provides a neat but unforced structure for presenting the complexities of the life you describe.

My suggestions for revision focus mainly on occasional wordiness, some unclear passages, and the introduction. The introduction is too long and detailed, I think: it immerses the reader in explanation before the point of the essay is clear. As you will see, I have suggested that you move some introductory sentences to the next paragraph, where they seem to fit well, and that you cut or condense some of the remaining sentences.

Although most of my suggestions appear in the margins, I have also made some changes in the expectation that editing would clarify my ideas. I hope you find the suggestions helpful and agree that they will strengthen your essay. Of course, the decisions on whether and how to implement them rest with you.

Sincerely,
Jane E. Aaron

NGUYEN'S EDITED ESSAY

A Good Woman

Use quotation marks for this saying?

A good woman means an industrious daughter, a devoted wife, and a loving mother. Thus ~~is the~~ *expressed* saying ~~that~~ has ~~been~~ a collective belief for many centuries in Viet Nam. ~~As soon as a female infant is born, it~~ *she* is given the middle name Thi—meaning *her* "female"—to emphasize ~~its~~ role (as a woman in later years.) ~~Then, in~~ growing up, th~~is~~ *e* child receives

Move this to 2nd sentence of paragraph 2?

Cut? Doesn't the name emphasize the role in child-hood, too?

See my letter: Reduce detail and length of introduction by moving these sentences and condensing this part?

lessons about a woman's duties and must practice what she learns. Parents wholeheartedly train their daughters to achieve the qualities expected of a woman. Should they forget *(OK to add?) their duty,* their neighbors promptly remind them. In a Vietnamese village, *a girl's family and* ~~the~~ entire community ~~helps, by words of~~ *contribute* praise and ~~by~~ punish-ment, to ~~bring up a female child to be~~ *raise her into* a good woman, whose ~~service, obedience, and generosity~~ bring *s* much

Should this sentence stress parents' responsibility rather than training (focus of the previous sentence)? Rephrase: Her parents are primarily responsible for her training.

repeated in 1st and last sentences of ¶

comfort to those around her. With the fear of retribution, the child grows into a woman who follows loyally the instructions of virtue *(?)* which determines her fate. From the moment *she* ~~her mind is mature enough~~ *can* ~~to~~ understand commands, *through her own marriage* ~~(to the day she is married~~ *and childbearing, a* ~~off, (to the time when she bears her own children, a~~ Vietnamese ~~woman~~ *(female?)* continuously tries to establish a good name as a diligent daughter, a submissive wife, and an altruistic mother.

Since her virtue continues beyond marriage and childbearing to the day and to the time are misleading

What does this clause refer to? Could the sentence be cut?

The idea of punishment is in the previous sentence, and loyalty and virtue could be introduced there as well, as modifiers for woman: a loyal virtuous woman.

Use female instead of woman when referring to the child as well as the adult?

Again –
female
instead of
woman? → *female?*

In order to be approved by everyone, a Viet-

namese woman must first be industrious. ~~This~~ begins

~~with her services at the house of her parents who~~
The child is kept
~~keep her~~ from idling with endless housework. ~~Already~~
By
~~at~~ the age of (nine,) she is the babysitter ~~of~~ her

always at 9,
or does the
age vary?
Perhaps: Before
the age of
eight or nine
or nine or ten
to make it
more general.

younger siblings. Carrying a baby on her back, she

spends the day sweeping the house, carrying messages,

and doing errands. As she grows older, she shares

more of the housework with her mother. Upon the

first crow of the rooster, she rises to brew tea

Moved because
the first line
doesn't apply
to the whole
sentence. → *at noon*

and prepare breakfast. Afterward, she does the

laundry by the river bank. ~~At noon~~ she cooks lunch

and has just enough time to tidy up the house before
         ∧
she prepares dinner. In the evening she goes to bed,

but only after having fixed the shirts or pants that

were torn or missing a button. (In keeping busy,) she

has no time to wonder and to dream, which often

result from idleness. *intend:* ~~She has no time for wondering~~
and dreaming, the pursuits of the idle.

Her training *add section*
at birth, when *from first*
paragraph as
suggested?
Then the
for *deleted*
part of this
sentence seems
unnecessary.

This phrase
implies that
she keeps
herself busy
to avoid
reverie. Perhaps
delete it and
rephrase to
sharpen the irony
I think you

2

I think you
need a better
transition
from childhood
to adulthood.
Perhaps: When
the girl becomes
a woman, she
must not
only work
diligently
but also
submit to
her husband.

Besides working diligently, a good Vietnamese

woman must also submit to her husband. She is ex-

pected to revere the man whom her parents have chosen

for her after they have accepted his valuable gifts.

Once married, she must show that she is unequal to
                                                appear
her husband. When husband and wife ~~are seen~~ to-

gether in the street, she usually keeps a respectful

3

distance behind him. She also ~~has to~~ acknowledge[s]

her inferior position in her speech. When addressed

by her husband, she always answers in a well-modulated

tone. In talking to him, she uses formal address; *[The semicolon shows the close relation between clauses.]*

~~E~~ven in the most intimate moments, she still ~~cannot~~ *may not*

use the familiar form of address. If she has per-

mission from her husband, she may speak / aloud, (her

opinions) but / *she* should not try to make ~~the~~ decision[s].

Whatever her husband says, she ~~will~~ *must* listen and not

[Could this be rephrased more simply: Silence is the way she demonstrates respect? If the implication about cultural encouragement is important, it should perhaps be stated more directly: The has learned [or has been taught] to show respect through silence.]

[contradict. ~~Remaining~~ silen[ce] is usually the most

encouraged means for her to be respectful.

Finally, to be ~~recognized~~ *viewed* favorably / a Viet-

namese woman must try to sacrifice herself for ~~the~~
it is
~~benefit of~~ the children ~~which are~~ her duty to bear.
at meals,
~~At mealtimes,~~ she eats little / repressing her hunger

with the gratifying consolation that her children are

growing taller and stronger. She must not dream of

any kind of luxur~~ies~~ *y*. Plain clothing gives her an

air of modesty and thrif~~tiness.~~ ~~Wearing~~ perfume or
might
lipstick ~~may~~ lead other people to condemn her as

wanton and irresponsible. Instead of beautifying
must
herself, she ~~should~~ give her children more food to

eat and better clothes to wear. She must also re-

frain from any kind of pleasure. She spends her

evening hours at home looking after the children

4

rather than at a nightclub or theater. A pack of

add nothing for herself and to stress the sacrifice?

cigarettes, a bottle of beer, or a few piasters lost

Could this be stated more simply? Perhaps: would mean less food for her children.

at the casino ~~can~~ deprive her children of their right

to be fed more. A Vietnamese mother does/everything

for the sake of her children.

every

In trying to be what one expects of her, a Viet-   5

namese (female?) (woman) ~~continues to~~ serve *ing* ~~if not~~ her parents

begins by

and siblings○ ~~then the husband and children of her~~

The changes here are a suggestion for recalling your 3-part structure, giving equal emphasis to childhood as to other parts.

~~own.~~ *Then,* Year after year, she humbles herself to make

her husband happy as a proud superior, from his

youthful days of good health to his time of age and

sickness. Day after day, she dedicates herself to

the welfare of her children even after they grow up.

In this lifetime of striving to be a good woman,

she sets ~~herself as~~ an illustrious example to other

women who are also trying to achieve the same de-

When she

sired qualities. ~~R~~ealiz~~ing~~ *es* her goal, she is the

The

pride of her parents, husband, and children. ~~P~~eople

Note that pride appears two sentences before.

around her are satisfied with her. They feel

(proud) and (sure of their lasting tradition) (*of?*) (in) bringing

up (*a?*) good (wom~~a~~n.) (*e?*) In any generation, they will always

have a good Vietnamese woman to admire. In any cen-

Do you mean that tradition is validated (or perhaps justified) by her success? If so, perhaps make that clearer: Her success validates [or justifies] their lasting tradition of bringing up a good woman.

tury, they will always have a slave to praise.

Effective ending.

THE AUTHOR RESPONDS:
COMMENTARY FROM THU HONG NGUYEN

When I was told that Jane Aaron would edit my essay, I was both surprised and curious. I must say that although it was a pleasant feeling that a professional editor, who must have edited the works of many popular and important writers, would now edit my essay, I could not help feeling nervous. I was also curious about what changes she would make on my essay. After all, the essay had been screened by my peers and instructor before it was sent into the contest. After I read over Ms. Aaron's comments, I was much impressed and felt that her editing was definitely necessary. From a piece of casual writing, she has turned my essay into professional work. I was both amazed and pleased how she suggested changes for some of my sentences and expressions that I was not satisfied with but did not know how to improve. My uneasiness soon left me and I was enthusiastically rewriting my essay using her suggestions. This is still my essay, but it is a stronger essay thanks to the editor's thoughtful comments.

NGUYEN'S REVISED ESSAY

A Good Woman

"A good woman means an industrious daughter, a   1
devoted wife, and a loving mother." This saying has
expressed a collective belief for many centuries in
Viet Nam. In a Vietnamese village, a girl's family
and entire community contribute praise and punishment
to raise her into a good woman who brings much comfort to those around her. With the fear of retribution, the child grows into a loyal, virtuous woman.
From the moment she can understand commands through
her own marriage and child bearing, a Vietnamese
female continuously tries to establish a good name
as a diligent daughter, a submissive wife, and an
altruistic mother.

In order to be approved by everyone, a Viet-   2
namese female must first be industrious. Her
training begins at birth, when she is given the
middle name Thi--meaning "female"--to emphasize her
role. Growing up, the child receives lessons about
a woman's duties and must practice what she learns.
The child is kept from idling with endless housework.
Before the age of nine or ten, she is the babysitter
for her younger siblings. Carrying a baby on her
back, she spends the day sweeping the house, carrying
messages, and doing errands. As she grows older,
she shares more of the housework with her mother.
Upon the first crow of the rooster, she rises to

brew tea and prepare breakfast. Afterward, she does
the laundry by the river bank. She cooks lunch at
noon and has just enough time to tidy up the house
before she prepares dinner. In the evening she goes
to bed, but only after fixing shirts or pants that
are torn or missing a button. She has no time for
wondering and dreaming, the pursuits of the idle.

When the girl becomes a woman, she must not
only work diligently but also submit to her husband.
She is expected to revere the man whom her parents
have chosen for her after they have accepted his
valuable gifts. Once married, she must show that
she is unequal to her husband. When husband and
wife appear together in the street, she usually
keeps a respectful distance behind him. She also
acknowledges her inferior position in her speech.
When addressed by her husband, she always answers
in a well-modulated tone. In talking to him, she
uses formal address; even in the most intimate
moments, she still may not use the familiar form
of address. If she has permission from her husband,
she may speak her opinions aloud, but she should
not try to make decisions. Whatever her husband
says, she must listen and not contradict. She has
been taught to show respect through silence.

Finally, to be viewed favorably a Vietnamese
woman must try to sacrifice herself for the children
which are her duty to bear. She eats little at

3

4

meals, repressing her hunger with the gratifying
consolation that her children are growing taller
and stronger. She must not dream of any kind of
luxury. Plain clothing gives her an air of modesty
and thrift. Perfume or lipstick might lead other
people to condemn her as wanton and irresponsible.
Instead of beautifying herself, she must give her
children more food to eat and better clothes to
wear. She must also refrain from any kind of
pleasure. She spends her evening hours at home
looking after the children rather than at a nightclub or theater. A pack of cigarettes, a bottle of
beer, or a few piasters lost at the casino would
mean less food for her children. A Vietnamese
mother does nothing for herself and everything for
the sake of her children.

In trying to be what everyone expects of her, a   5
Vietnamese female begins by serving her parents and
siblings. Then, year after year, she humbles herself
to make her husband happy as a proud superior, from
his youthful days of good health to his time of age
and sickness. Day after day, she dedicates herself
to the welfare of her children, even after they
grow up. In this lifetime of striving to be a good
woman, she sets an illustrious example to other
women who are also trying to achieve the same desired
qualities. When she realizes her goal, she is the
pride of her parents, husband, and children. The

people around her are satisfied with her. Her
success validates their lasting tradition of
bringing up good women. In any generation, they
will always have a good Vietnamese woman to admire.
In any century, they will always have a slave to
praise.

Questions on Nguyen's Essay

1. What is Nguyen's *purpose* in writing her essay? How do Jane Aaron's suggested changes help to strengthen Nguyen's purpose?

2. Aaron offers many comments on Nguyen's *introduction.* In general, her comments suggest that the introduction is too long and detailed and that the reader is immersed in explanation before the point of the essay is clear. Do you agree with Aaron's comments? What specific changes has she suggested? Study Nguyen's revised introduction. How do the changes strengthen not only the introductory paragraph, but the entire essay as well?

3. Aaron points out a number of unclear passages in paragraph 2. Study these passages and explain how and why they are unclear. How has Nguyen strengthened this paragraph in her revised essay?

4. Aaron also indicates a number of other unclear passages in other paragraphs. Examine these passages and discuss Aaron's suggested changes. Has Nguyen accepted these changes?

5. Aaron offers Nguyen many suggestions to avoid wordiness. Why, in general, is wordiness a problem for a reader? Study Aaron's suggestions and explain how the edited sentences make the essay more readable.

6. Does Aaron suggest any changes that you disagree with? Explain.

7. Nguyen tells us: "This is still my essay, but it is a stronger essay thanks to the editor's thoughful comments." Summarize the differences between the two drafts. Why is the revised draft stronger?

8. What have you learned about writing, reading, and the editing process from studying Aaron's comments on Nguyen's essay?

JOHN SIEGRIST, "RATTLESNAKE: A PALATABLE EXPERIENCE"

This section continues with Aaron's editing of John Siegrist's essay. Again we see Aaron's letter to Siegrist and her editing of the essay, followed by Siegrist's comments and his revised essay.

EDITOR TO AUTHOR:
JANE AARON'S LETTER TO JOHN SIEGRIST

Dear Mr. Siegrist:

Your essay is intriguing and usually quite clear: like all good process essays, it not only lays the steps out neatly but also makes an interesting point (about experimenting with the unfamiliar).

My suggestions for revision center on problems a reader might see in your essay. The explanations could be clearer in a few places, and sentences could sometimes be combined or condensed for greater conciseness and a smoother flow. In addition, paragraph 12, on various methods of preparing snake, could be revised to integrate information in paragraphs 2 and 15 about ways of preparing and serving snake and to provide a more inclusive and less awkward first sentence. Finally, the actor (the person performing the process) could be more consistent: you now shift among *one*, *I*, and *you* (sometimes stated and sometimes implied in imperative sentences such as "Place two fingers . . . "), or you use the passive voice ("This is usually accomplished . . . "). Shifting subjects are a common difficulty in process essays, and complete consistency is probably neither possible nor desirable. But I have suggested (in my editing) that you stick with *I* whenever possible because the passages in which you now use it seem the liveliest and most natural. *You* seems inappropriate because it would cast the reader as the actor when your message is to persuade the reader to try rattlesnake. *One* can work in isolated sentences, but it's hard to maintain without creating a stuffiness that would conflict with your essay's overall tone. Passives, though sometimes useful or necessary, tend to deaden prose and create confusion about who the actor is.

I have written suggestions and questions in the margins of your essay. When showing seemed easier than telling, I have made changes and usually explained them in the margins. I hope you agree that the suggested changes would make your essay even clearer and more readable then it already is. Of course, the decisions on revision are yours to make.

Sincerely,
Jane E. Aaron

SIEGRIST'S EDITED ESSAY

Rattlesnake: A Palatable Experience

Often may be less off-putting to readers, who can more easily say, "But not me."

People ~~usually~~ often alienate themselves from ~~things~~ the ~~and experiences which are not customary to their lifestyles.~~ new experiences They close their minds to ~~ideas~~ ~~which~~ (that) might prove enjoyable if ~~they would only~~ give n a try ~~them~~ ~~selves the opportunity to try something different.~~ This is the kind of resistance ~~met when one~~ I usually meet when I mention~~s~~ ~~the idea of~~ eating rattlesnake. *See my letter on the use of I.*

Restrictive clauses like this one usually begin with that instead of which.

Several changes in 1st paragraph eliminate unneeded words and help sharpen the meaning. The use of experiences in the 2nd sentence rather than 1st focuses attention on a key idea.

1

~~There are~~ people throughout the world ~~who~~ eat snake and find it not only palatable, but delicious. (People eat snake in sandwiches, ~~and~~ in soups, fried, or barbecued.) I was fortunate during my Air Force service to be stationed only thirty miles from the site of the most famous rattlesnake roundup, held annually in Texas. I ~~was able~~ not only ~~to find~~ found out how snake meat tastes, but ~~to~~ learn~~ed~~ how to catch, skin, and prepare the snake myself.

I suggest putting this information at the end of paragraph 2. (The editing here shows there are 4 variations.)

Editing avoids repeated I was in 2 sentences.

2

The first step in tasting fried rattlesnake is to collect the ingredients. ~~While~~ most of these can be found at any grocery store, but the main item, the snake, must be sought out in its own habitat. One thing must be said ~~before~~ to anyone who goes out to catch a rattlesnake: Be careful. A snake is like any other wild animal. It is timid until cornered, but then

3

In paragraph 6 it
sounds as if the
light shows
where the snake
is. If so, change to
is necessary
to illuminate
the darkened
areas? Or is
the gasoline
used to flush
the snake
out? And if
the light is
used merely
to show where
the snake is,
how do you
flush it out?
Or do you
shoot it in
its hiding
place?

it will fight to survive with ~~every ounce of energy.~~

                            places
The best ~~areas~~ to look for rattlesnakes are   4

                            Cliché? Instead
among rock piles, rock fences, heavy brush piles,   *say briefly what*
                    No   *happens when a*
and abandoned animal burrows. ~~Since~~ one ~~would not~~   *snake is*
              blindly   so   *cornered: ie, a*
want to reach into these places, a flashlight or   *poisonous bite,*
        ^   ^   *illness, maybe*
a   *death?*
mirror to reflect the sun into the darkened areas
^
is a necessity. I have heard of people ~~using hoses~~
              ˄   *snake's hiding*
              ˄ing
~~to~~ pour gasoline into the~~se~~ places, but ~~I feel~~ that

method is unsporting and creates an unnecessary fire

hazard.

family...
guests =   I
How many   ~~One should~~ take into account the amount of meat   5
people? Also needed ~~when looking for a snake.~~ A snake two feet
I suggest   *provides enough meat*
active voice long ~~would be all right~~ for two people. If a family
for example:
"a larger group is larger or guests are invited over, a snake four   *Antecedent*
of five or six   *unclear:*
requires..." or five feet ~~in length~~ is required. This ~~will~~ save   *Adequate*
                        long   ˄   *meat?*
Why hostess? ~~the hostess~~ the embarrassment of not having enough
Cut OK? to go around.

Change to killed Once the proper snake is found, it must be   6
or caught and   Many snake hunters ←—*Change*
killed since caught. ~~This is usually accomplished through the~~ *made it so set*
the next para.   *up possibility*
on your use ~~of~~ special poles or hooks, ~~The idea is~~ to pull *that this is*
method doesn't   and   *not the only*
describe the snake from its place of refuge, ~~use the pole to~~ *method, so*
catching?   *The hunter* *(es)*   *readers will*
Also, at the hold its head against the ground, then reach down   *be prepared*
end of this   *its* gaining the   *for yours.*
para., add and grab the snake behind ~~his~~ head, ~~This gives the~~ *Changes OK?*
a brief *control necessary to*   *This was unclear*
explanation ~~person control of the snake and allows it to be~~   *but I assume it*
of how the   *the snake*   *refers to grabbing*
hook-and- dropped into a burlap sack or other ~~suitable~~   *the snake.*
pole hunters
kill the snake?

container for transporting ~~back to the house.~~ home⊙

I am either too smart or too ~~big a~~ coward~ly~ to

Grabbing OK? ⁷attempt this practice. Since I don't like the idea
You describe of ~~coming within inches of~~ ↳grabbing an animal that has the
actual contact
in previous potential to kill me, I prefer to shoot the snake
paragraph.

from a (reasonable distance.) Any ~~type of~~ firearm will

Perhaps just
kill the
snake
instead of
ensure
that ...
picked up?

See query at ensure that the snake is dead before it is picked up;
paragraph 4
about where however, I use a small~caliber handgun because it
the snake is
when you destroys less meat. I shoot the snake in the head,
shoot it: leaving   intact
still in its ~~as~~ the body ~~is the part~~ to be cooked.
hiding place?

The ~~very~~ first thing to do ~~upon~~ after killing the

rattlesnake is to remove its head using a knife,
  a   an   a
~machete,~ axe, or even ~shovel.~ The fangs still con-

tain poison, and ~~even~~ an accidental scratch from them
                                   ↰the head is
could result in (serious medical problems.) Once) re-
                      I ↯ it   other
Illness or moved, ~~the head should be~~ buried to keep ~~stray~~ ani-
death instead
of the less mals from eating it and becoming sick. *"OK? Stray implies "lost"*
precise   *or "out of place."*
serious
medical The snake is now ready to be skinned and gutted.
problems? I remove the tail first and then attempt to cut a

straight line from one end of its belly to the other⊙

~~end.~~ This is fairly simple unless the snake's

muscles are still contracting; then it can be a
                              I
moving experience! If ~~you~~ find the snake trying to
                my   I
curl around ~~your~~ arm, ~either wait a little longer to

do the skinning or have a friend hold the body still.

7

8

9

way I learn my
(This ~~may show you~~ who ~~your~~ friends are.) A pair of

{Do you prefer scissors because it is easier to make a shallow cut with them? If so, I suggest moving this sentence to the end of the ¶ and saying something like: I find it easier to make a shallow cut with scissors than with a knife.}

scissors is much easier to use than a knife, but

either is fine. It is important to keep the cut

because penetrating
shallow ~~and try not to go into~~ the snake's organs,

~~as that~~ would contaminate the meat.

Once the cut is finished, the skin can easily   10

Does a snake skin have to be tanned? If so, say something like: The snake skin is worth saving; once tanned it can be used in...

be peeled back on each side of the snake's body. I

e
~~accomplish this by~~ plac~~ing~~ two fingers between the

snake's skin and the meat on the body and run~~ning~~ my

fingers the entire length on both sides ~~of the body.~~

s
The skin ~~will~~ peel away just like a banana's. The

for
snake skin is worth saving ~~and can be~~ used to make

belts, (hatbands, belt buckles,) and other ~~attractive~~

items.

the snake
The gutting ~~procedure~~ is very similar to ~~that~~   11

it I
~~of~~ skinning ~~the snake.~~ Place two fingers between

Organs OK?
Clearer than cavity, I think.

organs
the internal ~~cavity~~ and the meat of the snake's

Then I my
inner body. Run~~ning your~~ fingers the entire length

to
~~will~~ remove the guts in one clean ~~and effortless~~

(seems redundant.)

motion.

See my letter where I suggest these changes to provide a less awkward transition and a more inclusive introduction. (Even if you accept the value of these changes, you may prefer to make them differently. My changes are meant merely as suggestions.)

Skinned and gutted, the meat is ready to be
~~We now come to the actual preparation of the~~   12
prepared and served in any of
~~meat for cooking. There are~~ numerous ways ~~to pre-~~

~~pare any meat, and snake is no different.~~ The
a matter of
seasoning is ~~left up to one's~~ personal taste, as is
meat
the style of cooking. Snake can be steamed, fried,

It can be served in sandwiches or soups or alone as an appetizer or a main dish. It is especially good for a light meal or a refreshing change from beef, pork, chicken, or fish

baked, broiled, or even eaten raw. I prefer mine

barbecued,

Sentence moved from previous paragraph → fried, although I would like to try it barbecued.

Is barbecued the only method you haven't tried → Frying ~~rattlesnake~~ is probably *the* quickest and easiest ~~of all the~~ methods ~~to~~ *for* ~~prepare it.~~ *ing the meat* *I cut* The snake meat 13

Why do you prefer frying? (Just because it's quick and easy?) ~~must be cut~~ into portions which are easy to work with. ①find two- or three-inch lengths adequate.

Simplify? — ①use a deep-fat fryer, and while the oil is getting warm, I prepare the snake pieces. ①combine several ingredients, the amounts of which depend upon the ~~Combine?~~ number of pieces to be cooked. ①mix beaten eggs,

Sentences here could be combined and simplified as noted to give greater variety to the paragraph. (Note: almost all the sentences begin with I.)

Meaning the batter and the flour? If so, say: The batter and the flour give the pieces a light, crunchy coating when fried. pepper, and a little onion salt in a small bowl. ① dip the snake pieces into the mixture and then roll them in flour. This gives them a light covering *that* ~~which~~ becomes crunchy when fried.

frying The oil should be kept at a medium temperature: 14

The passives in this paragraph seem preferable to more sentences starting with I. — Too low a setting can cause the snake to fall apart, and too high a setting can cause the flour crust to harden too much. The meat should be ~~placed in the~~ *in the oil* ~~oil and~~ left ~~there~~ for not more than a few minutes *because* ᴬthe snake sections are similar to fillets of fish and *sections* fry very quickly. Once done, they should be removed *and ᵉᵈ of* ~~to~~ drain any excess oil. They are now ready to serve, and I guarantee everyone will be *a* waiting ~~in anticipa-~~ ~~tion of~~ th~~eir~~ first bite of rattlesnake.

The colon shows the close relation between these sentences. (The capital letter after the colon is optional but consistent with the style you set in paragraph 3.)

Agreement problem (everyone...their). OK to say the? Eating rattlesnake is a ~~rather~~ unique experience. 15

Something either is or isn't unique.

See comment at para. 12 in which I suggest you insert this information at the end of that para. If you do so, then you needn't start a new para. here

say pointless instead to avoid repetition from Using a fork?

It can be served as the main dish or as an appetizer.

It is especially suited when one ~~desires~~ a light meal

or a refreshing ~~change~~ from beef, pork, chicken, or

~~fish.~~ Using a fork to eat fried snake is almost (use-

less,) and one must rely upon the most basic of eating

utensils, the fingers.

Also, why is it useless or pointless?

Taste... flavor is redundant.

~~The taste of~~ rattlesnake meat has a flavor all   16

its own, close to that of armadillo.   Since most

people have not tried armadillo, I would describe ~~it~~
rattlesnake   _with a mild, slightly sweet flavor_⊙
as somewhat like turtle meat,ᶺ I won't lie and say
^

it tastes like chicken because it doesn't.   ~~It is a~~

~~meat with a very mild flavor, possibly just a little~~

(OK to put this info. here instead of two sentences later for the benefit of readers who haven't tried turtle?

If this sentence immediately follows the one about Chicken, a more explicit contrast seems needed. Perhaps: It is, however, exceptionally delicious!

~~sweet.~~   I can only verify that it does taste exceptionally delicious.

I think the shift to you in this paragraph is effective. You could go further and change most people to most of you.

I know (most people) will not have the opportunity   17
                                     try it if you have
or inclination to eat rattlesnake, but ~~if~~ the chance⊙

~~should arise, try it.~~   The taste is surprisingly

good, and the experience may open your mind to other
                            that
(culinary delights) ~~which~~ you have previously rejected.

Avoid the cliché?

Forget about those ideas you have of snakes, and

think of fried rattlesnake as one more way to experi-

ence life's variety ~~of food.~~   *Of food seems unnecessary. Omitting it ties the last sentence back to your introduction (about shutting off from experiences in general, not just eating experiences).*

THE AUTHOR RESPONDS:
COMMENTARY FROM JOHN SIEGRIST

I must admit to being a little surprised at the amount of editing Ms. Aaron did to my essay. This shock was lessened upon my reading the comments and finding that while numerous, the suggestions did not call for major revisions. I feel her comments give my essay that fine polish that only an experienced writer has the ability to give. I appreciated the chance to have my work edited and agree with most of her comments.

I incorporated Ms. Aaron's comments into my essay to give it a better flow from one idea to the next. This is the one element of writing I know I need to improve, and her ideas were clear and simple to use. The comments I did not use were the ones that I felt did not express my ideas in the context I had intended.

I have learned a great deal from the editing of my essay and am able to see where a little change can improve an essay considerably. My essay is now more polished and satisfying. I knew it had rough edges; I just need Ms. Aaron's comments to show me where they were.

SIEGRIST'S REVISED ESSAY

Rattlesnake: A Palatable Experience

People often alienate themselves from the unfamiliar. They close their minds to new experiences
that might prove enjoyable if given a try. This is
the kind of resistance I usually meet when I mention
eating rattlesnake.

1

People throughout the world eat snake and find
it not only palatable but delicious. I was fortunate
during my Air Force service to be stationed only
thirty miles from the site of the most famous rattlesnake roundup, held annually in Texas. I not only
found out how snake meat tastes but also learned how
to catch, skin, and prepare the snake myself.

2

The first step in tasting fried rattlesnake is
to collect the ingredients. Most of these can be
found at any grocery store, but the main item, the
snake, must be sought out in its own habitat. One
thing must be said to anyone who goes out to catch
a rattlesnake: Be careful. A snake is like any
other wild animal. It is timid until cornered; then
it becomes aggressive, fighting for survival.
Rattlesnake hunters must always keep in mind that
they are seeking a potentially dangerous animal.
Rattlesnake bites can cause serious illness and
sometimes, death.

3

The best places to look for rattlesnakes are
among rock piles, rock fences, heavy brush piles,

4

and abandoned animal burrows. No one wants to reach
blindly into these places, so a flashlight or a
mirror to reflect the sun is necessary to illuminate
the darkened areas. I have heard of people pouring
gasoline into snake's hiding places, but that method
is unsporting and creates an unnecessary fire hazard.

I take into account the amount of meat I need   5
prior to looking for a snake. A snake two feet long
provides enough meat for two people. A larger number
of people will require a larger snake. A good rule
of thumb is to allow one-half to one foot of snake
for each person. Keep in mind that as the snake's
length increases, so does its diameter, and this increases the amount of meat a large snake will yield.
Good judgment in selecting the proper size rattlesnake will save the embarrassment of not having
enough to go around.

Once the proper snake is found, it must be caught   6
or killed. Many snake hunters use special poles or
hooks to pull the snake from its place of refuge and
to hold its head against the ground. The hunter then
reaches down and grabs the snake behind its head,
gaining the control necessary to drop the snake into
a burlap sack or other container for transporting
home. This method keeps the snake alive until time
to cook the meat and ensures the availability of
fresh rattlesnake meat.

I am either too smart or too cowardly to attempt   7

this practice. I prefer to find a snake lying in a relatively open area and shoot it from a safe distance. Any firearm will kill the snake; however, I use a small-caliber handgun because it destroys less meat. I shoot the snake in the head, leaving the body intact to be cooked.

The very first thing to do after killing the rattlesnake is to remove its head, using a knife, a machete, an axe, or even a shovel. The fangs still contain poison, and an accidental scratch from them could result in illness or death. Once the head is removed, I bury it to keep other animals from eating it and becoming sick.

8

The snake is now ready to be skinned and gutted. I remove the tail first and then attempt to cut a straight line from one end of its belly to the other. This is fairly simple unless the snake's muscles are still contracting; then it can be a moving experience! If I find the snake trying to curl around my arm, I either wait a little longer to do the skinning or have a friend hold the body still. (This way I learn who my friends are.) It is important to keep the cut shallow because penetrating the snake's organs would contaminate the meat. I find it is easier to make a shallow cut using scissors rather than a knife.

9

Once the cut is finished, the skin can easily be peeled back on each side of the snake's body. I place two fingers between the snake's skin and the

10

meat on the body and run my fingers the entire
length on both sides. The skin peels away just like
a banana's. The snake skin is worth saving and,
once preserved, it can be used in making belts, belt
buckles, hatbands, and other items.

Gutting the snake is very similar to skinning   11
it. I place two fingers between the internal organs
and the meat of the snake's inner body. Then I run
my fingers the entire length to remove the guts in
one clean motion.

Skinned and gutted, the meat is ready to be   12
prepared and served in any one of numerous ways.
The seasoning is a matter of personal taste, as is
the style of cooking. Snake meat can be steamed,
fried, baked, broiled, barbecued, or even eaten raw.
It can be served in sandwiches or soups or alone as
an appetizer or a main dish. It is especially good
for a light meal and a refreshing change from beef,
pork, chicken, or fish.

I prefer snake meat fried because of the crisp   13
texture of the cooked meat, although I would like
to try it barbecued. Frying rattlesnake is probably the quickest and easiest method for preparing
the meat. I cut the snake meat into portions, two
or three inches in length, which are adequate for
serving and easy to work with. I use a deep-fat
fryer, and while the oil is getting warm, I prepare
a coating for the snake pieces which combines beaten

eggs, pepper, and a little onion salt. The amounts used will depend upon the number of pieces of snake to be cooked and personal taste. The snake pieces are dipped into the mixture, then rolled in flour. The batter and the flour give the pieces a light and crunchy coating when fried.

The frying oil should be kept at a medium tem-   14
perature: Too low a setting can cause the snake to fall apart, and too high a setting can cause the flour crust to harden too much. The meat should be left in the oil for no more than a few minutes be-cause the snake sections are similar to fillets of fish and fry very quickly. Once done, the sections should be removed and drained of any excess oil. They are now ready to serve, and I guarantee every-one will be awaiting the first bite of rattlesnake.

Eating rattlesnake is a unique experience.   15
Using a fork to eat fried snake is almost pointless, due to the fine texture of the meat, and one must rely on the most basic of eating utensils, the fingers. Rattlesnake meat has a flavor all its own, close to that of armadillo. Since most people have not tried armadillo, I would describe rattlesnake as somewhat like turtle meat, with a mild, slightly sweet flavor. I won't lie and say it tastes like chicken, because it doesn't. It is, however, exceptionally delicious.

I know most of you will not have the opportunity   16

or the inclination to eat rattlesnake, but try it
if you have the chance. The taste is surprisingly
good, and the experience may open your mind to other
foods that you have previously rejected. Forget
about those ideas you have of snakes, and think of
fried rattlesnake as one more way to experience
life's variety.

Questions on Siegrist's Essay

1. John Siegrist remarked in his commentary: "I must admit to being a little surprised at the amount of editing Ms. Aaron did to my essay." Were you surprised? What is it about the process of editing that makes a writer surprised, sometimes indignant, when he sees his work edited?

2. Jane Aaron tells us: "An editor is a kind of messenger between writer and reader, representing each to the other. On the one hand, the editor helps the writer state his or her message as effectively as possible. On the other hand, the editor represents the typical reader for whom the piece of writing is intended, anticipating his or her needs for information, clarity and readability." How has Jane Aaron helped Siegrist to state his message more effectively? How has she also helped you, the reader, to understand the essay better? What specifically do you find clearer and more readable in the revised draft?

3. Ms. Aaron identifies Siegrist's shift in person among "one", "I," and "you" as a major problem in his essay. Why does she suggest that he use "I" whenever possible? Why is "I" preferable to "you" or "one"? Do you agree with her suggestion? Locate specific passages in which Aaron suggested to Siegrist to revise his essay using "I" Why do these changes make Siegrist's essay more readable? How do they also help Siegrist achieve his *purpose*?

4. Ms. Aaron also comments: "Shifting subjects are a common difficulty in *process* essays, and complete consistency is probably neither possible nor desirable." Locate instances in which Aaron has suggested to Siegrist to use "you" or "one." Do you agree with her suggestions?

5. Study Aaron's editing of Siegrist's introductory paragraph. She writes to him: "Several changes . . . eliminate unneeded words and help sharpen meaning." Explain how Aaron's editing helps to sharpen Siegrist's meaning in this paragraph.

6. Siegrist writes in his commentary: "I have learned a greal deal from the editing of my essay and am able to see where a little change can improve an essay considerably." What are some of the "little" changes Aaron suggested that improved Siegrist's essay? How do these changes improve the essay as a whole?

7. Ms. Aaron suggested to Siegrist that he should combine information for greater conciseness. In paragraph 13 for instance, she edited sentences to combine and simplify. Study the editing of this paragraph. Explain the effect of the changes Ms. Aaron suggested? Has Siegrist combined information to make the essay more readable?

8. Ms. Aaron wrote to Siegrist: "I hope you agree that the suggested changes would make your essay even clearer and more readable then it already is. Of course, the decisions on revision are yours to make." And Siegrist comments: "The comments I did not use were the ones that I felt did not express my

ideas in the context I had intended." Which editing suggestions did Siegrist choose not to use? Find specific examples. Do you agree with his decisions?

9. Which of Aaron's comments did you find most helpful? What did you learn about reading, writing, and revising from studying Aaron's comments on Siegrist's essay?

10. Imagine that you are a professional editor preparing Siegrist's essay for publication. Are there any more changes that you would make? Annotate Siegrist's revised essay, as Aaron did with the original essay, explaining the changes you think are necessary and offering possible solutions. Also write a letter to Siegrist telling him what the strengths of his revision are and what still needs to be done.

GLOSSARY

abstract and concrete words An abstract word refers to an idea, quality, attitude, or state imperceptible to our senses: *equality, freedom, love, fearful, naive, courageous.* A concrete word, in contrast, refers to an object, person, place, or state that we can perceive with our senses: *magazine, bus driver, Hudson River, blushing, clear-eyed, howling.* Though abstract words are useful in conveying general concepts or impressions, they are too vague to create distinct sensory impressions in readers' minds. To make meaning precise and vivid, writers support abstractions with concrete words appealing directly to the senses of sight, hearing, touch, taste, and smell. See also **general and specific words**.

allusion A brief reference to a real or fictitious person, place, object, or event. An allusion can convey considerable meaning with few words: he was a Scrooge about money; her business tactics smacked of the robber barons. But to be effective, the allusion must refer to something readers know well.

analogy A comparison of two different things that uses some similarities between them as the basis for implying other similarities. An analogy differs from a **simile** or **metaphor** in that it involves a point-by-point rather than an overall comparison. It differs from **comparison and contrast** in that its aim is to find resemblances in two unlike things rather than to explore two related things through their common and contrasting qualities.

Like an **illustration,** an analogy adds specificity and vividness to expository writing. Brief analogies are useful for this purpose in many types of essay. "Smith fended off discovery in the grand manner of the Wizard of Oz: He sent his top subordinates out on lengthy, difficult field assignments, while generating such sound and fury from his corner office that secretaries trembled and middle managers feared to question even his most irrational statements." An extended analogy of a paragraph or more can help to clarify

423

an explanation by relating the thing being discussed to something more familiar; or it can strengthen an argument by using a known phenomenon to illustrate the potential impact of one whose effects are not yet apparent.

Analogy is frequently used in explanations to make an abstract topic more concrete or to make a complex topic easier to understand. In science, where abstraction and complexity are common, explanations often lean heavily on detailed analogies known as *models.* For example, an early model of the atom compared it to a miniature solar system, with a nucleus at the center (the sun) and electrons orbiting around it (the planets). The human brain is sometimes compared to a computer, an analogy that has helped researchers both to understand the operation of the brain and to refine the operation of the computer. That is, scientists use the similarities they have observed to predict other similarities, which they then test.

In expository writing it is not possible to test predictions. The reader must evaluate the validity of the analogy on the basis of its plausibility: Are the subject and the analogy similar enough to justify the writer's conclusions? This is an especially important question in argumentative and persuasive writing, where the conclusions are intended to shape readers' attitudes toward the subject. For example, political observers often contend that a current scandal is (or is not) another Watergate, or that U.S. policy in Central America will (or will not) lead the nation into another Vietnam. The reason the same analogy can be used by both sides in these debates is that no two situations are ever identical. Some aspects of U.S. policy in Central America resemble U.S. policy twenty years ago in Vietnam, while others do not. Therein lies the vulnerable spot of analogy as an argumentative tool. It stresses similarities while overlooking dissimilarities that may in fact be equally (or even more) significant. It cannot provide proof of an assertion or even hard evidence; it only suggests likelihood.

The writer using this technique therefore should carefully evaluate both the similarities and the dissimilarities between his or her subject and the chosen analogy. The analogy should be exploited up to but not past its logical limits. Every analogy breaks down if pushed too far—that is, if the comparison is extended to qualities of the two things that are not in fact similar. The solar system model of the atom, for instance, breaks down when the electrons' orbits are compared with those of planets; planets move in predictable and mostly parallel paths, while electrons do not.

The reader too should evaluate analogies with caution. Has the writer accurately identified similarities, and taken account of important dissimilarities? Has he or she extended the analogy too far? To what degree does the analogy depend on emotional rather than logical appeal? In the case of a parallel such as U.S. policy in Central America and in Vietnam, the emotional power of the comparison is strong. The writer knows most readers want to avoid "another Vietnam," and he or she uses this prejudice to influence their attitude toward the situation in Central America. The reader should be aware of this and should scrutinize the analogy for dissimilarities the writer may have ignored.

Analogy can also be used as a strategy for presenting a position. Amber Kennish's "Three Rounds with Dad" (p. 133) casts an argument between two antagonists as a boxing match. Here the analogy has no direct relationship to the subject; it simply helps Kennish to dramatize the conflict. Nevertheless, it does affect readers' perceptions of the essay's substantive arguments by describing them as weak or powerful ("a quick jab" versus "a blow to the gut"), and by showing one opponent bloodied and defeated by the other.

anecdote A brief narrative recounting an episode from personal experience.

argument and persuasion Writing that attempts to secure readers' assent to and support for the writer's position on an issue. Technically, *argument* uses facts and logic to win the reader's rational agreement, whereas *persuasion* uses an **emotional appeal** to induce readers to think or act in a certain way. Thus, someone arguing for capital punishment might make his or her case by presenting statistics indicating that nations that use it have lower crime rates than those that do not. Someone persuading readers to vote for capital punishment might contend that killing murderers is the only way to keep them from endangering the lives of innocent people. Argument and persuasion are so often used together, however, that they are not always distinguishable. Therefore, the term *argument* is often applied to both argumentative and persuasive writing.

Neither argument nor persuasion is a rhetorical strategy like **comparison and contrast, definition, process analysis,** and the other techniques commonly used to structure an essay. Rather, the writer of an argument works within whichever of these frameworks suits his or her needs. No matter what its strategy, an argument typically opens with one or more introductory paragraphs that outline the conflict and introduce the writer's thesis. The body of the argument consists of claims supporting the thesis and evidence to back up those claims.

For example, the **thesis** of Pamela Garrettson's "Prayer in America's Public Schools: Let's Not Start a Religious War" (p. 96) is that organized spoken prayer in public schools should not be legalized. One of Garrettson's claims in support of her position is that such prayer would make nonparticipants feel uncomfortable, undermining America's tradition of protecting minority religions. As **evidence** she describes her own unease at a Hindu service she attended. Another claim is that students are already legally free to pray in school. To back up this claim, Garrettson cites a relevant Supreme Court decision.

Many writers try to arrange their arguments so that each claim forms the topic sentence of a paragraph, and the rest of the paragraph consists of information related to that claim. This is a hard pattern to follow consistently but a useful organizing goal.

Two types of logic are commonly used in constructing an argument: inductive and deductive reasoning. **Inductive reasoning** involves moving from a collection of facts to a conclusion—that is, from particular cases to a generalization. A writer arguing in favor of rent-control legislation in his or her town might interview tenants in eight of the town's apartment buildings. Suppose most or all of these people report rent increases within the past year. The writer assumes that what is true in these particular cases is probably true for the town in general, and makes the claim that local rents are on the rise. The jump from representative but limited evidence (eight buildings) to a conclusion about all possible cases (every rental unit in town) is called an *inductive leap*. What is true of eight buildings may not in fact be true of the ninth or tenth. However, the inductive leap is a reasonable one, given the difficulty of gathering enough data to prove the writer's claim beyond doubt.

Deductive reasoning involves moving from a known fact about a whole class to a conclusion about one member of that class—that is, from the general to the particular. If a newspaper reported that the town council had passed a 5 percent increase for all local rental units, the writer could accurately conclude that the rent on the mayor's apartment would go up. In deductive reasoning, unlike inductive reasoning, the logical conclusion *must* be true if it is based on accurate premises. The deductive sequence—from the general to the particular—is called a **syllogism.** It comprises two premises and a conclusion:

—Major premise: All rents in town will increase by 5 percent.

—Minor premise: The mayor lives in a rented apartment.

—Conclusion: The mayor's rent will increase by 5 percent.

If either the major premise or the minor premise is false, the conclusion may also be false. For instance, perhaps the 5 percent increase is permitted but not mandatory (major premise). In that case, the mayor's rent might or might not go up. Likewise, if the mayor moves out of his apartment and buys a house (minor premise), his rent will not increase.

When deductive reasoning is used in expository writing, one of the steps in the syllogism may be implied rather than stated:

—Thanks to the general rent increase, even the mayor will soon have to pay 5 percent more for his apartment. (minor premise implied)

—Because the mayor is a tenant rather than a homeowner, he faces a 5 percent rent increase. (major premise implied)

—All local rents are going up 5 percent; and as we know, the mayor lives in a rented apartment. (conclusion implied)

In both inductive and deductive reasoning, the writer's **conclusion**—his or her claim—is based on facts drawn from personal knowledge or research. **Evidence** is what makes the claims in an argument convincing. If someone advocating rent control states that rents are on the rise, readers will want to know why he or she thinks so. If the writer's only support for this claim is a recent increase in his or her own rent, the conclusion carries little weight. Any inductive conclusion based on inadequate evidence is called a *hasty generalization*.

Other common pitfalls in argumentative writing are the *logical fallacies*—gaps or missteps in reasoning. These include ad hominem arguments, bandwagon appeals, begging the question, ignoring the question, and non sequiturs. Each of these fallacies is defined under *logical fallacies* in this glossary.

audience   That group of readers for whom a writer intends a particular work. To communicate effectively, the writer should consider readers' knowledge of the subject, their interests in it, and their biases toward it in choosing what to say and how to say it.

cause and effect   A writing strategy in which certain events are established to explain why other events happened. Cause-and-effect analysis involves identifying the links in a chain of events and demonstrating the connections between them. This type of reasoning is typically used to explain something that has already happened, or to predict a future result, or both.

Cause and effect is a popular technique in argumentative or persuasive writing. Often the writer uses a cause-effect relationship as the basis of the recommendation that comprises his or her **thesis:** "Cigarette smoking should be outlawed because it can cause cancer and other serious health problems." In this case the writer favors alleviating an undesirable effect (cancer and other diseases) by eliminating its cause (cigarette smoking). For the argument to be effective, the writer must show that the alleged cause really is a cause. That is, he or she must present evidence that smoking does in fact lead to health problems. To be thorough, the writer would also cite data indicating that eliminating cigarettes would cause a significant decrease in these illnesses.

Cause-and-effect analysis can be used to explain as well as to argue. For instance, instead of proposing that cigarettes be outlawed, the writer interested in smoking and health problems might focus on the nature of the cause-effect relationship. What particular qualities of tobacco smoke produce an adverse impact on the human body? Which organs and systems are affected, and in what ways? Cause-and-effect reasoning can also be used to show that one set of causes is more plausible than another. Some cigarette advertising aims at convincing readers that other factors besides smoking are responsible for the ailments commonly associated with tobacco.

Cause and effect is not an easy technique to use well. The writer who chooses this strategy faces the challenge of ordering and weighing incidents or conditions that may have overlapped in time, and whose relative importance may not be obvious. Only rarely is it possible to distinguish a clear causal chain: A caused B, which caused C. "The hurricane blew down our town's power lines, therefore we had no electricity, therefore we couldn't watch the news on TV." Most sequences of events—especially those worth writing about—are more complex, and thus harder to analyze.

In writing about a cause-effect relationship, it may be preferable to begin with effects and work backward to causes, or to begin with causes and move forward to effects. The choice usually depends on the type of case being made. An explanatory essay—one that asks "why?"—typically starts with an effect in the present and goes back to causes in the past. A high proportion of American marriages end in divorce—why? The United States and the Soviet Union have enough nuclear weapons to wipe out every city on the globe several times over; what are the reasons behind this buildup? A predictive essay—one that asks "what will happen if . . . ?"—more often starts with a cause in the present and goes forward to its probable effects in the future. How is America's high divorce rate likely to affect the next generation's attitude toward marriage? Given the current arms race, what are the chances of avoiding nuclear war?

Several common pitfalls should be kept in mind when using—or evaluating—cause-and-effect reasoning. One is confusing causes with effects. Has the arms buildup caused international hostility or resulted from it? A related problem is the post hoc fallacy—assuming that because one thing follows another in time, the first is a cause and the second is an effect. The writer must demonstrate that the relationship really is causal and not merely coincidental.

The question of necessary versus sufficient cause also arises here. Does a given situation exist only because some other situation or event preceded it? Could other causes have had the same effect? For example, suppose someone dies of lung cancer after ten years of smoking two packs of cigarettes a day. The writer may view smoking as a *necessary* cause of this person's death—that is, if the victim had not smoked cigarettes, he or she probably would not have developed lung cancer. However, many people who smoke two packs a day for ten years do not die of cancer. Therefore smoking is not a *sufficient* cause of death; some other factor must also have been involved.

Another common error in cause-and-effect reasoning is confusing a cause with a symptom or sign. A married couple, one of whom drinks heavily, files for divorce. Is drinking a cause of the divorce or a symptom of deeper incompatibility between the two partners? Similarly, a given situation may appear to be a cause when in fact it is a purpose. The League of Nations was formed for the purpose of preventing international wars in the future; but its cause lies in the conflicts of the past.

chronological order   A method of organizing an essay in which events are arranged as they occurred over time, from earliest to latest. Narrative often follows a chronological order.

classification: A writing strategy that involves dividing a subject into two or more component categories and then assigning each of its parts to one of these categories. Classification is a useful way to break down a complex topic into manageable segments. It can also help the writer analyze a subject more precisely by identifying each element within it according to a logical system.

The first step in classification, called *analysis* or *division*, consists of separating the subject into categories. In "Rock Around the World" (p. 83), Erik Field divides his rock-and-roll record collection into six categories: British Invasion, Motown, Memphis, the Los Angeles sound, the San Francisco sound, and New York punk. The second step is to place each of the subject's parts in the appropriate category. Under "British Invasion," for instance, Field mentions the Beatles, the Rolling Stones, the Kinks, the Yardbirds, the Who, and the Animals. By classifying individual bands geographically according to their origin and sound, Field is able to consider a large topic (rock-and-roll) in an organized, coherent fashion. He is also able to point out significant features of many different bands without becoming repetitive.

The simplest form of classification is the *binary* type, in which the subject is split into just two categories: items that possess a certain characteristic and items that lack it. The Rh factor in human blood is a binary classification. People whose blood contains this factor are labeled Rh positive, and those who lack it are Rh negative. This is obviously a very limited way of dividing up a subject, since it provides only one piece of information about the members of each category. Indeed, for the negative group, all we know is that its members do not share a certain quality—they need not be alike in any other way. Human blood, which is a complicated substance, is classified according to numerous other criteria besides the presence or absence of the Rh factor. The best known of these are the four major blood types. A, B, AB, and O, which comprise a *complex* classification. A complex classification provides at least one piece of positive information about all the members in each group.

When using classification, the writer must be sure to keep his or her categories consistent. Erik Field's classificatin of rock-and-roll, for example, is based on geography (which also corresponds with certain types of sound). To add a seventh category such as "blues" or "having a horn section" would make his system inconsistent—some bands could fall into more than one group. In any classification, the same principle should serve as the basis for all categories.

Once the writer has divided up the subject, he or she can go on to consider each category individually. This might involve naming the category, listing its members, discussing their common features, and noting important differences and similarities between it and other categories. Sometimes a category is further subdivided, as when Field separates his Memphis group into white (a combination of Southern rhythm-and-blues and country) and black (soul). Examining each component part helps the writer to convey a sense of the whole. He or she may reinforce this larger concept by beginning or ending the essay with either an overview or a general discussion of the subject.

cliché   A worn-out, overused expression that deadens rather than enlivens writing. Examples: *few and far between, fate worse than death, sea of faces, shot in the arm, tired but happy, viable alternative.*

climactic order   A method of organizing an essay in which elements—words, sentences, examples, ideas—are arranged in order of increasing importance or drama.

coherence   The quality of effective writing that results from clear, logical connections among all the parts so that the reader can easily follow the writer's thought process. Coherence requires logic, so that each point develops naturally from those preceding it, and organization, which arranges material in the way that best focuses and directs the reader's attention. See **parallelism** and **transitions**. See also **unity**.

colloquial language   The language of conversation, including contractions (*don't, can't*) and informal words and expressions (*hassle* for an argument or fight, *mad* for angry, *to party* for attending a party). Most dictionaries label such words and expressions *colloquial* or *informal.* Colloquial language is inappropriate in formal writing such as a college term paper or a business report. But sometimes it can be used selectively to relax a piece of writing and create a friendly intimacy. See also **diction.**

comparison and contrast   A writing technique in which the qualities of two subjects are examined in relation to each other. Comparison involves identifying both the similarities and differences between the subjects; contrast focuses on the differences (though it may make use of the similarities to do so). The two processes are closely related and are almost always used together. The effectiveness of comparison and contrast comes from its comprehensive review of the two subjects' attributes: In looking carefully at each part, both writer and reader gain a fuller appreciation of the whole.

Comparison and contrast can be used to structure an entire essay whose purpose is to evaluate two phenomena. Karen Kramer's "The Little Drummer Boys," for example, is a comparison of drummers and percussionists (p. 138). Or the technique can serve as one part of a larger essay, as in David Christman's discussion of the Dionysian versus the Apollonian aspects of tattoos in "Nietzsche and the Art of Tattooing" (p. 55).

Some comparison and contrast essays are explanatory, helping the reader to understand each subject better by exploring the likenesses and discrepancies between the two. "The Little Drummer Boys" is an explanatory essay, describing how drummers and percussionists differ in attitude, equipment, and performance style. Other comparisons are evaluative, aimed at proving that one alternative is preferable to the other. Evaluative comparisons are popular in advertising: Cereal X has no added sugar whereas Cereal Y has six teaspoons; Cereal X has more fiber; Cereal X has three times the vitamin nutrition of Cereal Y. In an essay, unlike an advertisement, the writer of an evaluative comparison must be careful to consider enough characteristics of the two subjects so that the weight of the **evidence** clearly favors one over the other.

The writer setting up either type of comparison and contrast begins by jotting down aspects of the two subjects that he or she plans to compare. In Kramer's essay about drummers versus percussionists, these include (1) equipment, (2) image and attitude, (3) style of playing, (4) personal appearance and behavior, (5) relationship to the band, and (6) love of equipment. Then, for each of these aspects, the writer notes the similarities and differences between the two subjects. For example, Kramer's "equipment" category would list the instruments played by drummers and by percussionists—some of them the same (drums and cymbals) and some not (triangles, sleigh bells, woodblocks, xylophones).

Once the elements of the comparison have been identified, the writer can choose between a subject-by-subject and a point-by-point structure. The subject-by-subject comparison describes the first subject completely and then the second. The writer's outline might look like this:

1. Drummers
   a. Equipment
   b. Image and attitude
   c. Style of playing (and so on)
2. Percussionists
   a. Equipment
   b. Image and attitude
   c. Style of playing (and so on)

A subject-by-subject comparison is most appropriate for a short essay whose purpose is to give an overall impression of each subject. In a longer paper, there is some risk with this format that each description will turn into a separate essay, losing the force of the comparison. For a thorough examination of the two subjects in relation to each other, the point-by-point format is usually preferable. Here, each paragraph or section of the essay covers one element of the comparison, with plenty of room for supporting details. The writer's outline might look like this:

1. Equipment
   a. Drummers
   b. Percussionists
2. Image and attitude
   a. Drummers
   b. Percussionists (and so on)

It is often possible and desirable to combine the two formats. Kramer's essay, for instance, opens with a brief subject-by-subject comparison of drummers and percussionists and then moves into a more detailed point-by-point comparison.

Kramer's **thesis** statement appears at the end of her second paragraph, between her subject-by-subject and her point-by-point comparisons. Her very first paragraph sets the stage for her thesis by creating expectations that the thesis then overthrows. The writer of an explanatory comparison (unlike an evaluative comparison) often need such a noncomparative introduction to show why the subjects' similarities and differences are of interest.

conclusions   The sentences that bring a written work to a close and provide readers with a sense of completion, with a sense that the writer has finished. Sometimes the final point in the body of an essay may accomplish this purpose, especially if it is very important or dramatic, but usually a separate conclusion is needed. It may be a single sentence or several paragraphs, depending on the length and complexity of the piece of writing, and it may include any of the following, or a combination, depending on the writer's subject and purpose.

1. A summary of the essay's main points.
2. A statement of the essay's main idea, if it has not been previously stated; or a restatement of the main idea incorporating information from the body of the essay.
3. A comment on the significance or implications of the subject.
4. A suggestion about how readers can use the information in the essay.
5. A recommendation that readers support a proposal or action, or that they take some action themselves.
6. A prediction for the future.
7. An example, anecdote, question, or quotation that reinforces the point of the essay.

Excluded from this list are several endings that are best avoided because they tend to weaken the overall effect of an essay: (1) an example, fact, or quotation that pertains to only part of the essay; (2) an apology for the writer's ideas, for the quality of the writing, or for omissions; (3) an attempt to enlarge the significance of the essay by overgeneralizing from its ideas and evidence; (4) a new idea that requires the support of an entirely different essay.

concrete words   See **abstract and concrete words**.

connotation and denotation   A word's denotation is its literal meaning: *Factory* denotes a building where goods are manufactured; *famous* denotes the quality of being well known. A word's connotations are the associations or suggestions that go beyond its literal meaning. Some connotations are personal and vary according to an individual's experiences. *Factory*, for instance, may connote a particular place, but it may further connote a judgment on the methods of production used within that place. Other connotations are more general, calling up similar associations for all who use or hear the word. Many groups of words with essentially the same denotation vary in their connotations. *Famous*, *eminent*, and *notorious* all denote the quality of being well known; but *famous* connotes celebrity and popularity among contemporaries *(famous actor)*, *eminent* connotes recognition for outstanding qualities or contributions *(eminent physician)*, and *notorious* connotes sensational, even unfavorable, recognition *(notorious thief)*. Each of these words can help shape a reader's responses to the person being described. But connotative words will backfire if they set off inappropriate associations— for instance, describing a respected figure as "a notorious teacher and scholar." Frequent reference to a dictionary will safeguard against such mistakes.

contrast   See **comparison and contrast**.

deductive reasoning   The method of reasoning that moves from the general to the specific.

definition   An explanation of the meaning of a word. Three main types of definition commonly appear in expository writing: lexical definitions, which summarize a term's meaning briefly, as in a dictionary; stipulative definitions, which specify a more limited meaning for a term in a particular context; and extended definitions, which explore a term's meaning in depth. A lexical definition is typically used to clarify a word that readers must understand in order to follow the writer's presentation. A stipulative definition enables the writer to use a word in a specialized sense that suits the purposes of his or her essay. An extended definition can fulfill either of these functions in more detail, or it can serve as the basis of a whole essay.

Lexical definitions usually characterize an object, phenomenon, or idea by classifying it in relation to other things. Such a definition normally gives the general category in which the term belongs and specific features that distinguish it from similar terms. A lexical definition of *anger* might be *a strong emotion* (general category) *of displeasure and belligerence* (distinguishing features). The term's roots might also be mentioned. One antecedent of *anger* is the Latin *angere*, "to strangle." In addition, lexical definitions sometimes include synonyms, other words that have approximately the same meaning: *wrath, rage, fury, ire*. The writer using a lexical definition in an essay chooses which of these elements to include on the basis of what readers need to know about the term in order to understand the sense in which the writer plans to apply it. If the writer's purpose is simply to clarify the meaning of a technical term, he or she may need only a phrase or two to define it. If the word may be unfamiliar and is important to the essay, a fuller definition will ensure that readers grasp it.

If the word being defined is central to the writer's goals, or controversial, or susceptible to different interpretations, a stipulative definition is appropriate. That is, the writer stipulates the special and limited sense in which the word will be used in the essay. Thu Hong Nguyen's "A Good Woman" (p. 188) opens with a stipulative definition: "A good woman means an industrious daughter, a devoted wife, and a loving mother." This definition represents traditional Vietnamese beliefs about the role of women, which is Nguyen's subject. Her essay as a whole comprises an extended definition, since she goes on to examine each phrase of her stipulative definition in more detail.

A lexical definition always reflects ordinary usage. While a stipulative definition narrows a word's meaning to suit a specialized purpose, it should not conflict with ordinary usage to a point that stretches readers' credulity. The lexical definition of anger, for example, is broad enough to fit the term in most common contexts. A stipulative definition for an essay on facial expressions might limit anger to mean "a frown or scowl accompanied by pursed lips, bared teeth, and/or flared nostrils." This definition is unusual, but consistent with readers' concept of anger. Someone could also define anger stipulatively as "a deep sadness and sense of loss," but to do so would be pointless, since readers are unlikely to accept such a definition.

An extended definition too should accord with ordinary usage. Often, however, the reason for writing an extended definition is that the term either has no clear meaning or is susceptible to different interpretations. Brenda Jacobs's "Handing Down Grace" (p. 106) tells of her realization that this phrase, like others she heard in the South, "struck a discordant note. . . . reason dictated that if grace were to be 'handed' anywhere, surely it would be sent in an upward direction." The purpose of an extended definition is usually to mirror a larger contradiction or an insight revealed by the writer's analysis of how the term is used. Jacobs's theme is not merely odd Southern expressions, but her own reconciliation with her Southern roots. Nguyen does more than describe the Vietnamese definition of a good woman; she subtly and then overtly deplores the subjugation of Vietnamese women.

denotation See **connotation and denotation.**

description The translation of a sensory image into words. By telling readers how something looks, feels, sounds, smells, or tastes, the writer enables them to share his or her experience. The thing being described may be a person, a place, an object, or even a state of mind.

Description appears in all kinds of writing. It can be used within any expository essay to convey a setting, introduce a character, or make other physical aspects of the piece more vivid. Or it can serve as the main strategy for an essay whose object is to recreate a segment of reality.

There are two general types of description: objective and subjective. An objective description emphasizes facts that could be observed by anyone: "It was a dark and stormy night, full of clouds, wind, and rain." This type of description functions mainly to paint a factual picture in the reader's mind. A subjective description, on the other hand, includes the writer's reaction or interpretation: "The sky was as dark as Helen's mood when we parted and as stormy as our good-byes." This type of description uses the picture it paints to transmit a mood. In doing so, it suggests why the writer thinks this picture is worth the reader's attention and may reveal something about the writer's attitude or values. Most descriptions combine objective and subjective elements: "Dark clouds hid the moon; gusts of wind and rain rattled the windows. It was the kind of night that makes you long for a cozy armchair in front of a fireplace." Such a description conveys both facts about the scene and clues to the writer's ideas about it.

Whether it is the essay's central focus or just one component part, a description always serves a purpose. Like every other aspect of the piece, it helps the writer to express his or her thesis. In a descriptive essay, the thesis typically takes the form of a **dominant impression.** That is, the writer tells readers about some person, place, object, or experience in a way that invests it with significance beyond its physical attributes. By sharing the writer's perceptions and viewpoint, the reader comes to understand and appreciate his or her interpretation as well.

Barbara Carter's "Momma's Cupboard" (p. 43), for example, is a descriptive essay about a pantry. Carter spends only a few sentences telling how the pantry looks. Most of her essay focuses on the exotic foods stored there and the childhood hopes and illusions represented by the pantry's contents. The essay's dominant impression is of "denials and broken dreams, the promise that never came." Carter selects and arranges the details of her description to convey this dominant impression.

The writer of a description can help to ensure success by following a series of steps. The first step is to identify the essay's topic and the dominant impression the description is meant to create. Next, he or she carefully observes the thing to be described. What are its most striking visual features? Does it have any special sound, feel, smell, or taste? Is it stationary, or do its motions help to characterize it?

The writer then chooses the most evocative and relevant details. A good description is not a catalog of facts, but an integrated picture which highlights significant qualities and omits those that do not contribute to the dominant impression. In a description of climbing a mountain, significant qualities might include the glare of sun on snow, the bite of cold wind on exposed skin, the crunch of boots on ice, the smell of wet wool, and the ache of tired muscles. Less significant would be the color of each climber's clothing, the number of rocks and trees along the path, or the brand of sunscreen used by the climbing party. Selectivity is essential in shaping an effective description.

Before putting words on paper, the writer should pick a **point of view.** This is something like the camera angle of a movie scene. For the description to feel authentic, the reader needs a sense of where the writer stands, literally and figuratively. Is this the viewpoint of someone indoors looking out? at the foot of a mountain looking up? on a high peak looking down? The point of view may be stationary or moving—for example, from the bottom of the mountain to the top, or in a panorama from side to side, or zooming in from a distance to a close-up. No matter how many elements the writer examines in the scene, his or her point of view should remain consistent. The description's dominant impression is the writer's impression, and it is established through the writer's eyes.

By the same token, elements in the description are arranged in a sequence that imitates the order in which a viewer might notice them. Frances Taylor's essay, "Carol" (p. 227) opens with Carol's most striking visual features—her mustache, her gold fillings—and then moves to the sound of her laugh, the tension of her body, her red tank top, and the sparkle in her eyes. With this picture vividly established, Taylor backs off to give us information about herself and the situation in which she met Carol. If Taylor had simply listed Carol's hair color, eye color, facial shape, and clothing, starting at the top of her head and moving to her feet, the description would be much less vivid and alive, for it would not reflect the way one person actually sees another.

Essential to an effective description is lively, specific language. Typical elements include concrete nouns and active verbs, adjectives and adverbs, and **figures of speech,** particularly similes and metaphors. Although adjectives and adverbs are often the most obvious way to make a description colorful, experienced writers recognize that the backbone of a verbal picture is its nouns and verbs. A writer telling about a climbing expedition, for example, might say, "After a long, difficult ascent we finally reached our goal." This sentence gives the reader only a vague sense of what the writer saw and felt. A more successful description would be, "After four days and nights of struggling up the mountain, we reached its snow-shrouded peak."

Similes and metaphors broaden readers' perception of the thing being described by comparing it with something else, usually something with well-known characteristics. A simile uses "like" or "as"; a metaphor does not. In using these figures of speech, the writer needs to consider not only obvious physical resemblances, but also how he or she wants the reader to react to the description. That is, similes and metaphors should contribute to the essay's dominant impression. To say, "Clouds drifted around the mountain peak like sheep in a meadow" creates a pleasant, pastoral mood. If this is not the writer's intention, he or she should choose a different comparison: "Clouds loomed over the mountain peak like portents of doom."

diction   A writer's choice of words to achieve a purpose and make meaning clear. Effective diction conveys the writer's meaning exactly, emphatically, and concisely, and it is appropriate to the writer's intentions and audience. **Standard English**, the written language of educated native speakers, is expected in all writing for college, business and the professions, and publication. The vocabulary of standard English is large and varied, encompassing, for instance, both *comestibles* and *food* for edible things, both *paroxysm* and *fit* for a sudden seizure. In some writing standard English may also include words and expressions typical of conversation (see **colloquial language**). But it excludes other levels of diction that only certain groups understand or find acceptable. Most dictionaries label these levels as follows:

> *Nonstandard:* words spoken among particular social groups, such as *ain't, yous, hisself,* and *nowheres.*
>
> *Slang:* words that become dated quickly and that may not be understood by all readers, such as *uptight,* for tense or inhibited, *bread* for money, and *honcho* for one in charge.
>
> *Regional* or *dialect:* words spoken in a particular region but not in the country as a whole, such as *poke* for a sack or bag, *holler* for hollow or small valley.
>
> *Obsolete:* words that have passed out of use, such as *fain* to mean happy or desirous (I *fain* would go.)

See also **connotation and denotation**.

division   Also called *analysis*. The method of development in which a subject is separated into its elements or parts.

dominant impression   The central idea or feeling conveyed by a description of a person, place, object, or state of mind.

effect   See **cause and effect**.

emotional appeal   In argumentative and persuasive writing, the appeal to readers' values, beliefs, or feelings in order to win agreement or inspire action.

essay   A prose composition on a single nonfiction idea or topic. An essay usually reflects the writer's personal experiences and opinions.

ethical appeal   In argumentative and persuasive writing, the sense of the writer's expertise and character implied by the reasonableness of the argument, the use and quality of evidence, and the tone.

evidence   The details, examples, facts, statistics, or expert opinions supporting any general statement or claim.

example   An instance or representative of a general group or of an abstract concept or quality. One or more examples may provide the basic structure for developing an essay.

exposition   The form of writing that explains or informs. Some essays whose primary purpose is self-expression or persuasion employ exposition to clarify ideas.

figures of speech   Expressions that imply meaning beyond or different from their literal definition used to achieve vividness or force. Among the more common are simile, metaphor, personification, and hyperbole. A *simile* compares two unlike things and makes the comparison explicit with *like* or *as*: "He buttered the bread like a bricklayer"; "The child cowered in the room like a frightened bird." A *metaphor* also compares two unlike things, but more subtly, by equating them without *like* or *as*: "Mud blanketed the town"; "Cars snaked down the turnpike." *Personification* is a kind of simile or metaphor that attributes human qualities or powers to things or abstractions: "The river surged angrily over the banks"; "The city turned a cold shoulder to me." *Hyperbole* is deliberate overstatement or exaggeration: "He had a mustache as big as a dust mop"; "I paced for hours." (The opposite of hyperbole is understatement, discussed under **irony**.)

formal style   See **style**.

freewriting   Also called *nonstop writing*. When students freewrite, they put pen to paper and continue to write without pausing to consider elements of composition such as grammar, sentence structure, word choice, or spelling. A useful way of getting started, freewriting quickly results in putting many ideas down on paper, ideas that can be developed into successful essays. For a detailed explanation by students of the benefits of freewriting, see "Students on Writing."

general and specific words   A general word refers to a group or class: *food, hobbies, clothing*. A specific word refers to a particular member of a group or class: *bread, coin collecting, socks*. General and specific are not exclusive categories but relative terms, as illustrated by the following chain from the most general to the most specific: *clothing, foot warmers, socks, wool socks, Fred's thermal wool socks*. General words are essential for referring to entire groups or classes, but they contribute little to vividness and often leave meaning unclear. Usually, the more specific a word is, the more interesting it will be for readers. See also **abstract and concrete words.**

generalization   A statement about a group or a class derived from knowledge of some or all of its members: "Holiday rituals create family memories" or

"Skyscrapers deprive cities of their human scale." The more instances the generalization is based on, the more accurate it is likely to be. A generalization is the result of inductive reasoning.

hyperbole   See **figures of speech.**

illustration   The use of examples to show how an abstract or general idea applies in real situations. As the term implies, illustration is a way of adding verbal pictures to exposition. This technique can be used in any piece of writing to clarify the meaning of a concept, support an assertion, or add specificity and vitality to a discussion that might otherwise be vague. Indeed, it is a rare composition that does not benefit from examples. Illustration also can serve as the main organizing strategy of an essay aimed at demonstrating the validity of an abstraction or generalization.

Not surprisingly for such a widely used technique, illustration is an umbrella term that covers a variety of applications. Some illustrations are highly specific and require scrupulous documentation, as when an anthropologist draws a conclusion about some ancient culture based on examples from a recently opened tomb. At the other end of the spectrum are semifictional examples intended to make an idea more vivid. Matthew Holicek's essay, "Look Out Behind You!" (p. 101) describes "slasher films" by using generalized examples that represent scenes in a number of movies: "The girls all love to take late-night strolls alone through the woods. . . . The boys, eager to impress the girls, prove their manhood by descending alone into musty cellars. . . ." A writer's choice of what type of illustration to use normally depends on the topic, **purpose,** and intended **audience** of his or her essay.

In an argumentative or explanatory paper, illustrations from primary sources are often essential for substantiating the writer's statements. If the goal is to analyze or refute another writer's position, all examples may be drawn from the subject's work. Monika Jerabek quotes lines and phrases from Sylvia Plath's poems throughout "Sylvia Plath: Electra Inspired" (p. 118) to document her observations about the relationship between Plath's poetry and her adoration of her dead father.

If the writer's goal is to present an original **thesis,** examples might come from primary and secondary sources, or from his or her own experience. In "Nietzsche and the Art of Tattooing" (p. 55), David Christman supports his statement, "Tattooing is an ancient art," with the example of an Egyptian mummy from 2000 B.C. Other illustrations in Christman's essay show tattooing practices in New Zealand, Japan, Central and South America, Borneo, Europe, and the United States, as reported in sources that Christman cites in his bibliography. In contrast, Ravenel Boykin Curry's "A Small

Town" (p. 63) draws on no outside sources. Curry's opening sentence is "Junior Boy is thirty-nine and he has made it." To illustrate Junior Boy's concept of "making it," Curry quotes him as promising himself "a telephone to talk to people." Though Junior Boy's life is far from luxurious, Curry establishes his success by describing in detail the installation of his first telephone.

Just as different essay topics require the writer to choose examples from different types of sources, the paper's subject and goals affect whether its examples are few or many, brief or extended. Some of theses are best supported with a large number of short examples. A writer defending an arguable generalization such as "There is too much violence in today's popular music" would do well to cite several different songs by different groups to confirm this observation. A more limited thesis, such as "Some current music videos show great imagination and creativity," might be substantiated with two or three detailed illustrations. Or the writer could choose a combination of examples, mentioning some videos briefly and describing one or two in depth. Usually the fewer the examples, the more detailed each one should be.

The writer should select both examples and the details within examples for their relevance to his or her thesis. In some cases it may also be appropriate to include illustrations that appear to contradict the thesis and then show why the thesis is nevertheless valid.

The placement of illustrations is important. It is best not to mix examples, but to treat one at a time, as thoroughly as necessary. Each one should appear close to the statement it supports—normally right before or right after it. If the bulk of the essay consists of one or more extended illustrations, the writer should be sure to present his or her thesis clearly at the outset, reinforce it by interpreting each example, and reiterate it in a closing summary.

image   A verbal representation of sensory experience—something seen, heard, felt, tasted, or smelled. Images may be literal: "The woman sat on the park bench"; "The street lights suddenly came on." Or they may be figurative: "The women perched on the park bench like old crows in their dark coats"; "Small eyes of light illuminated the street." (See **figures of speech.**) Through images, a writer touches the reader's experiences, thus sharpening meaning and adding immediacy. See also **abstract and concrete words.**

inductive reasoning   The method of reasoning that moves from the particular to the general.

informal style   See **style.**

introductions   The sentences that open written works and set the stage for what follows. An introduction to an essay identifies and restricts the subject while establishing the writer's attitude toward it. It may require a single sentence or several paragraphs, depending on how much readers need to know before they can begin to grasp the ideas in the essay. The introduction often includes a thesis sentence which states the main idea of the essay (see **thesis**). To set up the thesis sentence, or as a substitute for it, any of the following openings alone or in combination may be effective.

1. Background on the subject establishing a time or place or providing essential information.

2. An anecdote or other reference to the writer's experience illustrating the main idea or explaining what prompted the essay.

3. An explanation of the significance of the subject.

4. An outline of the problem the essay will address, perhaps using interesting facts or statistics.

5. A statement or quotation of an opinion that the writer disagrees with.

6. A quotation or question reinforcing the main idea.

A good introduction does not mislead readers by exaggerating the significance of the subject or the essay, nor does it bore them by saying more than is neccessary. A good introduction avoids two openings that are always clumsy: (1) beginning with "The purpose of this essay is . . ." or something similar; and (2) referring to the title of the essay in the first sentence, as in "This is not as hard as it looks" or "This is a serious problem."

irony   In writing, irony is the use of words to suggest a meaning different from their literal meaning. Some irony derives from *understatement*, from saying less than is meant. But irony can also suggest a meaning exactly opposite the literal meaning. Irony can be witty, teasing, biting, or cruel. At its most humorless and heavily contemptuous, it becomes *sarcasm:* "You have a real talent for failure."

logical fallacies   Flaws in reasoning that weaken or invalidate an argument. Some of the most common fallacies are listed below.

1. *Oversimplification,* overlooking or ignoring inconsistencies or complexities in evidence: "The problems in Nicaragua would be solved if the *contras* could drive the Sandinistas from power."

2. *Hasty generalization,* leaping to a conclusion on the basis of inadequate or unrepresentative evidence: "Every one of the twenty-five students polled supports the change in course requirements, so the administration should implement it."

3. *Begging the question,* assuming the truth of a conclusion that has not

been proved: "Deforestation in Brazil is necessary for economic development, so it should continue."

4. *Ignoring the question,* shifting the argument away from the real issue: "As a wife and mother, Geraldine Ferraro would be a sensitive vice-president."

5. *Ad hominem* ("to the man") *argument,* attacking an opponent instead of the opponent's argument: "She is just a student, so we need not listen to her criticisms of economic policy."

6. *Either-or,* presenting only two alternatives when there are more choices: "To do well in a competitive industry, you have to cheat a little."

7. *Non sequitur* ("it does not follow"), deriving a wrong or illogical conclusion from stated premises: "Since students pay high rents to live off campus, they should be able to have parties any time they want."

8. *Post hoc ergo propter hoc* ("after this, therefore because of this"), assuming that one thing caused another simply because it preceded the other: "After Gerald had his wisdom teeth out, he won the lottery."

metaphor   See **figures of speech.**

narration   A technique in which the writer tells what happened by relating a succession of events in a meaningful sequence. Narration is storytelling: the writer's purpose is not to present isolated facts but to describe one or more incidents in a way that shows both the chronological and thematic connections between them.

The simplest type of narration starts at the beginning and proceeds through the middle to the end. More complex forms involve shifts in time: the writer might start *in medias res*—at some significant point part way through the action—flash back to an earlier event and then forward again toward a conclusion. Whatever the sequence, it is important for the writer to identify a beginning, middle, and end before commencing. Having done that, he or she can decide how to structure the narrative so that its opening creates the right mood and its climax comes in the most effective place.

To use narration successfully, the writer must convey not only the order in which events occurred but the relationship implied by that order. Chronology alone—A happened, then B happened, then C happened—is boring and unimpressive. Indeed, readers faced with such an unadorned factual sequence are likely to add their own interpretation, which may or may not accord with the writer's intentions. It is the writer's job to give the story meaning by selecting, arranging, and presenting its elements in a way that guides the reader's interpretation. He or she does this by paying close attention to details, duration, direction, and development.

Details are the aspects of what happened that the writer chooses to include, to leave out, and to emphasize. Having chosen a subject and a thesis, the writer knows what his or her general sequence will be and what conclusion the reader is meant to draw from it. In "The Blanket Party" (p. 39), Terry Burns decided to start with a detail that suggests an ordinary summer night: "Crickets chirped in the grass. . . ." Burns then shatters the tranquility: ". . . as four men, dressed only in white government-issue underwear, made their way through the dark barracks." A good principle is to use every detail deliberately, including only those that contribute to the essay's purpose.

Duration refers to time—the schedule by which the subject is presented. In writing, unlike life, we can stretch out a moment or skip over a year. Whatever the writer describes at length, the reader will examine and consider closely. Whatever the writer skims through, the reader will assume is not very important. The decision of how much time to devote to an incident therefore depends on its significance, not on how long it took when it happened. Most narratives depict some events in full, omit others, and mention others only briefly. Such variety maintains the pace of the story and allows the writer to emphasize those scenes that add the most impact. Patrick Kinder Lewis's "Five Minutes North of Redding" (p. 150) opens with a short paragraph about the three hours before a train arrives, then spends a long paragraph on the few seconds when the train passes through. In this way he conveys the sense of a tedious wait before a crucial instant.

Direction is a sense of forward movement or flow. The reader should have an idea of where the essay is going from the beginning, and this idea should be reinforced as the narrative progresses. Careful attention to details and duration, plus effective **transitions** between sections, contribute to direction. Particularly important is leaving out any unnecessary scenes, sentences, or words that would slow the essay's momentum. A writer describing real events must be a ruthless editor, including only what is essential to his or her goals.

Development is the writer's arrangements of the elements in a narrative so that they not only keep the story moving but build toward a climax. The climax is the point near the end of the piece when its purpose becomes dramatically clear. To achieve this sense of revelation on the reader's part, the writer organizes events in a sequence in which each one seems to add new information and meaning to what has gone before. The result is a feeling of crescendo and a conclusion that is emotionally as well as intellectually satisfying.

Three other elements are important in narration. The first is **point of view**—the writer's indication of who is telling the story. This may be a first-person "I" representing the writer or some other main character. Or it may be a third-person "they," "she," or "he." The choice of point of view is based less on who has the most important role in the story than on whose perception of events the writer wants to convey.

Voice is the tone of the story—formal or informal, serious or humorous, ironic or earnest, dispassionate or sympathetic. Word choice, sentence length, and other aspects of style help the writer to create an appropriate voice for his or her narrative. In most essays, the voice should have enough personality to represent the writer (or other narrator) authentically, without being so idiosyncratic as to lose credibility.

Some narratives include *dialogue* to communicate significant events and ideas in the voices of the people involved. Dialogue may be direct ("Yes," she said) or indirect (She said yes). In a factual essay, the speakers' words should only take the form of direct diaglogue when they are quoted exactly. While there are advantages to reporting characters' actual speeches, it is rare for people to talk concisely and to the point for more than one or two sentences. Dialogue therefore should be used judiciously. Like all the elements of a narrative, it is valuable only when it advances the writer's **purpose.**

nonstandard English   See **diction.**

paragraph   A group of related sentences, set off by an initial indention, that develops an idea. By dividing continuous text into units, paragraphs help the writer manage ideas and the reader follow those ideas. Each paragraph makes a distinct contribution to the main idea governing the entire piece of writing. The main idea of each paragraph is often stated explicitly in a topic sentence, and it is supported with sentences containing specific details, examples, and reasons. Like the larger piece of writing of which it is a part, the paragraph should be easy to follow and clearly focused (see **coherence** and **unity**).

parallelism   The use of similar grammatical form for ideas of equal importance. Within a sentence, two or more elements of equal function and importance should always be parallel to avoid confusion: "The doctor recommends swimming, bicycling, or walking" is clearer and easier to read than "The doctor recommends swimming, bicycling, or that patients walk." But parallelism can also be an emphatic stylistic device either within or among sentences. When used among sentences, parallelism also clarifies the relations among ideas (see **coherence**).

personification   See **figures of speech.**

persuasion   See **argument.**

point of view   The position of the writer in relation to the subject. In description, point of view depends on the writer's physical relation to the subject; in narration, on the writer's place in the story and on his or her relation to it in time. More broadly, point of view can also mean the writer's particular mental stance or attitude. For instance, a smoker and a non-smoker might have different points of view toward smoking policies in a student lounge.

premise   The generalization or assumption on which an argument is based. See **syllogism.**

process analysis   An explanation of how something works, or how to do something. Just as **narration** tells *what* happened and **cause and effect** tells *why*, process analysis tells *how*. This is the strategy found in cookbooks, in instructions for playing a game or assembling a bicycle, and in descriptions of how the human heart operates or how a prince can secure political power. When used in an essay, process analysis begins with an overview of the subject and proceeds with a step-by-step discussion of each of its parts.

There are two types of process analysis: specified and informative. *Specified* process analysis tells the reader how to do something. John Siegrist's essay, "Rattlesnake: A Palatable Experience" (p. 217), is of this type, giving instructions on how to catch and cook a rattlesnake for dinner. *Informative* process analysis tells how something works. Sandra Casillas's "Cha-No-Yu, the Japanese Tea Ceremony" (p. 47) uses this technique to explain a Japanese ritual to American readers.

To understand how a process operates, we must know its **purpose** and the steps that comprise it. The thesis of a process-analysis essay tends to be simple: "how to prepare a rattlesnake meal" or "how a tea ceremony is conducted." The writer also should indicate why the process he or she has chosen to describe is of interest. Siegrist opens his essay with two paragraphs about food prejudices that often prevent people from trying new dishes and explains how he came to eat rattlesnake. Casillas conveys her reasons for writing about the Japanese tea ceremony with phrases like "the transition from chaotic modern life to the tiny tranquil chamber . . ." and a comparison of this slow traditional ritual with present-day high-speed technology.

Next, the writer identifies the steps in the process and describes each one in turn—the *analysis* part of the essay. Both Siegrist and Casillas use the second-person "you" in their analyses, suggesting that the reader is a participant. Siegrist also uses the first-person "I" when mentioning his own tactics and preferences. Other writers use the third-person "he," "she," "one," "they," or "it." The choice need not depend on whether the reader is actually likely to take part in the process being analyzed. Rather, the writer selects a mode of address that suits the subject and readers' probable reasons for being interested in it. A specified process analysis usually assumes the reader wants to learn to perform the steps described and phrases them either in the second person or in imperative commands: "Insert tab A into slot B." "Add a cup of water and stir." An informative process analysis may be about something the reader wants to understand, but in which he or she is not directly involved, such as how a hologram is made. In this case, the third person is often more practical: "The laser beam is split into two parts. One hits the object, while the other serves as a reference beam."

The steps in the process should be analyzed in a logical order. Any crucial ingredients should be specified, and unfamiliar terms identified, early enough to avoid confusion. A recipe that instructs, "Next add the egg yolks, beaten till lemon-colored" is harder to follow than one that says, "Beat the egg yolks till lemon-colored and add them to the mixture." Similarly, an explanation of holography should include definitions of "laser" and "reference beam." To be sure the analysis is clear, the writer should keep his or her **audience** in mind, covering each step in enough detail to be informative without becoming boring.

Organizing the essay in a logical order is more complicated when two or more steps take place at once. In a specified process analysis it is essential for the reader to be able to perform all the necessary actions in sequence, so the overlaps are usually small ones: "Turn cap clockwise while holding down tab with thumb." In an informative process analysis the writer may have to establish a sequence arbitrarily. Each step is described separately, but transitional phrases such as "at the same time" or "meanwhile" show when two or more steps are actually simultaneous.

If the process being analyzed is circular—photosyntehsis in leaves, for example, or the heart's pumping of blood—then the writer must also choose a starting point. Often the best place to begin is with a particularly visible step (sunlight hitting the leaf) or one that is somewhat familiar to readers (the initial thump of the heartbeat). For an especially complicated process, the writer might open with one relatively easy to explain aspect on which subsequent steps in the description can be based.

Process analysis is a technique applicable to a wide variety of subjects. Besides its more straightforward functions, it can be used humorously or ironically to explore a serious topic: "how to manage parents" or "how to take over a small country." Almost any "how" question offers material for process analysis, which is one of the most methodical ways to organize an essay.

purpose   The reason for writing, the goal the writer aims to achieve. The purpose may be to explain the subject so that readers understand it or see it in a new light; to convince readers to accept or reject an opinion or to act in a certain way; to entertain readers with a humorous or exciting story; or to express the thoughts and emotions inspired by a revealing or instructive experience. The writer's purpose overlaps the main idea—the particular point being made about the subject. In effective writing, the two together direct and control every choice the writer makes. See also **thesis** and **unity.**

rational appeal   In argumentative and persuasive writing, the appeal to readers' rational faculties—to their ability to reason logically—in order to win agreement or compel action.

rhetoric   The art of using words effectively to communicate with an audience.

satire   The combination of wit and criticism to mock or condemn human foolishness or evil. The intent of satire is to arouse readers to contempt or action, and thus it differs from comedy, which seeks simply to amuse. Much satire relies on irony—saying one thing but meaning another (see **irony**).

simile   See **figures of speech.**

slang   See **diction.**

specific words   See **general and specific words.**

standard English   See **diction.**

style   The *way* something is said, as opposed to *what* is said. Style results primarily from a writer's characteristic word choices and sentence structure. A person's writing style, like his or her speaking style, is distinctive. Viewed more broadly, style can range from formal to informal. A very formal style adheres strictly to the conventions of standard English (see **diction**), tends toward long, sophisticated sentences, and relies on learned words such as *malodorous* and *psychopathic.* A very informal style, in contrast, is more conversational (see **colloquial language**), tends toward short, uncomplicated sentences, and relies on words typical of casual speech such as *smelly* or *crazy.* The formality of style may often be modified to suit a particular audience or occasion: A college term paper demands a more formal style than an essay narrating a personal experience. See also **tone.**

syllogism   The basic form of **deductive reasoning,** in which a conclusion derives necessarily from proven or accepted premises. For example: The car never starts when it rains (the major premise). It is raining (the minor premise). Therefore, the car will not start (the conclusion).

symbol   A person, place, or thing that represents an abstract quality or concept. A red heart symbolizes love; the Statue of Liberty symbolizes the United States welcoming European immigrants; a cross symbolizes Christianity.

thesis   The main idea of a piece of writing, to which all other ideas and details relate. The main idea is often stated in a *thesis sentence* near the beginning of the essay, which asserts something about the subject and conveys the writer's purpose. Even when the writer does not state the main idea and purpose, the thesis governs all the ideas and details in the essay.

tone   The attitude toward the subject, and sometimes toward the audience and the writer's own self, expressed in choice of words and sentence structure as well as in what is said. Tone in writing is similar to tone of voice in speaking, from warm to serious, amused to angry, joyful to sorrowful, sympathetic to contemptuous.

transitions   Links between sentences and paragraphs that connect ideas and thus contribute to smoothness and clarity (see **coherence**). Some transitions are echoes of previous material that tie parts together and subtly indicate relationships: repetition and restatement can stress important words or phrases; pronouns such as *he, she, it,* and *they* can substitute for and refer back to earlier nouns; and parallelism can highlight ideas of similar importance (see **parallelism**). Other transitions are more obvious, stating the connections explicitly: transitional sentences beginning paragraphs or brief transitional paragraphs can help shift the focus or introduce new ideas; and transitional expressions can signal and specify relationships. Some common transitional expressions—by no means all—are listed below.

Space: above, below, beyond, farther away, here, nearby, opposite, there, to the right.

Time: afterward, at last, earlier, later, meanwhile, simultaneously, soon, then.

Illustration: for example, for instance, specifically, that is

Comparison: also, likewise, similarly.

Contrast: but, even so, however, in contrast, on the contrary, still, yet.

Addition or repetition: again, also, finally, furthermore, in addition, moreover, next, that is.

Cause or effect: as a result, consequently, equally important, hence, then, therefore, thus.

Summary or conclusion: all in all, in brief, in conclusion, in short, in summary, therefore, thus.

Intensification: indeed, in fact, of course, truly.

understatement   See **irony**.

unity   The quality of effective writing that resutls when all the parts relate to the main idea and contribute to the writer's purpose. A piece of writing must have a point, that point must be clear to readers, and they must see how every sentence relates to it. See **purpose** and **thesis**. See also **coherence**.

RHETORICAL
ARRANGEMENT

CONTEST RULES
FOR THE BEDFORD PRIZES
IN STUDENT WRITING

Bedford Books of St. Martin's Press is pleased to sponsor The Bedford Prizes in Student Writing, an annual contest designed to recognize outstanding essays written for freshman composition courses in the United States and Canada.

PRIZES

1. Each winner will receive a cash award of $175.00, to be sent by mail to the winner's home address.
2. Each instructor who sponsors a winning entry will receive a cash award of $75.00, to be sent by mail to the instructor's college address.
3. Formal certificates will be sent to the winning essayists, their instructors, and their departments.

CONTEST RULES

Eligibility and Deadline

1. The contest is open to any student enrolled in a freshman composition course at an accredited college or university in the United States and Canada.
2. Entries should be nonfiction prose essays—exposition and argument as well as narration and description—of at least 500 words. Research papers are also eligible. Fiction and poetry are not eligible. All entries must be written for and submitted for credit in a freshman composition course.
3. Although only final drafts will be judged, each entry must be accompanied by the writer's preliminary notes and drafts. Instructors may make such corrections and suggestions on prior drafts as they normally append to student papers, and the submitted version may be revised especially for entry in this contest along lines suggested by the instructor or by fellow students.
4. The contest runs on the academic year with deadlines for each semester. One set of winners will be chosen for both semesters and announced in the late fall. Entries for the fall semester must be postmarked no later than January 31, and entries for the spring semester must be postmarked no

452

later than May 31. *However, instructors are encouraged to submit entries at any time before these dates.* Entries should be submitted by mail to:

> The Bedford Prizes in Student Writing
> Bedford Books of St. Martin's Press
> P.O. Box 869
> Boston, MA 02117

5. There is no limit on the number of entries instructors may submit. Instructors are urged, however, to be selective in their submissions, sponsoring only those essays that in their judgment are of distinctively high quality. All entries will be judged for originality, clarity, organization, coherence, control of language and grammar, and, where applicable, reasoning and use of evidence.

Required Format and Accompanying Materials

6. Each entry must be typed, double-spaced, on one side of $8\frac{1}{2}'' \times 11''$ paper. The student's name should appear only on the first page of the entry in the upper right-hand corner, and the pages of the essay should be numbered. The entry should not bear the correction marks or comments of the instructor or other readers. The writer's preliminary notes and drafts should be stapled separately from the entry itself and labeled with the entrant's name.

7. Each entry must be accompanied by an official entry blank or a cover sheet containing the following information:
   Student's information: name, campus address, campus telephone number, home address, home telephone number.
   The student must also include a signed statement affirming that the essay is an original creation and that he or she has read, understood, and agreed to the rules and conditions of the contest.
   Instructor's information: name, department, college or university, address, office telephone number, home address, home telephone number, the specific assignment for the student's entry, instructor's signature.

Conditions

8. Entries must be original and may not infringe upon the rights of any third party.

9. All rights to an entry, including the copyright and other rights of reproduction and publication, are vested, upon its submission, in Bedford Books of St. Martin's Press. An entry is deemed submitted only upon its receipt by Bedford Books, which assumes no responsibility for the receipt or return

of any entry. *Students or instructors who want copies of the entries should make them before submission.*

10. Bedford Books of St. Martin's Press will publish a selection of the winning essays together in an anthology.

11. The decisions of the judges are final.

12. This contest is void where prohibited or restricted by law.

A complete list of winners, their college or university affiliations, and their sponsoring instructors will also be announced every year in *College Composition and Communication* and *College English.*